Clash of the Economic Titans: China and the United States

Chi Lo

Clash of the Economic Titans: China and the United States

Understanding China's Global Aspirations and Disruption

palgrave
macmillan

Chi Lo
Independent Scholar and Senior
Economist at a muti-national bank
Hong Kong, China

ISBN 978-981-95-2509-6 ISBN 978-981-95-2510-2 (eBook)
https://doi.org/10.1007/978-981-95-2510-2

This Palgrave Macmillan imprint is published by the registered company Springer Nature Singapore Pte Ltd.
The registered company address is: 152 Beach Road, #21-01/04 Gateway East, Singapore 189721, Singapore

To Margaret, Edwyn, Caroline and Arthur

Competing Interests The author has no competing interests to declare that are relevant to the content of this manuscript.

Also by Chi Lo

When Asia Meets China in the New Millennium—China's Role in Shaping Asia's Post-Crisis Economic Transformation, Pearson Prentice Hall, 2003

The Misunderstood China—Uncovering the Truth behind the Bamboo Curtain, Pearson Prentice Hall, 2004

Phantom of the China Economic Threat—Shadow of the Next Asian Crisis, Palgrave Macmillan, 2006

Understanding China's Growth—Forces that Drive China's Economic Future, Palgrave Macmillan, 2007

Asia and the Subprime Crisis—Lifting the Veil on the Financial Tsunami, Palgrave Macmillan, 2009

China after the Subprime Crisis—Opportunities in the New Economic Landscape, Palgrave Macmillan, November 2010

Thinking the Inevitable: China's Superpower Aspiration in the New Paradigm, Enrich Professional Publishing, March 2012

The Renminbi Rises: Myths, Hypes and Realities of RMB Internationalisation and Reforms in the Post-Crisis World, Palgrave Macmillan, July 2013

China's Impossible Trinity: The Structural Challenges to the 'Chinese Dream', Palgrave Macmillan, July 2015

Demystifying China's Mega Trends—the Driving Forces That Will Shake Up China and the World, Emerald Publishing, April 2017

China's Global Disruption—Myths and Reality, Emerald Publishing, January 2021

The Digital Renminbi's Disruption—Shaping the Global Economic, Financial and Policy Landscapes, Emerald Publishing, September 2022

Contents

1 **Introduction** 1

Understanding China Is Better than Underestimating China 1

Partial Understanding and Bad Policy 2

Not Knowing China 3

Not Knowing Thyself 4

2 **Why Has the World Got China so Wrong** 11

China-Bashing, Again… 12

… Because They Don't Like What They See 16

Understanding the Misunderstanding 17

How Different Is China? 18

Invisible and Visible Hands Working Together 21

No More Galapagos Critter 23

The Visible Hand That Is Not Understood 24

Misreading China at Your Peril 27

References 30

3 **China Rises When the West Sleeps** 33

Napoleon's Warning Comes True 35

GFC, A Turning Point for China's Rise 39

The Digital BRI Shock 43

A Global Disruption 46

A Change in Geopolitical Landscape… 46
… Benefiting ASEAN 47
From BRI to Debt Trap 49
BRI Ambition Scaled Back 51
No Point in Blindly Bashing China 52
References 54

4 Decoupling Versus Regionalism and "Collabetition" 57
Tariffs Don't Work as Intended 58
Decoupling, a Mutually Inclusive Incentive 59
China, a "Strategic Necessity" 60
Decoupling, Where? 61
What Is the Evidence Telling Us? 62
Shifts in Global Demand and Supply Chains 63
Regionalism Versus De-Globalisation 66
But Net FDI Has Dropped 67
Outward Direct Investment 69
New Sources of FDI 71
The Cost of Decoupling 72
New Paradigm of "Collabetition" and Impact 73
The EV Battleground 74
Boons and Banes 75
Impact on Energy Transition 76
Net-Zero, a Secular Trend 77
References 77

5 Capital Account Liberalisation, Opening a Can of Worms 79
Opening a Can of Worms 81
Controlled Liberalisation 82
The Inflow Channels 83
The Outflow Channels 83
The Two-Way Flow Channels 84
FTZs and Incentive Compatibility 86
Risk of Capital Flight 89
The Stock Connect Schemes 91
Debunking the Myths 93
Liberalisation with Chinese Characteristics 95

References 97

6 **Chinese Capital Flows, Friend or Foe** 99
The First Signs of Capital Outflows 101
Capital Flight Versus Capital Outflows 103
Drivers of Overseas Expansion? 107
The Changing Faces of Chinese ODI 111
ODI Face Changes Again 113
Pros and Cons of Exporting FDI 116
A Different Type of Investor 117
Capital Outflows Reflect Domestic Structural Changes… 119
… and Put Pressure on Development Finance 121
Crosscurrents 122
Another Serious Concern 124
Geopolitical Tensions on Chinese Investment 125
References 127

7 **The Reality of the BRI Disruption** 129
From Defensive to Offensive 131
The Strategic Importance 136
The Capital Linkage 137
It's a Sino-US Disruption 138
Overly Optimistic About the BRI 140
Commercial Reality 141
Political Suspicion 143
Still Going with International Norm 144
An Invisible BRI and Disruptions 146
Debt-Trap Finance, Myths and Realities 148
BRI Ambition Scaled Back 151
From BRI to Structural Rebalancing 153
References 155

8 **Trade War Turning the World Upside Down** 157
Even Partial De-globalisation Would Be Damaging 158
It's a Global Imbalance 159
Crushing the Chickens 161
The Chickens Fight Back 165
Confused by "Trumponomics" 168

Trump's Optimal Strategy 171
Relevance to China 172
Damage to the US 173
Collateral Damage and Contagion 176
Cold War Returning? 178
Appendix: Nash Equilibrium 179
An Example 180
Corner Solution (Winner Takes All) 181
References 181

9 Tech War of the Great Powers 183
The Core of Contention 184
China's AI Shock 186
Déjà vu and Global Impact 187
More than Just Geopolitical Rivalry 189
A Benign Disruption 191
The Digital Currency Fight 192
Digital Renminbi Challenging King Dollar 195
Is China Closing the Technology Gap? 199
Here Comes the Disruption 200
Fighting Back 201
The China Offensive and Limitations 204
The Disruption and Opportunity Cost 206
References 208

10 Digital Currency Competition and Disruption 211
Misunderstandings 212
Considerations for Investment & Reserve Asset 214
Bitcoin's Future 216
The Chinese Digital Competition 216
Controlled Anonymity 218
Disrupting the Global Payments System 219
Challenging the US 222
Disrupting the Banking System 225
Digital Renminbi Internationalisation 226
References 228

11 Creeping Renminbi Internationalisation Challenges King Dollar 229

It Starts with Oil 230
Linchpin of Dollar Supremacy 231
The Petro-Yuan's Threat 232
The Dollar's Boiling Frog Fable 234
A Gold-Backed Yuan 235
A Significant Step Forward 236
Incentive to Diversify Out of the Dollar 237
The Salami-Slicing Tactics 238
Add in the BRICS… 241
… and Africa 242
Gold and Renminbi Bonds 243
An Offensive Move by Stealth 245
Intriguing Thoughts 246
Eroding Funding for the US's Twin Deficits 246
Nudging Internationalisation Forward 247
"A Dollar for a Dollar" Strategy 248
Enter the Belt & Road Initiative 249
Geopolitical Implications 249
Is King Dollar in Danger? 251
The Practicality of "TINA" 253
Weakening the King Dollar 254
References 257

12 Is China Un-investible (Collapsing)? 259
Conventional but No Wisdom 260
There's More than Meets the Eye 261
Structural Transformation 264
What's New? 264
An Economic Paradox 265
A Revolutionary Change… 269
…That is Not Obvious 270
The New Reform Tactics 270
The China Risk 273
What is a Balance Sheet Recession? 274
The Curse of Debt-Deflation 275
Debt Risk 277
Wealth Destruction 279
Financial Engineering 279
Loss of Confidence and Deleveraging 280

Growth Sources 283
Why QE? 284
Conditions in China 284
Cost Versus Benefits 286
QE Not a Solution 287
A Lesson from Japan 289
References 290

13 A Reluctant Economic Superpower 293
The Optimists' Views 294
Japan's Turnaround 295
Structural Factors Boosting Japan's Wages 297
Mind the (r-g) Gap 298
A Policy Lesson for China 299
Supply-Side Expansion Alone Won't Work 300
Optimism on India 303
India's Advantages… 304
… Versus Reality 305
The Future 307
A Wrong Perception of China 308
The Chinese Motives to Move Up 310
Regional Partnership Challenging the US 311
A Reluctant Powerhouse 312
References 313

Index 317

About the Author

Mr. Chi Lo is the senior economist, Asia-Pacific, at a multinational bank based in Hong Kong. Chi's other positions in Asia included Asia Research Head for the British private property fund Grosvenor, chief economist and strategist for Asia at Standard Chartered Bank and research director for Greater China at HSBC in Hong Kong.

He was listed on the International Who's Who Professionals in 2000 and 2011 and has many years of international research experience in economics, financial markets and public policy & standards development, covering North American and Asian economies.

Before working in Asia, Chi was an economic advisor to the Canadian Treasury in Canada. His other experience includes international research firms in North America, regulatory bodies for securities trading in Toronto and London, and blue-chip international investment banks in North America, England and Asia.

Chi is the author of fourteen books on Chinese and Asian economic development and markets. He has published research work in international periodicals and newspapers and has appeared as a commentator on international media and speaker at international seminars, such as the United Nations, the World Economic Forum, Asian Development Bank, World Bank, House of Lords of the British Parliament, the European Commission and other central bank conferences.

He has taught economics and finance courses at various universities in Hong Kong and has spoken frequently at university finance courses and professional seminars in North America, Europe and Asia.

Chi did his economics graduate work at the London School of Economics and Political Science (LSE) in England and the University of British Columbia (UBC) in Canada.

Abbreviations

ABS	Asset-Backed Securities
AI	Artificial Intelligence
AIIB	Asia Infrastructure Investment Bank
BoJ	Bank of Japan
BoP	Balance of Payments
BRI	Belt and Road Initiative
CBDC	Central Bank Digital Currency
CCP	Chinese Communist Party
CDO	Collateralised Debt Obligations
CIPS	China International Payment System
CPTPP	Comprehensive and Progressive Agreement for Trans-Pacific Partnership
CSTC	Central Science and Technology Commission
DCEP	Digital Currency Electronic Payment
DLT	Distributed Ledger Technology
DM	Developed Markets
DOGE	Department of Government Efficiency
e-CNY	Electronic Chinese Yuan (or Electronic Renminbi)
EEU	Eurasia Economic Union
EM	Emerging Markets
EPI	European Payments Initiative
ESG	Environment, Social and Governance
ETF	Exchange-Traded Fund
EV	Electric Vehicles
FDI	Foreign Direct Investment
GCC	Gulf Cooperation Council

GFC	Global Financial Crisis
ICT	Information and Communication Technology
IMF	International Monetary Fund
IP	Intellectual Property
IPR	Intellectual Property Rights
IT	Information Technology
KPI	Key Performance Indicators
LLM	Large Language Model
m-CBDC	Multiple Central Bank Digital Currency
MLF	Mid-term Lending Facility
MPC	Marginal Propensity to Consume
NIRP	Negative Interest Rate Policy
NSF	National Science Foundation
ODI	Overseas Direct Investment
OMO	Open Market Operations
PBoC	People's Bank of China
PCT	Patent Cooperation Treaty
QE	Quantitative Easing
RCEP	Regional Comprehensive Economic Partnership
R&D	Research and Development
SAR	Special Administrative Region
SBT	Strategic Bitcoin Reserve
SDR	Special Drawing Rights
SOE	State-Owned Enterprises
SPFS	System for Transfer of Financial Messages
SWIFT	Society for Worldwide Interbank Financial Telecommunications
TINA	There Is No Alternative

List of Figures

Fig. 2.1	"Dual circulation" in China's new worldwide (*Source* Author)	15
Fig. 2.2	US trade balance (USD bn) (*Source* CEIC, author)	19
Fig. 2.3	China's growth contribution by GDP components (*Source* CEIC, author)	20
Fig. 2.4	Export growth of photovooltaic generators & lithium batteries since Covid-19 (*Note* *data only started in 2022. *Source* CEIC, author)	22
Fig. 2.5	Export growth of electric vehicles since Covid-19 (*Source* CEIC, author)	22
Fig. 3.1	Share of world exports (*Source* CEIC, author)	37
Fig. 3.2	Rising Chinese exports to ASEAN, Africa & Mexico since the trade war in 2018 (*Source* CEIC, author)	38
Fig. 3.3	China has increased investment in new market, esp. Asia significantly since 2018 (*Source* CEIC, author)	38
Fig. 3.4	China's BRI lending* has dropped since the official push in 2013 through 2017 (*Note* *approximated by total overseas lending. *Source* CEIC, author)	52
Fig. 4.1	Share of world exports (*Source* Statista, the World Bank, author)	58
Fig. 4.2	China's toal trade* with he G3 (*Note* *exports + imports with Japan, Europe & US, 12-month rolling sum. *Sources* CEIC, author)	62
Fig. 4.3	China's toal trade* with ASEAN (*Note* *exports + imports, 12-month rolling sum. *Sources* CEIC, author)	63

Fig. 4.4 China's total trade with ASEAN, Europe & N.America (*Note* *exports + imports, 12-month rolling sum. *Sources* CEIC, author) 64
Fig. 4.5 G3's imports* from ASEAN (*Note* *12-month rolling sum. *Sources* CEIC, author) 65
Fig. 4.6 Rising net FDI inflows* to ASEAN (*Note* *Balance of payments data. *Sources* CEIC, author) 65
Fig. 4.7 China's FDI share of country's total FDI* (*Note* 4-qtr moving average. *Sources* CEIC, HSBC, author) 66
Fig. 4.8 Falling FDI flows to China since late 2022 (*Note* *Balance of payments data, 4-quarter rolling sum. *Sources* CEIC, author) 68
Fig. 4.9 A narrowing gap* between BoP FDI inflows and utilised FDI (*Note* *BoP FDI inflows minus utilised FDI. *Sources* CEIC, author) 68
Fig. 4.10 Utilised FDI inflows* rose again in 2023 and 2024 (*Note* *12-month rolling sum. *Sources* CEIC, author) 69
Fig. 4.11 China has increased investment in Asia significantly (*Sources* CEIC, author) 70
Fig. 4.12 Average EV price by market (2023) (*Sources* Morgan Stanley, author) 75
Fig. 5.1 China's Gini coefficient suggests high income inequality (*Sources* World Bank, CEIC, author) 88
Fig. 5.2 Estimated over-invoicing of Chinese imports* (*Note* *value of Chinese import from Japan, the US and the EU minus value of exports from them to China. *Sources* CEIC, author's calculation) 90
Fig. 5.3 Chinn–Ito index of capital account openness (2021) (*Sources* Chinn–Ito index (KAOPEN), author) 94
Fig. 5.4 Renminbi-USD exchange rate trading volatility* risen (*Note* *approximated by the standard deviation of RMB-USD daily trading. *Sources* CEIC, author's calculation) 96
Fig. 6.1 China's basic balance* (quarterly basis) (*Note* *Current account balance + net FDI. *Sources* CEIC, author) 101
Fig. 6.2 A growing service trade deficit will keep eroding China' current account balance (*Sources* CEIC, author) 102
Fig. 6.3 China's net international investment remains small relative to other saving surplus countries* (*Note* *Data as of the third quarter of 2024. *Sources* Official data by governments, author) 103

Fig. 6.4 China's overseas direct investment (ODI) will continue to rise (*Sources* CEIC, author) 104
Fig. 6.5 China's errors & omissions and estimated non-FDI flows both showed rising capital outflows (*Note* *Change in FX reserves—C/A bal—net FDI flows, unadjusted for FX valuation effect as errors & omissions are data unadjusted for FX valuation effect. *Sources* CEIC, author) 107
Fig. 6.6 China's ODI (annual flows) (*Sources* CEIC, author) 108
Fig. 6.7 China has suffered diminishing marginal returns on investment (MRI)* (*Note* *5-year moving average. *Source* CEIC, author's calculation) 109
Fig. 6.8 China has cut ODI in DM and boosted ODI in EM (*Sources* Standard chartered, author) 113
Fig. 6.9 Net FDI flows* to China have turned negative (*Note* *Balance of payments data. *Sources* CEIC, author) 114
Fig. 6.10 China has been boosting ODI in metals and transport (*Sources* American Enterprise institute, author) 115
Fig. 6.11 China's structural rebalancing in progress (*Sources* CEIC, Author) 120
Fig. 6.12 Consumption and investment's contribution to China's GDP growth (*Sources* CEIC, Author) 121
Fig. 6.13 OECD FDI Restrictiveness index in 2023 (0 = open, 1 = closed. *Sources* CEIC, Author) 124
Fig. 7.1 China and the US shares of world exports (*Sources* Statista, The World Bank, author) 132
Fig. 7.2 Rising Chinese exports* to ASEAN, Africa and Mexico (USD bn) since the trade war in 2018 (*Note* *12-month rolling sums. *Sources* CEIC, author) 132
Fig. 7.3 China has increased investment in new markets, esp. Asia, significantly (USD bn) since 2018 (*Sources* CEIC, author) 133
Fig. 7.4 Chinese exports to the BRI countries, Europe & the US (*Sources* CEIC, author) 133
Fig. 7.5 China's export growth of photovoltaic generators & lithium batteries since Covid-19 (*Note* *Data only started in 2022. *Sources* CEIC, author) 134
Fig. 7.6 China's export growth of electric vehicles since Covid-19 (*Sources* CEIC, author) 134
Fig. 7.7 The invisible American shield (*Source* Author) 139

Fig. 7.8 China's foreign contracts continued to rise but revenue growth has stagnant* (*Notes* *12-month rolling sums; **Approximated by the value of completed projects. *Sources* CEIC, author) 142
Fig. 7.9 China's overseas lending* (*Note* *Balance of payments data. *Sources* CEIC, author) 152
Fig. 8.1 Share of China's net exports contribution to GDP growth (*Sources* CEIC, author) 160
Fig. 8.2 Targeted country-specific tariff rates on Asia, per US announcement on 2 April 2025 (*Sources* The White House, author) 163
Fig. 8.3 FDI inflows to Vietnam (registered capital) (*Sources* CEIC, author) 165
Fig. 8.4 FDI inflows to Vietnam (no. of licensed projects) (*Sources* CEIC, author) 165
Fig. 8.5 Total tariff rates on Asia under the reciprocal tariff framework (*Sources* The White House, author) 166
Fig. 8.6 Asian countries' fiscal and current account balances (2023/2024) (*Sources* CEIC, author) 169
Fig. 8.7 Cumulative foreign direct investment (FDI) (*Notes* *Data started in 2003 through 2023. **Data started in 1985 throgh 2023. *Sources* CEIC, author) 173
Fig. 8.8 Change in nominal exchange against the USD (*Sources* CEIC, author) 176
Fig. 9.1 Difference between US and China R&D spending (*Sources* CEIC, author) 187
Fig. 9.2 US internet boom (mid- to late- 1990s) boosted labour productivity growth (*Sources* CEIC, author) 188
Fig. 9.3 Renmimnbi trade settlement* (*Notes* *Data in 3-month moving average. **Mainland China + HK + Taiwan. *Sources* CEIC, author) 196
Fig. 9.4 Renminbi's share in global foreign exchange reserves (*Sources* IMF COFER, author) 197
Fig. 9.5 Intellectural property rights earnings (*Sources* CEIC, author) 199
Fig. 9.6 Intellectural property rights payments balance (*Sources* CEIC, author) 200
Fig. 9.7 China's exports to the BRI countries have far outpaced those to Europe & the US (*Sources* CEIC, author) 202
Fig. 9.8 China's R&D spending is catching up with the US level (*Sources* CEIC, author) 203
Fig. 9.9 Growth of the "Big Fund" (*Sources* CEIC, author) 203

Fig. 10.1 Bitcoin's long (10-year) and short (1-year) price volatilty far exceeds traditional assets (*Sources* Forbes, author) 215
Fig. 10.2 The two-tier system of DCEP (*Source* Author) 218
Fig. 10.3 Value of cashless payments (*Sources* BIS, author) 223
Fig. 10.4 Rising China-Russia trade* (*Note* *Exports + imports, 12-month rolling sum. *Sources* CEIC, author) 223
Fig. 10.5 The correspondent bank model (*Source* Author) 226
Fig. 11.1 Linchpin of the dollar's supremacy (*Source* Author) 232
Fig. 11.2 Share of global payments currencies (March 2025) (*Source* SWIFT, author) 233
Fig. 11.3 Number of new US sanctions by year (*Source* Compiled from US Treasury by author) 238
Fig. 11.4 Shares of USD and renminbi in global reserves (*Source* IMF, author) 240
Fig. 11.5 China-Africa trade* (USD billion) (*Note* *12-month rolling sum. *Source* CEIC, author) 242
Fig. 11.6 China trade with South Africa & Nigeria* (USD billion) (*Note* *12-month rolling sum. *Source* CEIC, author) 243
Fig. 11.7 China's gold reserves (million onces) have been rising as renminbi internationalisation moves ahead (*Source* CEIC, author) 244
Fig. 11.8 US twin deficits require persistent funding from the world's saving (*Source* CEIC, author) 247
Fig. 11.9 Strategic importance of the Middle East in China's expansion strategy (*Source* Author) 248
Fig. 11.10 The share of other smaller currencies* in global reserves has surged since 2000 (*Note* *Total global reserves excl. USD, euro, yen, pound sterling, Swiss franc and renminbi. *Source* IMF, author) 252
Fig. 11.11 US chronic current account deficit* reflects its savings deficit (*Source* CEIC, author) 255
Fig. 11.12 Top current account deficit countries (2024) (*Note* *12-month rolling sum. *Source* Trading economics, author) 256
Fig. 11.13 US bond yield follows Fed funds rate movement (with a correlation coefficient of 0.8) (*Source* CEIC, author) 257
Fig. 12.1 China's import value fell in 2023–2024 but volume continued to rise (*Source* CEIC, author) 262
Fig. 12.2 Household expenditure > income growth => no economic collapse (*Source* CEIC, author) 263

Fig. 12.3 China's household disposable income growth > nominal GDP growth (*Source* CEIC, author) 263

Fig. 12.4 Industries migrating inland* (*Source* CEIC, author) 266

Fig. 12.5 China's consumer willingness to spend* has not recovered to pre-Covid level (*Note* *China's National Bureau of Statistics survey. *Source* CEIC, author) 268

Fig. 12.6 China's private-sector investment growth (*Source* CEIC, author) 268

Fig. 12.7 China's corruption index* (*Note* *A higher score = less corruption. *Source* Transparency International, author) 271

Fig. 12.8 Number of patent cooperation treaty (PCT) applications by China as a share of US and Japan applications (*Source* World Intellectual Property Organization, author) 273

Fig. 12.9 A debt-deflation spiral of balance sheet recession (*Source* Author) 276

Fig. 12.10 Debt-to-GDP ratio (%) for non-financial sector (2022) (*Source* BIS, author) 278

Fig. 12.11 China's debt-to-GDP ratio (%) (*Source* BIS, author) 281

Fig. 12.12 Year-over-year change in China's domestic debt-to-GDP ration (%) (*Source* BIS, author) 282

Fig. 12.13 PBoC's balance sheet growth (*Source* CEIC, author) 285

Fig. 12.14 China's share of merchandise & service exports in global markets (*Source* Statista, author) 287

Fig. 12.15 China's (r-g) gap* is too small for boosting GDP growth under debt-deflation (*Note* *1-year real loan prime rate (LPR) minus real GDP growth rate. *Source* CEIC, author) 290

Fig. 13.1 Nikkei 225 index rose to record high in November 2024 (*Source* CEIC, author) 294

Fig. 13.2 Japan's (r-g) gap is conducive to boosting growth (*Source* CEIC, author) 296

Fig. 13.3 Japan's old-age & female labour participantion rate (*Source* CEIC, author) 297

Fig. 13.4 Japan's total accession & separation rates rising to post-Covid high (*Source* CEIC, author) 298

Fig. 13.5 The BoJ only cut interest rate more than a year after the stock market crash (*Source* CEIC, author) 299

Fig. 13.6 China did not suffer from the devastating asset bubble collapse as Japan did (*Source* CEIC, author) 301

Fig. 13.7 Japan: Increase in manufacturing capex failed to reflate income growth (*Note* *Capital expenditure in manufacturing & equipment, and intellectual property. *Source* Morgan Stanley, author) 302
Fig. 13.8 Indian stocks (SENSEX) have outperformed Chinese stock (CSI 300) since 2022 (*Source* CEIC, author) 303
Fig. 13.9 China's foreign direct investment inflows have slowed down sharply (*Source* CEIC, author) 304
Fig. 13.10 China's corruption* has improved while that of India's has worsened since Covid-19 (*Note* *A larger index = less corruption. *Source* Transparency International, author) 306
Fig. 13.11 India has the lowest R&D spending compared with China and the US (*Source* CEIC, author) 307

CHAPTER 1

Introduction

Understanding China Is Better than Underestimating China

US President Donald Trump started a trade war with China again in 2025, after doing so in his first presidency in 2018. This time the trade conflict has included all trading partners of the US, i.e. the world. It is a vivid example of misunderstanding China leading to misguided policies creating geopolitical risks and global economic disruptions. This book is about analysing China's emergence on the global stage and understanding its superpower aspiration (clash with the US) by assessing it from different, hidden, aspects and questioning conventional wisdom, which often are just conventional views without much wisdom (in my view), through rigorous research thoughts backed by data and evidence.

China and the US are locked in severe competition for global leadership. China is rising quickly to challenge the US's Number One status, raising fears and antagonism between the two countries and, more generally, between the developed world led by the US and the developing world led by China. With rising geopolitical tensions and misinformation inundating the world, it is all the more important to have better understanding about China and its role in the global system so that the world can respond according to informed decisions and solid analysis but not hearsays and biases. As ancient Chinese military strategist Sun Tzu said, know yourself and your enemy, and you will win every battle.

C. Lo, *Clash of the Economic Titans: China and the United States*,
https://doi.org/10.1007/978-981-95-2510-2_1

However, Mr. Trump's trade war, which uses punitive tariffs and export restrictions, against China has totally missed this point by not knowing China and not even knowing his own country on any sound economic basis. As an introduction to analysing the great power competition for global leadership between these two big powers, this trade war contains crucial evidence, implications and illustrations for the danger of misguided policy and investment reactions. A crucial question is why China has been so assertive in fighting back the US punitive tariffs, defying the world's expected that it would not retaliate tit-for-tat?

Hence, this introduction, through the trade war, sets the stage for the discussion in the rest of the book about China's superpower aspirations and disruption. Generally, the economic, financial, technological and geopolitical challenges that China is posing to the US, and the resulting global disruptions, are often not thoroughly understood. This book seeks to fill the void of partial understanding of China and debunk myths, hypes and distorted analyses through rigorous research thoughts and data analysis made simple for non-technical (non-mathematical) readership.

However, things can change a lot due to Mr. Trump's mercurial behaviour and, generally, the evolving US foreign policy on competing with China. Fear not. The discussions in this book are about mega trends and structural developments that will last for a long time for analyses, reassessment and references.

Let us start with the trade war and see what it tells us about the clash of the Titans—China and the US.

Partial Understanding and Bad Policy

Fundamentally, using tariffs to correct a current account (or in a narrower sense, trade) deficit is flawed when the external deficit is a result of domestic savings-investment imbalance, i.e. deficient savings and excessive investment. The savings deficiency may come from excessive consumption (i.e. insufficient private-sector savings) or fiscal deficit (i.e. excessive public-sector spending), or both. This is the case in the US as manifested in its chronic (at least over 20 years) twin deficits – fiscal deficit + current account deficit. In 2024, the US had a fiscal deficit of 6.4% of GDP[1] and

[1] The safety guideline for a fiscal deficit, based on international experience, is 3% of GDP, above which economic problems, such as current account deficit, loss of confidence, capital misallocation, debt-currency crisis etc., will emerge.

a current account deficit of 3.9%; i.e. it had a twin deficit of 10.3% of GDP that needs massive funding from foreign savings.

Trying to use trade (and/or exchange rate depreciation) policies to correct a trade deficit will not work if the underlying problem of savings-investment imbalance is not corrected. This is simple economics, but it is amazing that the Trump administration has ignored it and focused on partial analysis to push for trade wars, including a weak dollar policy,[2] to fight China. This is like a dog barking up the wrong tree.

Not Knowing China

Misunderstanding China is a bigger mistake than barking up the wrong tree in response to the rise of China on the global stage. Forcing decoupling from China to reduce US dependence on Chinese imports is not as simple as Mr. Trump thinks. For example, production of iPhones could move elsewhere, and India (even onshoring back to the US) has been mooted. However, it will be very costly and easier said than done. Why?

This is because China has a comparative advantage (the very economic tenet that the Trump administration has chosen to ignore) in logistics, manufacturing supply chains and engineering. It is thus not surprising that China dominates in the production of smartphones and many other products because it is far cheaper and more efficient to produce them there. Decoupling production from China by brute force will raise global prices of these products as supply chains are reconfigured and distorted.

The trade war is an external economic shock on the US in terms of what it can import (which is a supply problem), and on China in terms of finding markets for its exports (which is a demand problem). However, China has the capacity, policy tools and resources to make up for this demand deficiency that the trade war with the US has inflicted.

Domestically, China has ample room to stimulate consumption, which accounts for a low percentage of GDP (less than 40% in 2023). There is scope for large increases in fiscal spending on measures to boost personal consumption, or science and education (which would extend its lead over

[2] The so-called "Mar-a-Lago Accord"—a plan proposed by Stephen Miran, chair of Trump's Council of Economic Advisers—tries to coordinate with America's trading partners to weaken the dollar to reduce the US trade deficit with these other countries.

the US in technology and engineering), or the environment and healthcare. Beijing can also make it easier for tens of millions of citizens to move from the countryside to towns and cities.

Externally, China can expand into new markets outside the developed world, as it has been doing through the Belt and Road Initiative (BRI) network since the last trade war with the US in 2018. Indeed, China's total exports to the BRI countries have surpassed its exports to Europe and the US combined in recent years.

The point is that China can make up for the deficiency of aggregate demand resulted from the Sino-US trade war without resorting to "dumping" them on the rest of the world. How about the US?

Not Knowing Thyself

While Mr. Trump thinks in very simplistic terms that tariffs are a panacea for curing the US trade deficit with China by hitting Chinese exports, the supply-side adjustments that the US has to make in such a trade war are far more complicated than what he sees. The adjustments would need years of increased investment, training, infrastructure, etc. However, arguably, this may not be happening easily because Trump's mercurial policies are making the challenge of this adjustment all the greater.

The on-again, off-again tariffs, combined with the drastic public-sector spending and job cuts implemented by the newly created Department of Government Efficiency (DOGE) have wreaked havoc on private and public sectors' confidence alike. Consider moving production to the US. That will require massive upfront investment. Yet because of all the policy and incentive disruptions from Trump's erratic policy moves, no firm can be sure about the economic environment even three months ahead, let alone through his four-year term. Globally, the disruption to the supply chains is creating a massive amount of uncertainty and damaging comparative advantages and, thus, destroying the disinflationary benefit of globalisation.

Even America's trade deficit may worsen as opposed to the trade war's intention. Mr. Trump's rhetoric is to bring back manufacturing jobs. On "Liberation Day"—2 April 2025 when he announced punitive tariffs (ranging from 30 to 65%, and later elevating to 145% for China) on all trading partners—he declared that his sky-high tariffs would cause jobs to "come roaring back into our country". Not long after, Commerce Secretary Howard Lutnick pushed this point to its limit in a television interview by saying "The army of millions and millions of human beings screwing in little screws to make iPhones – that kind of thing is going to come to America".

One should wonder what on earth they are trying to bring back to America. Manufacturing jobs today make up less than 10% of US employment because the US is a high value-added knowledge-based economy. The average manufacturing worker earns much less than the average service-sector worker. Trump's policy to bring back factory jobs from overseas would mean a significant drop in the average manufacturing wage in the US. This is because Mr. Lutnick may want Americans "screwing in little screws", but America's businesses are not going to pay high wages for that type of work. Developing countries all want to move up the value chain, create high-pay jobs to escape the so-called "middle-income trap".[3] But Trump's policies (or shall we call it "Trumponomcs") go backwards by moving his advanced country back into the low-wage trap that poor countries have tried hard to get out.

In other words, the Trump rhetorics are looking to the past, not the future. Even if his policies were successful in reviving American manufacturing, it would not create good jobs for workers in the de-industrialised parts of the economy. Cars these days, for example, are made by robots, with the best companies employing more engineers, researchers and designers than manual workers. The production-line work is low-pay low value-added that an advanced economy like America should not focus on. It is the service and knowledge sectors that really matter and make America great.

So, Trump's policies seem to be shooting himself in the foot. They will almost surely destroy America's longstanding trade surplus in those high value-added services and erode its technological edge. That does not bode well for America in its competition with China for global power in the long term. The damage on the US will be particularly serious under his destructive policy on America's considerable soft power: tourism is falling off the cliff, foreign students are discouraged from studying in the US and foreign (mainly Chinese) scientists are expelled, the rule of law

[3] The "middle-income trap" refers to a situation where a country's economy stagnates or slows down significantly after reaching a middle-income level (with per-capita annual income roughly between USD5,000 andnUSD14,000, according to the World Bank's definition), preventing it from progressing to a high-income status.

is being tested, and the president is waging a war on America's leading universities.

The erosion of its soft power makes the long-run prospects for the US even bleaker, *ceteris paribus*, because universities produce the advances in science that are the cornerstone of America's technological dominance. China, meanwhile, has built many high-quality universities over the past decade, producing more than 8 million university graduates each year, with half of them having STEM degrees. China has also produced more STEM PhDs than the US, with China's strategic focus on building a large, research-driven workforce in critical technologies being a key driver in this trend.

All this makes understanding China all the more important both for the sake of managing China's superpower inspiration and for the US's self-reflection to position itself in accommodating the rising power of China. The following is the plan of the book.

Chapter 2 decodes the factors behind the divergence of views on China's economic evolution by drawing on socio-economic evidence and data and differences in political ideologies and cultural values. The discussion highlights the characteristics and changing dynamics underlying China's peculiar economic system that have puzzled many, especially those in the West. The approach of the analysis is to question conventional wisdom, debunk myths, reveal the misunderstandings and ignorance about China's superpower inspiration, and assess China from "hidden angles" and reveal the danger of misreading China and the resulting misguided policy and investment responses to China's emergence.

Chapter 3 analyses how China emerges on the global stage while the West sleeps on the wheel. The focus is on how China's rapid economic and geopolitical expansion and technological advancement are defying America's protectionist policies but also creating misunderstanding and fears about its growing economic clout intensifying geopolitical risks. I also challenge the conventional wisdom that China is using "debt-trap" finance and economic expansion to reap massive benefits at the expense of other nations; China also suffers from ill-judgement.

Decoupling has been a key US policy to compete with China, forcing changes in global policy and business decisions and international trade and investment flows. By analysing trade and capital-flow data, Chapter 4 reveals the fallacy of using punitive tariffs and export restrictions as tools to correct America's massive trade deficit and contain China's global emergence. The analysis highlights that (1) shifts in global demand have led to the development of "reverse supply chains" but not decoupling, (2) the trend of negative net foreign direct investment in China is not a sign of imminent danger to the world, and crucially, (3) the emergence of a new paradigm of collaboration-cum-competition when the US-led de-globalisation clashes with the China-led regionalism. All these issues have profound global implications that need better understanding and more research.

Opening up the capital account is another mega trend unfolding in China. This trend is creating significant impact on the global policy and investment landscape, and causing confusion, fears and hype among the international community that China is competing with the US for global power. Chapter 5 assesses the motivation and optimism and pessimism about China's capital account liberalisation and discusses its "controlled liberalisation" process that has puzzled the world. The analysis debunks the myths behind Beijing's policy moves, which many observers have mistaken as big steps towards capital account opening, reveals the incentive incompatibility problems that China optimists have overlooked, implicit capital controls, and other distorted understanding behind the liberalisation measures.

Crucially, China's capital account liberalisation has turned it from being a net foreign direct investment (FDI) recipient to a significant FDI exporter. Chapter 6 explores the dynamics of these outflows, dispels the myth of capital flight while addressing the risk of it, and reveals the evolving structural forces behind China's foreign investments and their geopolitical and financial impact.

China's capital outflows could even be a catalyst for reforming the global development finance model that has been dominated by the interest of the rich countries, Chapter 6 argues. The implications from my analysis are that (1) China is challenging the US's global financial clout, (2) the world needs to change the way it assesses China's investment and capital flows and (3) the US and the developed world need to reassess the way they run the development finance model to compete with China for global influence.

Chapter 7 zooms in to examine one particular aspect of China's capital outflows, the Belt and Road Initiative (BRI) which underpins China's long-term strategic expansion on the global stage. The international community has either partial knowledge about the BRI's strategic importance or distorted views on its impact on the Chinese and global economic development. This chapter assesses whether the BRI has actually gained traction (as the optimists believe), examines its impact on China's economic rebalancing efforts (which have been misunderstood) and exposes the fallacy of the China critics' view that China is using "debt-trap diplomacy" under the guise of the BRI to "conquer the world". Unlike the fear of pessimists, the BRI is under many constraints that prevent it from disrupting the global balance of power any time soon.

I examine the strategic and economic competition that lie behind the US-China trade war in Chapter 8 and "tech war" in Chapter 9 and argue with theoretical and empirical evidence that the global disruptions, possibly including military conflicts, are results of (1) a lack of understanding by the Trump administration about global economics and China's development, and (2) a "non-Nash" strategy of Trump's mercurial policy, which is not some erratic un-systemic moves as commonly seen by many observers.

The highlight of my tech war analysis is China's AI shock—DeepSeek—in early 2025, which has prompted the world to focus attention on Sino-US geopolitical tensions. However, as I argue in Chapter 9, this AI shock has also exposed a problem of collusion in America's tech industry that has hampered global innovation and competition. Geopolitics and, ironically, America's policies designed to impede China's AI innovation have pushed China to speed up its AI innovation and development that could disrupt the global system.

The Sino-US tech war is also fought over the digital currency platform. Chapter 9 also reveals the problems with the Bitcoin reserve that the US is building, which cryptocurrency advocates never talk about, the digital currency fight between China and the US, the digital renminbi's challenge to King dollar, and the disruptions of the digital fight to the global system.

Chapter 10 follows on with the digital theme by assessing the different approaches of the two powers to developing digital currencies, with China spearheading the creation of a central bank digital currency (CBDC) and the US leveraging market forces for developing cryptocurrencies. The discussion contains food for thought for other countries that are considering the creation of their CBDCs.

The analysis extends to the political economy aspect of China's digital disruption to the global payments system and challenge to the US dollar's global status. The Russo-Ukrainian war adds to the world's incentive to reduce US dollar risk and reliance on the US dollar-dominated payments system. China could potentially leverage on this development to breakup the global US dollar-centric system and expand the digital renminbi's international role to challenge the hegemony of the US dollar. The "digital currency war" between the two great powers will create disruption to the global financial system and regulatory regime which this chapter seeks to reveal.

The slow but steady progress on renminbi internationalisation has been eroding the US dollar's global supremacy since 2009 indiscernibly like the boiling frog fable. Chapter 11 reveals the renminbi's creeping internationalisation and the hidden trends that most in the public have ignored—notably Beijing's "salami-slicing" tactics and "a dollar for a dollar" strategy in hitting the US financial foundation. Behind all these is a little-known development that China may have quietly and slowly amassed enough financial clout quietly in redirecting global dollar liquidity away from the US. While "TINA" (a situation where There Is No Alternative) can keep King dollar's throne for more years, structural forces from the global savings-investment imbalance are building to weaken the dollar in the coming years so that even without the China challenge, King dollar's global influence is on the decline.

The last two chapters assess and challenge the conventional views that China has become un-investible (i.e. collapsing) and will be overtaken by Japan and India as economic superpower. I argue, with evidence, that the world has dwelled on the stock of China's past problems while it should reassess China's growth outlook based on its new structural reform directions. Chapter 12 reveals an economic paradox that has not been properly understood by both the West and even the Chinese, discusses the little-known revolutionary change in the Chinese system and reform tactics by President Xi Jinping (which most in the West see as power grab), dispels the fallacy that China is falling into a balance sheet recession, and refutes the policy prescription of quantitative easing as advocated by many so-call experts.

The last chapter challenges the validity of the global assumption that China wants to become an economic superpower. In the discussion, I address the two big questions that have caught global attention since the end of the pandemic, namely optimism on Japan getting out of its thirty-year debt-deflation quagmire and India replacing China and the US as the world's economic superpower. I challenge the conventional wisdom of these arguments with evidence and data that have been overlooked or ignored and reveal (1) the lessons that China can learn from Japan, and (2) the partial understanding about the developments in the three countries that could lead to misguided policy reactions and investment decisions. In the end, China may end up as a reluctant superpower.

CHAPTER 2

Why Has the World Got China so Wrong

At the turn of the millennium, the global balance of power has undergone a seismic shift without much notice. While the West has grappled with internal and geopolitical challenges, China has steadily, and quietly, ascended to become a dominant force in global economics, technology and diplomacy. The preparation for the achievements started decades ago with its economic reforms in the early 1980s, when China endeavoured to get its people out of poverty and into better life quality. In 40 years, China had lifted 800 million people out of poverty—the level of income of less than USD1.9 per day according to the World Bank's definition.

China's development efforts showed that it had determined right in the beginning not to stay a sweatshop forever. So, they went after talent. If they did not have it, they threw money at it by bringing in experts (both local and foreign) and building universities to train future technocrats and leaders. If they did not have the equipment, they followed the textbook script of international trade by exchanging domestic surplus labour for foreign machinery and capital they needed. By 2010, the returns on these investments were manifested in the size of the Chinese economy which had grown into the second largest in the world, surpassing Japan and trailing after the US. The world started to take notice.

While China was laying low and strengthening their economic powerbase, the US was too engaged with wars in the Middle East—noticeably Iraq and Afghanistan. When the US finally woke up to the reality by

C. Lo, *Clash of the Economic Titans: China and the United States*,
https://doi.org/10.1007/978-981-95-2510-2_2

2010, they did not like what they saw. But China never looked back or stopped. It kept pouring resources funded by the country's high domestic savings into high-tech industries, like electric cars, batteries, solar panels, renewable energy, semiconductors, aeroplanes, aerospace, photovoltaics, etc., even before the tech competition with the US even started.

In 2024, China dropped another bombshell onto the world by showing off its military strength, including the possession of the 12,000 km-range intercontinental ballistic missiles, the sixth-generation fighter jets, the 076 electromagnetic catapult amphibious assault ship and the KJ-3900 radar planes and their wolf-packed drones (Aytekin, 2024; Gan, 2024; Sweetman, 2024; Yu, 2024). These developments have further awakened the US and its allies to the reality that "China is coming", intensifying the shift of the US foreign policy on China from constructive engagement to strategic competition since the first Trump administration in 2017 (Winkler, 2023).

China-Bashing, Again...

Since China's emergence, there has been a deep mistrust and negative bias developed among the developed nations, led by the US, on China's progress. This has led to a sharp rise in China-bashing stories again since 2018 after a retreat of anti-China sentiment between 2010 and 2013. A survey in 2022 by Cambridge University and YouGov (a British-based international research and data analytics firm) showed that negative views on China soared to new highs in almost two-thirds of the 26 countries surveyed (de Waal, 2022), with most of the negative sentiment coming from the US and its allies.

Without understanding China properly, this attitude is dangerous and could risk the world running erroneous policies and business and investment decisions, aggravating geopolitical tensions and, thus, increasing the probability of military conflicts. While research and media coverage on China abound, they often do not help much to better understand the Middle Kingdom because in the public domain, guesstimates, conjectures, *a priori* reasoning from dubious assumptions, misinformation and media-generated hallucinations are reiterated so often that they are taken as facts.

To put it bluntly, when a lie about China is told a thousand times, it becomes the truth. The demagoguery of contemporary populism ensures that clamour about China needs no evidence at all to fuel it! The proliferation of distorted news and propagandas on social media, augmented by artificial intelligence fraudulent practices, has aggravated the situation.

How ridiculous can it get? Consider the reporting on China's Covid-19 outbreak in early 2020. A major international newspaper published an opinion piece by an academic calling China "the real sick man of Asia" and accusing its government of covering up the health crisis.[1] While there is nothing wrong with exposing any possible wrongdoings, but both the author and the publisher provided no evidence at all to support the claim, at which Beijing took serious offence.

Similarly, another international newspaper reported that "the most fateful consequence of the official silence was that it facilitated the exodus of some five million people in the weeks before the city (of Wuhan) was quarantined on January 22, thus helping to transport the virus all over the country and overseas" to underscore their narrative of China covering up the serious state of the virus outbreak.[2] This was total nonsense and showed that the reporters were either ignorant about China or distorted the evidence to fit their narrative and agenda.

Those who know China should know that most if not all of these five million people were migrant workers who always went back to their hometowns during the Chinese New Year (and other major Chinese festivals) for family reunion. They left early (before the city of Wuhan was locked down) because they had to get home before the New Year, not because the city government "facilitated the exodus". China has almost 300 million migrant workers, or floating population,[3] who travel back home from the cities where they work every Chinese New Year for family reunion. That is why many observers call this Chinese-New-Year travel the largest migration on earth.

So, the problem with misreading China, and, hence, the analysis about its global relations and disruption, has a lot to do the contamination and abuse of public information and hidden agendas, aggravated by socio-cultural differences in doing the analysis. The latter is highlighted by the

[1] "*China Is the Real Sick Man of Asia*," by Walter Russell Mead, The Wall Street Journal, February 3, 2020.

[2] See "*Coronavirus: the cost of China's public health cover-up*," by James Kynge, Sun Yu and Tom Hancock, Financial Times, February 7, 2020.

[3] In 2023, China had 298 million migrant workers, comprising more than a third of the Chinese workforce.

fact that what is understood by the West of China is often not the same understanding by China of the West. These problems have created an expectation gap between what the world expects China to deliver and what China can actually, and want to, deliver. This gap has become a key factor in creating global political tensions and market volatility, and in hyping the fears about China's global ascent.

Many observers also tend to see China in the lens of inscrutable oriental tropes (The Economist, 2024), blinding them from understanding China properly. Very often, it is not that China is inscrutable, but that many China critics, especially American hawks, simply do not like what they see or hear, or are simply being naïve about the happenings in China. Many China critics do not know the Chinese language and cultural and have never set foot on China but rely on public information twisted by distorted views and analysis.

In fact, Chinese President Xi Jinping has expressed his thinking about the global system and China's role in it more clearly and more frequently than any other Chinese leaders. He often takes time to explain in detail what he thinks about most issues under their policy agenda. For example, in announcing the "dual circulation" policy framework in May 2020 at the Politburo meeting, Mr. Xi and the leadership made it very clear that the strategy was to counter global hostilities and global demand shift by strengthening the domestic sector as the primary driver for economic growth (the internal circulation) while still engaging, but reducing reliance on, the external sector to sustain stable growth and resilient investment (the external circulation) in the face of rising strategic competition with the US.

He went into details in explaining a new paradigm of increasing global uncertainties and geopolitical hostility that, ironically, would create new opportunities for China as the US global leadership flounders. This paradigm reflects Mr. Xi's new worldview that the global system will be divided into three main regions, Asia, North America and Europe, with each region being led by a super-regional power. This will lead to the rise of regionalism with strong intra-regional economic linkages alongside de-globalisation with weak inter-regional linkages. The rest of the world will fit in somewhere among these regions.

In the dual circulation framework, China sees its internal circulation sitting in the centre of Asia, engaging regional and global capital, financial and technological markets for enhancing domestic growth and driving regional growth (Fig. 2.1).

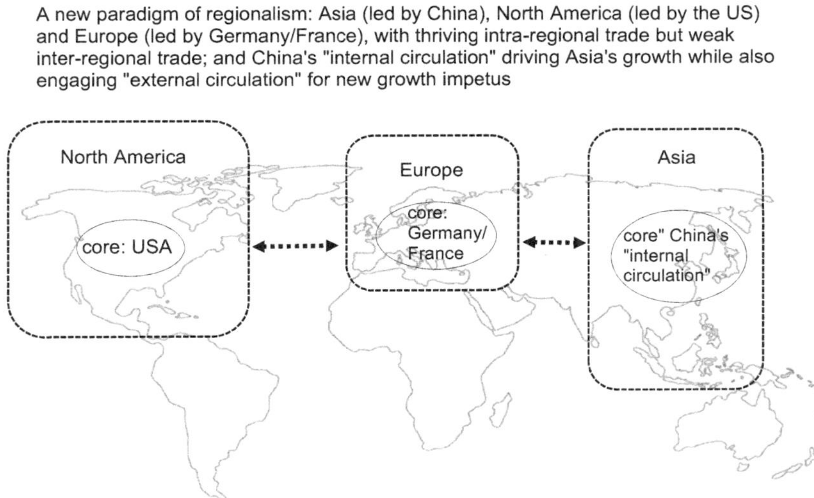

Fig. 2.1 "Dual circulation" in China's new worldwide (*Source* Author)

The external circulation in China's policy thinking is a paradigm focusing on the US as the global demand hub which is built on globalisation and reflects the US's post-World War global leadership and international cooperation. But this model is failing, in Mr. Xi's view, due to the withdrawal of the US from the global stage, or in other words the return of the US to isolationism and protectionism.

So, the Chinese leadership believes that de-globalisation, leading to economic decoupling and breaking up of the global supply chains, is a secular trend that will threaten China's long-term stability. Rising geopolitical tensions and exogenous shocks such as the Covid-19 health crisis have aggravated this global structural change. Hence, China can no longer rely on global integration as a growth driver; it must focus on domestic demand, or the internal circulation, to hedge against external risks.

… Because They Don't Like What They See

China's new worldview and development strategies are, thus, designed as a defence against geopolitical and external economic shocks. However, the West mostly sees them as an offensive policy to reshape the world order by imposing Chinese values and system design. Antagonism, suspicion and geopolitical tensions ensue, and these are often aggravated by distorted information and ignorance about the workings of the Chinese system and political economy.

Notably, when Mr. Xi talked about a "community of shared future for mankind" and an end of the "Cold War mentality and camp confrontation model", he was not being cryptic. He explicitly called for an end to US hegemony towards a multipolar world order where different political and economic systems could coexist as equals and the Western democracies should not be seen as the only and right model. All these were explicitly discussed and disseminated in his policy statements and writings.

So, what seems to be unsettling for the China critics, American hawks in particular, is not the inscrutability of China but the clarity of its vision and the effectiveness of the Chinese leadership's execution of the strategies to realise the vision. China's Belt and Road Initiative, its technological and scientific advancement and its growing diplomatic influence in the Global South[4] are not secret strategies at all.

The real question is not about what China wants, as China critics see, but about whether the US can come to terms with China's ascent to the global stage. Can the American hawks break their binary thinking mode of "either us or them" to engage constructively with a world where different systems and values must find ways to coexist and cooperate, rather than dominate or contain each other?

[4] Global North and Global South refer to a categorisation of countries based on their defining characteristics with regard to socio-economics and politics. According to UN Trade and Development, the Global South broadly comprises Africa, Latin America and the Caribbean, Asia and Oceania.

Understanding the Misunderstanding

In the grand scheme of things, the West's misunderstanding of China's progress arises not from a single factor but from a combination of factors including cultural, political, economic, and geopolitical divergences, with each factor contributing to a skewed perception.

China's hybrid economy blends state intervention with market dynamics. This often creates distorted views among Western analysts who are accustomed to neoliberal models and criticise the Chinese model without being able to recognise the adaptability and local characteristics of the Chinese approach, such as the role of state-owned enterprises in strategic sectors and the long-term vision of the leadership.

For example, China's Communist Party-led socialist system emphasises long-term planning and centralised governance. This basic set-up runs against the liberal ideals of Western democracies and, thus, makes them see the Chinese system as inherently restrictive and suppressive. However, this view has led to underestimation of China's capacity to drive growth and address challenges like poverty, banking crisis, asset bubbles, etc. This also explains why despite decades of crisis prediction by some "China experts" in the West, China still stands like an island in the storm.

Add in China's unique cultural and historical perspectives, the misunderstanding of China becomes even more distorted because, simply, if you do not live in China and have not gone through its political and economic volatilities over the past 50 centuries, you will never get it. China's Confucian heritage and collectivist values prioritise social harmony, state stability and territorial integrity. These values contrast sharply with Western individualism and freedom of choice even at the cost of social and political instability and territorial disintegration.

Many "China experts" seem to have ignored, or even to be unaware of, the legacy of the Century of Humiliation[5]—a period in Chinese history that began with the First Opium War (1839–1842) and ended in 1945 with China emerging out of the Second World War by gaining a permanent seat at the United Nations Security Council. The legacy makes

[5] The century-long period of humiliation was characterised by the decline, defeat and political fragmentation of the Qing dynasty, which led to demoralising foreign intervention, annexation and subjugation of China, notably by the imperialist powers of Britain, the US, Japan, Russia, France, Germany, Austria-Hungary, and Italy racing to "lease (by brute force)" Chinese harbours and ports, and scrambling for their own spheres of influence. In the Chinese history, this period is known as the "scramble for concessions".

China focus on sovereignty and self-reliance more than anything else. However, Western narratives often misinterpret this as aggression rather than resilience and self-defence.

Concepts such as “socialism with Chinese characteristics” lack direct Western analogues. This often leads to mistranslation, distorted thinking or dismissal. China’s domestic focus on stability and incremental reform under state guidance also clashes with the Western practice of political liberalisation, free market mechanism, and “shock treatment” style of reform. Throw in media misrepresentation and exaggeration through opinionated, sentimental, headlines and unsubstantiated and biased information, a picture of Chinese authoritarianism exploiting human rights and suppressing freedom overwhelming achievements in poverty reduction, infrastructure progress and technological innovation becomes “mainstream thinking” in the West. This is no different from selective framing shaping public opinion to view China through a lens of “evil axis”.

How Different Is China?

Contrary to the popular belief that China is a centrally planned economy where everything is decided in Beijing, China is one of the most decentralised economic systems in the world (Mok & Wu, 2013; Jin, 2023). A similar erroneous conventional belief is that exports are driving China’s economic growth, but they are not.

Take the export-driven view on China, which US President Donald Trump and many of his advisors also hold to justify their tariff war against China in the belief that the US-China trade deficit could be eliminated by hitting Chinese exports with punitive tariffs. This is wrong even on the basis of simple economics. The root cause of the chronic and large US-China trade deficit is the US’s saving-investment imbalance, with America’s national savings falling far short of its investment. Without addressing this fundamental problem, hitting China will only divert the US trade deficit from China to other countries, as evidence has shown (Fig. 2.2).

As for China, evidence shows that since the 2007–2008 Great Financial Crisis (GFC), net exports have not contributed much to China’s economic growth.[6] In fact, for most years since the GFC, net exports

[6] We consider net exports (total exports minus total imports), instead of gross exports, because in the expenditure approach of national income accounting, net exports are one

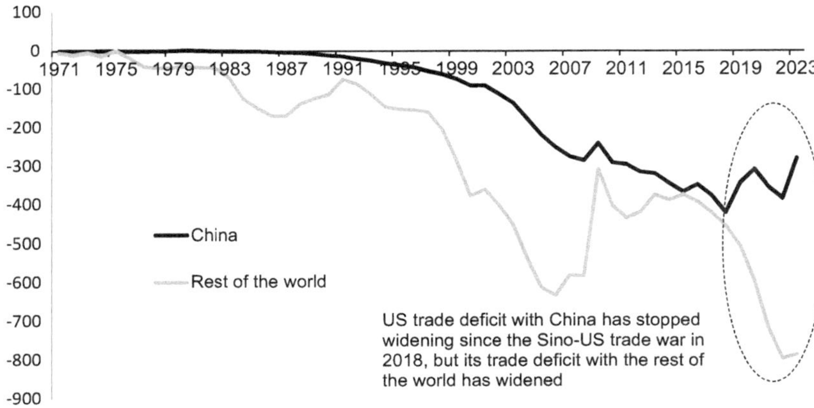

Fig. 2.2 US trade balance (USD bn) (*Source* CEIC, author)

were a drag on GDP growth (see negative contribution by net exports in Fig. 2.3). Those who think that by imposing punitive tariffs on Chinese exports would hurt China's economic growth badly and could address a trade deficit with China are "frogs in a well".

Equally amazing is the belief that China is still a centrally controlled economy. Beijing started decentralising the economy in the 1990s (Lo, 2015, pp. 58–61). Since then, China's local authorities, including provinces, cities, villages and townships, have controlled about 85% of total government spending. By comparison, for OECD countries and the US, only about a third and 45%, respectively, of total government expenditure happen at local level.

This means that provinces and large municipalities in China have an immense degree of autonomy over the way they run their respective economies. Furthermore, they compete with each other fiercely to achieve their key performance indicators (KPIs) set out by the central government. At the economy level, there are companies competing with each other fiercely in the market for profit maximisation and/or other commercial goals.

of the four components for GDP growth. The other three components are consumption, investment and government spending.

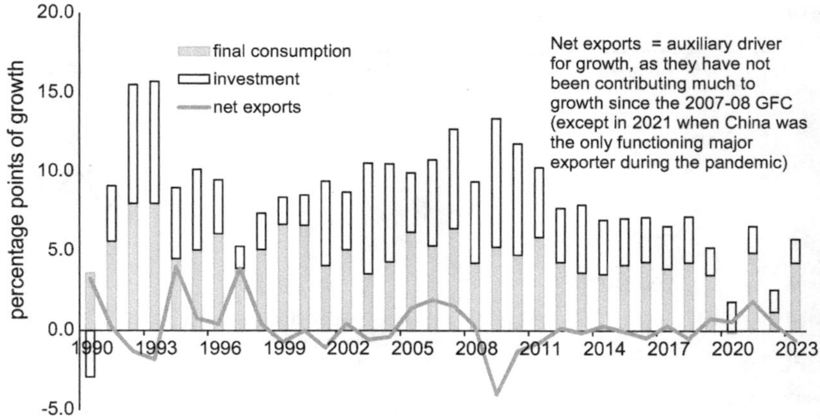

Fig. 2.3 China's growth contribution by GDP components (*Source* CEIC, author)

This set-up has created a policy and business environment that is constantly shifting so that both governments and companies have to keep evolving to adapt to the changes. On any day at any time, there is a province running a highly effective new policy that allows it to gain an advantage over other localities. But low barriers to entry allow other localities to copy this new policy quickly, feeding into the competition process and, thus, making the economic environment highly dynamic. The process allows the state to move in unison with the economy instead of slowing it down, as is the case in many countries.

The role of the central government in all this is to set broad objectives and manage personnel changes to achieve these objectives but not to strictly control who does what to achieve some rigid targets, as many in the West still assume. Keen competition between the localities drives the dynamics of this system, making it work, as outperformance will mean promotion and rewards by the central government. In other words, in "China Inc" the central government is the board of directors and human resources department, presiding over an army of local CEOs who have immense degrees of autonomy over their own companies. This is not a perfect or right model and it is not for every country, but this is how things work in China that we have to understand.

Take the solar industry as an example. After decades of development, the central government decided in 2011 to speed up the industry's growth as a strategic goal by introducing substantial government incentives, such as tax benefits, provision of cheap credit and promotion opportunities for officials who outperform the relevant KPIs. Within a few years, there were solar companies and patents related to research on solar technology emerged all over China.

In 2013 China became the world's leading installer of photovoltaics. In 2015, it surpassed Germany as the world's largest producer of photovoltaic energy. Two years later, China became the first country to have more than 100 GW of total installed photovoltaic capacity. In 2024, Chinese firms were the industry leaders in almost all of the key parts of the solar industry supply chain, including polysilicon, silicon wafers, batteries, and photovoltaic modules, with its share in all the manufacturing stages of solar panels exceeding 80% since 2022 (IEA, 2022).

Invisible and Visible Hands Working Together

This system is somewhat paradoxical, hence, incomprehensible to most Western analysts. This is because while the system is incredibly decentralised, it is also incredibly effective at mobilising the country for centrally decided objectives. In economic sense, this is like having both the invisible hand (market incentives) and visible hand (government directives) working together to drive the system.

Imagine if you put all the countries in North America, the European Union and North Africa (whose total population roughly equals that of China's) under a common leadership who decides on common objectives and the career path of all the officials in these countries based on their achievements of the KPIs in their respective countries. Of course that is not possible, one would say, and this exactly why the West cannot understand China.

However, this system works for China. It has been mobilised to its full extent on engaging leading edge semiconductors and innovations since the US's imposition of export restrictions and trade/tariff obstacles in 2018. As a result, exports of some high-tech products, such as lithium batteries, electric vehicles and photovoltaic generators, have grown exponentially (Figs. 2.4 and 2.5).

This evidence shows that the US hawkish trade policy had been unsuccessful in stopping China's tech progress and that Chinese companies had

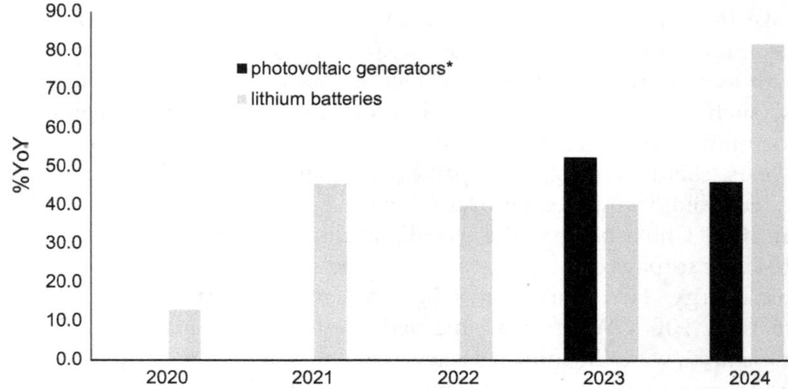

Fig. 2.4 Export growth of photovooltaic generators & lithium batteries since Covid-19 (*Note* *data only started in 2022. *Source* CEIC, author)

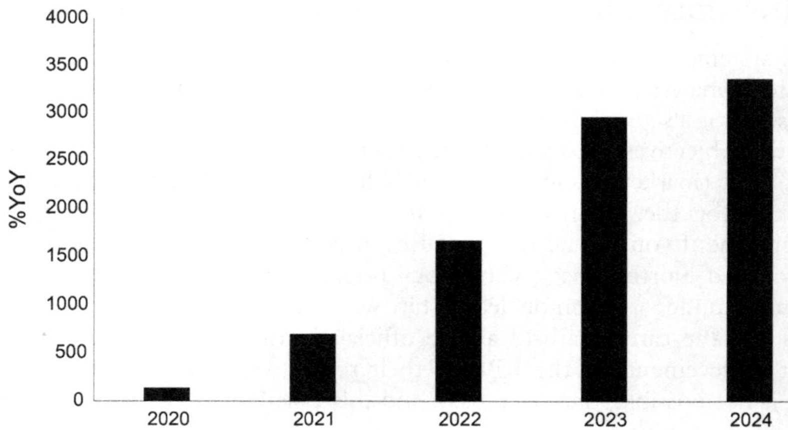

Fig. 2.5 Export growth of electric vehicles since Covid-19 (*Source* CEIC, author)

embraced a survival strategy that reflects the adage of "what does not kill you makes you stronger". Once the Chinese mobilisation machine is ignited after getting an objective, you cannot stop or beat them. In other words, once you have hundreds of thousands of PhDs, technicians, companies and officials mobilised to compete and work simultaneously within the same "China Inc" to make something happen, it will happen.

So, if the US does not want China to develop a certain technology, the very last thing it wants to do is to make the Chinese mobilise the full strength of the system on it. However, without understanding the Chinese characteristics, it has made precisely this mistake. By implementing all the tariffs and export restrictions the US was effectively, and ironically, pushing China to ramp up its formidable economic mobilisation power to becoming a tech (AI) powerhouse as quickly as possible.

No More Galapagos Critter

Furthermore, research and surveys found that since the 2018 Sino-US trade war 90% of Chinese companies were considering expanding overseas (HSBC, 2024; Shen, 2024). This attitude is a complete change in China's corporate mindset from the mid-1990s and early 2000s, when Chinese companies sought strong government protection for survival. China's export competitiveness and speedy technological progress in the face of US policy obstacles stand in defiance of the so-called "Galapagos Island Syndrome"—which refers to isolated business development that will only survive in the home market but not outside—that the world saw infect Chinese companies in the early to mid-2000s (Ezell & Atkinson, 2014).

All these developments raise questions about whether a trade war would serve American interests. To put it differently, America might have waged a trade war with China that is self-defeating due to its ignorance about the Middle Kingdom's characteristics and economic evolution. While Chinese companies upgrade their supply chains and adapt to the global demand shift and rising geopolitical tension, American manufacturers have had to deal with higher input costs and disrupted supply networks because of their government's anti-China policies.

Ironically, by forcing China to decouple from the US, America's protectionist policies seem to have eroded its global influence, albeit slowly. This can be seen in the increase in the usage of the renminbi in international payments, which has ranked consistently fourth and fifth most widely used currency for global payments in the SWIFT system, and the creeping progress of renminbi internationalisation. We shall discuss these issues in the following chapters.

The Visible Hand That Is Not Understood

Another aspect of the Chinese "visible hand" system that the West often finds incomprehensible or does not want to understand, because it runs against their "invisible hand' liberalism belief, is the ability to allocate losses to different players in order to make system-level changes to contain/diffuse any potential crisis. This is indeed something very difficult, if not impossible, for most other governments to do. It also explains why no debt-currency and banking crises have happened in China despite decades of "expert" prediction.

A recent example of the system allocating losses to prevent a crisis from erupting was seen in the real-estate industry in 2021 when Chinese property giant Evergrande failed. The government recognised there was a housing bubble and President Xi issued a policy directive of "houses are for living in, not for speculation" to all levels of government to handle the situation. Since then, various measures (including cuts in mortgage rate, selective expansion of credit, reduction in the down payment, a programme to turn unfinished property projects into social and rental housing, etc.) were implemented to ensure the bubble would not burst into a systemic crisis but instead would deflate gradually, and ensure that the losses were borne by real-estate developers and speculators but not too much by society as a whole.

This "visible hand" allocating losses to minimise the systemic impact is a key reason why China has not suffered a property (or banking) crisis and a recession in the modern era. Beijing engages in "controlled demolition" and tries to ensure that the country does not suffer massive crises like what the US and some other countries have repeatedly gone through, for instance. It is just a different approach of economic management and not to argue which is a better system. However, many Western observers have simply ignored this China characteristic and claimed that China was covering up the true losses because it had an authoritarian, and hence inferior, system of economic management.

Granted, no system is perfect. Weaknesses of the Chinese system are all too well-known—corruption, moral hazard, over-investment leading to excess capacity, suppression (whatever that means and applies to), lack of freedom of choice, etc. However, even on understanding about China's shortcomings (and often picking on them with the intention of demonising them), many Western analysts are ignorant about many negative aspects of the Chinese economy. So, they are often barking up the wrong tree in their criticism without providing constructive analysis on helping to understand China better.

One example is local protectionism. There is a perverse incentive for local officials to protect their local companies by giving them policy advantages over companies from other provinces. This results in outcomes that hurt everyone's interests and impede overall economic growth. But this issue seldom features in the China debate. The point is that ignorance about China creates both positive and negative biases in global opinions.

Ultimately, everything in the Chinese system relies on the wisdom of the government, or Communist Party to be more precise, to mobilise the system to achieve the policy objectives. The perverse incentive is a risk to the system. If the leadership loses its wisdom or if the objectives are ill-thought, the whole country will be working towards the wrong direction, potentially creating disasters down the road.

In fact, this is the "key man" risk that China and the world face when President Xi Jinping re-centralised power by making himself president for life in 2018. Many observers argue that this was precisely the control problem of the Chinese system, but that it would not happen in democratic countries where the system is driven by the "invisible hand of the market".

Really? Evidence shows that the "control problem" also happens in free market economies but in different forms, in my view, collectively called market failure. Big players (including politicians, investors, companies, etc.) often have significant controls on economic and financial activities in a liberal system. Either implicitly or explicitly, they take the forms of monopolies, oligopolies, lobby groups, collusion, etc. The "invisible hand of the market" then becomes "benefits for shareholders or vested interests". However, what is good for shareholders is not always good for the society or country.

For instance, it is almost insane, in my view, that we have had three generations in the West where the best and brightest went to work in the finance industry engineering convoluted schemes just to make money out of nothing. Granted, many of the financial engineering activities have produced real economic benefits and contributed to wealth creation. But many have also amounted to rent-seeking and wealth transfer, leading to moral hazard problems and finally financial crises.

The US subprime crisis in 2008, which led to the GFC in subsequent years, is the best example in recent memory (Lo, 2010, chapter 1). From a society perspective, these activities resulted from the control by the "invisible hand" and are hardly good use of precious human resources—they contributed to wealth destruction rather than wealth creation, as the subprime crisis showed.

Understanding China properly is imperative to enable the world to manage the disruption that its global superpower aspiration will create. Misunderstanding China has led to an irony of the world's opinion on China's global role. It is worried about the global disruption that China would cause when it thrives, and it is also worried about the disruption when it collapses. Quite often, the world does not seem to know whether China would thrive or collapse, or what do China's actions mean.

To be fair, the misunderstanding about China has also been aggravated by socio-cultural differences in the analytical process. This is highlighted by the fact that what is understood by the West of China is often not the same understanding by China of the West. These problems have created an expectation gap between what the world expects China to deliver and what China can actually, and want to, deliver. This gap has become a key factor in creating global political tensions and market volatility, and in hyping the fears about China's emergence to the global stage.

Past mistakes about reading/judging China abound. When it joined the World Trade Organization (WTO) in 2001, for example, many thought that China would liberalise to become a democracy. Since Japan, Taiwan and South Korea had all moved in that direction after joining the WTO, the pattern was clear: Once a country was wealthy enough, its growing middle classes demanded a say in the government.

That turned out to be wrong. China has actually moved more towards political centralisation since President Xi Jinping took the helm in 2013. This has led to a concern that China's economic collapse would be inevitable because it has defied for too long the widely held view that political openness was necessary for sustaining economic development. China's exceptionalism of high growth without political openness should end ultimately, according to this logic. So, its growth rate would collapse to commensurate with its closed political system, sending devastating effects to the global system.

A less dramatic view is that China would get stuck in the "middle-income trap", just like many other emerging economies that do not make it to the rich-income country status after decades of high growth. The concern about China's future growth has, in turn, raised a practical concern about China disrupting the world order by pursuing currency devaluation as an escape route to its potential growth disaster, thus triggering future currency wars. We shall examine these issues in the following chapters.

China's history of surprising the world goes even earlier. Before Deng Xiaoping's economic liberalisation in 1978, most China watchers did not think that China would undertake serious economic reforms and usher in the longest period of fast economic growth in world history. But it did. And earlier yet, it was inconceivable that a large country like China would lose the Opium War so decisively to a relatively small British naval fleet and ended up having to cede Hong Kong. And it did.

With hindsight, it turns out that the Chinese system actually fares reasonably well against capitalism. Human beings are not evidently too bad at deciding what human beings should work on if they are being thoughtful and strategic about it. In fact, the China model follows the textbook model of an economy that is run by a benevolent authority who sets an objective function to maximise the country's wellbeing, subjects to a set of budget/policy constraints.

China's rise on the global stage is a testament to its resilience, adaptability and strategic vision. While the West has been "sleeping on the wheel", China has seized the opportunity to reshape the global order. The West must wake up to this reality and take decisive action to secure its future. The coming years will be pivotal in determining the global balance of power. The question is not whether China will continue to rise, but whether the West can rise to the China challenge.

Misreading China at Your Peril

What could happen if the world keeps misreading China? Political scientist Graham Allison, a professor at Harvard Kennedy School, has given us some clues. He coined the term "Thucydides Trap" to describe the historical tendency for established superpowers and upstart rivals to go to war with each other. This becomes a model widely applied to the US and China tensions in recent years. With American policies towards China getting more aggressive, Professor's model warns that default antagonism towards China could elevate the risk of catastrophic military conflict in the future. There are better options for pursuing US objectives, but they must start with a proper understanding of China.

Thucydides was right that when a rapidly rising power seriously threatened to displace a major ruling power, there was a discombobulation that, historically, led to war. In the last five centuries, according to Professor Allison's research, this situation happened 16 times with 12 of them resulting in war (Allison, 2017).

The ongoing China-bashing, which often evolves to demonising China, confuses more than clarifies the misunderstandings. Negative biases emerge as many China bashers deny China's progress but become aware that China is catching up quickly, with some areas even displacing the US as the predominant player. Notably, China owns most supply chains and an increasing number of technology, green and clean products and projects. These include solar panels, lithium batteries, electric vehicles, artificial intelligence and windmills, just to name a few.

The danger in demonisation is both an overestimation and an underestimation of the China challenge because opinions are distorted and can lead to foolish reactions. What complicates the situation is the fact that China has significantly increased its military capabilities. This changes the military balance dramatically. Arm race is an arena where great power rivals could easily, through misunderstandings and miscalculations, end up finding themselves in a war that neither intended nor wanted.

As China challenges America's global supremacy, misreading each other's intentions and actions could lead them into the dangerous and deadly Thucydides Trap. The ongoing underestimations and misapprehensions of the dangers inherent in the Sino-US relationship could contribute to upsetting the world's precarious balance and tipping it to a major war. Even a business-as-usual attitude may not prevent the potential clash between two titans because when a rising power (China) is threatening to displace a ruling power (the US), accidents could occur, leading to crises with disastrous outcomes that would otherwise be contained.

Thucydides' powerful insight stemmed from two key drivers of the clash dynamics: the emerging power's growing entitlement and ego, which translate into its demand for recognition and a bigger say on sovereign and strategic matters, and the existing power's fear, insecurity and determination to defend the *status quo.* In the Thucydides case of the Peloponnese war in the fifth century B.C., Athens had emerged over 50 years as a steeple of civilisation, yielding advances in philosophy, drama, history, architecture, democracy and naval and military prowess. This threatened Sparta, which for more than a century had been the ruling power on the Peloponnese peninsula.

As Athens' power and influence grew, so too did its ego and persistent demand for recognition and changes to previous arrangements to reflect new realities of its emerging power. The Spartans saw the Athenian posture as unreasonable, ungrateful, instigating and threatening to the system it had built and within which Athens had thrived. The parallel of this historical precedent is a relevant illustration of China's global ascent challenging the US-led international order which has, until recent years, provided leadership and global peace and prosperity since the end of World War II.

The rise of China has upset the world's balance of power because never before in history has a nation risen so quickly and on so many dimensions of power. Within a single generation, China has emerged from being a country that did not appear on any international league tables to the top ranks in the economic, investment, foreign trade and technology aspects. In 1980 when China started to open up to the world, its economy was smaller than that of the Netherlands. But within two decades, it rose to become the second largest economy in the world by beating Japan in 2010.

More crucially, like Athens back in the ancient Greece, as China's clout grows its leaders have become more confidence and assertive and want international recognition. The arrival of President Xi Jinping as China's new paramount leader in 2013 marked the watershed of the change in China's attitude towards itself and the world. When Deng Xiaoping started China's economic liberalisation in 1978, he pursued a policy of "hide and bide" by laying low in its foreign relations to achieve and preserve stability and gain access to overseas markets. The policy was for China to bide its time and hide its capabilities.

However, Mr. Xi ended the hide and bide era by transforming China's growth engine from export-led (i.e. Mr. Deng's foreign market access policy direction) to domestic-driven (i.e. a self-confident and self-reliant policy), and by pursuing an active foreign policy that is increasingly assertive in advancing China's interests. The Belt and Road Initiative, in my view, is a crystalisation of Mr. Xi's change in attitude. It lays bare the essence of his "Chinese Dream"—the rise of a 5,000-year-old civilisation with over 1.4 billion people is not a problem to be fixed. It is an emerging secular force to be reckoned with by the world.

Nevertheless, a Sino-US clash leading to disastrous disruption in the global system is not inevitable. As Professor Allison's study of the Thucydides Trap showed, four out of the 16 cases of power competition did not end in bloodshed. Those successes, and the failures, offer pertinent lessons for global leaders. When the parties avoided war, it required significant and painful adjustments in actions and attitudes on both the parts of the challenger and the challenged. This means that minimising the inevitable global disruption due to the emergence of China requires tremendous efforts and understanding China better and properly is an imperative step.

Now let us move on to assess China's superpower aspiration and the disruption it has created (and will create in the future) and decode the misunderstanding about China on the global stage.

References

Allison, G. (2017). Destined for War: Can America and China Escape Thucydides's Trap? Houghton Mifflin Harcourt.

Aytekin, E. (2024). China flexes muscles with first intercontinental ballistic missile test in 44 years. *Anadolu Agency*. 28 September. https://www.aa.com.tr/en/asia-pacific/china-flexes-muscles-with-first-intercontinental-ballistic-missile-test-in-44-years/3344378

De Waal, J. R. (2022). China's reputation declines while America's gets a boost. *YouGov UK*. October 24. https://yougov.co.uk/international/articles/44996-chinas-reputation-declines-while-americas-gets-boo

Ezell, S., & Atkinson, R. D. (2014). *The Middle Kingdom Galapagos Island Syndrome: The Cul-De-Sac of Chinese Technology Standards*. Information Technology & Innovation Foundation.

Gan, N. (2024). China fires ICBM into Pacific Ocean in first such public test in decades as regional tensions flare. *CNN World*. September 26. https://edition.cnn.com/2024/09/25/asia/china-icbm-test-pacific-ocean-intl-hnk/index.html

HSBC. (2024). China's going global. *HSBC Global Banking and Markets*. 2 October. https://www.gbm.hsbc.com/en-gb/insights/market-and-regulatory-insights/china-going-global

International Energy Agency. (2022). *Special Report on Solar PV Global Supply Chains*. IEA Publications.

Jin, K (2023). Economic Decentralization: China's Recipe for Success? (Webcast) *China&US Focus*, China-United States Exchange Foundation. 4 July. https://www.chinausfocus.com/videos/economic-decentralization-chinas-recipe-for-success

Lo, C. (2010). *China After the Subprime Crisis: Opportunities in the New Economic Landscape*. Palgrave Macmillan.

Lo, C. (2015). *China's Impossible Trinty, the Structural Challenges to the "Chinese Dream."* Palgrave Macmillan.

Mok, K. H., & Wu, X. F. (2013). Dual decentralization in China's transitional economy: Welfare regionalism and policy implications for central-local relationship. *Policy and Society, 32*(1), 61–75. https://doi.org/10.1016/j.polsoc.2013.02.002

Shen. M. (2024). More Chinese firms keen to expand overseas, survey finds. *SHINE.CN*. June 13. https://www.shine.cn/biz/economy/2406139523/

Sweetman, B. (2024). China's big new combat aircraft: a technical assessment. *The Strategist, Australian Strategic Policy Institute*, 31 December.

The Economist. (2024). *Helping America's hawks get inside the head of Xi Jinping, November 21.* https://www.economist.com/china/2024/11/21/helping-americas-hawks-get-inside-the-head-of-xi-jinping

Winkler, S. C. (2023). Strategic Competition and US-China Relations: A Conceptual Analysis. *The Chinese Journal of International Politics, 16*(3), 333–356.

Yu, Z. (2024). Has China unveiled its sixth-generation fighter? *Think China, SPH Media Limited*. 30 December. https://www.thinkchina.sg/technology/has-china-unveiled-its-sixth-generation-fighter

CHAPTER 3

China Rises When the West Sleeps

The statement "Beware the quiet man. For while others speak, he watches. And while others act, he plans. And when they finally rest... he strikes[1]" describes aptly the rise of China to the global stage when the West is sleeping on the wheel. Arguably, many of the fears about China's rise have been exaggerated due to ignorance about the Middle Kingdom's development process.

Since 2010 when China overtook Japan as the second largest economy in the world, it has repeatedly surprised the developed world, especially the US, with progress in economic, financial and technological aspects. The surprise, or shock, does not necessarily come from product superiority but from the scope of technological innovation and the speed of the progress that the West did not expect.

Consider China's aerospace progress. In 1969 the US landed on the Moon. Twenty-eight years later in 1997, the US successfully sent robotic landers and rovers to Mars. China landed on the Moon 44 years after the US did in 2013. But only 8 years after going to the Moon, China deployed its Zhurong rover on Mars in 2021. The speed of the Chinese catching up to the American space programme development was phenomenal.

[1] This is a famous but unattributed quote appeared in the 2018 movie "Vice" that follows Dick Cheney on his path to becoming the most powerful vice president in American history.

C. Lo, *Clash of the Economic Titans: China and the United States*, https://doi.org/10.1007/978-981-95-2510-2_3

One may argue that the Chinese achieved all these because it learned from the US and other advanced countries by sending students to study, who later brought back the technological know-how. That is a fact. But the point is that China has built upon the basic knowledge it has acquired and climbed the learning curve swiftly so that it has moved up the technology ladder even when the US cuts off technological transfer. This is underscored by China's scientific progress that came after the US launched the so-called "China Initiative" programme[2] in 2018 that have expelled many Chinese and Chinese-American scientists from the US, cut the number of Chinese students admitted to US universities, and sharply curtailed US-China scientific exchange (Greenfield, 2024) on national security concerns.

Even in the production of advanced semiconductor chips, which the US aims at curbing its growth since the Biden administration through export restrictions and tariffs, China has exhibited rapid progress in self-production and product upgrades that has repeatedly shocked the world by refuting the conventional view that its semiconductor industry would stumble at the technology frontier due to the US-led tech export restriction policy started in the early 2020s. The first shock came when Huawei launched its high-end Huawei Mate 60 smartphone in August 2023. The 7-nanometer chip powering the new phone showed that China's self-sufficiency in semiconductor design (by HiSilicon, owned by Huawei) and manufacturing capabilities (by SMIC) were catching up at an alarming pace that no one had expected before.

Then in early 2024 Huawei and SMIC announced that they would be mass-producing the 5-nonometer chips in new Shanghai production facilities, further fuelling fears about leaps in their next-generation chip prowess. Later in the year, Huawei started shipping a new chip, the Ascend 910C, for artificial intelligence use (Pan, 2024). This new chip is comparable to Nvidia's advanced H100 chip, which was produced in 2023 but banned by the US government from exporting to China for

[2] The "China Initiative" is a now-defunct US federal program created that sought to counter the threat of economic espionage and trade secrets theft conducted by or for the benefit of the communist regime in China. It was launched in November 2018 by the Trump administration and overturned in February 2022 by the Biden administration. When it was still in effect, the programme was widely criticised for not only being ineffective but also facilitating numerous instances of racial profiling and discrimination against Asian American and Asian immigrant scientists, researchers and academics. Despite opposition, there are efforts at the time of writing to reinstate the programme.

national security reasons. However, the US export controls failed to arrest Huawei's progress. Just a few months after launching 910C, in April 2025 Huawei started shipping an upgraded version 910D AI chip to its business partners in China for testing. The new chip is expected to help fill a void in the Chinese AI market left by increased US chip export controls.

Granted, these new chips are still a generation behind the developed world's cutting-edge ones of 3-nonameter chips. However, they show that China is still able to move at a shockingly fast pace in making advanced chips, despite the US-erected trade obstacles, and underscores my point that China has built sufficient scientific knowledge to move ahead by itself without relying on foreign technological transfer. President Xi Jinping's remarks to Dutch Prime Minister Mark Rutte during his China visit in March 2024 summed up China's tech development resolve: "No force can stop China's scientific and technological development" (Chiang, 2024).

In general, China has been pushing for a shift in the global balance of power quietly since the turn of the millennium. It has steadily ascended to become a dominant force in global economics, technology and diplomacy while the West grapples with internal challenges and geopolitical fatigue. This process has created some blind fears and suspicions among many in the West; see discussion below. Nevertheless, the West was not unaware of China's potential. It had ignored it until the early twenty-first century. In fact, prediction of China's emergence as a superpower went back to as early as the Napoleonic days.

Napoleon's Warning Comes True

Napoleon purportedly appreciated China's potential as a world power and cautioned against "waking the sleeping dragon". China's subordination into the Western powers in the 1839–1842 Opium War and its economic decline as the "sick man" of East Asia for the rest of the nineteenth century and the first half of the twentieth century only dulled, but never extinguished, the anticipation that sooner or later China would dominate the world again.

China's economic progress in recent years has raised again the debate on, and the fear of, China's looming ascent to superpower stature. An early Chinese breakthrough that "woke" up the world came in October 2003, when China launched its first human into space (before landing on the Moon). This made China the only country in the world after the US and the former Soviet Union to have conquered the space.

The Western media have also sounded alarm about China's efforts to expand and diversify its access to sources of oil in the Middle East, Africa, Latin America and even Canada. Even today, the industrial world still infers from the "giant sucking sound" created by the flood of cheap Chinese goods into their markets displacing local manufacturing jobs that China has moved up the value chain after becoming the world's factory in the late 1990s and early 2000s. Meanwhile, analysts have also pondered the implications for global security of China's military modernisation effort, which started in the 1980s, and its pledge to develop a "revolution in military affairs with Chinese characteristics".

It is the expansion of China's economic cum diplomatic influence that revives the suspicion and fear about China's ambition to become a superpower. American media has long highlighted the Chinese diplomacy in search of long-term sources of oil and the impact of China's growing oil import on petrol prices that American consumers have to pay. Beijing's purchase of US Treasury securities that finances the American twin (fiscal and current account) deficits, America's ongoing threat to name China a currency manipulator in order to pressure Beijing to appreciate the renminbi against the US dollar, and Chinese attempts to buy American companies and assets all underscore China's large trade surplus with the US that lies behind the "blame/fear China" sentiment.

China's rapid development in heavy industries, notably steel and shipbuilding, reflects the dramatic advances that its economy has made since economic reforms started in 1978. Fears about such Chinese industrial dominance prompted US President Trump to issue executive orders in late 2024 and early 2025 to protect and revive the US shipbuilding and steel industries (Levy & Boak, 2024; Penley, 2025), even though the US does not have any comparative advantages in these industries. Meanwhile, the ubiquity of Chinese goods serving the average consumer at Walmart, Target and the likes, and of Chinese-made clothing and daily goods in upscaled department stores underscores how much China's competitiveness has made it the world's factory.

Chinese exports have also been moving up the value chain, with rising market share in higher value-added exports such as construction services, white goods and machinery and equipment. This means that cheap Chinese production cost is spreading up the value chain. Hollowing out of the American production base by the Chinese is a feeling of *déjà vu* all over again.

Nevertheless, despite the US tariffs and other trade barriers against Chinese exports, they have not work as intended. Since the Sino-US tariff war started in 2018, China's global share of exports has risen while that of the US has fallen (Fig. 3.1). This is because Chinese firms have responded by shifting production and trade to other countries, notably in ASEAN[3] Africa and Latin America (Mexico in particular) to skirt US tariffs and trade restrictions (Figs. 3.2 and 3.3). Far from isolating China, the US tariffs have forced Chinese firms to diversify, innovate and expand in other countries, enlarging China's global footprints.

Naturally, China's economic expansion comes with diplomatic influence across the globe. Through projects such as the Belt and Road Initiative (BRI), China has established itself as a key player in global infrastructure development, fostering stronger ties with developing nations. Different from the West's expansion approach, which often prioritises short-term gains, China's diplomatic strategy focuses on pragmatism, long-term planning and building enduring partnerships. By investing in developing nations, notably in Africa, Latin America and Southeast Asia, it

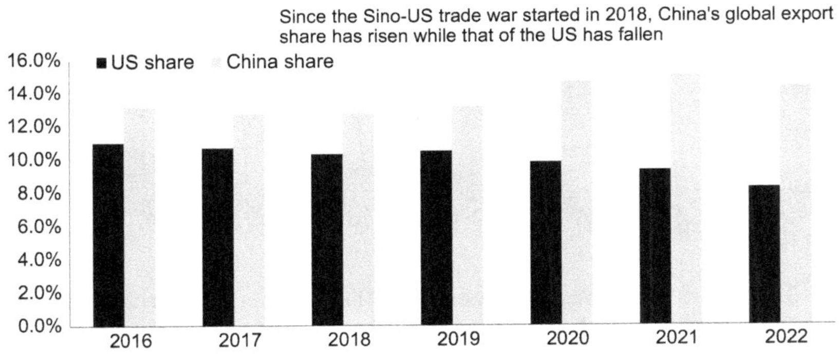

Fig. 3.1 Share of world exports (*Source* CEIC, author)

[3] The Association of Southeast Asian Nations (ASEAN) is an inter-governmental international organisation, comprised of Indonesia, Vietnam, Laos, Brunei, Thailand, Myanmar, the Philippines, Cambodia, Singapore and Malaysia.

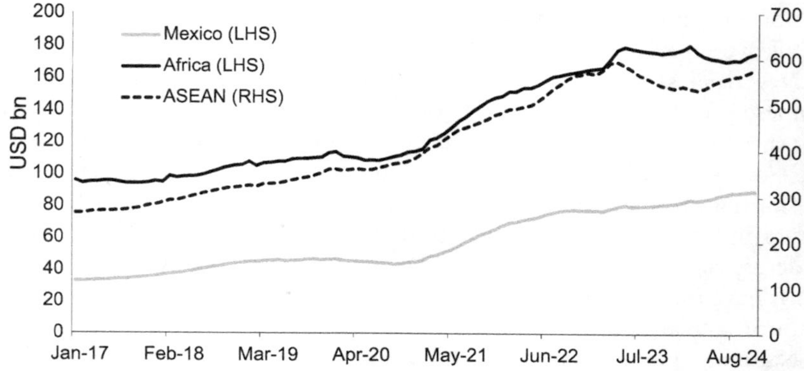

Fig. 3.2 Rising Chinese exports to ASEAN, Africa & Mexico since the trade war in 2018 (*Source* CEIC, author)

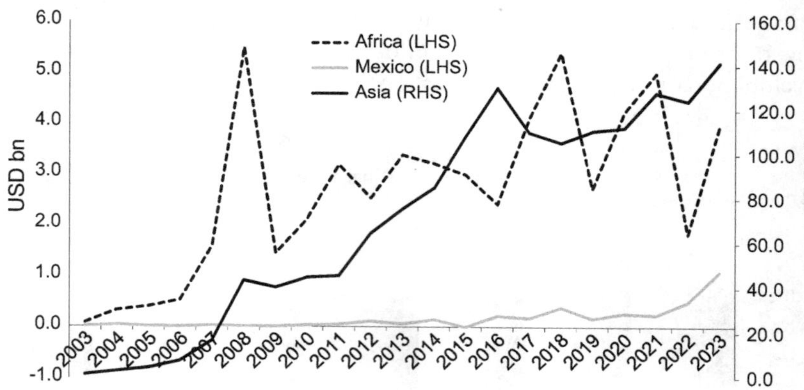

Fig. 3.3 China has increased investment in new market, esp. Asia significantly since 2018 (*Source* CEIC, author)

has not only secured access to critical resources but also created a network of allies that supports its global agenda.

What is interesting is that these days, the world talks about the economic ascent of China causing concerns in the global system as if it does not know how to deal with a new and stronger China. Critics have forgotten that back in the ancient times (notably between the first and late thirteen century), China was an economic superpower. Its economic supremacy went into a protracted decline during the Qing Dynasty that spanned from 1644 to 1911.

Hence, strictly speaking, China's economic ascent is an economic comeback. However, China's development trends since the turn of the millennium are not as straightforward as they were in the old days. Global geopolitical and socio-economic forces are more complicated nowadays. The Chinese economy and development process, in a hybrid system that combines market forces with planning mechanism, are also more intriguing these days, making proper understanding of China difficult.

GFC, A Turning Point for China's Rise

In the 2007–2008 subprime crisis, China was part of the problem in creating an unbalanced world where its savings surplus was funding the West's (notably the US's) savings deficit. In the post-crisis adjustment process, it should be part of the solution. But trying to be a solution is not easy. On one hand, the developed world has to understand China and give it time and room to change. On the other hand, the developed world itself has to make painful structural changes. China also needs to realise its limitations in the restructuring process and keep up with the reform momentum. Making the West to better understand China and the global rebalancing process is not easy because there is a wall of negativity about the Middle Kingdom to climb and overcome in the Western opinion.

Since the US subprime crisis, China has been seen as pursuing a domestic policy of government-driven growth at all costs, complemented by a beggar-thy-neighbour international policy. It is true that China's economy is dominated by a statist direction. Its foreign economic expansion and trade practices are ringing loud alarm. Its stable foreign exchange rate policy has kept the renminbi (which is also called the yuan) undervalued for years, leading to international outcry of foul play. Its purchases of foreign strategic resources, such as oilfields, mines and physical and financial assets around the world by state-owned companies are raising international political as well as economic tensions.

Many Western analysts and observers see these moves as a dramatic change in China's policy towards aggressive expansion in the form of economic invasion. However, there is more to the truth than meets the eye. From China's perspective, these moves are a result of a government making tough choices under growing economic and political constraints in the face of an increasingly hostile external environment. No doubt, some of China's policy moves, such as the drive to acquire overseas resources, are prompted by strong special interest groups. But so are many of the policy moves by the developed world. The point is that ignorance about China's development will only make misunderstanding it worse, and that could lead to misguided reactions to the challenges and disruptions that the emergence of China brings.

From these perspectives, the 2007–2008 Global Financial Crisis (GFC) that followed the US subprime crisis represented a turning point in the global economy for the rise of a new economic leadership. This is because the finances of the developed world governments were over-stretched, with huge debt burdens dragging on their growth. They could hardly afford another crisis with their economic power significantly weakened. In a broader perspective, the GFC also destroyed public confidence in fiat money as a result of the global central banks' monetisation (aka quantitative easing) policy to contain the Crisis. All this not only opened an opportunity for the rise of Bitcoin and other cryptocurrencies as a protest against irresponsible money-printing and poor monetary policy management but also the search for an alternative global economic leadership other than the US.

The dark horse for the new global economic leader might be China, given its significant economic reforms, accumulation of wealth and expansion momentum. And the global leadership change could start with the Chinese currency. This is because economic development since the GFC suggests that the basic functions of money (as a unit of account, a medium of exchange and a store of value) of the G3 currencies (US dollar, euro and Japanese yen) might have been eroded significantly. This has opened up a window of opportunity for the Chinese renminbi to rise as an alternative global currency, challenging the US dollar's global dominance in the longer term.

Indeed, I have argued elsewhere (Lo, 2013, Chapter 1) that some powerful structural shifts were unfolding behind the G3 currencies and the emerging markets, giving rise to some distinctive trends that were conducive to the rise of the renminbi even before the GFC. They include the weakening of the US dollar's global dominance, the uncertainty of the euro and the structural decline of the yen. The GFC aggravated these weakening trends of the G3 currencies. Meanwhile, even with a largely closed capital account, the global market influence of the renminbi has continued to rise.

While the US dollar always dominates as a unit of account, the outlook for this dominance seems to have weakened as an increasing number of countries have tried to reduce US dollar risk by diversifying out of dollar assets. Of the five most actively used international payments currencies in the SWIFT system—US dollar, euro, pound sterling, yen and renminbi—only the yuan stands out as the one that will most likely experience an increase in international usage in the coming years.

Being a new component currency of the Special Drawing Rights[4] (since October 2016) and with Beijing continuing to liberalise China's capital account, the renminbi will become a growing part of the global financial infrastructure. Notably, China's creation of the Asian Infrastructure Investment Bank, the Silk Road Fund, the New Development Banks and the usage of its domestic policy banks for international lending are all instrumental in boosting the role of the renminbi and, hence, China's influence, under the Belt and Road Initiative (BRI) that spans from China through Asia, Africa to Europe.

After the GFC, most of the world's major currencies have failed to serve as a store of value by failing to deliver stable positive return both in nominal and real terms. Since the currency war[5] in 2010, global currency market volatility has risen sharply. The Swiss franc and the Japanese yen have become negative yielding currencies since 2015. The euro, the Swedish krona and the Danish krone also do not provide any reasonable stable non-zero returns. The Canadian, Australian and Kiwi dollars, Norwegian krone, Brazilian real and South African rand all have been stuck with volatile downward trends that are influenced by commodity prices.

Although the US dollar and pound sterling are still providing the store of value function (at the time of writing), could the renminbi emerge

[4] *The Special Drawing Rights, or SDR, is an international reserve asset, created by the International Monetary Fund in 1969 to supplement official reserves in its member countries. The value of the SDR is currently based on a basket of five major currencies: the US dollar, euro, the Japanese yen, pound sterling and Chinese renminbi (the latter was included in the basket in October 2016).*

[5] Currency war is, in essence, rounds of competitive devaluation when a country seeks to gain a competitive advantage over other countries by devaluing the exchange rate of its currency against other currencies. The term was coined by former Brazilian Finance Minister Guido Mantega in 2010, when he opined that a currency war broke out in the aftermath of the US subprime crisis. This view has since been echoed by many other government officials, analysts and the financial media from around the world.

as an alternative over time in a world of financial instability? That's the question that many global players are asking. The dollar and sterling have been more volatile, and often providing lower yield, than the Chinese renminbi. Granted, there are structural problems behind the yuan, and it is not fully convertible on the capital account yet. But who else does not have structural problems?

China differs from most other countries in that it has a long-term strategic vision and a stronger resolve to reform. It is, arguably, the biggest country in the world implementing the largest number of structural reforms. Beijing's ambition to make the renminbi a global reserve currency is compatible with its incentive to keep the currency stable and strong over time, despite all the short-term noises about devaluation.

Regarding the medium of exchange function, an increasing amount international payments are settled in non-US dollar currencies, with the yuan being one of the beneficiary currencies. This means erosion of the US dollar's global dominance. A strong challenger to the US dollar seemed once to be the euro. The creation of the eurozone raised the expectation that Brussels might be able to attract an ever-increasing number of countries into the euro-zone system which, in turn, would mean an ever-increasing demand for the euro as a medium of exchange in the global markets.

However, the "European dream" to become another global power centre running with the US-led global framework has been disrupted by the geopolitical conflicts in countries in emerging Europe, notably Ukraine, and by the upheavals across the Arab world. Britain's vote on 23 June 2016 to exit from the European Union, an event that financial market dubbed as "Brexit[6]", was a significant blow to global confidence in the European dream and, hence, the euro.

In the 2000s, there was also the commodity boom that increased the demand for US dollar and, hence, further strengthened the dollar's role as a global medium of exchange as nearly all commodities are priced in US dollar. However, that demand for dollar has abated following the commodity bust since 2013. The table will turn only when global trade and the commodity cycle re-accelerate markedly again. But that has

[6] Brexit is an abbreviation for "British exit", which refers to the 23 June 2016 referendum by British voters to exit the European Union (EU). Withdrawal from the European Union has been a right under Article 50 of the Treaty on European Union of EU member states since 2007.

not happened as the US-led de-globalisation and ongoing eruption of geopolitical risks and regional wars have held back global demand growth.

The question is when global trade finally accelerates again, where would the biggest momentum come from? Given the difference in growth dynamics between the developed and emerging worlds, long-term global trade growth is likely to take place mostly in the emerging markets. Indeed, China has been promoting regionalism to spread its economic influence and as a means to counter de-globalisation. Over the long term, the China-led trade growth will likely increase the usage of the renminbi at the expense of the G3 currencies, especially when one considers China's ambitious BRI strategy.

The Digital BRI Shock

This brings us to China's digital Belt and Road Initiative which could become a global disruptive force by strengthening China's economic transformation and altering the global economic and political dynamics. The digital BRI is also an illustration of China's expansion when the West sleeps on the wheel.

Thank all this to the Covid-19 health crisis which gave China an opportunity to advance its BRI in digital form. The pandemic has laid bare the inequalities of the digital divide between the rich and poor nations. China's digital BRI expansion provides these nations with the much-needed capital and technology to combat diseases and spur growth. But it has also enhanced China's global influence, notably in the emerging economies.

Strategically, the digital BRI reinforces China's diplomatic approach of drawing its neighbours towards its economic embrace and complements its "dual circulation" policy[7]. This development has increased the developed world's suspicion on China's global ambition and will continue to create geopolitical tensions. However, it will also open up new global investment and growth opportunities, especially for Asia.

[7] China's "Dual Circulation" strategy, announced in May 2020 by the Chinese Communist Party, is an economic policy for rebalancing the country's economy by prioritising domestic consumption. Strategically, it is a policy to counter geopolitical hostility by strengthening the domestic sector while still engaging, but reducing reliance on, the external sector to sustain stable growth and resilient investment in the face of strategic competition with the US.

China's digital BRI is a rebranding of the existing BRI. It underscores my argument in Chapter 2 that the Chinese system is adaptive, flexible and competitive, contrary to the conventional thinking that it is a rigid system driven by central planning. The Covid-19 health crisis threatened China's BRI by choking off its equipment supplies and workers for the projects and forcing many developing nations into economic crisis and debt distress. In response, China redirected its energies to the BRI's digital development by sharing Chinese artificial intelligence (AI) technology for digital diagnostic systems, monitoring solutions and medical supplies with the partnering countries to fight the pandemic.

There are two components advancing the digital BRI. They are the Digital Silk Road and the Health Silk Road, launched in 2015 and 2016, respectively. The pandemic accelerated their development. The digital BRI is expected to boost China's economic and political influence by facilitating its internationalisation process and will, thus, consolidate President Xi Jinping's "Chinese Dream" to make China a global force, eventually that is. The process, however, will inevitably disrupt the global system by reshuffling the global power balance.

What are these two digital BRI components and how do they work? The Digital Silk Road aims at improving the recipient countries' telecommunications networks and digital technologies, including AI capabilities, cloud computing, e-commerce, surveillance technology, mobile systems, smart cities and other digital economic areas (Triolo et al., 2020a). It is also part of China's dual circulation policy by seeking cooperation with Asia on the digital economic and medical aspects. The latter is manifested in the Health Silk Road (see below), where China has established a China-ASEAN public-health cooperation mechanism to combat infectious diseases.

Some estimates suggested that a third of the BRI participating countries were working with China on Digital Silk Road projects (Chan, 2019). Notably, Africa, the Middle East and parts of Eastern Europe, Latin America and Southeast Asia badly need affordable and reliable technology to expand broadband internet coverage and communications networks. The pandemic had widened the inequality of the digital divide between the poor and rich nations. China's Digital Silk Road-related investments helped fill the poor nations' need and spark economic growth by providing them with critical technological infrastructure.

However, much of the debate in the West about China's digital BRI has focused on the risks of espionage and surveillance (Eder et al.,

2019; Fidler, 2018) and ignored the digital cooperation and development aspects. China's digital expansion has only become a serious concern since the Sino-US trade war started in 2018. But its information and communications expansion to the developing economies actually started in the late 1990s, with Chinese tech giants Huawei and ZTE building much of Africa's digital infrastructure. By 2017, China's digital financing in Africa surpassed the combined funds from African governments, multilateral agencies and the G7 nations (ICA 2017). The African Union[8] also launched in 2017 the Smart Health Monitoring Room using ZTE technology. Chinese e-commerce and Fintech platforms have also focused their expansion on Southeast Asia through the Digital Silk Road.

In other words, China has been paving the way for the developing countries to use Chinese technology while the West has been ignoring them or sleeping on the wheel. Crucially, the pandemic has increased the developing world's acceptance of and demand for Chinese telecommunications and surveillance tools for fighting the health crisis. This has enabled Beijing to link the Digital Silk Road to the Health Silk Road (Lancaster et al., 2020), which is an informal global health cooperation on infectious disease prevention and information sharing, medical assistance and traditional medicine development (Cao, 2020).

Under the Health Silk Road, China had pledged to send Covid-19-related equipment and medical assistance to foreign partners and make Chinese vaccine a "global public good" by joining COVAX—the vaccine partnership that pooled government funds together to subsidise vaccine access for poor countries and ensure equitable global distribution. Though COVAX ended in December 2023 as the pandemic passed, China's influence lingered on. Due to the insufficient number of homegrown coronavirus cases for doing the testing, the Chinese sent their vaccines to partner institutions overseas for third phase trials, with at least 16 countries participating in 2020. Many of them signed agreements with their Chinese counterparts to purchase doses or manufacture the vaccine for local distribution. The whole aid programme thus allowed China to extend its influence through the Health Silk Road.

[8] The African Union was set up in 2002 and contains 55 member countries in Africa.

A Global Disruption

The Digital Silk Road-Health Silk Road combo is a cheaper and more efficient way for China to expand the BRI than its traditional form of capital-intensive infrastructure options. It also allows China to raise its national image on the global stage and leverage on the increased influence to challenge the existing global powers. Furthermore, the digital BRI has boosted China's export of digital surveillance technologies to countries that seek to fight Covid-19 by monitoring quarantines and sorting populations in an effort to safely restart local economies.

However, all this has increased the worries of China critics about the risks of espionage and abuse of surveillance capabilities and created geopolitical tensions. Politics aside, there is also a technological aspect of the disruption that will affect the future landscape of the global tech industry and its supply chains. To the extent that the Digital Silk Road helps recipient countries to better manage their digital communications networks, where data management, filtering and content surveillance are part of the digitalisation process, it could accelerate a fracturing of the global internet in two ways:

- An internet bifurcation into a Chinese-led system and a non-Chinese internet led by the US (Chin 2019).
- A divergence of tech-management policies and regulations adopted by those countries that use the Chinese system from those that do not (Triolo and Allison 2020b).

Digital transformation does spur economic development. China sees its burgeoning digital economy as a success story for sharing with other countries. Thus, its effort on expanding the digital BRI will only intensify, though it will not be smooth sailing along the way. Geopolitical tensions will rise, but so will a new investment and growth landscape.

A Change in Geopolitical Landscape...

Arguably, Covid-19 has transformed global politics and the foreign policy priorities of many countries, especially the developing world (Ngeow, 2020). For China, its digital BRI has provided an important policy frame to increase its influence on the health governance of the developing world,

Asia in particular, and direct BRI investments to basic public health and enlarge its role in the supplies of medical products and services.

Even before the pandemic, China supplied the world market almost half of the basic personal protective equipment (Brown, 2020), such as surgical masks and gloves, respirators, protective garments and medical googles and shoe covers. Its export of these supplies were not only crucial for the poor nations to fight Covid-19 and other diseases but had also helped Beijing claim regional, or even global, leadership in health governance, especially when the West lagged behind China in providing Covid-19 management to the emerging markets.

China will continue to expand its global medical supply chain and investment through the Health Silk Road and make inroads into manufacturing and exporting sophisticated medical products. The developing nations' limited manufacturing capabilities of these medical products and their acceptance of Chinese technology will facilitate China's expansion into producing basic health equipment in the industrial parks that have already been built under the BRI. This expansion will not only help China establish a central role in the regional and global medical supply chains but also expand its diplomatic influence across the developing world.

… Benefiting ASEAN

Rising Sino-US tension and wariness in the developed world of dependence on China's protective gear and basic medical supplies have made Southeast Asia, ASEAN in particular, an ideal destination for China to build offshore production bases for its medical equipment and supplies. ASEAN is a crucial region for China's digital BRI expansion as it has been for the traditional BRI, especially when these countries received China's medical assistance and advice during the Covid-19 health crisis.

Strategically, the ASEAN region lies on the sea route of the BRI which enabled China to exert influence over the China Seas, many parts of which are also claimed by other Southeast Asian nations. Beijing appears to be focusing on economic expansion, while keeping an "uneasy peace" by slowly asserting its influence in the waters. This approach has created geopolitical tension, with some Asian countries suspecting China of pursuing a strategy of encircling Asia with a "string of pearls"—a network of ports connecting China's eastern coast to the Middle East—to boost its strategic clout and maritime access (See map). India, among others, asserts that Beijing designed such a "string" to make China the hub of a new order in Asia and the Indian Ocean. It worries that by establishing dominance along major trade routes, China is trying to redraw Asia's geopolitical map.

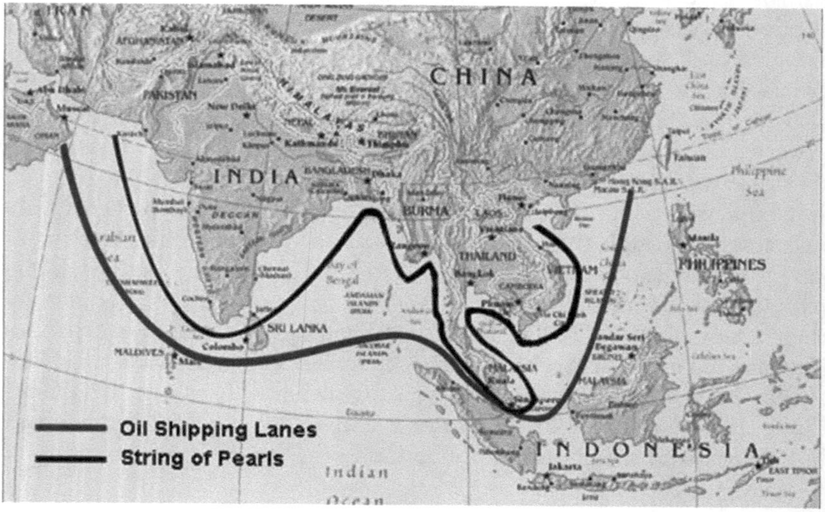

China's grand vision of the BRI's sea route is to build new port infrastructure that links to its inland transport networks, increases the number of international sea routes, improves logistics by enhancing the usage of information technology, dismantles trade and investment barriers and deepens financial integration by greater usage of the RMB. Strategically, China has engaged the region with a multi-aspect approach to accommodate the different stages of economic development of these countries. Poor countries get more Chinese assistance, trade and investment in the construction of basic public-health infrastructure, while rich economies get more scientific exchange and management cooperation through health professionals and scientists.

From the Health Silk Road perspective, the purpose is to integrate the digital functions in the different countries' healthcare systems. This does not only make them more efficient but also promotes China's digital health and biotechnological standards and, hence, increases its regional influence. This is exactly China's new worldview under its dual circulation policy that sees its internal circulation sit in the centre of

Asia while engaging regional and global capital, financial and technological markets for enhancing domestic growth and driving regional growth (see Chapter 1). Ultimately, all this reveals Beijing's BRI vision to draw China's neighbours closer to its economic embrace as a long-term development strategy to counter external exigencies and global demand shift.

It is clear that the strategic objective of the BRI is aimed at building a massive network of trade and infrastructure by China in the developing world. This initiative is not only crucial for China's traditional exporters of manufactured goods and for the state-owned heavy industries that build infrastructure projects. It is also important for building China's economic future by developing emerging technologies, such as blockchain, big data, virtual reality, artificial intelligence and the Internet of Things[9].

From BRI to Debt Trap

The West has criticised China's increasingly assertive foreign economic policy through its BRI as a practice of neo-mercantilism (Blackwell & Tellis, 2015) and "debt-trap diplomacy" (Chellaney, 2017). These views argue that China had sought to advance its economic and geopolitical influence by purposely ensnaring some of the developing countries in unsustainable loans-for-infrastructure deals. Such a suspicion should not be surprising because development finance is an area of economic prowess dominated by the developed world institutions, including the World Bank, the Asian Development and the European Bank for Reconstruction and Development.

The conventional wisdom is that the heavier the debt burden on the recipient country, the greater China's leverage becomes when the country is being forced to sell to China stakes in Chinese-financed projects or hand over management to Chinese state-owned investors. Concerns about China's debt-trap finance have found their way into some countries' foreign policy circle, aggravating the geopolitical tensions (The White House, 2018; Hurley et al., 2018). Critics of China's BRI assume that

[9] The Internet of Things is the network of physical devices, vehicles, home appliances and other items embedded with electronics, software, sensors, actuators and connectivity which enables these things to connect and exchange data, creating opportunities for more direct integration of the physical world into computer-based systems. The purpose is to increase economic efficiency and benefits with less human intervention.

its economic interests are maximised when its lending partners are in financial distress. However, there is no proof for this claim.

The debt-trap view also assumes that China could maximise its economic and geopolitical interests by ensnaring its BRI partners in debt distress. However, evidence shows that China does not always reap the alleged economic benefits and that it is often a victim of its lending missteps. Pushback from BRI recipient countries has increased, leading to a decline in BRI investment since 2020. More importantly, domestic criticism on the BRI has emerged, which will scale back, though not stop, President Xi Jinping's BRI ambition.

Anecdotally, China's lending to Venezuela has been the single most important evidence of its debt-trap finance backfired. Venezuela is the largest recipient of Chinese official finance, with the China Development Bank lending the bulk of more than USD60 billion between 2007 and 2017[10]. Since China is the world's biggest oil importer and Venezuela has the world's largest oil reserves, the commercial rationale for the loans was strong for financing long-term oil partnership between the two countries.

Yet, with Venezuela in the depths of economic and political crises since 2013, the China-Venezuela loans-for-oil relationship has gone badly wrong. The collapse of Venezuela's economy means that it has not been able to make loan repayments and even oil shipment to China. In sum, Venezuela has gone from being a geopolitical asset for China in Latin America to being a liability.

Some other BRI projects have also gone wrong. For example, Sri Lanka's Mattala Rajapaksa International Airport, which opened near Hambantota in 2013, is still the emptiest airport in the world. Hambantota's Magampura Mahinda Rajapaksa Port is largely idle, as is the multibillion-dollar Gwadar Port in Pakistan. Chinese lending and investment in other BRI countries, including Afghanistan, South Sudan and Angola, have also reportedly gone wrong.

All this shows that China debt-trap finance has not achieved its intended purpose of gaining economic and geopolitical benefits through the BRI, as many observers alleged. China might just be following the footsteps of the Western governments, businesses and multilateral development finance institutions in the 1930s and 1970s when they found

[10] According to data from the Carnegie-Tsinghua Centre for Global Policy as of 2017.

themselves in unsustainable debt relationships that hurt debtors and creditors alike.

BRI Ambition Scaled Back

The BRI problems have caught domestic attention in China. Since June 2018, there have been signs of discontent from policy advisors, academics and even government officials with President Xi's ambitious policy agenda. One of the criticisms focuses on his excessive "foreign aid" to countries in Africa and the Middle East with obvious reference to his BRI projects. The public airing of such a criticism may indicate the emergence of a consensus that Beijing should scale back its BRI ambition.

Macroeconomic forces have also prompted President Xi Jinping to scale back his BRI ambition. When the BRI was launched in September 2013, China enjoyed a current account surplus with huge foreign exchange reserves close to USD4 trillion. Its steel, cement and construction industries were plagued by excess capacity with "hungry" engineering firms looking for new markets. Such a macroeconomic backdrop justified lavish lending to foreign governments in exchange for lucrative construction and engineering contracts. However, by 2019 China's current account surplus had almost disappeared and its foreign exchange reserves had shrunk to USD3 trillion. Greater regulatory scrutiny of BRI projects and more caution on overseas lending have naturally become an economic necessity.

As a result, the push for BRI expansion has faded, even if it retains political importance. This can be seen in the drop in China's foreign loan data. After an initial surge during the official push for BRI expansion in 2013 through 2017[11], the growth rate of China's external loans (a proxy to lending to the BRI countries) has fallen despite a growth spike between 2020 and 2021 which was due to increase in Covid-related (not BRI related) lending (Fig. 3.4). Also note that these numbers have limitations. China does not report any detail breakdowns on foreign lending flows, such as the loans' destinations, purposes and recipients, or any breakdowns between its official lending and private-sector lending. So, it is tricky to draw definite conclusions from the aggregate data.

[11] Foreign (BRI) loan growth was disrupted in 2015 and 2016 when Beijing imposed capital controls to stem capital flight during chaotic market conditions. Loan growth rebounded in 2017 as normal market conditions returned.

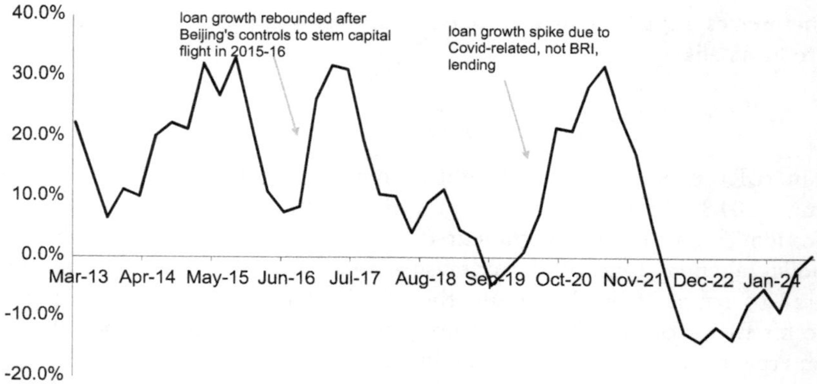

Fig. 3.4 China's BRI lending* has dropped since the official push in 2013 through 2017 (*Note* *approximated by total overseas lending. *Source* CEIC, author)

A lot of loans to foreign engineering and construction projects are hidden in the form of Chinese bank lending to state-owned contractors in the domestic system. While the Chinese government may have tighter scrutiny of these loans, thus making it harder for the recipient countries to abuse the Chinese loans, it also means there are no details on cross-border transactions for monitoring and analysis. So, the actual foreign lending (including to the BRI countries) is almost certainly higher than the official data suggests, though the growth trends should not differ much.

No Point in Blindly Bashing China

In sum, the BRI faces constraints on both the supply side and the demand side. On one hand, tighter financing and more stringent project controls are forcing Chinese engineering and construction firms to be more vigilant. On the other hand, the recipient countries are becoming more careful about agreeing to Chinese-funded projects, as they seek to avoid becoming financially trapped by Beijing.

From the political perspective, the BRI is still moving forward, and China is still signing more countries into the network. There were 54 countries joining the BRI in 2017, shortly after its inception. By 2023, the number of BRI countries had grown to 150 (Table).

BRI countries 2017
Total 54

Albania	Papua New Guinea
Armenia	Philippines
Azerbaijan	Poland
Belarus	Romania
Bosnia and Herzegovina	Serbia
Bulgaria	Slovak Republic
Cambodia	Slovenia
Cameroon	Somalia
Comoros	South Africa
Côte d'Ivoire	Sri Lanka
Croatia	Tanzania
Czech Republic	Thailand
Egypt, Arab Rep.	Timor-Leste
Estonia	Turkey
Georgia	Turkmenistan
Hungary	Ukraine
Indonesia	Uzbekistan
Iraq	Vietnam
Kenya	Yemen, Rep.
Latvia	
Lebanon	
Lithuania	
Madagascar	
Malaysia	
Maldives	
Moldova	
Mongolia	
Montenegro	
Morocco	
Myanmar	
Nepal	
NewZealand	
North Macedonia	
Pakistan	
Panama	

BRI countries 2023
Total 150

Afghanistan	Djibouti	Madagascar	Slovak Republic
Albania	Dominica	Malawi	Slovenia
Algeria	Ecuador	Malaysia	Solomon Islands
Angola	Egypt, Arab Rep.	Maldives	Somalia
Antigua and Barbuda	El Salvador	Mali	South Africa
Argentina	Equatorial Guinea	Malta	South Sudan
Armenia	Eritrea	Mauritania	Sri Lanka
Austria	Estonia	Micronesia, Fed. Sts.	Sudan
Azerbaijan	Ethiopia	Moldova	Suriname
Bahrain	Fiji	Mongolia	Syrian Arab Republic
Bangladesh	Gabon	Montenegro	Tajikistan
Barbados	Gambia, The	Morocco	Tanzania
Belarus	Georgia	Mozambique	Thailand
Benin	Ghana	Myanmar	Timor-Leste
Bolivia	Greece	Namibia	Togo
Bosnia and Herzegovin	Grenada	Nepal	Tonga
Botswana	Guinea	New Zealand	Trinidad and Tobago
Brunei Darussalam	Guinea-Bissau	Nicaragua	Tunisia
Bulgaria	Guyana	Niger	Turkey
Burundi	Honduras	Nigeria	Turkmenistan
Cabo Verde	Hungary	Niue	Uganda
Cambodia	Indonesia	North Macedonia	Ukraine
Cameroon	Iran, Islamic Rep.	Oman	United Arab Emirates
Central African Republi	Iraq	Pakistan	Uruguay
Chad	Italy	Panama	Uzbekistan
Chile	Jamaica	Papua New Guinea	Vanuatu
Comoros	Jordan	Peru	Venezuela, RB
Congo, Dem. Rep.	Kazakhstan	Philippines	Vietnam
Congo, Rep.	Kenya	Poland	Yemen, Rep.
Cook Islands	Kiribati	Portugal	Zambia
Costa Rica	Korea, Rep.	Qatar	Zimbabwe
Côte d'Ivoire	Kuwait	Romania	
Croatia	Kyrgyz Republic	Russian Federation	
Cuba	Lao PDR	Rwanda	
Cyprus	Latvia	Samoa	
Dominican Republic	Lebanon	Saudi Arabia	
Czech Republic	Lesotho	Senegal	
	Liberia	Serbia	
	Libya	Seychelles	
	Lithuania	Sierra Leone	
	Luxembourg	Singapore	

Source: Green Finance & Development Centre, as of June 2024

In a way, Beijing's attempts to reset the BRI's direction as a multilateral endeavour that respects international norms are making an impact. But the economic, regulatory and political constraints on the BRI's expansion and ambition mean that the concern about its disruption to the global balance of power should not be exaggerated. There are benefits that the BRI will bring to the global system, and if that is seen as a disruption because it forces the existing global powers to rethink their international policies and contribution to the world, it would be a benign disruption.

There is no point in blindly fearing or bashing China without understanding properly what is happening with the Middle Kingdom and its experiences.

References

Blackwell, R. D., & Tellis, A. J. (2015). *Revisiting US Grand Strategy Toward China*. Council on Foreign Relations, Council Special Report No. 72, March.

Brown, C. (2020). *COVID-19: China's Exports of Medical Supplies Provide a Ray of Hope*. Peterson Institute for International Economics, March 26.

Cao, J. (2020). Toward a Health Silk Road – China's Proposal for Global Health Cooperation. *China Quarterly of International Strategic Studies, 6*(1), 19–35.

Chan, J. H. (2019). *China's Digital Silk Road: The Integration of Myanmar—Analysis*. *Eurasia Review*, April 30. https://www.eurasiareview.com/30042019-chinas-digital-silk-road-the-integration-of-myanmar-analysis/

Chellaney, B. (2017). *China's Debt-trap Diplomacy*. Project Syndicate, January 23.

Chiang, S. (2024). *Xi tells Dutch prime minister: No force can stop China's tech advance*. CNBC Tech. March 27. https://www.cnbc.com/2024/03/28/xi-to-dutch-pm-no-force-can-stop-the-pace-of-chinas-tech-advance.html

Eder, T. S., Arcesati, R., & Mardell, J. (2019). *Networking the "Belt and Road – The future is digital"*. Mercator Institute for China Studies, August 28. Retrieved from https://merics.org/en/tracker/networking-belt-and-road-future-digital#:~:text=Innovation%20and%20the%20Digital%20Silk,and%20Road%20Initiative%20(BRI).&text=In%20Europe%2C%20the%20UK%20and,of%20their%205G%20telecoms%20networks

Fidler, M. (2018). *African Union Bugged by China: Cyber Espionage as Evidence of Strategic Shifts*. Council on Foreign Relations, March 7. https://www.cfr.org/blog/african-union-bugged-china-cyber-espionage-evidence-strategic-shifts

Greenfield, N. M. (2024). *Study shows drastic decline in US-China scientific exchange*. University World News, 11 July. https://www.universityworldnews.com/post.php?story=20240711122935490#:~:text=As%20of%20September%202021%2C%20federal,disruption%20of%20international%20scientific%20exchange.

Hurley, J., Morris, S., & Portelance, G. (2018). *Examining the Debt Implications of the Belt and Road Initiative from a Policy Perspective*. Centre for Global Development, CGD Policy Paper 121, March.

Lancaster, K., Rubin, M., & Rapp-Hooper, M. (2020). *Mapping China's Health Silk Road*. Council on Foreign Relations, April 10. https://www.cfr.org/blog/mapping-chinas-health-silk-road

Levy, M., & Boak, J. (2024). *Trump vows to block Japanese steelmaker from buying US Steel, pledges tax incentives and tariffs*. AP News, Associated Press. December 4. https://apnews.com/article/us-steel-nippon-trump-biden-steelworkers-1b0fb38077ff0a6b68e64a184f270bac

Lo, C. (2013). *The Renminbi Rises: Myths, Hypes and Realties of RMB Internationalisation and Reforms in the Post-Crisis World*. Palgrave Macmillan.

Ngeow, C. B. (2020). *COVID-19, Belt and Road Initiative and the Health Silk Road: Implications for Southeast Asia*. Friedrich Ebert Stiftung. Singapore. October.

Pan, C. (2024). *Huawei's AI chips take another step forward as Chinese firms look for Nvidia alternatives*. The South China Morning Post. 29 September. https://www.scmp.com/tech/big-tech/article/3280306/huaweis-ai-chips-take-another-step-forward-chinese-firms-look-nvidia-alternatives

Penley, T. (2025). *Trump's plan to revive US shipbuilding sends 'critical signal' to China amid flaring trade tensions: Expert*. FoxBusiness, Fox News. March 6. https://www.foxbusiness.com/media/trumps-plan-revive-us-shipbuildings-sends-critical-signal-china-amid-flaring-tensions-expert

The White House. (2018). *How China's Economic Aggression Threatens the Technologies and Intellectual Property of the United States and the World*. White House Office of Trade and Manufacturing Policy, June.

Triolo, P., & Allison, K. (2020). *Will the Battle Over Huawei Kill Globalization? The China Project*. February 21. https://thechinaproject.com/2020/02/21/will-the-battle-over-huawei-kill-globalization/

Triolo, P., Allison, K., et al. (2020). *The Digital Silk Road: Expanding China's Digital Footprint*. *Eurasia Group*, 8 April.

CHAPTER 4

Decoupling Versus Regionalism and "Collabetition"

Fears about China's "giant sucking sound" hollowing out other countries' jobs have morphed into fears about its "banging sound" invading the world's economy and dominating it with the Chinese system. The blind fears have led to misguided policies, notably trade and investment protectionism, led by the US through tariffs and export and foreign investment restrictions to force China to decouple from the global system since 2018.

From a macroeconomic perspective, imposing punitive tariffs to create/protect domestic growth by hurting the foreign country is fundamentally flawed. This is because the net impact of tariffs on the economy of the country that imposes them, in terms of output and employment, is quite uncertain. Tariffs provide protection for some domestic industries and encourage import substitution. That could increase employment and domestic income.

However, those industries with large exposure to the tariffs could suffer a decline in employment due to rising input cost and possibly become targets of retaliatory tariffs. If these downside effects were to negate or even overwhelm the positive impact from import tariff protection, that would result in a net negative effect on domestic growth. Indeed, the US Federal Reserve's (Fed) research analysed the 2018 US tariff war on China and found that the net impact on US growth and employment was negative, *ceteris paribus* (Flaaen & Pierce, 2024).

C. Lo, *Clash of the Economic Titans: China and the United States*, https://doi.org/10.1007/978-981-95-2510-2_4

Tariffs Don't Work as Intended

Evidence shows that the US protectionist policies did not work in containing China's expansion. They will likely not work in the future because China is not sitting on its hands. It has responded not so much by retaliatory protectionist measures but more by climbing the technology value chain to improve competitiveness and by developing new export markets. This can be seen in the rise in China's global share of exports since 2018 when the Sino-US tariff war first started.

Far from isolating China, the US tariffs imposed by Donald Trump in his first presidential term (many of which were either kept or raised by the Biden administration) have forced Chinese firms to diversify, innovate and expand in other countries, enlarging China's global footprints. As a result, China's global share of exports has risen since 2018 while that of the US has fallen (Fig. 4.1) as Chinese firms shifted production and trade to other countries, notably in ASEAN, Africa and Latin America (Mexico in particular) to skirt US tariffs and trade restrictions.

These developments raise questions about whether using trade war and protectionism to force decoupling from China would serve American interests. While Chinese companies upgrade their supply chains and adapt to the global demand shift and rising geopolitical tension, American manufacturers have had to deal with higher input costs and disrupted

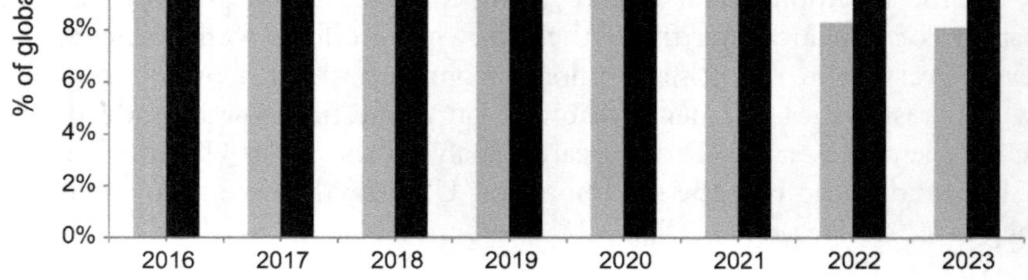

Fig. 4.1 Share of world exports (*Source* Statista, the World Bank, author)

supply networks because of their government's China-containment policies.

Ironically, by forcing China to decouple from the US, tariffs and trade restriction policies seem to have eroded America's global influence, albeit slowly. This can be seen in the increase in the usage of the renminbi in international payments, which has ranked consistently fourth and fifth most widely used currency for global payments in the SWIFT system, and the creeping progress of renminbi internationalisation.

Another international development resulted from the US's protectionist and decoupling policies is a "reverse supply chain", where China has become an essential input supplier to other developing countries instead of just absorbing their inputs for self-production. This development has helped China expand and integrate deeper into the regional (and global) supply chains, refuting the decoupling argument.

In the grand scheme of things, to counter the protectionist and decoupling forces, China has been building regionalism to counter de-globalisation. This has created another issue that the global debate on China's economic ascent has missed—a new paradigm of what I call here "collabetition" where global competition and collaboration with China increases simultaneously. The resultant profound global implications are completely different from what decoupling and de-globalisation imply.

Decoupling, a Mutually Inclusive Incentive

Contrary to conventional wisdom, decoupling is not only an American incentive to reduce its risk exposure to China. It is also a Chinese incentive to reduce its dependence on foreign technology. This bilateral incentive also underlies the drive for de-globalisation and breaking up of the global supply chains.

The new tariffs that Donald Trump imposed on Chinese imports at the onset of his second presidential term in 2025 have reinforced the common view held in the US that decoupling is about reducing imports to safeguard or repatriate US jobs, and to ensure the national security of the American civil and military infrastructure. Contrary to its former "constructive engagement" policy, the US sees China as a strategic competitor since the first Trump presidency in 2018 and is thus seeking to reduce what it sees as the risk of its economic dependence on China.

China has countered this change in US foreign policy with its "dual circulation" strategy.[1] Arguably, this is China's decoupling effort through a strategic policy shift to hedge against the US risk by switching its policy focus to economic control from economic growth. In this context, the goal of the dual circulation strategy is to boost the domestic sector as the key growth driver, reduce dependence on foreign technology and products by import substitution and draw upon its domestic economic powerbase to achieve dominance in global competitiveness, overseas investment and global supply chains, and to drive regional (especially Asian) growth.

China, a "Strategic Necessity"

From a global perspective, the US strategic moves against China, especially under the Trump administration's erratic misguided intentions, or planned chaos, have made the Middle Kingdom look more stable, predictable and "rules based". Under this situation, decoupling from China will not work because an increasing number of countries are building better trade and diplomatic relations with China as a way to hedge against the US risk. Evidence shows that China has become a larger trade partner than the US for most countries in the world (Rajah & Albayrak, 2025). In 2023, 145 countries or about 70% of the world trade more with China than with the US. Among these countries, China was the largest bilateral trading partner for 60 economies, compared to only 33 for the US.

The hawkish foreign and protectionist policies of the US are going to push even more countries towards China's economic embrace. Countries that have been overly dependent on the US for trade will inevitably seek to diversify to hedge the US risk. Meanwhile, China will continue to expand and strengthen foreign trade with its enormous and increasingly competitive manufacturing sector. Seeking to expand multilateral and bilateral

[1] China's "dual circulation" strategy, announced in May 2020 by the Chinese Communist Party, is an economic policy for rebalancing the country's economy by prioritising domestic consumption. Strategically, it is a policy to counter geopolitical hostility by strengthening the domestic sector while still engaging, but reducing reliance on, the external sector to sustain stable growth and resilient investment in the face of strategic competition with the US.

free-trade agreements and lowering tariffs have become Beijing's key policies to counter Washington's decoupling push (Duan, 2024; Xinhua, 2024). The US protectionist approach will only facilitate China's global reach.

This political-economic development enhances the strategic appeal of China on the global stage. In a bipolar world of superpowers, the US and China are keen competitors in nearly all economic, technology and even military domains. Given China's growing influence and dominance in many key industries, ignoring progress in its development and its changing international economic and financial relations risks creating a massive blind spot in policy and investment strategies.

Decoupling, Where?

There is no evidence yet for China decoupling from the US and global system. Not only is Sino-US trade continuing to rise, but there is also a significant increase in trade and investment between ASEAN[2] and China, despite geopolitical, regulatory and economic shocks. The increase in China-ASEAN connection reflects a change in the global supply-chain structure that vindicates China's dual circulation economic strategy to boost regionalism to counter de-globalisation and the rise of geopolitical risks.

Even the fall in net foreign direct investment (FDI) inflows to China is not necessarily a sign of China decoupling. This is because the decline also reflects an increase in China's outward investments under it "external circulation" tactic in the dual circulation framework to capture the shift in global demand and supply-chain structure. Nevertheless, Beijing's scrutiny of foreign firms on corruption, fraud, espionage and national security grounds in 2023 and 2024 did hurt foreign sentiment in China and revived discussions about China breaking away from the global system. Such talks have also revived fears about the breaking up of the global supply chains and fuelling the arguments against investment in and trade with China and Asia.

[2] The Association of Southeast Asian Nations (ASEAN) is an inter-governmental international organisation, comprised of Indonesia, Vietnam, Laos, Brunei, Thailand, Myanmar, the Philippines, Cambodia, Singapore and Malaysia.

What Is the Evidence Telling Us?

Despite the trade war with the US, Covid-19 health crisis, US-led restrictions on tech exports and technology transfer to China, and other trade restrictions such as tariffs, China's total trade with the G3 economies (Japan, Europe, and the US) has continued to rise, defying market expectations (Fig. 4.2). In Asia, China's trade with ASEAN has not only risen steadily but also accelerated after the Sino-US trade war in 2018. This has raised ASEAN's share in China's total trade with Asia to over 30% from around 18% in 2010 (Fig. 4.3), suggesting that the region has become more reliant on trade with China.

All this is not evidence of decoupling. China's sticky trade relationship with the G3 and its increase in trade with ASEAN have happened because of 1) China's development policy that sees itself as a driver for Asian growth, 2) China's reaction to the global demand shift and 3) the change in the global supply chain structure. Nevertheless, if US President Doanld Trump's draconian tariff war policy against China persists, it may change the trade dynamics between the two big powers and increase

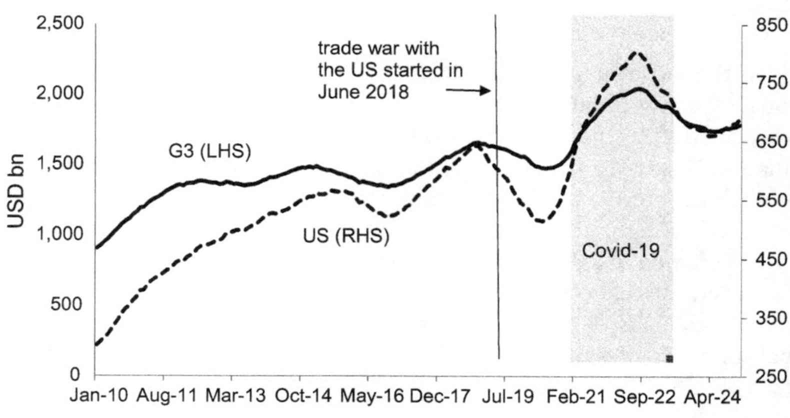

Fig. 4.2 China's toal trade* with he G3 (*Note* *exports + imports with Japan, Europe & US, 12-month rolling sum. *Sources* CEIC, author)

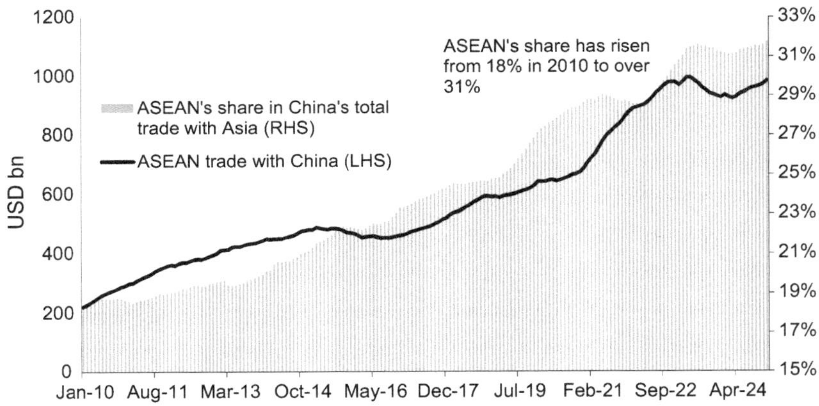

Fig. 4.3 China's toal trade* with ASEAN (*Note* *exports + imports, 12-month rolling sum. *Sources* CEIC, author)

decoupling pressures at least between China and the US. This is a crucial geopolitical risk that needs monitoring.

In its dual circulation strategy, adopted since May 2020, China sees itself moving into a new paradigm where the global system would be divided into three main regions: Asia, North America and Europe, with each region being led by a super-regional power. Naturally, China sees itself as the leader in Asia. This strategy aims at using China's domestic growth impetus (the "internal circulation") to drive both internal and regional growth and leveraging on intra-regional trade and capital flows (the "external circulation"). This regional strategy has manifested in the increase in trade with ASEAN, with has surpassed North America since 2019 as China's second largest trading partner after Europe (Fig. 4.4).

Shifts in Global Demand and Supply Chains

Since the Sino-US trade war, the G3 economies, especially the US, have increased imports sharply from ASEAN to reduce reliance on Chinese imports (Fig. 4.5). In fact, the trade war has resulted in trade diversion rather than trade destruction. This is also not evidence for "reshoring" or even "friend-shoring", that the Americans want to see. The trade diversion instead reflects a shift, not a breakage as many have misunderstood, of

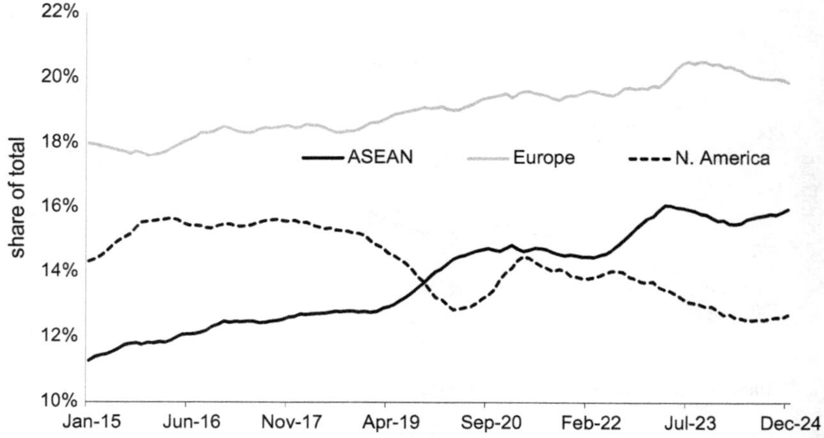

Fig. 4.4 China's total trade with ASEAN, Europe & N.America (*Note* *exports + imports, 12-month rolling sum. *Sources* CEIC, author)

Asia's supply chains. The depth and scale of existing manufacturing operations in Asia, along with continued cost-competitiveness and network externalities prevailing in the region have prompted such shift.

However, buying more from ASEAN does not necessarily mean buying less or decoupling from China due to the so-called "China + 1 strategy".[3] This is a corporate strategy for multinational companies to keep producing in China for the local market and move some capacity elsewhere, notably to ASEAN, to manage potential supply-chain disruption due to economic, political and other considerations, such as the Covid-19 health crisis. The rising FDI trend to ASEAN (Fig. 4.6) underscores such strategy, with the Sino-US trade war further boosting the incentive to relocate.

Official data shows that more than one-third of FDI flows to ASEAN's manufacturing sector comes from Northeast Asia, with China's share rising quickly, especially in Indonesia, Vietnam and Thailand, in recent years (Fig. 4.7). This highlights the growing connectivity between the

[3] The China + 1 strategy, also known as Plus One or C + 1, is a supply chain strategy that encourages companies to minimise their supply chain dependency on China by diversifying the countries they source inputs from. The goal is to reduce the risk of over-relying on a single country for sourcing and manufacturing.

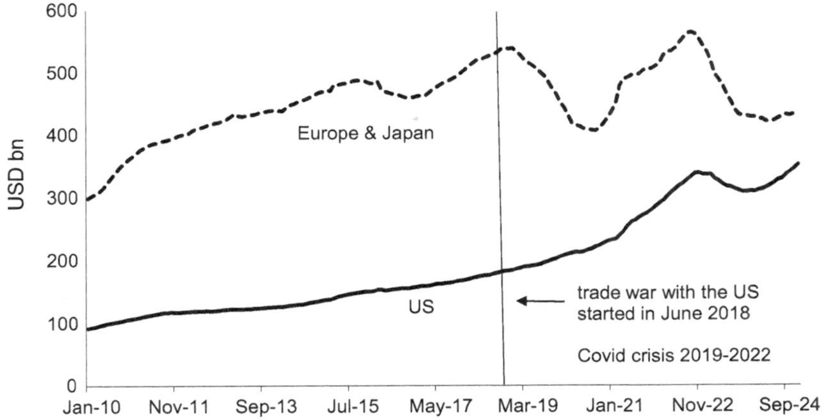

Fig. 4.5 G3's imports* from ASEAN (*Note* *12-month rolling sum. *Sources* CEIC, author)

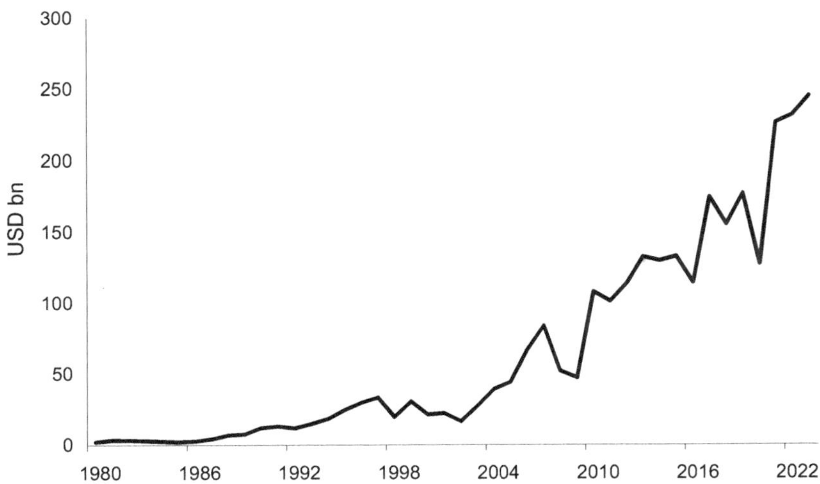

Fig. 4.6 Rising net FDI inflows* to ASEAN (*Note* *Balance of payments data. *Sources* CEIC, author)

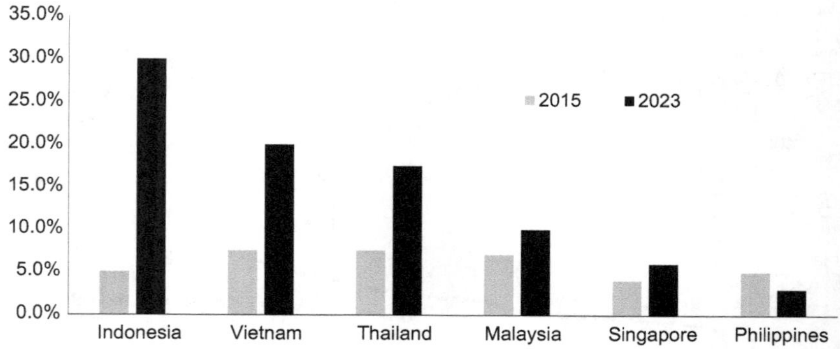

Fig. 4.7 China's FDI share of country's total FDI* (*Note* 4-qtr moving average. *Sources* CEIC, HSBC, author)

Chinese and ASEAN economies and reflects further supply-chain integration between China and ASEAN but not decoupling. In the conventional supply chains, ASEAN ships components and goods to China, which then sells to the world markets. That makes China the world's factory.

However, this supply-chain dynamics have reversed in recent years, with China supplying ASEAN with products that power the region's exports to the world. This shift in the supply-chain integration process has expanded the world's factory to include both China and Asia that, in turn, boosted Sino-ASEAN trade to more than the amount of the Sino-US trade (see Fig. 4.4).

Regionalism Versus De-Globalisation

In addition to using its internal growth impetus to drive domestic and regional growth, China's dual circulation policy also seeks to cooperate with ASEAN in the digital economy and promote the Health Silk Road initiative (see Chapter 2) by establishing a regional China-ASEAN public-health cooperation mechanism to fight diseases such as Covid-19.

To leverage on the regional capital flows and investment opportunities, China encourages its domestic companies to increase investment in ASEAN, thus reducing the amount of net FDI inflows to China at any given level of gross FDI flows. To address geopolitical concerns, especially in the South China Sea, Beijing is seeking regular dialogue with the regional governments and trying to speed up the negotiations on the code of conduct in the region and maritime cooperation.

From a macroeconomic perspective, all these developments will, in my view, lead to the rise of regionalism with strong intra-regional economic linkages against a de-globalisation backdrop. Asia's supply chains have proven highly resilient to starve off disruptions to the global system. Their shift, as discussed above, is an adaptation to the global demand change and geopolitical tensions. This resilience forms the basis for long-term investment in Asia and China which remains in the core of the supply chains.

So, there is no clear evidence that economic decoupling has become a trend. Even the increase in investment outflows from China does not represent decoupling, as I argue below. They reflect Beijing's efforts to boost regionalism to counter de-globalisation and the rise of geopolitical risks. The change in the global supply-chain structure integrating China deeper into the regional supply chains is the strongest evidence against decoupling. The international trade and policy crosscurrents could lead to a new paradigm that encompasses onshoring, reshoring and friend-shoring. This suggests that when the US-led de-globalisation meets the China-led regionalism, they could end up increasing global competition and collaboration, simultaneously, with China and produce some profound global implications that the public debate has not considered.

But Net FDI Has Dropped

The sharp drop in China's net FDI since late 2022 (Fig. 4.8), according to China's balance of payments (BoP) data, has intensified the market's fear about the world decoupling from China by not investing in China. Some observers even argued that the FDI outflows were a sign of foreign firms de-risking or friend-shoring their businesses (Atkins, 2023). In other words, they are leaving China for good.

However, there is more to the truth than meets the myopic eye of the pessimists. China has two FDI data series. The State Administration of Foreign Exchange (SAFE) reports quarterly balance of payments (BoP) data which includes foreign firms' undistributed profit and unremitted profits. The Ministry of Commerce (MoC) reports monthly utilised FDI data which does not include the profits numbers.

Hence, the value of the BoP FDI data is usually larger than the utilised FDI data. Reinvested earnings of foreign firms have accounted for as

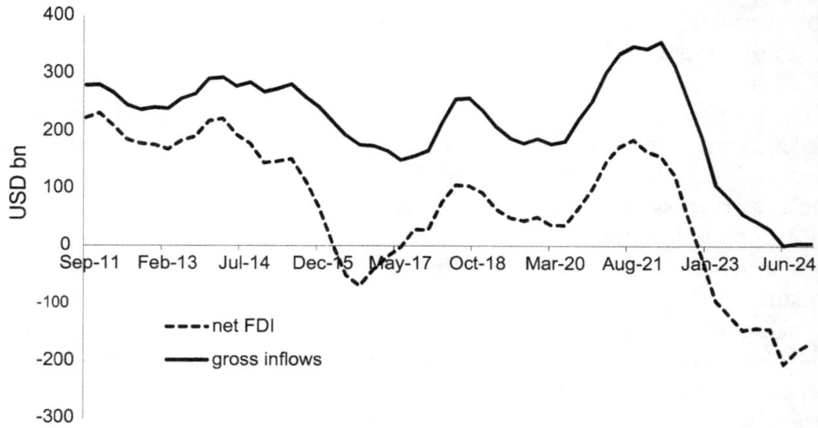

Fig. 4.8 Falling FDI flows to China since late 2022 (*Note* *Balance of payments data, 4-quarter rolling sum. *Sources* CEIC, author)

much as 80% of the data gap between BoP and utilised FDI (Brooks, 2024). Evidence shows that this data gap has been narrowing since 2013–14 and turned negative since 2022 (Fig. 4.9). What is happening?

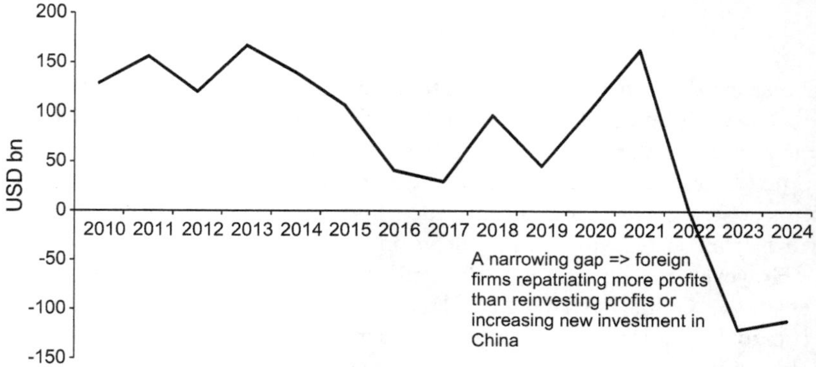

Fig. 4.9 A narrowing gap* between BoP FDI inflows and utilised FDI (*Note* *BoP FDI inflows minus utilised FDI. *Sources* CEIC, author)

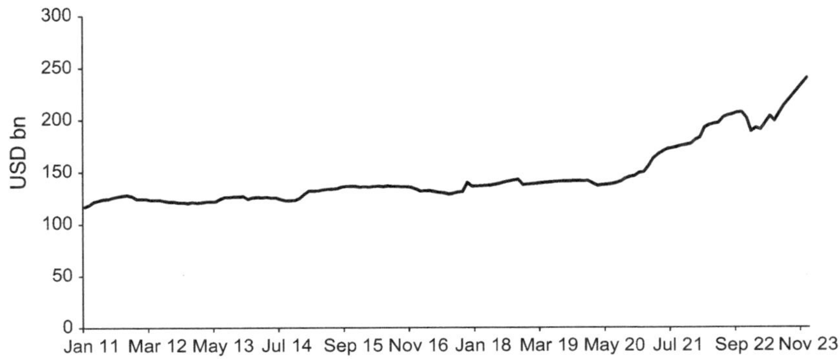

Fig. 4.10 Utilised FDI inflows* rose again in 2023 and 2024 (*Note* *12-month rolling sum. *Sources* CEIC, author)

The data gap between these two FDI data series gives a clue as to whether foreign firms are deserting China. The declining trend of the gap implies that BoP FDI dropped more significantly than utilised FDI, suggesting that a big part of the declining, and later negative, data gap likely reflected foreign firms repatriating profits (hence the plunge in BoP FDI) to a greater extent than they reinvested their earnings or increased new investment in China (represented by utilised FDI). Furthermore, monthly data showed that utilised FDI flows rebounded in 2023 and 2024 (Fig. 4.10), accounting for the narrowing of the FDI gap in Fig. 4.9.

The point is that there is no evidence for significant asset sales (i.e. investment withdrawal) by foreigners. So, the claim that foreigners are leaving China for good does not stand up to scrutiny.

Outward Direct Investment

Also eroding China's net FDI inflows is the sharp rise in China's outward direct investment (ODI) in recent years, as China tries to secure its supply chains and diversifies its manufacturing base by shifting production to countries where exports are not subject to US tariffs. China's ODI is notably apparent in the ASEAN region (Fig. 4.11). By increasing their investments in Asia, these overseas Chinese firms have been able to source components and inputs from China for making exports to the US that are shipped from Asia. Hence, the Chinese content of US imports from Southeast Asia has risen, offsetting the decline in direct US imports from China. This indirect route for Chinese exports to the US (via Asia) arguably defeats the US's purpose of replacing Chinese imports by Asian imports in the trade war.

Crucially, this increase in China-Asian connection reflects a structural change in the global supply-chain with China integrating further with the regional supply chains but not decoupling (see discussion above). This approach also vindicates Beijing's economic development and expansion strategy by boosting regional relationship to counter the decoupling and de-globalisation forces and the increase of external hostility against China.

Meanwhile, the worry about FDI outflow hurting China's economic growth has been exaggerated. China does not depend on FDI to finance its development, as many observers erroneously think. This is because FDI only accounts for about 3.0% of China's total investment. Rather, FDI is important for China as a channel for technological and business management know-how transfer. Furthermore, FDI brings in international market discipline, which helps to enhance the competitiveness of domestic enterprises and improve governance.

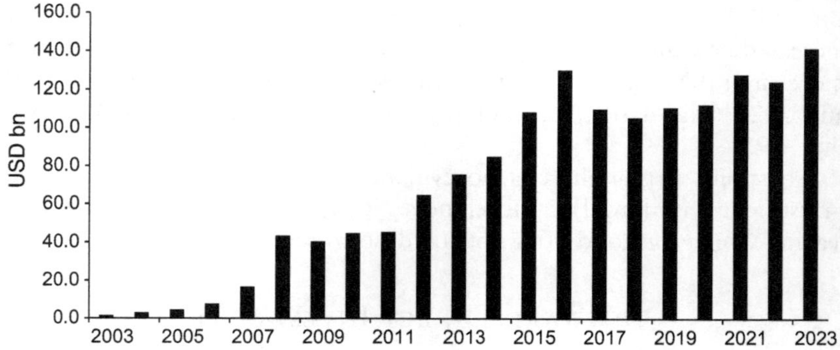

Fig. 4.11 China has increased investment in Asia significantly (*Sources* CEIC, author)

New Sources of FDI

While America's strategic competition foreign policy is reducing US FDI (and portfolio investment) in China, especially in sectors that the US deems strategic to its national interest, the Middle East (especially the Gulf Cooperation Council, or GCC, countries) is ready to step up its investments in China amid improving diplomatic and economic relations. The six GCC nations—Saudi Arabia, Kuwait, the United Arab Emirates, Qatar, Bahrain and Oman—have sovereign wealth funds totalling an estimated USD4 trillion, but less than 2.0% of this is invested in Asia, including China. This situation is set to change because this investment capital would grow to US$10 trillion by 2030, with USD1 to 2 trillion allocated to China (Yu, 2023). This could potentially offset the decline in US FDI in China. Furthermore, some FDI could flow to China by stealth when players skirt the US government's restrictions on directly investing in China by repackaging their investments in financial hubs such as the UAE and sending the money to China (and Asia).

There are signs of increasing engagement between the GCC and China which coincide with the acceleration of China's renminbi internationalisation momentum since March 2023 when Saudi Arabia announced that its state-owned oil and gas company Aramco would build oil refineries with China with construction starting in 2026 (Gnana, 2023), and that it would join the China-led regional security and trade club, the Shanghai Cooperation Organisation (Al-Atrush, 2023). The latter is an important sign of Saudi Arabia's improving diplomatic relationship with China which should help advance their talks on trading oil in renminbi.

In May 2023, the UAE signed three agreements with Chinese nuclear energy organisations, giving China an entry point into the GCC region. Then in August 2023, the BRICS bloc (comprising Brazil, Russia, India, China and South Africa) expanded its membership by adding six countries, including Saudi Arabia and UAE. In the third quarter of 2023 alone, Saudi Arabia, UAE and Qatar signed investment and partnership agreements with China worth at least USD5 billion, covering sectors in energy, research and development, industrial/green projects and finance.

The list of events and agreements will grow as Sino-Middle East cooperation increases.

While the FDI outflow data gives China critics the firepower to argue for a decline of China's prowess (Sharma, 2023), they are ignoring this development of new FDI flowing into China from the Middle East (and other countries, especially Asia) at their peril. This changing investment dynamics argue that FDI flows to China are undergoing a transitional phase with outflows led by the US being replaced by inflows from the Middle East and Asia over time. There is no conviction that China is decoupling.

The Cost of Decoupling

Decoupling China is easier said than done, just as multinational corporations' (MNCs') "China + 1" strategy is easier proposed than implemented. The experience from the Covid-19 pandemic lays bare the truth that when China shuts down, Asia (to where many MNCs have diversified their production bases) also shuts down because of the close integration of China in the regional supply chains through intra-regional trade and Chinese ODI in Asia.

China is not perfect. However, as many MNCs can attest, many regional countries lack size, scale, skills and efficient infrastructure, among other shortcomings. By contrast, China offers advantages that make decoupling impractical, including its size, well-financed infrastructure network, educated labour force, an efficient transportation and communication networks, a safe system and improving quality control, etc.

Take Vietnam, whose economy is less than 3.0% of China's. Should MNCs move their production from China to Vietnam, it would quickly exhaust Vietnam's capacity. Companies could go to India. Those who have done so can attest that India's infrastructure is not capable of replacing production and distribution in China. Labour quality is another major factor. World Bank research shows that 97% of Chinese aged 15 and older were literate as of 2020 (the latest data available), but India's literacy rate was only 76% in 2022 (Wei, 2024).

The incentive to decouple from China will remain as countries strive to avoid China-related risk. However, the extensive interdependence between the economies of China and the US and other countries argues that complete decoupling would be both impractical and implausible.

The German ifo Institute research estimates that a decoupling between the West and China, based on a 25% increase in import tariffs and a doubling of non-tariff barriers on both sides, would cost all countries dearly in terms of economic growth. China's real GDP growth could fall by over 2% points and those of the developed countries, including the

European Union (excluding Germany), the US, Germany and Australia by between 0.5% points and 1.5% points, depending on their intensity of the economic relations with China.

Granted, economic models do not necessarily represent the reality, but the message is clear: A decoupling of the developed world (led by the US) from China would lead to substantial losses on both sides and beyond as the world economies are closely connected to both China and the West.

New Paradigm of "Collabetition" and Impact

Hence, in my view, it is unlikely that the West or China will go for complete decoupling. The US and European economic strategies are striving to strengthen their economies and reduce dependency on China through diversification. The same goes for China, whose dual circulation strategy aims at boosting domestic consumption and internal production capability (especially in the tech sector) to de-risk the West.

Implementing these economic strategies will lead to stronger competition between China and the West. However, the close ties between the economies will remain, resulting in ongoing collaboration. Ultimately, a landscape of "collabetition" (collaboration-cum-competition) may arise out of China-led regionalism.

This new paradigm will involve tougher competition between countries, with players in the West striving to keep their technology edge over emerging players from China. However, there will also be new possibilities for cooperation as Chinese companies move up the innovation and high value-added ladder.

The most consequential aspect of even a partial US-China decoupling is likely in technology. Sino-US security competition is increasingly embedded in the two countries' domestic industrial and technological policies. From a macroeconomic perspective, technological decoupling could hurt global growth in the long term by reducing international trade flows, misallocating resources to production when the country does not have a comparative advantage, and restriction of cross-border knowledge diffusion. These could take the forms of reshoring, onshoring and friend-shoring, trade fragmentation and protectionism.

From an investment perspective, there could be short- to medium-term benefits on, and disruption to, the commodities sector. This is because Sino-US tech competition, especially in AI, means large investments in the high-tech sector and data centres and a subsequent surge in power consumption. The rise of electric vehicles, for example, could lead to a surge in power consumption around the world, creating stress on the existing power infrastructure in the major economies.

The West pursuing de-risking through onshoring/reshoring/friend-shoring will lead to relocation of the world's manufacturing, resulting in a steady rise in capital investment in the manufacturing sector. The trend has driven a cyclical manufacturing recovery in the global economy after the pandemic and an increase in demand for industrial commodities until the 2025 trade war hit. If the demand momentum is sustained in the long term, it could provide a strong support for commodity prices, *ceteris paribus*.

On the back of technology decoupling initiatives, US and China's electricity consumption will likely rise sharply in the years to come to satisfy the expected explosive growth of energy-intensive AI data centres and other high-tech development. The natural gas and nuclear power industries are well-primed to meet this surging energy demand as renewable energy solutions have yet to sufficiently scale up to replace fossil fuels.

The EV Battleground

The decoupling-collabetition battleground has manifested heatedly in the electric vehicles (EV) market, with China catching up swiftly in EV and battery production and exports and eroding the US's industry leadership status. This competition has implications not only for geopolitical tensions but also global energy transition. The latter, again, is another area that public discussion on China's role in the global economy has missed.

As has become the norm with technological advancements in various sectors in recent years, China has forcefully blown the rest of the world out of the water in terms of EV production and sales. One advantage that has greatly helped its head start is its dominance of global supplies of several critical resources, such as lithium and graphite. These are crucial components of battery electric vehicles. Lithium-ion battery technology is currently the most efficient (and by far the most widely used) method of powering EVs. China is controlling 60% of global lithium supplies, giving it a huge advantage in becoming the front runner in the development of the technology.

Facing such rising and formidable challenge, in May 2024 the US-imposed tariffs of 102.5% on imported Chinese EVs. The EU and Canada also followed suit by imposing tariffs ranging from 45% (by the EU)

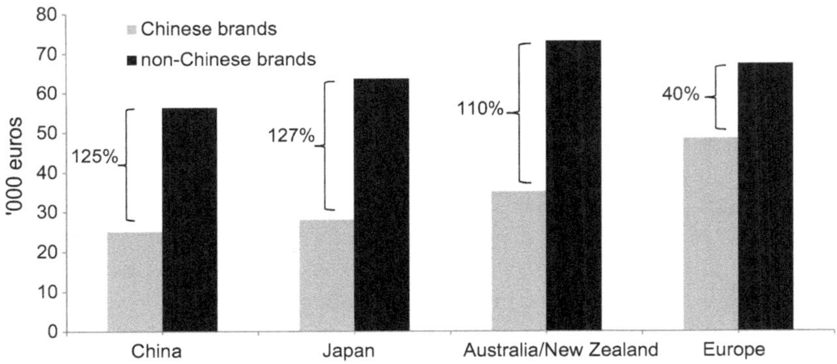

Fig. 4.12 Average EV price by market (2023) (*Sources* Morgan Stanley, author)

to 100% (by Canada) on Chinese EV imports. Such measures have not only created economic winners and losers but could also have profound implications on the world's transition to a net-zero economy.

China exports no EVs to the US at the time of writing. So, the US administration's EV import tariff is essentially symbolic. However, the EU's tariffs could have material impact: Chinese EVs accounted for almost 20% of the EV market in Europe in 2023, and the share is expected to rise to 25% in 2024 (T&E, 2024). Furthermore, the estimated 40% cost advantage of Chinese EVs in the European market is much smaller than in other markets (Fig. 4.12). The EU's 40% tariff rate could eliminate China's competitive advantage in the European market.

At the time of writing, the EU's new tariffs are provisional, pending negotiation results. They may be reduced if Chinese producers can prove that they get lower government subsidies than the EU has estimated. Furthermore, if China could reach an agreement with the EU to reduce the volume of Chinese EV exports to Europe, the new tariffs may not be implemented at all.

Boons and Banes

In general, the tariff obstacle may prompt some Chinese EV makers to consider locating their production facilities to the US and export from there. That could help create jobs and boost manufacturing and tax revenues in the US. However, such incentive of the Chinese firms could be offset by the US government's hawkish policy on Chinese investment in the US.

So, the primary victims of the tariffs appear to be Chinese EV exporters in terms of profits and jobs. But the tariffs will likely also hit European and American consumers as domestic producers could raise EV prices, or keep them high, in the face of less competition. Producers from smaller countries could also suffer as they could face higher competitive pressure from China if it diverts its exports to Europe and the US to other markets. There may also be a risk of larger countries imposing protectionist measures on Chinese EV imports.

Impact on Energy Transition

Crucially, by making EVs dearer in Europe and the US than they would otherwise be, the tariff protection would delay the transition from conventional air-polluting fossil-fuel powered cars. Since EVs can play an important role in the world's transition to a net-zero economy, arguably, some subsidies for EV production are a second-best policy.

Furthermore, in the absence of a sufficiently high global carbon tax to incentivise energy production and consumption transition, a globally efficient subsidy rate for EV production should be set high enough to encourage the transition. From this perspective, tariffs on EVs are a distortion to this balancing policy act and the global initiative of net-zero transition.

Finally, the new tariffs could create two opposing forces in the global markets. On the positive side, shutting Chinese EVs out of the European and US markets could prompt China to export EVs elsewhere, especially to the Belt and Road Initiative countries, enabling those countries' consumers to access cleaner transportation and thus supporting the net-zero initiative.

On the negative side, although the diversion of China's EV exports to countries with small domestic automobile industries will only have a limited negative impact, the adverse effect on countries with a large automobile industry, such as Japan, India, South Korea, Mexico, Spain and Brazil, could be significant as their EV manufacturers would come under greater competitive pressure. These countries may feel the need to follow the European and American tariff moves, which will not only disrupt global trade but also erode the global energy transition initiative.

Net-Zero, a Secular Trend

Despite the ebb and flow of government policy, net-zero transition is a secular trend. It will get stronger with a clearer direction than it does today when the global powers finally find a way to cooperate on a common energy transition policy via a combination of an EV subsidy scheme, a common tax on carbon emissions and a common mechanism for allocating the emissions.

The private sector can play a critical role in the energy transition process. As pools of capital that can be allocated across a range of assets, investment funds can be used to direct substantial financial resources towards sustainable and green initiatives. Market estimate puts the financing needs for the net-zero transition at over USD6 trillion a year between 2024 and 2030, with transportation and energy systems having the biggest funding needs. However, global climate financing was estimated at only a little over USD1 trillion in 2022 (Allen & Overy, 2023).

The huge funding gap underlies the attraction of energy transition as a long-term investment theme. However, the clash between China and the US in their foreign and trade policies, many of which are due to America and the developed world's misunderstanding about China's economic reality and development, is eroding this global energy transition initiative and risking putting the future world on a dangerous path of natural disasters.

References

Al-Atrush, S. (2023). *Saudi Arabia moves closer to joining Chinese security club*. Financial Times, Dubai. March 30.

Allen & Overy. (2023). *How big is the net Zero financing gap?* Allen & Overy LLP in Climate Policy Institute, September.

Atkins, B. (2023). *Manufacturing Moving Out Of China For Friendlier Shores*. Forbes. August 7. https://www.forbes.com/sites/betsyatkins/2023/08/07/manufacturing-moving-out-of-china-for-friendlier-shores/

Brooks, R. (2024). *Is China financially decoupling?* The Brookings Institution. May 9.

Duan, J. (2024). China aims to clinch more free trade agreements, vowing increased openness. *Belt and Road Portal, Xinhua News Agency*. January 30. https://eng.yidaiyilu.gov.cn/p/07RKQKIL.html

Flaaen, A., & Pierce, J. (2024). *Disentangling the Effects of the 2018–2019 Tariffs on a Globally Connected U.S. Manufacturing Sector. The Review of Economics and Statistics* (pp. 1–45). MIT Press Direct. September 16. https://www.justinrpierce.com/index_files/flaaen_pierce_tariffs_manufacturing.pdf

Gnana, J. (2023). *Saudi Aramco will start construction of 300,000 b/d refinery in China*. S&P Global. 26 March. https://www.spglobal.com/commodity-insights/en/news-research/latest-news/crude-oil/032623-saudi-aramco-signs-agreements-to-build-refinery-in-china

Rajah, R., & Albayrak, A. (2025). China versus America on global trade. *Lowy Institute, Indo-Pacific Development Centre*. 30 January.

Sharma, R. (2023). *China's rise is reversing*. *Financial Times*, Opinion. November 19. https://www.ft.com/content/c10bd71b-e418-48d7-ad89-74c5783c51a2?accessToken=zwAGC24sHiiQkdPBC9cb5BhI19OtiXTFeDxRog.MEYCIQCL1w52Qk4sHrknigqlA5iF3alRnIFVkOGaZ3KRNkvkKQIhAJQGCXFOsikWRkFosZwbD2Sr3GL8vaKNLGUkShK3wFkh&sharetype=gift&token=6221b5cd-0248-45c7-a830-0a2e21ef05a3

T&E. (2024). *How Europe can use tariffs as part of an industrial strategy*. Briefing paper, European Federation for Transport and Environment. March 27. https://www.transportenvironment.org/articles/how-europe-can-use-tariffs-as-part-of-an-industrial-strategy

Wei, S. J. (2024). *Is India's Economy overhyped?* Project Syndicate. April 17. https://www.project-syndicate.org/commentary/india-must-implement-reforms-to-become-economic-superpower-by-shang-jin-wei-2024-04#:~:text=According%20to%20the%20World%20Bank,two%20countries%20is%20much%20smaller.

Xinhua (2024). China to cut import tariffs on certain goods to expand domestic demand. *The State Council, The People's Republic of China*. December 29. https://english.www.gov.cn/news/202412/29/content_WS677084bec6d0868f4e8ee577.html

Yu, E. (2023). Beijing's Mideast Pivot Aims to Fuel Boom in Investment. *The Wall Street Journal*, printed edition. July 8. Also appeared online as A Trillion-Dollar Opportunity: China's Pivot to the Middle East Set to Fuel Investment Boom. July 7. https://www.wsj.com/articles/a-trillion-dollar-opportunity-chinas-pivot-to-the-middle-east-set-to-fuel-investment-boom-1f4bb5a2

CHAPTER 5

Capital Account Liberalisation, Opening a Can of Worms

The opening up China's capital account and its capital outflows are two major issues that have created a lot of confusion and distorted analyses which have, in turn, led to fears about China's policy and global expansion intentions. Indeed, China's capital account development will have significant global impact in the coming decades for at least two reasons.

Firstly, the capital-flow dynamics will move into totally new economic and policy paradigms in which China will operate. Secondly, the unique way that China is liberalising its capital account shows Beijing's conflicting objectives of opening up and retaining controls. This has resulted in a "half-baked" capital account convertibility approach that has no precedence to it. This is what makes most of the Western world puzzled and worried because there is a lot at stake in its impact on the world economy.

The second point follows from the fact that the process of liberalisation will bring tremendous policy challenges to Beijing as the Impossible Trinity[1] (Mundell, 1963, Fleming, 1962) that comes with capital account convertibility will force the Chinese government into a policy choice dilemma between monetary autonomy and exchange rate control. The

[1] The Impossible Trinity, also known as the Trilemma, is policy-choice problem based on the Mundell-Flemming model which states that it is impossible for a country to have control of all three of the following variables at the same time: A fixed exchange rate (i.e. control of the exchange rate), an open capital account (i.e. free capital flows) and an independent monetary policy (i.e. control of the interest rate).

C. Lo, *Clash of the Economic Titans: China and the United States*, https://doi.org/10.1007/978-981-95-2510-2_5

transition from a close to an open capital account is also fraught with risks (Lo, 2013, Chapter 6), which could create unintended consequences not only for the Chinese economy but also for the global system.

Given the potential risks and formidable challenges, why does China still want to engage in capital account liberalisation? While many analysts have argued that making China's capital account fully convertible is, and will remain, Beijing's top policy priority, this view is myopic because it ignores the changing global and domestic dynamics since 2014 that have prompted Beijing to downgrade its policy priority for capital account liberalisation in exchange for domestic growth protection. Beijing's policy focus with regard to capital account convertibility will continue to shift from time to time because it has to protect the country from the potential shocks of opening up the capital account.

Hence, Beijing has proceeded with caution by installing a controlled process through investment quotas, stock market connection schemes and the establishment of free-trade zones. Apart from the free-trade zones, these control schemes can be categorised into three channels, namely the inflow channels, the outflow channels and the two-way-flow channels. The first two categories are straightforward, but they are skewed towards allowing more inflows than outflows. The two-way-flow category is more complicated and, as a result, has generated a lot of hype and crooked analysis that I seek to clarify in this chapter.

The creation of free-trade zones in various parts of China has also generated blind optimism on the speed of China's capital account liberalisation and renminbi internationalisation. In particular, most market players seem to have ignored an incentive incompatibility problem behind the free-trade zones in this round of the opening up compared to the last round in the 1980s. They made irrelevant and erroneous comparisons with the old free-trade zones that China set up to jump-start economic reforms under paramount leader Deng Xiaoping.

Three mega trends are growing out of the capital account liberalisation trend. They are.

1. the start of Chinese capital outflows, which many observers confuse with capital flight from time to time and do not have a clear understanding of the outflow dynamics,
2. the Belt and Road Initiative, which is a crucial part of China's capital outflow dynamics and Beijing's currency globalisation and economic rebalancing strategies, and

3. the internationalisation of the renminbi, which is the path that will take the Chinese yuan to become a global reserve currency eventually.

We shall deal with these mega trends and their global disruption in the following chapters.

Opening a Can of Worms

The crucial question is why China wants to open up its capital account, given the many domestic challenges that its economic transition creates, including slowing economic growth momentum, a weak financial system, unbalanced growth that is still dependent on investment, and an ageing population? Indeed, making the capital account convertible is like opening up a can of worms (Lo, 2015, Chapter 2) because market forces will compel China to make deep-rooted changes to the system that could undermine the stability of the Communist Party.

Perhaps Beijing sees more benefits than harm of an open capital account. Liberalising capital flows is an external force for it to push through domestic financial liberalisation, which will help put the domestic economy on a sustainable path in the long term (Parsad & Rajan, 2008). In particular, capital account liberalisation allows Chinese households to diversify the risks and returns of their savings portfolio internationally, enables Chinese companies to enhance their marginal returns on investment, which have been declining in the domestic economy for many years, and pushes domestic financial reform by creating competition for the domestic banks which are protected by government monopoly and dependent on captive domestic funding sources.

In the end, for the renminbi to become a global reserve currency, free capital flows are a basic requirement as both portfolio and direct investment flows will have to be freed for both the domestic and foreign private sectors.

Meanwhile, liberalisation of capital inflows will also produce crucial collateral benefits by allowing increasing foreign participation in China's financial markets to improve domestic liquidity in both the banking sector and the capital market (Kose et al., 2009). Other segments of China's financial sector, especially insurance, will be forced open to foreign competition which, with effective regulations, will lead to significant efficiency gains.

Furthermore, an open capital account could help boost Shanghai to become an international financial centre, an ambition that Beijing announced as early as in 2009 (Cainey, 2010; ChinaDaily, 2024; Huaxia, 2023), by forcing through domestic structural changes to facilitate the move towards a flexible exchange rate regime and deepening domestic financial reforms. The latter will, in turn, help rebalance the economy away from manufacturing-based investment-led growth to service-based consumption-led growth. Meanwhile, a flexible exchange rate will free up monetary policy to tackle domestic macroeconomic objectives, i.e. allow Beijing to tackle the Impossible Trinity by retaining monetary autonomy for handling domestic demand management needs (Prasad, 2009).

Despite years of liberalisation effort, China's capital account remains very closed, according to the International Monetary Fund's Annual Report on Exchange Arrangements and Exchange Restrictions (AREAER[2]). This underscores my long-held argument that China had only been willing to open its capital account at a very slow pace, despite the views of many financial market players that China was pursuing capital account convertibility swiftly.

Contrary to many market players' simplistic assumption that Beijing would want to liberalise the capital account quickly, the government is not in a hurry to do so and does not have a timeline for doing that. However, the fact that Beijing has increasingly engaged in relaxing its capital account restrictions in recent years to promote the internationalisation of the renminbi (albeit in an asymmetric way where inflows restrictions are relaxed more quickly than outflows) shows that it does have a genuine intention to open up the capital account.

Controlled Liberalisation

Contrary to may "experts" assertion, the liberalisation process will move at a pace that the Chinese leadership deems appropriate; no one can push it. To show its caution on managing the potential volatility that capital account opening will entail, Beijing has created a system of controlled and calibrated liberalisation for both inflows and outflows. Arguably, in

[2] The AREAER is a set of binary measures that reflect the existence of any restrictions on a large number of categories of capital inflows and outflows. See https://www.imf.org/external/pubs/nft/2014/areaers/ar2014.pdf. These measures change only when there is a major policy change to the specific capital account items.

designing these control schemes, Beijing aims at having the cake and eat it in the sense that it wants to reap the collateral benefits of financial openness and retain control of the pace of capital account convertibility at the same time. Broadly speaking, these control schemes fall into three categories: the inflow channels, the outflow channels and the two-way flow channels.

The Inflow Channels

These include the Qualified Foreign Institutional Investor (QFII) scheme, launched in 2002, and the Renminbi Qualified Foreign Institutional Investor (RQFII), launched in 2011. The QFII scheme allows qualified foreign institutional investors to convert foreign currency into renminbi and invest mainly (80% of the quota) in Chinese onshore equities and some renminbi-denominated fixed-income instruments.

The RQFII scheme allows qualified foreign institutional investors to use offshore renminbi funds to invest in Chinese onshore equities and renminbi-denominated fixed-income instruments. There is no restriction on the mix of equities and fixed-income instruments that the foreign institutions can invest in under the RQFII scheme.

However, in September 2019, the State Administration of Foreign Exchange (SAFE) announced the removal of investment quotas for both the QFII and RQFII. The removal aimed at simplifying the investment process for foreign investors in China in order to attract more long-term foreign investment and further integrate China's capital markets with the global financial system.

While quotas are gone, foreign investors still need to obtain a licence from the China Securities Regulatory Commission (CSRC), register with the State Administration of Foreign Exchange (SAFE) the amount of investment they intend to bring into China, and meet certain qualification requirements, including being financially sound and having good credit. Then in 2020, the QFII and RQFII schemes were brought together under a single regulatory framework called the Qualified Investor (QI) scheme.

The Outflow Channels

Other than outward direct investment by Chinese companies, there is only one portfolio outflow channel opened up for local Chinese to invest overseas. It is through the Qualified Domestic Institutional Investor (QDII) scheme, which was launched in 2006. It allows local Chinese domestic financial institutions, including commercial banks, insurance companies, securities companies, trust companies and fund management companies, to invest in an approved list of offshore markets and financial products. Local Chinese retail investors can only invest overseas by buying investment products these QDII institutions created for sale.

As of July 2024, the latest data available, Beijing had granted USD167 billion QFII quotas to 189 qualified foreign institutions. That was up 86% from 2015, or only an average increase of 8.6% a year in 10 years. Compared with the rapid relaxation of capital inflow regulations, which basically put no cap on foreign portfolio inflows now, the restrictive outflow quotas suggest Beijing's preference for attracting more portfolio inflows than allowing outflows in its capital accounting opening process.

The government proposed a second QDII scheme, called QDII2, in 2013 which will permit high net-worth Chinese individual investors with at least RMB1 million (or USD160,000) in assets to invest overseas directly through designated domestic financial institutions; they do not have to buy QDII products as required under the first QDII programme. But at the time of writing, the QDII2 scheme still has not been launched as Beijing has downgraded the policy priority of capital account liberalisation and renminbi internationalisation due to domestic concerns (which we shall discuss later).

The Two-Way Flow Channels

These channels come in two forms: free-trade zone (FTZ) and stock connect scheme. Shanghai launched its FTZ in September 2013, followed by Guangdong, Fujian and Tianjin in 2015. Within the FTZs, in principle, foreign investors are free to invest in economic sectors except those specified on the so-called "negative list".[3] Foreign financial institutions are free to set up shop in the FTZs and engaged in cross-border capital

[3] Such "negative list" approach means that foreign investment in China is generally permitted, unless the respective project or entity falls within a negative list. Foreign investment in areas falling under a negative list is still subject to restrictions or prohibitions. In other words, due to the restrictions imposed by the negative list and other operational and regulatory restrictions, foreign investors are not really free to invest in the designated free-trade zones.

account transactions under a more liberal FTZ-set of regulations than the rest of the country. Shanghai has been the pilot FTZ for China to experiment with more capital account liberalisation.

Within the FTZs, foreign financial institutions are free to process cross-border renminbi settlements under current account transactions and foreign direct investment inflows to the zones without the need to seek approval from the People's Bank of China (PBoC). Foreign companies in the FTZs are allowed to source funds from offshore for the exclusive use inside the respective zones where they reside only, and these funds cannot be used to invest in securities or to extend loans further.

The foreign firms within the zones can also settle foreign exchange transactions among each other involving the renminbi at any time without the need for approval from the authorities. Approved private investors can set up banks, financial leasing companies, consumer finance companies and other financial entities within the FTZs, while approved foreign-invested banks can set up branches, subsidiaries or upgrade existing sub-branches to full branches.

The stock connect schemes are an alternative approach for Beijing to control the process of capital account liberalisation by allowing cross-border equity investment by a broad range of local and foreign investors, including retail investors. In November 2014, Beijing launched the Shanghai-Hong Kong Stock Connect scheme, which allows mainland Chinese investors to trade selected Hong Kong and Chinese stocks listed in Hong Kong and allows foreign investors to trade selected Chinese A-shares[4] listed in Shanghai. And in August 2016, the State Council approved a similar scheme, the Shenzhen-Hong Kong Stock Connect. Since the stock connect schemes do not have investment quotas, its advent has render the QFII, RQFII and QDII quotas irrelevant, though they are still being used at times.

Some other two-way flow channels are the Mutual Fund Recognition scheme (launched in 2015) and the Cross-boundary Wealth Management Connect Scheme in the Guangdong-Hong Kong-Macao Greater

[4] A-shares refer to onshore Chinese shares that trade on the two Chinese stock exchanges, the Shanghai Stock Exchange and the Shenzhen Stock Exchange. These are shares of mainland Chinese companies and were historically only available for purchase by mainland citizens. Since 2003, selected foreign institutions are allowed to purchase them through the Qualified Foreign Institutional Investor (QFII) and Renminbi Qualified Foreign Institutional Investor (RQFII) quotas.

Bay Area (launched in September 2021). These programmes allow mainland Chinese and Hong Kong mutual funds and wealth management products to be distributed through banks in each other's markets through a streamlined vetting process.

New controlled schemes will continue to be introduced as a way for China to open up its capital account and retain control on the process at the same time. The inflow and outflow channels are quite straightforward, but the two-way flow channels are complicated and have generated a lot of confusion and hype in the financial markets, with many observers churning out partial analysis contaminating rational thinking. Let's consider the FTZs first.

When the idea of establishing the FTZs in China was first announced in 2013, it generated a lot of excitement and hype about acceleration of China's structural reforms, capital account convertibility and renminbi internationalisation. In principle, the creation of the FTZs is a step towards deeper changes. However, more than a decade after their implementation, there has been no acceleration in China's capital account liberalisation, as the optimists expected. Instead, Beijing has downgraded its policy priority for, though not halted, capital account and renminbi convertibility since 2016. What is wrong with the optimists' expectations? Crucially, no one has questioned whether the incentives for the various FTZ stakeholders are compatible.

FTZs and Incentive Compatibility

Incentive compatibility is the single most important factor determining whether the FTZs will be able to deepen China's structural reforms. The FTZs will not be a game changer until the incentive problem is resolved. Arguably, the FTZs are "financial cousins" of the Special Economic Zones (SEZs) which China set up in the early 1980s to kick-start economic reforms by providing preferential tax treatments, supportive bureaucracy and market mechanism for foreign (and later domestic) firms to manufacture and export from the SEZs. They were successful in transforming China into the world's factory. Now the FTZs' focus is on commerce and finance, which is a natural next step up the value chain of economic reforms.

From a policy perspective, Beijing used the SEZs as a tool to build political and public support for economic reforms in the 1980s and 1990s by unleashing "animal spirits" in these patches of market mechanism, i.e.

by allowing people to get rich through private incentives. After more than four decades of fast growth, the Chinese economy is facing growth fatigue. So, Beijing is trying to replicate the success of the SEZ model by creating the FTZs to revive economic vigour. However, things are not as simple as they were 40 years ago when incentive compatibility was not a problem.

The incentives to reform the economy were aligned among the SEZs' stakeholders, including the central government, local governments and economic agents. Since the onset of economic reform, China has pursued a supply-expansion development model by building, investing and producing first and assuming that demand will follow. This model worked. Together with globalisation, the SEZs incentivised all the stakeholders to focus on production and, hence, on getting rich by expanding China's aggregate demand through exports.

The economic interests were further cemented by an implicit social contract struck between Beijing and the people after the Tiananmen Square incident in 1989. Until the early 2000s, most Chinese had faith in their national leaders and accepted the post-1989 social contract in which the Party provided rising living standards in return for the people not questioning its monopoly of power.

However, the social contract started to break down after the turn of the millennium, as mounting corruption and political changes have impaired the system and created an increasing amount of social grievances. Firstly, income and wealth inequality have become more serious as the country has grown richer (Fig. 5.1). This has raised the awareness among the bottom strata of society that it is higher level policy, not just corruption and the incompetence of local officials, which bars them from sharing the benefits of economic growth and liberalisation.

Secondly, the wealthy and the intellectuals are taking more interests in politics and the reform process to protect or fight for their interests, or even to take part in the rent-seeking activity that has emerged as a by-product of economic reforms.

It is thus clear that there is an incentive incompatibility problem in the system that is going to haunt the FTZs. Many of the vested interest groups that supported economic reforms to get rich are now turning against deeper reforms, as they realise that more reforms will destroy their rent-seeking opportunities. Furthermore, the intellectuals realise that upward mobility is capped and any advancement one manages to gain through hard work can be taken away by the elite group because the

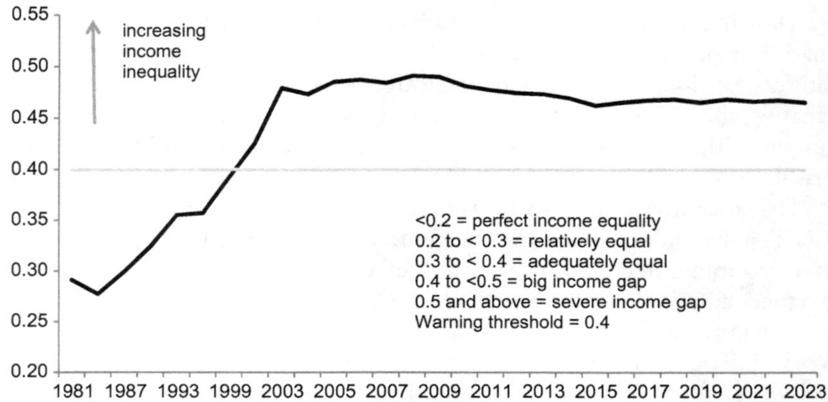

Fig. 5.1 China's Gini coefficient suggests high income inequality (*Sources* World Bank, CEIC, author)

elites can do and get what they want at will. Many intellectuals are, thus, turning away from reforms for the suspicion that more reforms would only benefit the elites more and deepen social inequality further.

Since the FTZs are focusing on finance and commerce, which are more fluid activities than manufacturing, as one can move capital around much more easily than fixed assets, incentive incompatibility is a serious problem in the FTZs. Accelerating the capital account and renminbi convertibility are almost impossible in the presence of this problem as free capital flows will only lead to systemic instability. Why is that?

Unlike the SEZs, where all stakeholders share a common economic incentive driven by animal spirits, the FTZs stakeholders have different incentives. The central leadership wants to deepen reforms, which inevitably involves more advanced capital account and currency convertibility. But the local authorities and many vested interest groups resist deeper changes so as to protect and maximise their short-term gains. Meanwhile, the public, especially the intellectuals, wants accountability from the government and more equal distribution of wealth.

Risk of Capital Flight

These conflicting interests have created a risk of massive capital outflow as people seek better opportunities elsewhere or ways to escape from financial repression and related problems. The risk and pressure of capital flight were evident in 2015 when massive capital outflow caused a capital account deficit in China for the first time in more than 30 years, put significant depreciation pressure on the renminbi, prompted heavy intervention by the PBoC and led to a massive loss of USD700 billion in foreign exchange reserves.

Contrary to the expectations of the optimists, potential capital flight is the single most important obstacle to Beijing making fund flows between the FTZs and other parts of the country fungible even though it allows free capital account and renminbi flows within the FTZs. This is because by allowing free access to the FTZs by other regions, China would effectively open up holes in its capital account and risk opening the floodgates for capital flight.

China's chronic over-invoicing problem may be indicative of a strong incentive for capital flight if the floodgates were opened. When over-invoicing, a Chinese firm inflates its import bill by charging the import price of some commodity much higher than the actual cost. By reporting an inflated import bill to the Chinese customs, this allows the passing of capital overseas, with the foreign (exporting) entity crediting the excess amount into its Chinese counterpart's bank account outside of China.

One, though imperfect, estimate for over-invoicing is the difference between China's import values and the export values of its corresponding trading partners. In principle, after allowing for the small foreign exchange rate differences used in the different official reporting systems, they should be the same. However, the data shows that China's inflated imports bills had been getting larger for many years (Fig. 5.2), suggesting a rising incentive of illegal capital outflow, until 2014 when the government tightened up controls. Nevertheless, there has been no sign yet for the over-invoicing problem to improve.

This phenomenon seems to run contrary to the perception of rising hot money flowing into China that many observers alluded to. Note that the two sets of data do not necessarily contradict each other as they correspond to two different incentives (or two disjoint sets, technically): one is local capital wanting to get out of China (the over-invoicing problem), and the other is foreign capital wanting to come into China (the hot

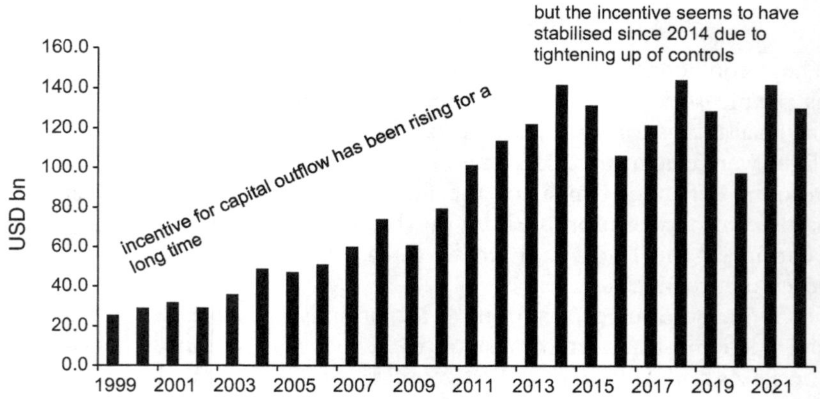

Fig. 5.2 Estimated over-invoicing of Chinese imports* (*Note* *value of Chinese import from Japan, the US and the EU minus value of exports from them to China. *Sources* CEIC, author's calculation)

money inflow issue). The players in these two sets are different and have different views on China's investment environment. Furthermore, the over-invoicing problem has a persistent rising trend, but the hot money inflow is volatile from year to year and does not have a trend.

So, China's closed capital account is barring capital flight from taking place. This is also why Beijing will continue to restrict any freely convertible financial activities between the FTZs and the rest of the country in the medium term to avoid creating leakages for capital flows. Establishing rules for what financial institutions can do in the FTZs is meant to address this loophole problem, which is induced by incentive incompatibility among the FTZs' stakeholders. To play safe, China will likely keep its asymmetric stringent capital control, which is to allow capital to come into the country much more easily than allowing it to go out.

Realistically, the FTZs are not likely to be a game changer for deepening China's structural reforms until the incentive problem is resolved. They will remain experiment zones for onshore renminbi convertibility and capital account liberalisation until Beijing thinks it's time to roll them out nationally. This practice is meant to minimise the possibility of massive capital flight that could destabilise China's financial system while at the same time to maximise the collateral benefits of opening the capital account at a controlled pace within Beijing's tolerance limits.

The Stock Connect Schemes

The biggest dissatisfaction with the discussion on China's structural reform mega trends is the lack of serious economic research and empirical support, which has manifested in some observers providing "expert" views that contaminate the understanding and proper analysis of China. Underscoring this point is the large number of analyst reports on the launching of the stock connect schemes providing superficial and distorted views on its effects on China long-term structural changes and impact on the international investment community.

Like the Shanghai-Hong Kong Stock Connect scheme, the Shenzhen-Hong Kong Stock Connect is a cross-boundary investment channel that connects the Shenzhen Stock Exchange and the Hong Kong Stock Exchange. Under these stock connect schemes, investors in each market are able to trade shares in the other market using their local brokers and clearing houses.

The two stock connect schemes are controllable and expandable channels for mutual market access between the Mainland and Hong Kong by a broad range of investors. Eligible investors in Mainland China can buy eligible shares listed on the Hong Kong Stock Exchange via their own local brokers, while Hong Kong and international investors can buy eligible Shanghai- and Shenzhen-listed shares through their brokers in Hong Kong as well.

Northbound (Hong Kong buying Chinese stocks) and southbound (Mainland Chinese buying Hong Kong stocks) trading will be subject to separate sets of daily quotas, which are calculated on a netting basis throughout each trading day. There was an annual aggregate quota for the Shanghai-Hong Kong Stock Connect, but it was scrapped when the Shenzhen-Hong Kong Connect was launched without any annual quota restrictions. The daily quota limits the maximum net buy value of cross-boundary trades under each scheme. The northbound daily quota has been set at RMB13 billion while the southbound daily quota at RMB10.5 billion for each of the two schemes.

The key characteristics of the stock connects are the ban on arbitrage activity, their closed-loop design and the exclusive use of offshore renminbi liquidity for funding the trading under the schemes. These mean that:

- Chinese investors who buy Hong Kong shares must sell the shares back in the Hong Kong market. Similarly, Hong Kong and international investors who buy Chinese shares in Shanghai and Shenzhen must sell the shares back in the respective Chinese stock exchanges.
- No price arbitrage is allowed for the inter-listed stocks between Hong Kong and China's stock exchanges. The sales proceeds must go back to their home market bank accounts; they must not be used for other purposes, such as buying other assets or goods and services, in the destination market.
- All trades under the schemes are transacted in renminbi, with all the foreign exchanges between Hong Kong dollar and renminbi to be done in Hong Kong only; i.e. the transactions of the stock connect schemes only uses offshore renminbi in Hong Kong.

This Shenzhen-Hong Kong Stock Connect scheme could potentially be a game changer for foreign portfolio investment in China by allowing international investors access to the universe of "new China" stocks in technology, media, healthcare, communications and consumer services companies listed on the Shenzhen Stock Exchange. In other words, the stock connect schemes offer hundreds of choices to foreign investors to monetise the new growth engines of China. This also helps allocating capital to the new China economy, which is mostly private-sector driven.

The abolition of the annual net quota of the Shanghai-Hong Kong Stock Connect to coincide with the decision of not setting an annual quota for the Shenzhen-Hong Kong Stock Connect was also a step towards liberalising the capital account and, in principle, deepening the internationalisation of the renminbi. This is because in a balanced market where selling and buying forces are equal, trading under the stock connect schemes will go on uninterrupted because the net buy quotas will not be hit. All this should help improve Chinese stock liquidity, attract more foreign participation in China's stock market, improve two-way flow for portfolio investments and increase the demand for RMB. All these are instrumental in improving the chance for MSCI to include all Chinese shares in its global index in the future.

Debunking the Myths

However, in the proliferation of analyst reports on the Shenzhen-Hong Kong Stock Connect when it was launched, there was a wave of positive comments and praises for the scheme in fostering China's capital account liberalisation, on- and off-shore market convergence, renminbi internationalisation , improvement in capital allocation and MSCI inclusion of the Chinese shares in its global emerging market index. While the broad direction of these views was correct, there were also a lot of blind optimism and erroneous views that distorted proper understanding and assessment of the schemes and, hence, the structural forces behind China's mega trend of capital account and financial market liberalisation.

Notably, some head of research of a major international bank in Hong Kong argued that "the abolishment of overall quotas can be seen as an indication that China's capital liberalisation is maturing..." (Mackel, 2016). This was a causal and irresponsible statement unsubstantiated and refuted by research evidence. But still, it created a hype about China's financial reforms in the banking community and brought many blind followers!

The Chinn-Ito index, a measure of capital account openness of more than 180 countries in the world with a scale of 0 (completely closed capital account) to 1 (completely open capital account), shows clearly that China's capital account (with an index of only 0.163) was quite closed in 2021, the latest update available at the time of writing (Fig. 5.3). This is consistent with the conclusion of the IMF AREAER's assessment (see above). It argues clearly that China's opening-up process was still at an early stage. According to this evidence, China's capital account is even more closed than Nigeria, and is clearly a long way away from catching up with other open markets, such as Hong Kong, Japan, Singapore, the UK and the US.

The introduction of the Shanghai-Hong Kong Stock Connect scheme in late 2014 would not by any remote chance have boosted China's capital account convertibility in any significant way because the scheme is only a baby step towards liberalising China's capital account due to its closed-loop design. As explained above, the closed-loop mechanism does not really allow free capital flows in and out of the country. Essentially, it only extends the boundary of capital controls on mainland Chinese capital to Hong Kong. It does not even allow price arbitrage between the onshore and Hong Kong markets for inter-listed stocks.

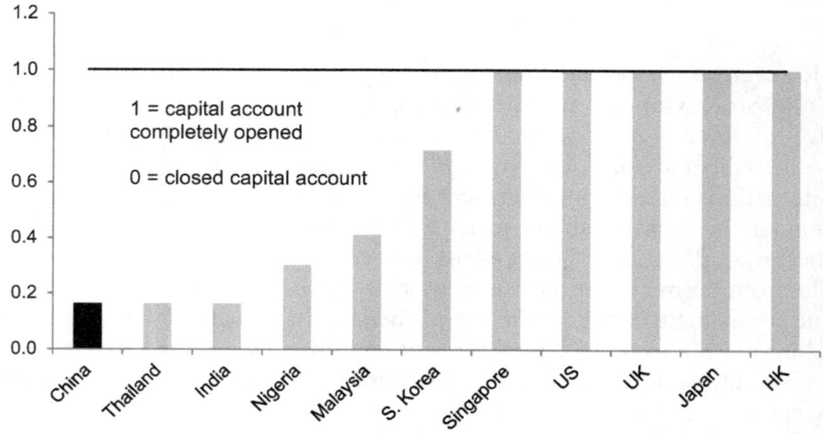

Fig. 5.3 Chinn–Ito index of capital account openness (2021) (*Sources* Chinn–Ito index (KAOPEN), author)

For example, if the stock price of Ping An Insurance, China's second largest insurance company that is inter-listed in both Hong Kong and Shanghai, is trading higher in Shanghai, an investor cannot buy the shares in Hong Kong and sell them in Shanghai through the Stock Connect scheme to arbitrage the price differences. This restriction prevents hedging and price convergence by limiting liquidity and asset flows between Hong Kong and Shanghai/Shenzhen. Obviously, this refutes those naive views that the stock connect schemes would lead to price convergence swiftly and would be a significant step towards opening China's capital account.

Furthermore, the regulatory requirement that all foreign exchange trades for settling the Stock Connect trades must be done in Hong Kong using only its offshore renminbi funds shows clearly that Beijing still wants to keep the onshore market segregated from the offshore (Hong Kong) market by using offshore renminbi liquidity only to support the Stock Connect schemes. The purpose is to shield the onshore stock market and monetary regime from offshore volatility. This argues against the view that China would move fast to open its capital account and allow price convergence between the on- and off-shore markets in the short term.

Others also argue that the daily net quotas are a risk control measure against speculative flows. This is only partly right. It cannot deny the fact that these quotas, together with the closed-loop cross-border flow design of the schemes, are de facto capital controls. Risk can be controlled through other means such as a circuit breaker mechanism, which China tried but failed miserably in 2015 (Stafford & Wildau, 2016), instead of quotas.

If the Shenzhen-Hong Kong scheme assumes the same trading/demand pattern as the Shanghai-Hong Kong scheme, where there are significantly more southbound trades than northbound trades, the two stock connect schemes will shrink the offshore (Hong Kong) renminbi pool over time. *Ceteris paribus*, this will hinder renminbi internationalisation but not encourage it as many observers have wrongly assumed.

Granted, there are certainly benefits to be had from the stock connect schemes, and they are a step forward towards capital account liberalisation and deepening renminbi internationalisation by increasing foreign incentive to hold and use renminbi. However, expectations on the pace of changes and the delivery of results should be realistic. From the financial market's perspective, demand for "new China" stocks has to be justified by fundamentals. The stock connect schemes do not change the fundamentals, but China's macroeconomic management and reform policies do.

This brings up the credibility issue, which is the ultimate factor (in my view) at this stage of China's market development in affecting international demand for Chinese shares, especially the retail-dominated new China stocks. China needs to build credible markets that earn investors' trust. Kicking the habit of making discretionary changes to trading rules that distort investors' entrance to and exit from the Chinese markets and improving market transparency are the ways to go.

Liberalisation with Chinese Characteristics

In sum, China is opening its capital account, but it is also retaining significant control over the extent and pace of the opening-up process. It is only dismantling the capital controls slowly, but even that is sufficient enough to bring about pressures from the Impossible Trinity to force the Chinese authorities to choose between controlling the exchange rate or the interest rate (Lo, 2015, Chapters 1 and 10).

Indeed, since 2010, the PBoC has started exiting its monetary policy monopoly, notably by loosening up the trading of the renminbi, widening its trading band with the US dollar and changing the calculation of the "fixing" mechanism to make it more market-driven.[5] The increase in the volatility of the renminbi exchange rate over the years, as seen in the renminbi's exchange rate volatility approximated by the standard deviation of the exchange rate from its average value (Fig. 5.4), shows that the PBoC has been freeing up the exchange rate, albeit slowly, in exchange for retaining its monetary autonomy (i.e. controlling the interest rate). Making renminbi trading more flexible by further widening of its trading band with the US dollar[6] can be expected as Beijing continues to reform the foreign exchange rate system.

While China is moving to open the capital account slowly, with a stated goal of freeing the renminbi exchange rate from administrative control, it

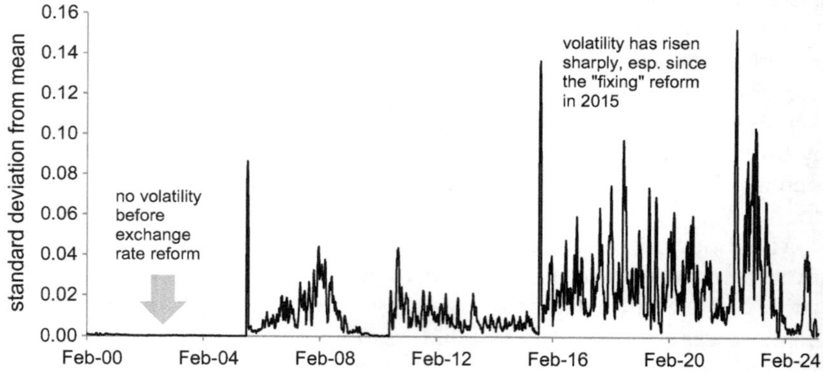

Fig. 5.4 Renminbi-USD exchange rate trading volatility* risen (*Note* *approximated by the standard deviation of RMB-USD daily trading. *Sources* CEIC, author's calculation)

[5] The People's Bank of China (PBoC) manages the renminbi, or yuan, by fixing a daily exchange rate (hence the term "fixing") against the US dollar and posts it as the official trading rate at the beginning of each trading day in the onshore market. The market then trades renminbi against US dollar within a 2% band above and below the fixing throughout the day. The PBoC sets the fixing every trading day, hence the name daily fixing. This mechanism does not apply to the offshore renminbi, or CNH, market in Hong Kong or other offshore centres.

On 11 August 2015, the PBoC changed the calculation of the fixing from basing it on the moving average of the closing rates of the previous 10 trading days to the closing rate of the previous day.

[6] At the time of writing, the trading band is set at 2% above and below the daily fixing.

is unclear what its final objective is. A fully convertible capital account and renminbi may not be the endgame that Beijing wants because that would mean giving up control completely. Free market practice is not consistent with the Communist Party's ideology. Rather, Beijing may want a capital account that is largely open but not open enough to let market forces dominate the system. It still wants to exert some degree of control on capital flows.

Indeed, some academics have argued that the long-term approach for China to resolve the Impossible Trinity might be capital account convertibility combined with some sort of soft controls in the form of quotas and registration systems for capital flows (Yam, 2011). It is not a completely free capital-flow regime, but capital flows and exchange rate movement will be much freer than they are today.

Arguably, this means that Beijing may still want to defy the Impossible Trinity by having the cake and eat it (i.e. partial capital account convertibility with some controls on both the exchange rate and interest rate). Call this capital account liberalisation with Chinese characteristics. Time will tell what form the endgame will take and whether China will be successful in its effort.

The risk to the world economy is that such a "half-baked" approach to capital account convertibility has not been tested before. So, its potential impact on the global system is unknown. What is certain is that as Chinese capital persistently flows out on a massive scale for the first time in China's modern economic history, it will shake up the prevailing rules of the game of the global investment and regulatory framework, as we shall discuss in the following chapter.

References

Cainey, A. (2010). Shanghai Building an International Financial Center with Chinese Characteristics. *Booz & Company*. https://www.academia.edu/34838518/Shanghai_Building_an_International_Financial_Center_with_Chinese_Characteristics

ChinaDaily (2024). China ups efforts to build Shanghai into strong international financial center. *Xinhua*. June 9. https://www.chinadaily.com.cn/a/202406/19/WS66728b92a31095c51c509c22.html

Fleming, J. M. (1962). Domestic Financial Policies Under Fixed and Floating Exchange Rates. *IMF Staff Papers, 9*, 369–379.

Huaxia (2023). Xi stresses expediting building Shanghai into modern socialist int'l metropolis. *Xinhua*. December 3. https://english.news.cn/20231203/8486fcc77bed43aea9741e3479f06ce4/c.html

Kose, A., Prasad, E., Rogoff, K., & Wei, S. J. (2009). Financial Globalisation: A Reappraisal. *IMF Staff Papers, 56*(1), 8–62.

Lo, C. (2013). *The Renminbi Rises: Myths, Hypes and Realties of RMB Internationalisation and Reforms in the Post-Crisis World*. Palgrave Macmillan.

Lo, C. (2015). *China's Impossible Trinty, the Structural Challenges to the "Chinese Dream."* Palgrave Macmillan.

Mackel, P. (2016). *Asian FX: RMB – Connecting to Shenzhen*. HSBC Global Research, 17 August.

Mundell, R. A. (1963). Capital Mobility and Stabilization Policy Under Fixed and Flexible Exchange Rates. *Canadian Journal of Economics and Political Science, 29*, 475–485.

Prasad, E. (2009). Is China's Growth Miracle Built to Last? *China Economic Review, 20*(1), 103–123.

Prasad, E., & Rajan, R. (2008). A Practical Approach to Capital Account Liberalisation. *Journal of Economic Perspectives, 22*(3), 149–172.

Stafford, P., & Wildau, G. (2016). *China u-turn stokes circuit breaker debate*. Financial Times. January 11. http://www.ft.com/cms/s/0/4d692706-b845-11e5-bf7e-8a339b6f2164.html#axzz4K0ER7f8W

Yam, J. (2011). *A Safe Approach to Convertibility for the RMB*. Chinese University of Hong Kong Institute for Global Economics and Finance, Hong Kong, Working Paper 5.

CHAPTER 6

Chinese Capital Flows, Friend or Foe

In this chapter, we discuss capital outflows in the context of overseas investments including direct investment, lending, portfolio investment and arbitrage activities by Chinese companies and investors. We shall also address the issue of illegal capital outflows that are not driven by the same forces behind the investment and lending decisions. Crucially, a new trend has emerged since 2022 with China turning into a foreign direct investment net exporter for the first in its economic history.

The great emigration of China capital was not on the world's radar screen until around 2013 when non-foreign-direct-investment (non-FDI) outflows started to increase and caught the attention of the financial markets. A flurry of big cross-border mergers and acquisitions (M&A) by Chinese companies since 2013 further attracted international attention to China's overseas direct investment (ODI), raising the developed world's suspicion and fears about the motivation of outflows and their impact on the global economic order.

Chinese capital outflows set three milestones in 2016. First, annual ODI crossed USD100 billion for the first time. Second, with increasing outflows and stagnant inflows, 2016 marked the beginning of a declining net foreign direct investment (FDI) trend, which turned outright negative in 2022. Finally, 2016 was the first time that saw China's private sector accounting for more than half of ODI. These shifts argue that there is a

C. Lo, *Clash of the Economic Titans: China and the United States*,
https://doi.org/10.1007/978-981-95-2510-2_6

need for a change in the way that the world looks at China's international capital/investment flows.

From the Western perspective, the main question has been whether China's state-owned enterprises (SOEs) armed with cheap financing from the Chinese policy banks would upset the rules of the international economic order, either by scooping up strategic assets around the world or by leading a charge for increased Chinese geopolitical influence through channels such as the Belt and Road Initiative (BRI) strategy.

There has been limited understanding about the changing faces of China's private- and public-sector ODI. Nevertheless, the Chinese investment behaviour is quite different from international practices and could disrupt global markets and prompt policy responses to counteract China's ODI expansion. A more recent phenomenon is that China's ODI has shifted from developed markets (DM) to emerging markets (EM) due to a rise in geopolitical risk.

Emigration of Chinese capital is a mega trend with far-reaching implications on development finance, government policies and the global asset markets and investment landscape. However, there is misunderstanding about the driving forces behind China's capital outflows and misguided views on their implications on both global and China's development. In particular, many observers tend to lump China's capital outflows together with capital flight and believe that the Chinese system would crash and send seismic shocks across the global system. In this case, China's capital outflow would be a time bomb destabilising the world economy at some point in the future.

There is also a perception, thanks to prominent media headlines, that when Chinese private capital flows out to buy foreign assets, it is mostly illegal capital outflow with the investors trying to flee a corrupted and collapsing system. However, evidence suggests that this is not entirely true, and that China's private entrepreneurs are mostly rational investors seeking profit maximisation in overseas markets. Chinese private firms have strong incentive to go abroad to enhance their returns on investment which has been suffering from persistent diminishing margin returns in the domestic market.

The emergence of China as the world's largest investor while it is still a developing economy is raising important questions about its global policy implications and the challenges that it will bring to the global market norms and practices. In some ways, Chinese capital-raising activity to finance their overseas investments could be a catalyst for improving development finance for the developing world and prompting the existing multilateral development banks to strive for efficiency gains. But in other ways, they could be a disrupting force to the global norms and governance standards. This double-edged sword of China's capital outflows is creating challenges for China as an emerging international investor and financier and for the global system to accommodate this "new kid on the block".

The First Signs of Capital Outflows

For decades, the world only saw one-sided strong capital inflows to China due to China's closed capital account and a rising surplus in its basic balance. The basic balance is approximated by the sum of the current account balance and net FDI into china. These strong inflows put persistent appreciation pressure on the renminbi exchange rate. But things started to change after 2007, when China's basic surplus started to decline which at the same time also eroded the support for the renminbi. Between 2013 and 2016, the renminbi exchange rate came under persistent depreciation pressure owing to significant capital outflows from the financial and capital accounts on the back of a declining basic surplus (Fig. 6.1).

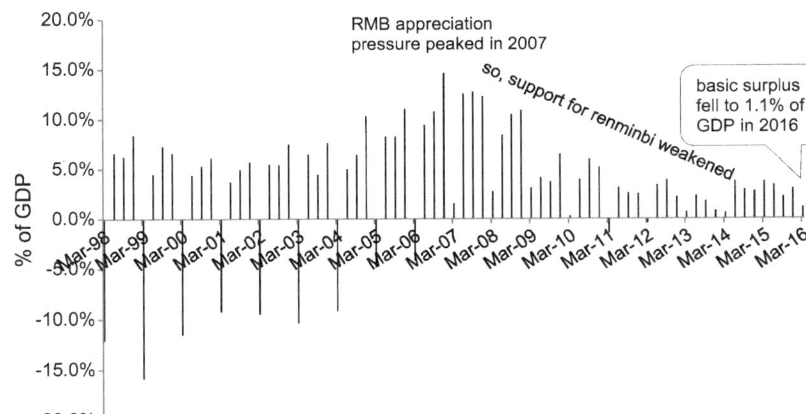

Fig. 6.1 China's basic balance* (quarterly basis) (*Note* *Current account balance + net FDI. *Sources* CEIC, author)

This change in the fortune of the renminbi was the first sign of capital outflows from China. It also suggested that the structural underpinning for the renminbi from China's external accounts had deteriorated. The drop in China's basic surplus in 2007 owed mainly to net FDI outflows and a widening service account deficit that reduced the current account surplus in the basic balance.

This structural change in China's external accounts should not be surprising as China rebalances towards consumption-led growth, but with an underdeveloped domestic service sector, demand for service imports (notably outbound tourism, education, and financial, commercial and legal services) rises sharply. So, its service trade deficit is expected to continue to grow and erode the current account surplus over time (Fig. 6.2), *ceteris paribus*.

Net FDI outflows will likely continue also, as the increase in Chinese ODI will overwhelm FDI inflows in the medium to long term. Notably, China's net international investment position remains small as compared to other major saving surplus economies, such as Japan, Germany and Singapore (Fig. 6.3). This suggests that China still has large room for overseas investment expansion. Indeed, China's ODI is on a structural rising trend due to Beijing's encouragement for Chinese capital to go

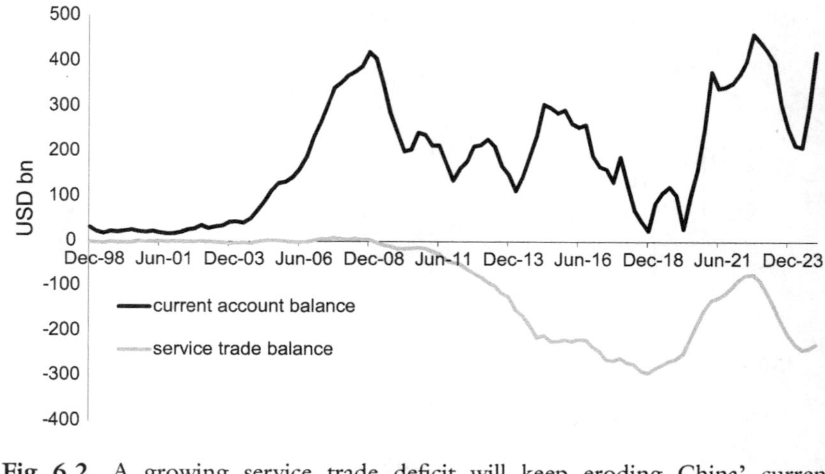

Fig. 6.2 A growing service trade deficit will keep eroding China' current account balance (*Sources* CEIC, author)

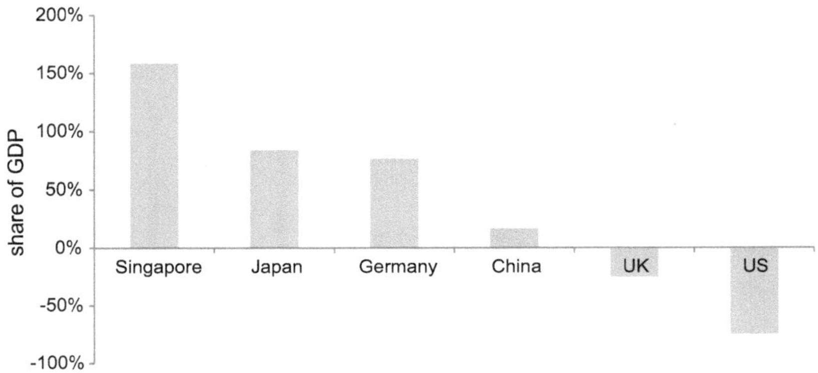

Fig. 6.3 China's net international investment remains small relative to other saving surplus countries* (*Note* *Data as of the third quarter of 2024. *Sources* Official data by governments, author)

global (e.g. the Belt and Road Initiative) and diminishing returns on domestic investment owing to excess capacity. Annual ODI flows have increased from an average of 0.5% of GDP a year in the early 2000s to an average of 5.0% between 2019 and 2023, while cumulative ODI has risen from 2.7% of GDP to 64.0% (Fig. 6.4).

From a currency perspective, does this structural rise in capital outflow argue for a long-term decline in the renminbi? Not necessarily. A broader portfolio of international assets will strengthen China's balance of payments (BoP) position by generating a large overseas income stream, just as Japan's surge in ODI in the 1980s and 1990s created income flows that enabled it to keep running a current account surplus. That, in turn, supported the Japanese yen exchange rate, despite a dwindling trade surplus. For the world, the structural increase in China's ODI will be positive for asset prices as it increases the demand for overseas assets.

Capital Flight Versus Capital Outflows

Many analysts, including some of those who call themselves "China experts", have sounded a loud alarm that China's capital outflows reflected the economic ills in the country prompting capital to flee. Some have even predicted banking or debt-currency crises would trigger capital

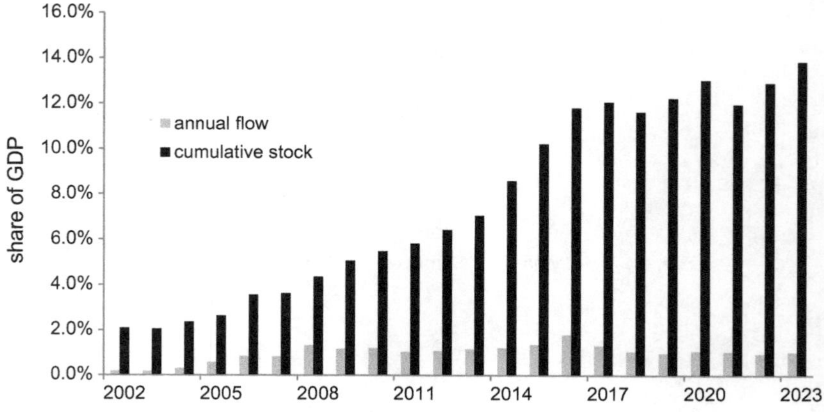

Fig. 6.4 China's overseas direct investment (ODI) will continue to rise (*Sources* CEIC, author)

flight and force Beijing to massively devalue the renminbi. These views not only show a lack of understanding about China's development but are also fundamentally flawed.

The issue that has caused apprehension and confusion about China's capital outflows is non-FDI outflows, which are volatile but have nevertheless exhibited a rising trend. They include portfolio investment (or hot money) flows, trade credit flows, foreign lending and borrowing by Chinese companies, interest rate arbitrage flows and illegal capital outflows. China does face a risk of capital flight, due to a combination of socio-political and economic factors, but it is not an imminent risk that could crush the Chinese system any time soon. Furthermore, non-FDI flows are not representative of the driving forces behind China's capital outflows. The problem is that estimating non-FDI outflows is tricky because no one has a clear picture of these flows and there are no standard ways to estimate these flows.

Some observers and analysts cited the sharp drop in China's foreign exchange reserves between late 2015 and early 2016 despite a large trade surplus and net FDI inflows as evidence for rampant capital flight from the capital and financial accounts of China. A detailed examination of the data argues that this was not entirely correct because the valuation effect on China's foreign reserves (due to exchange rate changes) and other factors had distorted the picture.

China reports its foreign reserve holdings at face value in US dollar terms. So, even if it makes no changes to its portfolio holdings, but if the foreign exchange value of the non-US dollar portion of the reserve assets (which was estimated at about 40% of the total [Troutman, 2013]) falls, the headline foreign reserve value shows a decline. This was indeed what happened between 2015 and early 2016, when the world's major currencies dropped by more than 20% against the US dollar.

Research (Troutman, 2013) shows that China's foreign reserves consist of foreign assets denominated in seven major currencies, including the euro, yen and pound sterling, with the euro accounting for two-thirds of the non-US dollar portion. It is obvious that the sharp fall in these major currencies against the dollar had the effect of reducing significantly the dollar value of China's foreign reserves, *ceteris paribus*.

My estimation shows that this valuation effect reduced the value of China's foreign reserves by a total of USD399 billion in the second half of 2015 (or 57% of the USD700 billion loss in reserves estimated by the financial market for the whole year), giving a false signal of rampant capital outflows. While the estimates of the loss in reserves may be subject to debate, because no outsiders know the true composition of China's foreign reserve portfolio, the rationale of the valuation effect behind the drop in its foreign reserve value is robust.

Other factors during that period also distorted China's headline foreign reserves value. They included the transfer of at least USD168 billion of funds by Beijing from its foreign reserves as a capital injection into the policy banks between the second quarter of 2014 and the second quarter of 2015, a notable decline in the fixed-income asset value in the foreign reserve portfolio due to market conditions and the repayment of foreign debt by Chinese companies.[1]

[1] During 2013 and the first half of 2014, when expectation of renminbi appreciation ran high and the onshore-offshore interest rate gap was large (with offshore rates much lower than onshore rates), many domestic Chinese entities borrowed in foreign currency (mainly USD) and swapped the proceeds into renminbi (thus increasing capital inflows). The total amount of these foreign corporate debts was estimated at USD1 trillion in 2015. But since renminbi expectation turned negative in mid-2014, these entities unwound their foreign liabilities by selling renminbi for US dollar to repay their foreign debts, thus increasing capital outflows.

According to the Bank for International Settlements (BIS), this repayment of foreign debt amounted to USD235 billion in the third quarter of 2015. My estimation put the total repayment at USD330 billion in the second half of the year. The point is that this debt-repayment was legitimate capital outflow but not capital flight. Crucially, the repayment of foreign debt reduced China's debt vulnerability. It also left the country's net international financial position completely unchanged. This was because the fall in the foreign currency assets of the central bank (which supplies foreign exchange to the Chinese companies in exchange for domestic currency) was matched dollar-for-dollar by the fall in foreign currency liabilities of the Chinese corporations. Most analysts and the media focused exclusively on the fall in the official foreign exchange reserves but ignored the identical decline in the corporate sector's foreign liability.

Meanwhile, there is no accurate data for China's non-FDI outflows, as part of them are distorted by rent-seeking activity and capital flight. One way to estimate China's non-FDI flows is to subtract the current account balance and net FDI inflows from the change in foreign reserves. These non-FDI flows fluctuated widely between the early and mid-2000s but nevertheless showed a worsening trend of outflow between 2009 and 2016. This was echoed by the errors and omissions account in China's balance of payments data (Fig. 6.5), which was used by some analysts as a proxy for illegal capital outflows.

Another big part of the outflows, about 30% of net financial outflows in late 2015, came from large foreign currency loans to foreign entities. These loans were extended by the China Development Bank, the country's main policy bank assigned with a significant foreign lending mandate, and other state-owned banks. Despite being part of capital outflows, these transactions should also have no impact on China's net international financial position because the fall in the central bank's foreign exchange asset should be matched by the increase in foreign currency assets of the domestic banks by a similar amount.

All these are not to deny the fact of China's capital outflows, which some observers have confused with capital flight. The point is that after allowing for the valuation effect and the special factors that could have reduced the value of China's foreign exchange portfolio, actual capital outflows were much smaller than the headline estimates suggested. From an economic development perspective, non-FDI outflows will continue to rise as Chinese investors/savers and banks diversify their investment

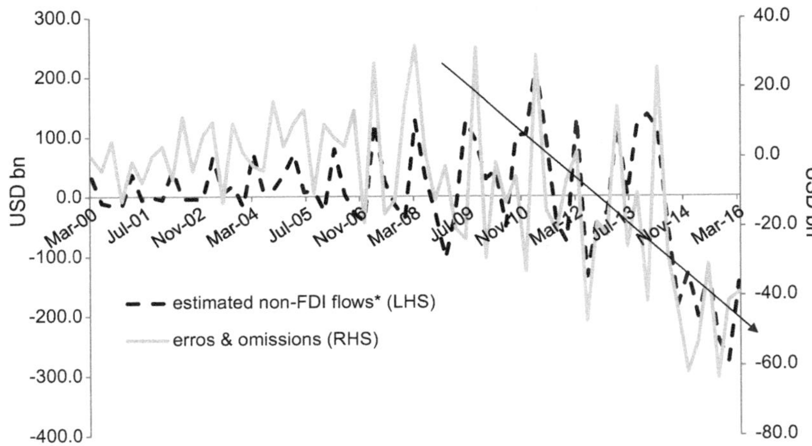

Fig. 6.5 China's errors & omissions and estimated non-FDI flows both showed rising capital outflows (*Note* *Change in FX reserves—C/A bal—net FDI flows, unadjusted for FX valuation effect as errors & omissions are data unadjusted for FX valuation effect. *Sources* CEIC, author)

and lending portfolio overseas in the coming decades on the back of slow capital account opening by Beijing.

Drivers of Overseas Expansion?

What about overseas direct investment, or ODI, by Chinese companies? A wave of big cross-border M&A by Chinese companies during the mid-2000s raised many eyebrows. Led by state-owned ChemChina's USD43 billion bid for Swiss Syngenta, a global leader in agricultural science and innovation formed by merging the agrochemical businesses of AstraZeneca and Novartis, and private insurance giant Anbang's USD13 billion offer in 2016 for Starwood Hotels, China's announced foreign acquisitions[2] totalled more than USD100 billion in 2016 for the first time on China's records.

[2] Not all the announced M&A succeeded. A notable example was Anbang's bid for Starwood Hotels, which failed in the eleventh hour.

Indeed, China's ODI grew by an annual compound rate of 14% between 2008 and 2014 (Fig. 6.6), but the robust trend was disrupted by the Beijing's deleveraging process in 2015 to rein in the country's financial excess by cutting funding for many, including overseas, investments. However, despite strong growth, the stock of China's ODI has remained small relative to other major surplus economies (see Fig. 6.3), suggesting that there is significant room for expansion by China in the future.

In the grand scheme of things, increasing Chinese ODI simply reflects a secular trend of Chinese expansion into the global markets by increasing its global investment share that would be normal for an economy of its size and financial heft. The question is what drove the large Chinese expansion overseas that has become a trend and made the world suspicious and worried?

China's macroeconomic environment is an important factor, augmented by government policy support which adds momentum to its ODI expansion. Excess capacity has led to diminishing marginal returns on investment in the domestic economy for many years (Fig. 6.7). This was the fundamental factor for driving Chinese companies to look overseas (hence capital outflow) for enhancing their return on investment. Realising the diminishing returns problem, President Xi Jinping started a wave of structural reforms and economic deleveraging when he took office in 2013. But these measures have cut GDP growth from

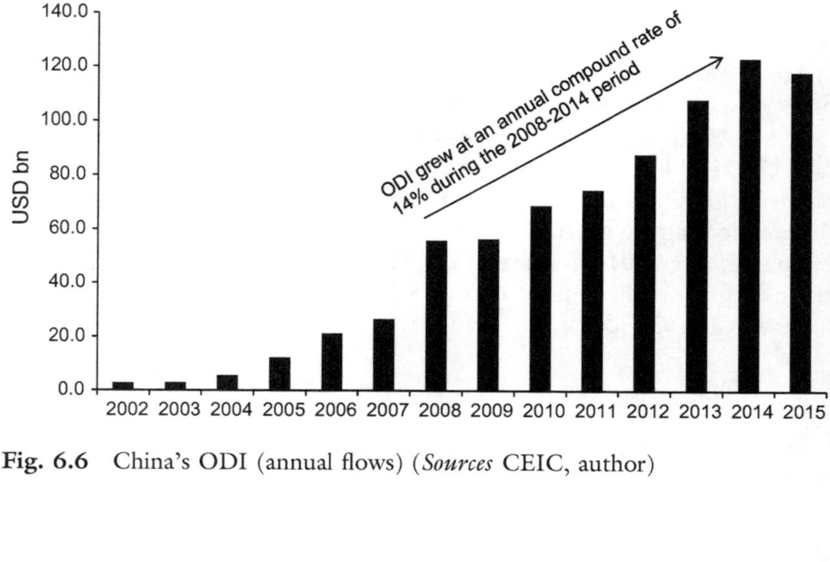

Fig. 6.6 China's ODI (annual flows) (*Sources* CEIC, author)

double-digit rates seen in the 1990s and 2000s to less than 7% a year since 2015. While the reforms eventually boosted investment returns in the economy (see Fig. 6.7), they created short-term uncertainty for investment in the domestic markets which added to the incentive for capital outflow.

A strong renminbi exchange rate that appreciated significantly between the mid-1990s and the mid-2000s also facilitated China's ODI expansion by making it cheaper for Chinese companies to purchase overseas assets. Once started, the ODI expansion has not stopped. Despite the short-term noises about renminbi weakness and fears about devaluation, the yuan is likely to remain a stable currency with a strong bias over the medium to long term because of Beijing's policy goal of making it a global currency eventually. This policy should support the secular flow of China's overseas direct investment as part of the renminbi internationalisation efforts. And the overseas investments will bring in foreign earnings to boost the current account surplus, providing support for the renminbi exchange rate.

Vigorous government support in terms of streamlining the regulatory approval process and providing cheap funding via the state and policy banks has played a crucial role in helping Chinese companies to push into the international markets. In 2014, for example, the State Council

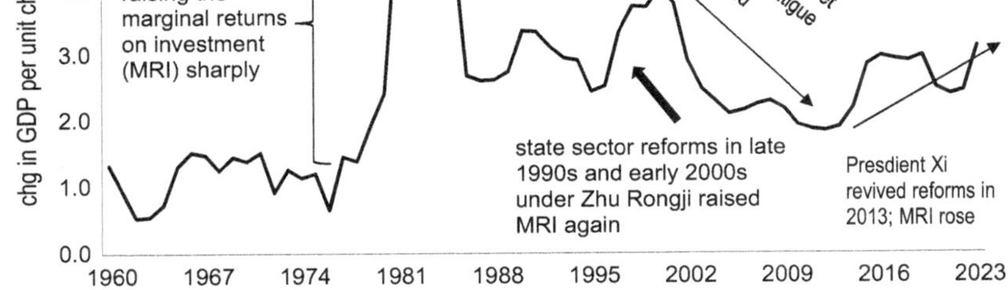

Fig. 6.7 China has suffered diminishing marginal returns on investment (MRI)* (*Note* *5-year moving average. *Source* CEIC, author's calculation)

revised the regulatory approval process under the "Catalogue of Investment Projects Subject to Government Confirmation" by exempting small and medium-sized (less than USD1 billion) Chinese overseas investment projects from seeking approval from the National Development and Reform Commission. They only need to file the applications for reference. This has significantly reduced red tape and the threshold for ODI projects.

In another move to facilitate liquidity for overseas investment, the People's Bank of China (PBoC) in 2015 lowered the threshold for multinational corporations (MNCs) to launch cross-border two-way renminbi fund-pooling services. After the change, domestic and foreign subsidiaries of the same MNC, including Chinese companies, can transfer funds freely among themselves through the fund-pooling scheme without the need for approval from the PBoC. This offers MNCs more flexibility and choices in foreign currency financing so that allocation of foreign currency funds can be made more efficient within the same group.

At the company level, there have been microeconomic incentives put in place for Chinese investment to go overseas in the forms of:

1. Vertical integration: manufacturing companies expanding overseas up or down their respective value chains to achieve resources integration and reduce costs.
2. Horizontal integration: overseas M&A or greenfield investment[3] to gain access to foreign markets.
3. Acquisition of foreign technology or brands: overseas M&A to acquire advanced technology, know-how and/or internationally recognised brands.
4. Diversification: acquiring productive overseas assets that are unrelated to the host company's domestic core business.

Prior to 2013, vertical and horizontal integrations were the main driving forces for Chinese ODI. Since 2013, acquisition of foreign technology and brands and diversification needs have become the key driving forces, reflecting the changing structure of the Chinese economy.

[3] A green field investment is a form of foreign direct investment where a parent company builds its operations in a foreign country from the ground up. In addition to building the new production facilities, these projects can also include the building of new distribution hubs, offices and living quarters.

The share of Chinese ODI driven by acquisition of foreign technology or brands and diversification has been rising over the years, from my estimate of 17.5% of the total in 2008 to 38.0% in 2023. This increase comes at the expense of the ODI driven by the vertical and horizontal integration incentives. This, in turn, reflects some structural changes that are going on in Chinese ODI amid a rising trend of outflows.

The Changing Faces of Chinese ODI

Once upon a time, China's ODI was a matter of SOEs doing resource and infrastructure deals. However, that picture has changed since 2013 when mega foreign M&A deals were announced by Chinese companies. The range of investment interests has also broadened from the traditional energy and materials to consumer goods, financial services, technology, entertainment, hospitality, industry and property.

Despite prominent media headlines of property deals, such as Anbang's purchase of the Waldorf-Astoria Hotel in New York and Soho China's purchase of a stake in the GM Building during the peak of ODI expansion between 2015 and 2016, real estate accounted for a small share of China's total overseas investment.

Crucially, this share fell from an already small 8% in 2016 to only 1% in 2023. This dispels the popular notion that when Chinese private entrepreneurs buy foreign assets, they are squirrelling money away (by buying overseas properties which involve large outlays) for the day when they must flee a collapsing country or the corruption investigators. The pattern of ODI is more consistent with the explanation that China's private companies are seeking to maximise profit on the hunt for new market opportunities and portfolio diversification.

The change in the ODI interest reflected the growing role of Chinese private firms in driving overseas investments and becoming bolder in pushing into the foreign markets. Big private firms favoured North America and Europe, where they accounted for almost a third of all Chinese M&A activity by value in the years before the peak ODI period of 2015–2016. Meanwhile, almost all M&A deals in natural resources were still made by SOEs.

So, what happened to Chinese investment in 2013 that made the year a watershed for China's ODI? In that year, China's overseas investment was dominated by two giant deals. First was CNOOC's USD15.1 billion acquisition of Nexen, a Canadian oil and gas company with global offshore production sites and major holdings of oil sands. Then there was the USD7.1 billion purchase of US pork producer Smithfield Foods by Chinese meat firm Shuanghui International (renamed WH Group later).

CNOOC's acquisition was the largest ever at the time by a Chinese firm, topping Chinalco's USD12.8 billion investment in Rio Tinto in 2008, and it followed the same path of a Chinese SOE scouring the world for natural resources to feed the nation's economic boom. On the other hand, WH Group's purchase marked a new direction in China's ODI because WH Group, based in Henan province, was the first private company to make a foreign acquisition valued over USD5 billion.

These giant deals had implications for the changing nature of China's ODI—in addition to state-backed firms securing massive natural resource deals, private firms were joining the chorus of overseas investors on a large scale with more diverse interests. The purchase of Smithfield actually followed Dalian Wanda's USD2.6 billion purchase in 2012 of AMC Entertainment, the world's largest chain of movie theatres in the US. Energy and metals remained the prime targets for SOEs, but a growing share of ODI had come from private firms engaged in finance, entertainment, agriculture, real estate and technology.

There was also a change in the geographical focus for China's overseas investment between 2013 and 2022, when developed countries become the top investment destination. More and more Chinese firms were looking to established markets to tap wealthy consumers or acquire products and technology that were not available at home including management expertise, high-tech products and even safe foods. Leaving Hong Kong aside, the top three ODI destinations for China were the US, Australia and the UK, while France, Canada and Germany were also in the list of top ten destinations.

This evidence of diversified Chinese ODI dispelled some of the political and media scaremonger views that Chinese giant "invincible" state firms, backed by cheap funding from home, were trying to gobble up the world's scarce natural resources. Two takeover deals announced in April 2014 highlighted China's diversified ODI interests. On one hand, state-owned MMG's USD5.9 billion deal to buy a copper mine in Peru from the Anglo-Swiss commodity trader Glencore Xstrata was of the old practice. On the other hand, the purchase by Nanjing Cenbest (a subsidiary of the private Chinese conglomerate Sanpower) of UK department store chain House of Fraser reflected the new scope of Chinese ODI.

ODI Face Changes Again

China's ODI has undergone some significant changes again since 2022. Firstly, its geographical focus has shifted from developed markets (DM) back to emerging markets (EM), thanks largely to the rise in Sino-US geopolitical tension. China's ODI in the developed countries, notably the US, has dropped sharply since 2019, reflecting divestment as DM's hostility, led by the US, towards China increases. To manage the DM hostility, China has increased significantly its ODI in EM, including the BRI countries (Fig. 6.8).

This shift in ODI pattern also reflects China's export reorientation to EM as a way to counter the rise in DM hostility towards China. Since the Sino-US trade war started in 2018, China has increased sharply its exports to EM, especially to ASEAN and Latin America.

Meanwhile, US foreign direct investment in China has remained large, with the cumulative amount tripling that of China's ODI in the US. However, as bilateral tensions escalate China may put up invisible trade barriers, such as putting some US companies operating in China on its "unreliable entity" list on national security concerns as retaliation. This will not only deter American investment in China but will also make other foreign investors, notably those US ally countries, reduce investment or

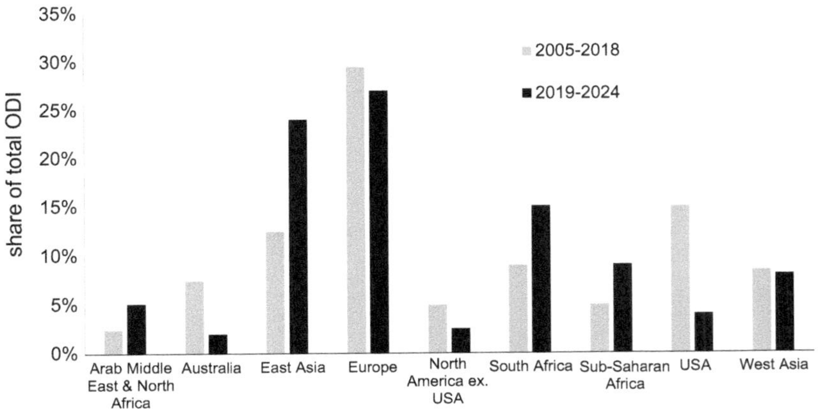

Fig. 6.8 China has cut ODI in DM and boosted ODI in EM (*Sources* Standard chartered, author)

hesitate to invest, in China due to policy uncertainty from both China and the US. This will add pressure to further slowdown foreign direct investment in China and aggravate the negative net FDI trend that emerged in 2022 (see below).

Secondly, the rapid increase in ODI has turned China into a net FDI exporter since 2022 from a net FDI recipient. This means that net FDI flows to China have turned negative (Fig. 6.9). The rise in geopolitical tension between China and the US has aggravated the negative trend by reducing foreign (notably US) investment in China and increasing profit repatriation by foreigners from China.

Despite China's pledge to remain open to foreign investments, even long-term foreign investors have turned hesitant on investing in the Middle Kingdom for fearing to be caught in the crossfire of the escalating geopolitical tensions. Since the Sino-US competition/tension is not expected to end anytime soon, the outlook for FDI inflows, especially by the US and DM in general, to China is not bright. With ODI continuing to expand but inward FDI remaining muted, China will likely become a persistent net FDI exporter.

Furthermore, the sharp contraction in FDI inflows reflects a reshuffling of global supply chains amid rising global protectionism. Even as

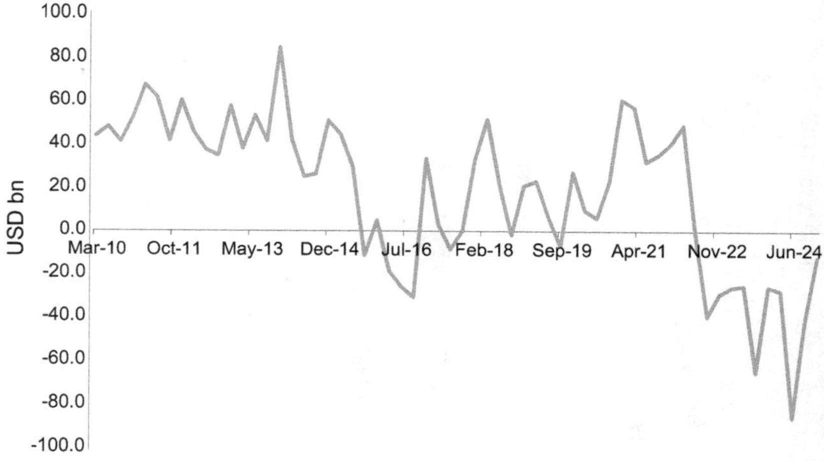

Fig. 6.9 Net FDI flows* to China have turned negative (*Note* *Balance of payments data. *Sources* CEIC, author)

Chinese companies increase investment abroad and most foreign companies are unlikely to exit the China market (but rather opting for a "China + 1" and "investing in China for China's domestic market" strategy), the shifting FDI trends mean that more production capacity will be installed outside China. Meanwhile, as China increases its ODI, it is adding to its overseas assets and national income. This will expose China's foreign investments and their expansion plans to political risks and uncertain returns.

Thirdly, while still focusing on energy and technology, China has tried to diversify its overseas investments into metals and transport since 2019 (Fig. 6.9). However, all these sectors are becoming vulnerable to protectionist policies and could be on the frontline of geopolitical friction. Furthermore, although the share of ODI by China's private enterprises has increased sharply, ODI by state companies is still large and they could be a political obstacle for China to expand its overseas investments (Fig. 6.10).

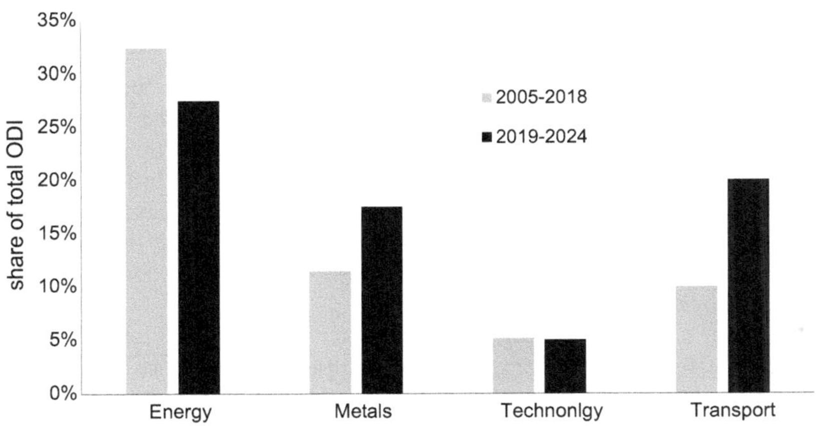

Fig. 6.10 China has been boosting ODI in metals and transport (*Sources* American Enterprise institute, author)

Pros and Cons of Exporting FDI

All this means that China is facing headwinds in investing overseas but at the same time suffering a decline in FDI inflows. Nevertheless, these crosscurrents are unlikely to change the trend of China turning into a net FDI exporter as its economy matures. This change is not inherently bad, but it does have pros and cons to the Chinese system.

On the positive side, ODI is a way to export China's excess capacity, increasing the investment scope for Chinese companies and, thus, helping to enhance marginal returns on investment by leveraging cheaper labour, resources or technology abroad. Strategically, China can secure supply chains (e.g. raw materials, energy) through ODI to enhance long-term economic security.

Of course, there is no free lunch. Acceleration of ODI could amount to hollowing out of some domestic industries, hurting job creation and growth at home. Furthermore, when overseas investments underperform, ODI will hurt overall corporate profits and, by extension, China's economy and asset prices. There is also a negative impact on the renminbi exchange rate in the short-term stemming from negative net FDI flows when capital outflows overwhelm inflows.

However, as Japan's experience shows, the long-term impact of being a net FDI exporter could be positive for China because more ODI means an increase in foreign assets held by Chinese companies. These assets will produce long-term income flows back to China, boosting its current account surplus and supporting the renminbi exchange rate, *ceteris paribus*. To the extent that more Chinese ODI increases the usage of and demand for renminbi, they will also facilitate renminbi internationalisation.

In sum, China becoming a net exporter of FDI signifies the maturation of its economy and the global competitiveness of its enterprises. This development aligns with the national strategy of "going global" and reflects the progress of China's reform and opening-up policy. Domestically, it facilitates the internationalisation of Chinese companies and the currency. Globally, it also promotes economic growth, international trade and industrial cooperation to counteract the forces of de-globalisation and US protectionism and isolationism.

A Different Type of Investor

In terms of the evolution process, China's ODI is a unique phenomenon because China is emerging as one of the world's largest investors with its investment footprints across the globe while it is still a developing economy. This development raises many questions about China's investment style and behaviour. What kind of challenges are they creating to the global norms and how should the world react/position for the wave of China's overseas investment in the coming decades?

Evidence shows that China's overseas investment is indeed quite different from the international norm in that it focuses a lot on developing countries with poor governance, although it is also expanding rapidly into the developed world. The US has been the biggest ODI destination for China until 2018 when bilateral relationship deteriorates. However, what attracts global attention is its significant investment in poor African countries (including the Democratic Republic of Congo and Angola) and Latin America (such as Venezuela and Ecuador), where poor governance is an issue for most international investors. Such Chinese investment behaviour is quite different from the world's major investors and may reflect the political forces behind the Chinese investments and the opportunistic nature of the Chinese investors.

Generally, empirical evidence shows that in addition to factors like market size and availability of natural resources that determine the flows of FDI, there is also a strong correlation between global FDI flows and good governance environment (Dollar, 2015). The reason is that an environment with better property rights, transparency and the rule of law should enhance investment profitability. So, this environment should attract more investment, *ceteris paribus*.

However, this did not seem to apply to China until around 2018 when Chinese investment style started moving towards international norms and standards. In the early 2000s, China's ODI was mostly attracted by countries that offered natural resources and only weakly attracted by large market size. Crucially, it did not bear any correlation with the governance environment, as approximated by the index of the rules of law and intellectual property rights (Dollar, 2015). This seems to suggest that China's ODI was indifferent to the governance environment.

This practice still persists, despite some improvement in China investment attitude. Although China invests a lot in South Africa, which has relatively better governance than other countries in Africa, it also invests heavily in Angola, Congo and Sudan, where poor governance persists (according to the corruption perceptions index rankings by Transparency International[4]). The same ODI indifference attitude exists in China's investment in Latin America where it invests heavily in both countries that have relatively better governance structure, such as Brazil, and countries that have not, such as Venezuela and Ecuador (Transparency International, 2024).

However, it will be inappropriate to jump to the conclusion, as some do, that China is focusing on investing in poor governance countries simply because it also does not have a good governance culture either. Although it does seem true that corporate governance is not a major factor in the Chinese ODI decision-making process, that may be due to the fact that many of China's jumbo overseas investments are still made by SOEs, which do not come under the same pressure as private firms to produce good returns on their investments.[5] Since SOEs answer to the government, not shareholders, their overseas investments in poor governance countries are often politically driven by state-to-state deals rather than market-driven profit maximisation incentives.

Such Chinese ODI behaviour has raised some important questions. For the world, the question is whether China is sustaining poor governance in some countries via state-to-state investment deals. In some cases, Chinese ODI are indeed supporting local political elites and, thus, helping them to hold onto their corrupt regimes. For example, if it were not Chinese investment and money, Venezuela (ranked highly corrupted by Transparency International, at 178 out of 180 in the 2024 corruption perceptions index) would likely have no choice but to turn to the International Monetary Fund and other multilateral development banks for funding in exchange for policy and economic reforms to stabilise its economy back in 2015–2016.

For China, the question is whether it is getting the best returns on its ODI by using public money. With diminishing marginal returns on

[4] A country's score indicates the perceived level of public-sector corruption on a scale of 0 (highly corrupt) to 100 (very clean). A country's ranking indicates its position relative to the other countries in the index. The index for 2024 includes 180 countries and territories, with Denmark being ranked as the most-clean country (ranking number 1) in the world and South Sudan the most corrupted (ranking number 180).

[5] Empirical evidence shows that state firms typically are inefficient and unprofitable as compared to their private-sector counterparts in the domestic economy. So, the state firms would behave the same and produce the same inferior returns in their overseas investment.

domestic investment (see Fig. 6.7), it makes perfect sense for China to invest overseas to diversify and enhance investment returns. Earnings on China's ODI could help the country finance its public pension scheme and the social safety net to cater for needs of an ageing population. So, it is in China's best interest to invest overseas with sound management and principles. However, its ODI behaviour is not always generating the desired results.

Chinese private firms generate much higher returns on investment than SOEs in the domestic economy. Presumably, they would be able to do the same in overseas investments. Evidence from Chinese investment in Africa suggests that this had been the case (Chen et al., 2015). Small and medium-sized Chinese firms investing in Africa typically did not invest in natural resources, which were typical giant state-to-state deals, but in services and manufacturing. These investments were determined by the local endowments of labour, capital and skills, which are characteristics of profit-maximising investment. But even if the private Chinese firms are generating high returns on their ODIs, overall ODI efficiency is still being dragged down by the inefficient big SOEs' investments.

Capital Outflows Reflect Domestic Structural Changes...

The changing dynamics of China's capital outflows and overseas investments are closely linked to the structural changes in its economy, which will continue to evolve in the coming decades with far-reaching impact on the global system and investment landscape. In terms of investment in, and capital flows to, poor governance countries, China is making changes, albeit slowly, to follow global norms of better governance and environmental standards. This change is, in turn, linked to its domestic economic structural shifts.

The key motivation for China to invest in developing countries with poor governance, notably in Africa and Latin America, was to gain access to natural resources to cater for its huge industrial development appetite. In the 1990s and 2000s, China's growth model was very resource-intensive, demanding a large amount of the world's energy and raw materials and driving up global commodity prices. This growth appetite prompted it to look for more natural resources even in risky environments, including those countries with poor governance structure.

All this has changed since 2010 as the supply of commodities has increased and the structure of China's growth model has shifted away from industrial-based investment-led towards service-based and consumption-driven activities, which are not that resource-intensive. In particular, since 2013 China's new economy, as represented by the tertiary sector, has grown larger than the old economy, as represented by the secondary sector (Fig. 6.11). This suggests that a process of "creative destruction" has been in progress, where the new sectors, such as movie and entertainments, e-commerce, online sales and insurance, have shown robust growth replacing old sectors, such as property and infrastructure. Consumption has contributed an average of 3.8 percentage points to GDP growth each year since 2009, compared to investment's contribution of 3.2 percentage points (Fig. 6.12).

As a result of this shift in demand and supply, commodity prices have come down and China's import needs for raw materials have fallen. Furthermore, many of China's ODI in poor governance countries have not worked out well, but Chinese entrepreneurs are increasingly demanding better returns on their investments abroad, including state-backed projects. The combination of these factors will reduce China's capital flows to, and investments in, the natural resource sector and countries with poor governance.

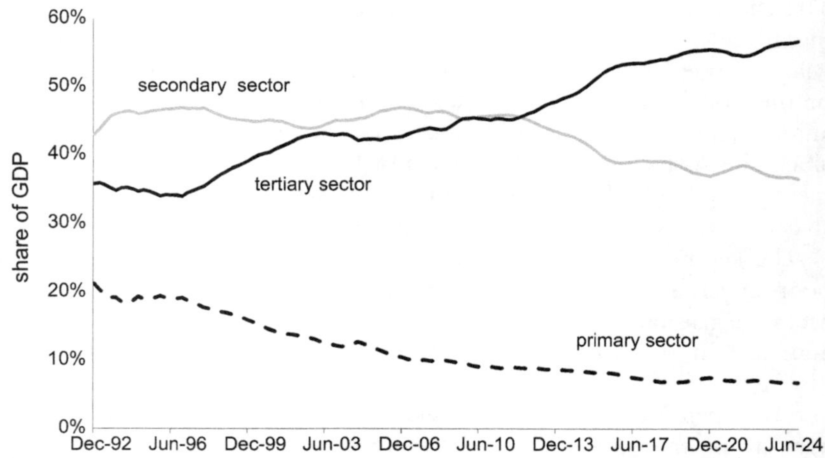

Fig. 6.11 China's structural rebalancing in progress (*Sources* CEIC, Author)

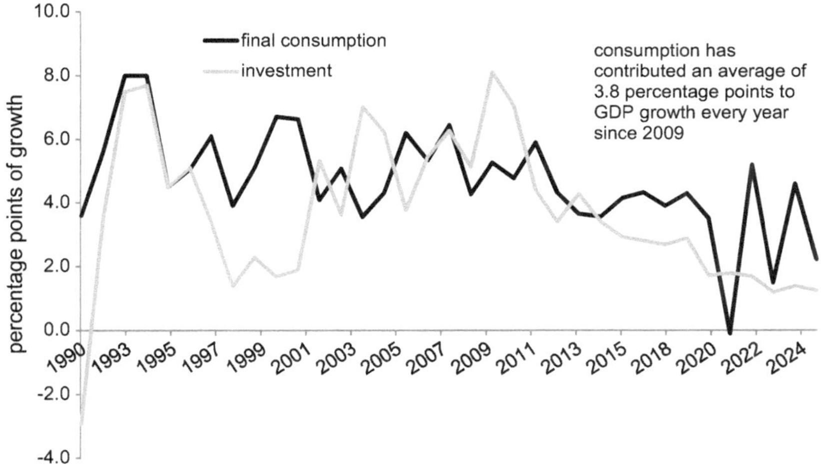

Fig. 6.12 Consumption and investment's contribution to China's GDP growth (*Sources* CEIC, Author)

… AND PUT PRESSURE ON DEVELOPMENT FINANCE

Meanwhile, many Chinese private firms are looking to invest abroad in a wide range of sectors, and to increase investment in both the developed world and in emerging markets with relatively good governance structure, including environment and social protection. However, these environment, social and governance (or ESG) factors have always been thorny issues for the World Bank and other multilateral development banks in their financing conditions for infrastructure projects in the developing world. This is because they have been imposing standards that reflect the preferences of the rich sponsoring countries while ignoring the realities that the developing country recipients face.

China has identified this problem and sided with the developing nations, which have been voting with their feet by welcoming Chinese financing and by turning away from the other multilateral development banks as the main source of infrastructure financing. The developing nations' preference to Chinese funding can be seen in their strong positive response to the formation of the Asia Infrastructure Investment

Bank (AIIB),[6] with countries that are not so friendly to China, such as Vietnam, India and Indonesia, signed up as founding members. The AIIB's attempt to develop workable safeguards to address environmental and social damages by infrastructure projects but without the long delays and high costs of the existing multilateral development bank practices is a welcome innovation in improving efficiency in development finance.

If the AIIB's objectives are properly implemented, China may end up modifying global norms by making them more align with developing countries' preferences, thus bridging gaps in Western-led multilateral development banks and promoting inclusive, sustainable and efficient infrastructure investment. In other words, by focusing on sustainable infrastructure, technological innovation and good governance, the AIIB can drive meaningful reforms in development finance by making the traditional financing players more responsive, efficient and inclusive.

Such success, however, depends on all players maintaining high standards and avoiding the pitfalls of debt dependency and geopolitical influence. The potential force by China to usher in reform of the financing practice should be seen as a positive disruption to the prevailing Western-dominated development finance model and should be encouraged.

Crosscurrents

In the longer term, Beijing's strategies of internationalising the renminbi and encouraging Chinese companies to go global, notably through the BRI programme, are steps to liberalise the capital account. In other words, these measures should make capital outflows from China easier. Moreover, there is already a broad trend of Chinese households and companies diversifying their wealth and investment internationally. The emigration of Chinese capital is a gradual secular trend but not a sudden short-term phenomenon. So, its disruption to the global markets should

[6] The Asian Infrastructure Investment Bank (AIIB), started operation in December 2015, is a multilateral development bank and international financial institution that aims at collectively improving economic and social developments in Asia. It is the world's second largest multi-lateral development institution. Headquartered in Beijing, China, the bank has 110 members, including 12 prospective members from around the world (as of December 2024). The breakdown of the 110 members by continents are as follows: 42 in Asia, 26 in Europe, 22 in Africa, 10 in Oceania, 8 in South America and 2 in North America.

prompt gradual changes but not sudden shocks, as some China critics fear.

From China's perspective, there is no smooth sailing for investment outflows. A medium-term impediment to Chinese capital outflows is debt. Chinese companies mostly rely on debt to finance overseas investments, with the key funding source coming from domestic commercial and policy banks. The rapid corporate debt build-up since 2010 has already made the international community worry about a systemic crisis in the Chinese banking system.

After the US subprime crisis, Beijing launched a massive RMB4 trillion (USD58 billion at the then prevailing exchange rate) credit injection programme to counteract the subprime crisis impact on the domestic economy. Subsequent years of borrowing have pushed China's total (public and private sectors) debt to over 280% of GDP in 2023 from 160% before the subprime crisis.

However, slowdown in Chinese growth, deterioration in corporate earnings and tightening cash flows have eroded companies' debt servicing and repayment ability significantly. An increasing portion of new credit has been used to keep companies afloat and to service existing debt. This has resulted in deteriorating asset quality at the Chinese banks, with the official non-performing loan (NPL) ratio rising from less than 1% in 2011 to a peak of 1.75% in early 2016 and hovering at an average of 1.6% since then.

While this ratio is much lower than the unhealthy NPL threshold of 5.0%, many market players have estimated that China's true NPL ratio could be 4 to 5 times higher (Tang et al., 2024). The problem is structural, due largely to the presence of hidden debts incurred by the local government financing vehicles and the property sector's structural decline.

If the debt risk intensifies, on one hand it could hinder China's capital outflows from the official ODI channel and on the other hand accelerate hot money and illegal capital outflows due to a loss of confidence in the Chinese system. Nevertheless, with a high savings rate, a relatively closed capital account, an implicit guarantee policy (although Beijing is retreating from it gradually) and government ownership of the major banks, China's debt problem may not necessarily manifest in a banking or a debt-currency crisis, as many experts have predicted. But a damaged banking system could seriously impair the financing ability of Chinese companies for overseas investment.

What all this means is that the world's concerns about China's capital outflows flooding the global markets and wreaking havoc on the development finance world is overblown. Meanwhile, China's capital outflows through the BRI expansion, which has seen the number of participating countries rise from 54 in 2017 to 150 in 2023, will have far-reaching impact on the world's economic and political environment in the coming decades. However, this topic has not been well-understood, with hype and distorted information clouding rational analysis. I shall address these issues in the next chapter.

Another Serious Concern

Before we look at the BRI, let us address another serious issue—the shifting balance between Chinese capital outflows (the ODI), which is on the rise, and inflows of FDI, which is slowing down. This shift reflects a significant asymmetric investment environment in China. Despite its reputation as a magnet for foreign investment until 2022 when net FDI turns negative, China runs one of the most restrictive FDI regime in the world, according to the OECD's FDI Restrictiveness Index, even compared with other big emerging economies, such as Brazil, India, Mexico, South Africa and Chile (Fig. 6.13).

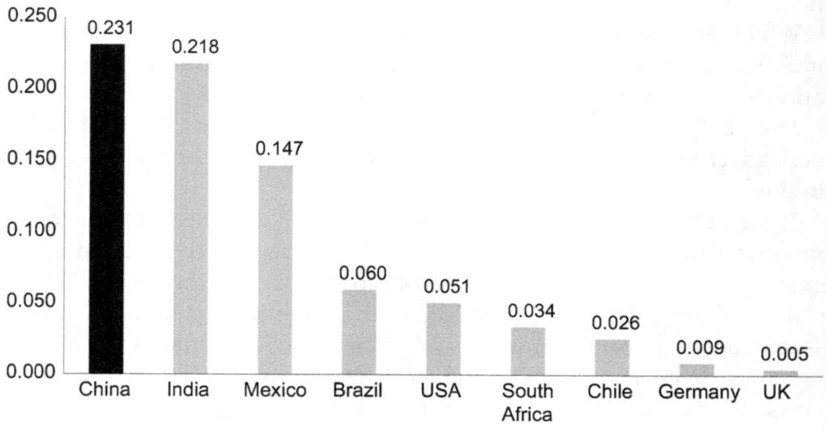

Fig. 6.13 OECD FDI Restrictiveness index in 2023 (0 = open, 1 = closed. *Sources* CEIC, Author)

This asymmetry is unhealthy and is generating a lot of concerns among other countries regarding an uneven playing field in China, where Chinese firms are free to invest as they please in advanced economies while many foreign firms face enormous invisible barriers to enter the Chinese market. This problem has become the biggest irritant for foreign countries, sowing the seed for protectionism, decoupling and geopolitical tensions as the developed world, led by the US, feels a pressure to impose some sort of a "reciprocity" standard on Chinese investment inflows.

While no one can force China to open up its FDI regime to match the liberal countries' levels, development since 2018, when the US started a trade war with China under the first Trump administration, shows that the US and its close allies have started to close their doors to Chinese investments. Underlying the China-containment policy (Teixeira, 2019) is a problem of mistrust which, arguably, is partly due to China's mischievous behaviour in the early days of its overseas investment expansion.

Though China has made improvement on adherence to the global standards of trade and investment, the mistrust problem has persisted as many countries have continued to dwell on the stock of China's past problems even China has moved on. This anti-China bias is not conducive for the world to accommodate the rise of China as a major international creditor. Admittedly, there is still a lot for China to do to prove itself a responsible global player, many governments, especially in DM, are uncertain and apprehensive about their countries' strategic interest being hurt by China's massive capital flows.

Geopolitical Tensions on Chinese Investment

The US, notably, has long taken a vigilant stance against China on its investment in US strategic sectors. Its Committee on Foreign Investment in the United States (CFIUS) is responsible for reviewing proposed foreign acquisitions of US assets that could potentially have national security implications.[7] Deals involving Chinese firms have faced more CFIUS reviews than those from any other countries. However, until the change in the US foreign policy on China from constructive engagement to strategic competition in 2017, it was unclear if the larger number of

[7] CFIUS is an interagency body chaired by the Treasury Department. It has the power to review, force modifications and even recommend that the president block certain foreign investments if they could harm national security.

reviews reflected particular concern over Chinese ODI in the US or simply the fact that there were more Chinese firms seeking overseas investment in the US.

Since taking over as US President for the second time in early 2025, Donald Trump has intensified the anti-China policy. His "America First Investment Policy" (The White House, 2025) executive order signalled that the hardline approach that he took towards China on national security in his first administration would continue. The order, signed in February 2025, is aimed at making it harder for China and the US to invest in each other but easier for the US and its allies to invest in each other. It is a strong signal that the US is determined to force decoupling from China because nothing in the order suggests its provisions could be rolled back even if US-China relations were to improve in the future.

In general, the order seeks to significantly increase scrutiny and restriction on inbound investment by China and outbound investment by US firms, and to make sure Chinese firms with access to US capital markets live up to US standards. The order also names China as one of the "foreign adversaries", with measures aiming at restricting proposed investment from China into the US as well as from the US into China through heightened scrutinisation and bureaucratic means. The order also specifically calls for restricting Chinese investments in US critical infrastructure, technology and energy.

What is damaging, from a geopolitical tension perspective, is the executive order's review of one of the most important compromises between China and the US—a deal that allows US regulators to audit China's audits to ensure Chinese firms listed in the US comply with US laws. China ignored such US request for years until Congress passed the Holding Foreign Companies Accountable Act (HFCAA) in 2020, giving China an ultimatum that Chinese firms would be delisted from US stock exchanges if the US could not supervise their audits. Concerned that audits could reveal state secrets, Beijing first delisted some state firms deemed sensitive to be part of the compromise, then signed an agreement with the US in late 2022 and began complying.

So, the deal worked. However, by going back on the agreement, Trump's America First policy has sabotaged the marginal improvement on the bilateral relationship with China achieved in the Biden administration. It also underscores the point that while China is making improvement on adhering to international standards, the US continues to dwell on China's past problems and carry out misguided actions. Thank this to the blind negativism without better understanding China and acknowledging any improvement it has made.

With many other governments following the US footstep on reviewing and scrutinising Chinese ODI projects, it is clear that there is an increase in international scepticism of the merits of welcoming Chinese investments in a country. This scepticism begs a larger question: Is Chinese ODI so different from other countries that merits special caution? There is no clear-cut answer, in my view, as China's ODI is driven both by political and market motives. But the opaque and cosy relationships between the Chinese government and Chinese companies and their heavy investment in countries with governance problems do add to such scepticism and mistrust in Chinese overseas acquisitions.

To be fair to the Chinese, it may also be possible that the rapid rise of China's economic power is inducing anxiety, prompting foreign governments to review Chinese projects out of fear of losing out to an economic rival. It is possible that they could use national security concerns as an invisible barrier to block Chinese deals. Indeed, some Western nations and their politicians are worried about Chinese ODI not always for well-defined reasons (GaoYan, 2021; Gertz, 2016).

So, on their part, these governments need to define more clearly their strategic objectives in relation to their policies towards Chinese investments, but not just rely on ad hoc reviews, distorted information and vague and sentimental reasons to block certain investments. In other words, governments should have well-defined policy parameters for assessing the merits of Chinese ODI in their countries and a predictable process for determining if any projects have crossed their line of security concerns.

References

Chen, W., Dollar, D., & Tang, H. (2015, August). *Why Is China Investing in Africa? Evidence from the Firm Level*. Brookings Institute.

Dollar, D. (2015, January). *United States-China Two-Way Direct Investment: Challenges and Opportunities*. Brookings Institute.

GaoYan, Q. (2021, July 22). Political Risk Distribution of Chinese Outward Foreign Direct Investment. *International Journal of Emerging Markets, 16*(6), 1202–1227.

Gertz, G. (2016, August 12). *Will the West Welcome or Shun Chinese FDI?* The Brookings Institution.

Tang, M. Liu, P., & Tsang, R. (2024, April 15). *China Banks Brace for Tide of Bad Property Loans*. S&P Global. https://www.spglobal.com/ratings/en/research/articles/240415-china-banks-brace-for-tide-of-bad-property-loans-13068811#:~:text=We%20project%20NPL%20ratios%20for,term%20imbalances%20in%20the%20economy

Teixeira, V. (2019). The United States' China Containment Strategy and the South China Sea Dispute. *Central European Journal of International Security Studies, 13*(3), 166–193.

The White House (2025, February 21). *America First Investment Policy*. The White House, Presidential Actions.

Transparency International. (2024). *Corruption Perceptions Index 2024*. https://www.transparency.org/en/cpi/2024

Troutman, K. (2013, December 24). *A World of Known Unknowns: A Closer Look at the Allocation of China's Foreign Exchange Reserves*. The Peterson Institute for International Economics.

CHAPTER 7

The Reality of the BRI Disruption

The US and some countries see China's Belt and Road Initiative (BRI), launched by President Xi Jinping in late 2013 when he visited Central Asia and Southeast Asia, as an aggressive Chinese expansion move. However, there is more than meets the eye. For better understanding, one needs to assess it from China's perspective in the context of the global geopolitical development. Arguably, the BRI started off as a defensive strategy. But as geopolitical tension between China and the US intensifies since 2018, the BRI has turned offensive to counter external hostilities.

Due to insufficient understanding of the BRI, it has generated not only fears and criticism but also optimism and hype about its potential geopolitical and economic impact on the world's balance of economic and political powers. Distorted information, and exaggerated fears have often overwhelmed rational thinking, clouding the assessment of the BRI's far-reaching impact on the global economy. In particular, many observers assume that BRI was a well-planned strategy by Beijing to accelerate the rise of China on the global stage, challenging the supremacy of the US and the developed world.

From a political economy perspective, the BRI is indeed a new kind of Chinese diplomacy—one that shifts from a defensive stance to a proactive strategy focusing on enhancing national security by countering American containment. However, like the renminbi internationalisation project,

C. Lo, *Clash of the Economic Titans: China and the United States*, https://doi.org/10.1007/978-981-95-2510-2_7

Beijing faces constraints on delivering the BRI results despite a strong incentive to make it work.

A related problem of the BRI is the so-called "debt-trap" diplomacy that has created fears about Beijing wreaking havoc on the global system by stirring political and financial storms. The worry is valid, but its ultimate global impact may not turn out as what many observers and critics have expected. China will get hurt too if it pushes such money politics too far.

The BRI is also evidence of China's long-term development vision that many Western analysts have tend to ignore. It was launched 7 years before Beijing's announcement (in May 2020) of its "dual circulation" economic strategy, which includes an "internal circulation" that focuses on boosting the domestic sector as the primary economic growth driver and an "external circulation" that engages (but does not rely on) the global market to foster economic growth and resilience. The BRI clearly fits in the external circulation as a tactic to survive and counter the US's protectionist and containment policies.

A crucial point about the global impact of the BRI that China optimists have overlooked is the extent of the reaction of global powers, who have every incentive to prevent Beijing from realising its ambition. Even many of China's Eurasian neighbours, who have warm relations with China, also fear that their interest could be compromised if China were to achieve primacy. The resultant political pushback constitutes a strong constraint on Beijing's efforts to push the BRI programme, thus limiting its expected impact. Such international reactions have also created negative geopolitical consequences by disrupting the global supply chains and intensifying de-globalisation, thus pushing the world into a negative sum game with rising political tensions.

The US has led the China-containment policy but, arguably, headed in the wrong direction by pursuing protectionism and isolationism. This is because by using foreign and trade policies that hurt friends as well as competitors, the US is creating precisely the political-economic running room China needs for advancing its interests via the BRI. For example, by squandering its influence in the Middle East and Asia, it is opening the door to greater Chinese sway in these regions. Washington could have some material influence on many parts of Beijing's BRI project, but only if it first could manage to stop self-destructing. In any event, the BRI is a serious factor when it comes to global disruption not only because of the huge network of influence that Beijing is building but also because of the clash between China and US interests.

From Defensive to Offensive

The Sino-US trade war that started since 2018 has vindicated the effectiveness of the BRI to defend China against US tariffs and export restrictions. Simultaneously, China's expansion in new BRI markets is an offensive strategy fighting back at the US containment policy. Evidence has shown that US protectionist measures have not hurt China's economy as much as conventional wisdom has it. However, US President Donald Trump still sees imposing punitive tariffs on China's exports to the US as an effective way to reducing US dependence on Chinese goods, reshoring manufacturing and protecting domestic industries, and containing a threat to national security that the US believes China's global expansion poses.

Data from Trump's first trade war with China in 2018 and 2019 shows that tariffs did not work as intended. Far from isolating China, the US tariffs (many of which were either kept or raised by the Biden administration between 2021 and 2025) have forced Chinese firms to diversify, innovate and expand in other countries, enlarging China's global footprints. As a result, China's global share of exports has risen since 2018 while that of the US has fallen (Fig. 7.1), as Chinese firms shifted production, trade and investment to BRI countries, notably in ASEAN, Africa and Latin America (Mexico in particular), to skirt US tariffs and trade restrictions (Figs. 7.2 and 7.3).

China's BRI expansion has been proven an important counteracting factor to the US trade war on China which conventional thinking has overlooked: International trade is not static, as many observers have assumed. China's export expansion to other markets has offset the fall in exports to the US. Over the years, China has been exporting more to the BRI countries than to Europe and the US (Fig. 7.4) both because of trade expansion with these markets and, more importantly, an increase in the number of countries joining the BRI. The latter reflects an increase in resentment of the US global policy, especially its frequent use of economic and financial sanctions, since 2017.

Arguably, these trade and investment shifts are imbedded in the dual circulation strategy that Beijing put together in 2020 to counter Trump's "America first" policy that he put together in his first presidential term

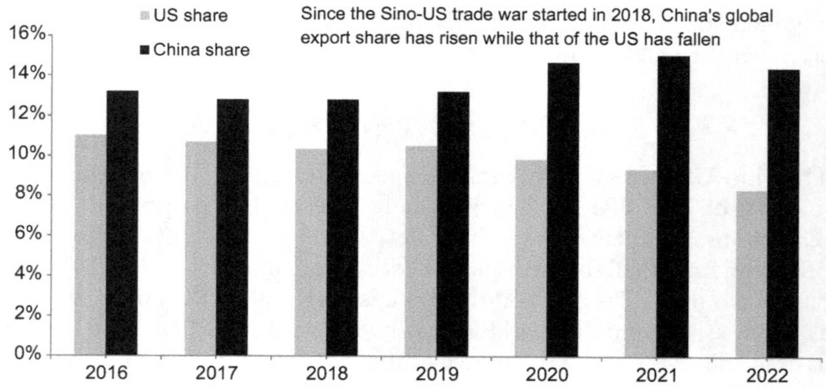

Fig. 7.1 China and the US shares of world exports (*Sources* Statista, The World Bank, author)

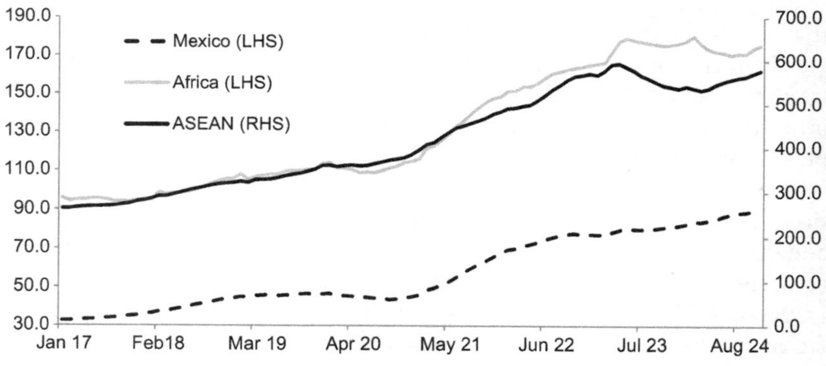

Fig. 7.2 Rising Chinese exports* to ASEAN, Africa and Mexico (USD bn) since the trade war in 2018 (*Note* *12-month rolling sums. *Sources* CEIC, author)

(2017–2021). Crucially, Beijing's strategy of sustaining China's growth through expanding domestic demand and reducing reliance on exports also reflects a change in Beijing's strategic thinking from cooperating with the US to preparing for "struggle" under intense geopolitical tension.

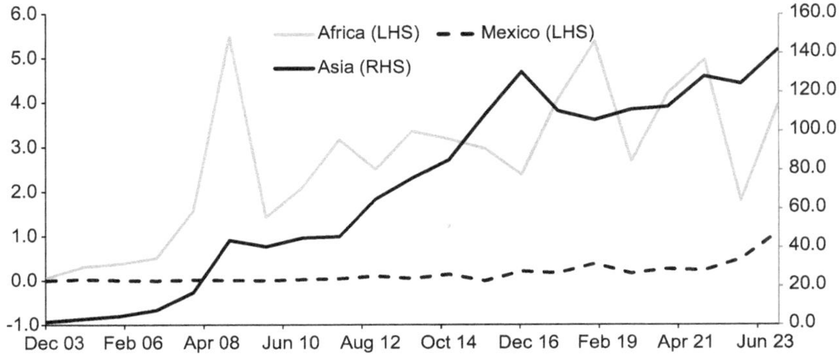

Fig. 7.3 China has increased investment in new markets, esp. Asia, significantly (USD bn) since 2018 (*Sources* CEIC, author)

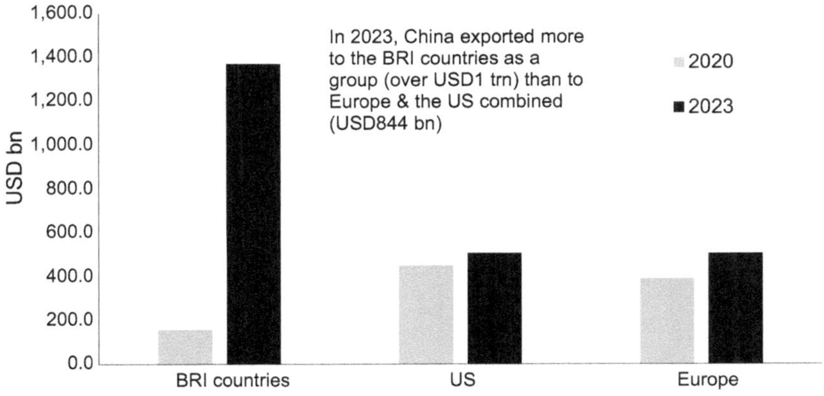

Fig. 7.4 Chinese exports to the BRI countries, Europe & the US (*Sources* CEIC, author)

Demonstrating this struggle, with some success, Chinese exports grew by an average of 10% a year between 2019 and 2022, despite the US trade obstacles, thank mostly to the trade expansion with the BRI countries. Crucially, exports of some new economic sectors, such as lithium batteries, electric vehicles and photovoltaic generators have grown exponentially in recent years (Figs. 7.5 and 7.6); and many emerging market countries are big buyers of these products.

Chinese companies seem to have embraced a survival strategy that reflects the adage of "what does not kill you makes you stronger".

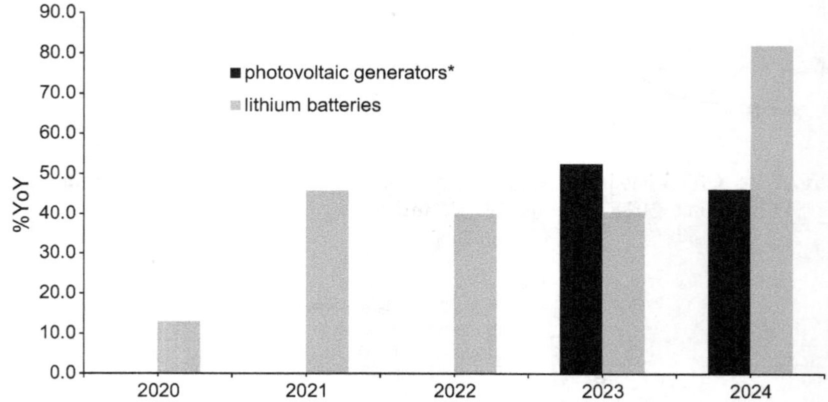

Fig. 7.5 China's export growth of photovoltaic generators & lithium batteries since Covid-19 (*Note* *Data only started in 2022. *Sources* CEIC, author)

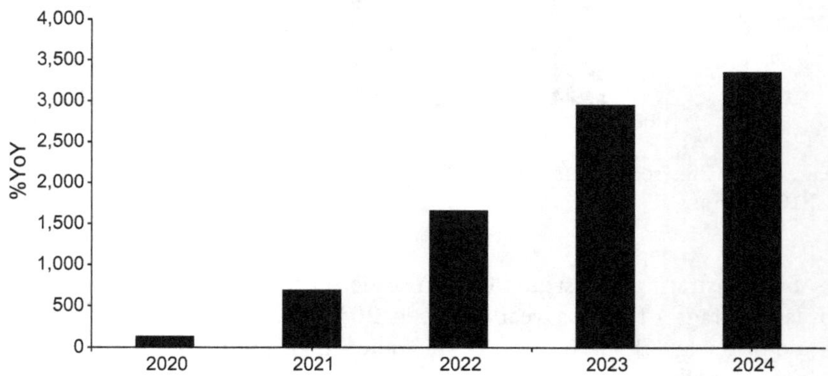

Fig. 7.6 China's export growth of electric vehicles since Covid-19 (*Sources* CEIC, author)

Surveys in 2024 indicated that 90% of Chinese companies were considering expanding overseas (HSBC, 2024; Shen, 2024). This is a significant change in Chinese corporate attitude from the old mindset of hiding behind the wall of government protection for survival, which prevailed in the mid-1990s and early 2000s, to a new progressive thinking of breaking the boundaries to strive and thrive since the launching of the BRI.

These developments also raise questions about whether a trade war would serve American interests. While Chinese companies expand and upgrade their supply chains under the BRI and adapt to the global demand shift and rising geopolitical tension through Beijing's dual circulation strategy, American manufacturers have had to deal with higher input costs and disrupted supply networks because of their government's China-containment policies and protectionism.

Ironically, by forcing China to decouple from the US, America's tariffs and trade restriction policies seem to have eroded its global influence, albeit slowly. This is reflected by the gradual increase in the usage of the renminbi in international payments, which has ranked consistently fourth and fifth most widely used currency for global payments in the SWIFT system, and the creeping progress of renminbi internationalisation. These not-easily-discernible events are further evidence of China emerging on the global stage while the West is sleeping on the wheel.

Furthermore, by diverting trade and investment from the US to other parts of the world, China's BRI has created growth opportunities both for itself and partner countries. From an Asian perspective, this diversion has boosted intra-regional trade with China as the driver, thus benefitting the regional economies. It has also ushered in a structural change in the regional supply chains that integrates China more closely with Asia, refuting the decoupling narrative but underscoring China's external circulation tactic by boosting regionalism to counter de-globalisation and geopolitical risks. More trade wars and decoupling policies by the US will only force China to open up even more to position itself as the world's opportunity at a time when the US is turning inward.

While China's dual circulation and BRI strategies could help protect it from external exigencies and allowing it to expand its global influence, it could also reveal its domestic problems, just like opening the capital account could open a can of worms, as we discussed in Chapter 5. Much will depend on China's resolve and ability to restructure the economy. For sustained economic resilience, domestic consumption must grow along with expansion of global trade and investment networks, i.e. China will need to implement its dual circulation strategy effectively. Only time will tell how it will work out.

The Strategic Importance

The BRI aims at achieving long-term economic and political objectives. It is, arguably, a "one stone kills three birds" strategy that will help China achieve international, domestic and political objectives in the long term by opening up new trade, investment and technology development opportunities. These initiatives will reshape the global balance of economic power and, inevitably, create disruptions along the way (Lo, 2017, chapter 8). The BRI has two routes which many in the West do not seem to distinguish:

- A land route called the Silk Road Economic Belt that includes countries on the ancient Silk Road through Central and West Asia, the Middle East and Europe.
- A sea route called the 21st Century Maritime Silk Road that links China's port facilities with the African coast through South and Southeast Asia, moving up through the Suez Canal to the Mediterranean.

Domestically, the BRI aims at exporting China's excess capacity by creating new markets for Chinese manufacturers, construction firms, capital goods makers and manufacturers. This should enhance domestic investment returns and stabilise GDP growth over the longer term. The project envisages building roads, railways, pipelines and industrial corridors across the participating countries, requiring billions of tonnes of steel and cement, hundreds of thousands of workers, tens of thousands of cranes and diggers and numerous new dams, power stations and power grids. It also aims at connecting all BRI countries by internet networks driven by Chinese technology.

Internationally, the BRI investments should unleash an infrastructure boom by connecting China with Asia, Europe and Africa by land and by sea. This could boost renminbi internationalisation by encouraging its usage in both trade and financial transactions. Politically and strategically, the BRI is a tool for Beijing to secure foreign trade and investment relationships to counteract major trade pacts that have excluded China, and to breakout of the US foreign policy that blocks China's expansion eastward (see below).

The whole BRI vision aims at building a massive network of trade, investment (especially in infrastructure) and technology for China to expand into countries in Asia, Central Asia, the Middle East, Europe, Africa, America and Latin America. It should also go a long way to deepen renminbi internationalisation when the Chinese currency is used for payments. The oil-producing Middle East region, which lies on the east–west land route of BRI, is of particular strategic importance to China due to its linkage with the major oil-consuming regions. Establishing a major influence in the oil-producing Middle East will enable China to also exert influence on trading with the major energy-consumption regions.

The geopolitical aspect of BRI is an especially important strategic vision of Beijing. The Chinese Communist Party (CCP) has started changing its foreign policy stance from defensive to proactive since President Xi Jinping came to power in 2013. The policy shift aims at making China an independent politico-economic pole in the world, which is reflected in President Xi's "Chinese Dream" that aims at transforming China from a regional power to a global geopolitical power eventually. Successful transformation will give China the opportunities to strengthen its national and economic security and stimulate economic development. However, before China can become an influential global player, it must first solve its internal socio-economic problems.

The Capital Linkage

Despite China's strong trade linkages with many regional economies and the BRI initiatives to extend these connections, its influence from a capital perspective is still limited. However, China wants to change this limitation both to serve the purpose of exporting its excess capacity at home and increase its soft power in Asia (and other parts of the world when the situation allows) through money politics, although it also realises that there will be resistance from some countries.

For example, while Vietnam allows anti-China protests to emerge on the surface, it still accepts Chinese investment in energy projects such as hydro and coal for meeting energy needs. China also invests in and finances many projects in Cambodia and Laos, especially in energy projects, with Chinese state-owned enterprises (SOEs) outcompeting many other countries in terms of pricing.

Even though these developing countries need a lot of capital for development, it does not mean that China could get its way to extend its influence through money politics. This is because there is domestic political consideration by the Asian countries and there is keen competition from other regional players, notably Singapore, South Korea and Japan which also have a strong financial influence in the region.

The BRI also faces funding limitations. Most of the Southeast Asian foreign debt is owed to multilateral development banks, notably the Asian Development Bank and the World Bank, a situation that reflects the existing world financial order forged after the Second World War. These debts are predominately denominated in US dollar and Japanese yen, thus exposing the debtor countries to foreign exchange risk. These development banks also often push the borrowers to use contractors from the countries that fund the projects. Japan has had immense influence in the region through the Asian Development Bank, as many Japanese firms have moved production offshore to ASEAN to take advantage of cheap labour and natural resources.

China wants to change this situation and increase its power through the BRI projects in the region. This means that capital-starved countries, such as Indonesia, Vietnam and Cambodia, often find it difficult to turn away Chinese investments and financing sources. Chinese institutions are also very keen on finding foreign opportunities and are willing to do deals on competitive terms. Hence, demand meets supply. This jostling for power by China in the Asia–Pacific has benefited many Southeast Asian countries. However, it also means more competition, and tension, with other countries with presence and interest in the region.

It's a Sino-US Disruption

However, the major frustration to China's expansion and threat to its national security is America's policy "pivot" to Indo-Pacific since 2017. Such a pivot is an extension of the US's "Asia pivot" policy under the Obama administration (2009–2017) and aims at deterring China from becoming a dominant power in the Asia–Pacific region. Consider the distribution of US treaty allies in Asia–Pacific. They span from north to south of the Pacific Ocean, from Japan and South Korea through South and Southeast Asia to Australia, forming an invisible "American shield" that blocks China's expansion to the east (Fig. 7.7).

Fig. 7.7 The invisible American shield (*Source* Author)

Thus, the BRI expands to the West from China. However, such expansion clashes with the US "Silk Road" project, which Washington launched in 2011 and aims at building connections between Afghanistan and Central Asia, South Asia and the Middle East. So, the US sees China's BRI expansion as a threat to its national security. Washington hopes to enlist India and Japan in its effort to counter the influence that Beijing is gaining across the world through the BRI framework.

Meanwhile, China is also trying to involve Japan and India in its BRI network. By persuading them into collaborating on BRI projects and deepening economic relations with these two countries, Beijing hopes to gain their trust gradually. It is also trying to convince Delhi to strengthen cooperation in the Bangladesh-China-India-Myanmar Economic Corridor, a plan which the four nations drew up in 2013. China reckons that pursuing this economic project would help ease tensions between Beijing and Delhi and lead to significant bilateral trade and strategic benefits (Lo, 2017, chapter 8). By enlisting Japan in the BRI plan, China hopes to secure influence in Northeast Asia by breaking the US strategic alliance in the region and gain a strategic leverage on managing the Korean Peninsula.

In the grand scheme of things, China is using the BRI to mitigate territorial and regional disputes. At the same time, it is deepening its military and political cooperation with Russia to counterbalance the US influence in the Asia–Pacific region and Central Asia. Moscow and Beijing have agreed to link the BRI with the Russian-led Eurasian Economic Union,[1] an economic union of states that also includes Armenia, Belarus, Kazakhstan and Kyrgyzstan, which lies along the BRI route.

Thus, putting all the blame on China for upsetting the global balance of power is myopic. Sino-US tensions lie in the heart of this disruption which, arguably, is inevitable due to the rising influence of China challenging the global supremacy of the US. Through the BRI, Beijing is creating deeper economic and political integration with its neighbouring countries and beyond, stretching to Africa, Europe and Latin America so that China will not be isolated in case of a Sino-US confrontation and that it will still be able to pursue its geopolitical and geo-economic agendas despite the increase in US hostility. Beijing is also using the BRI to strengthen its national security by improving relations with countries with which it has territorial disputes or political tensions.

Overly Optimistic About the BRI

When China held the two-day BRI forum in Beijing in May 2017 and outlined action plans for building new trade and investment global networks, the world thought that China had an integrated implementation strategy to expand its global influence. Optimists argued that the BRI would bring significant economic benefits to the global economy through China's financial support for, and enhanced policy coordination with, the BRI countries. But critics fear that it would just be a ruse for

[1] The Eurasian Economic Union (EEU) is an economic union of states located primarily in northern Eurasia. A treaty establishing the EEU was signed in 2014 by the leaders of Armenia, Belarus, Kazakhstan, Kyrgyzstan and Russia, and came into force on 1 January 2015.

China's self-economic and political interests. Both positive and negative views stem from too much hype about the BRI's potential achievements.

The truth is that there is no implementation plan and no official BRI projects as such! While the May 2017 forum explained, for the first time, President Xi Jinping's vision and intentions of his BRI idea, it provided no details of any strategy or project list. Those who claimed to be able to provide the strategic details did so out of imagination. The BRI is not a coherent trade and investment plan but a series of wide-ranging projects that serve Beijing's economic and political aspirations, whatever they may be (Oliveira et al. (2020). There is no timeline and signposts for when it will be completed because the BRI development is a moving target on Beijing's agenda.

Meanwhile, different levels of the Chinese government have used the initiative as an excuse to launch investment projects. The media and many analysts have assumed that all these were BRI projects, even though they might not have any official BRI status. Many of these projects were planned and initiated before President Xi took office but were folded into the grand narrative of the BRI. When Beijing launched the BRI, it talked about 67 or so countries would be included in the network, but it also said that there would be no geographical restrictions. This has been the case indeed, as the country list had grown to 150 in 2023. The truth is that what actually gets built depend on individual deals struck between Chinese and foreign firms, subject to diplomatic negotiations between the governments.

The BRI is a vision based on an evolving concept. Notably, the initial BRI policy document called for building six economic linkages across the Eurasian landmass, but it did not specify the routes of connection or target any specific industries and infrastructure projects. This left open the possibility of any projects any routes depending on the evolvement of the political objectives and environment.

Commercial Reality

Critics often doubt the commercial viability of many of the so-called BRI projects, and there is no lack of examples of failure. China's foreign project data seems to show that the BRI projects did have difficulties in generating revenues. Chinese foreign engineering and construction projects enjoyed more than a decade of steady revenue growth. But that growth peaked in 2018, three years after Beijing prioritised the BRI, and has remained stagnant since then (Fig. 7.8).

A macroeconomic explanation for the slowdown in this foreign income growth was the fall in commodity prices in 2014 and 2015. Since most of China's foreign projects were focused on resource extraction, income from these projects were hit hard by the decline in commodity prices. However, subsequent data shows that despite continued rise in newly signed foreign contracts, foreign revenues growth remained stagnant.

More importantly, the rising gap between the contracted projects and realised revenues (see Fig. 7.8) raises the suspicion that many Chinese firms were probably responding to political pressure by rushing to sign all sorts of phony deals and then letting them quietly rot away. Indeed, many provinces and cities have sent overseas delegations to find projects and signed MOUs to satisfy the political directive, regardless of the viability of the projects. When there is no follow-up of implementation on the projects, there is of course no revenues generated.

Incentive of the Chinese firms aside, there is also an economic limitation on the BRI expansion. Some of the countries participating in the BRI scheme have poor economic fundamentals, such as large fiscal and current account deficits. So, Beijing is taking on greater default risk by investing in them or by providing them with capital. A wider use of the renminbi

Fig. 7.8 China's foreign contracts continued to rise but revenue growth has stagnant* (*Notes* *12-month rolling sums; **Approximated by the value of completed projects. *Sources* CEIC, author)

in these countries may also expose China to foreign exchange risk. For example, China swaps renminbi for country X's currency at the prevailing exchange rate. If country X uses the funds to buy Chinese machinery, but China does not spend currency X at once to buy goods from the host country X, it would be exposed to foreign exchange risk if and when currency X depreciates.

Furthermore, politics may also backfire on China. Given China's poor track records on operating in foreign countries, including clashes in work ethics and the lack of human rights in labour treatment, a major increase in the scale of China's external activities could increase the risk of damaging Beijing's political image or creating instability in the host countries. Expansion of Chinese influence throughout central and South Asia will also create tensions with major players in those regions.

However, weighing the opportunities against the risks, BRI may still be a positive force for global markets by fostering new trade and investment links. The key is for China to abide by international norms and rules in its initiatives. It is still too early to judge whether the BRI will succeed or fail in achieving its intended goals because building new trade networks and infrastructure will take a long time. Meanwhile, BRI enthusiasts have overstated the ability of China's new financing channels, notably the Asian Infrastructure and Investment Bank (AIIB), to fund infrastructure investment in the economies along the BRI routes.

Political Suspicion

Development bankers have argued that Asia's infrastructure deficit is not a result of a lack of funding but of viable projects. This has led many critics to argue that while China had money it might still struggle to find profitable projects to invest in, but it would still channel funds into commercially nonviable strategic projects to bolster its economic security or boost growth in its impoverished regions and to establish political influence in the recipient countries.

India, in particular, has been very critical of China's BRI, persistently criticising its connectivity projects for "overriding sovereignty" of other nations (Krishnan, 2017; PTI, 2023) and seeing China's port-building exercise in the Indian Ocean, notably in Sri Lanka and Pakistan, as a platform for military expansion. In general, many countries also suspect that

China's BRI diplomacy is a ruse for advancing its economic and geopolitical interests, despite Beijing's assurance of its purpose of building a community of common interest.

The truth is probably a bit of both. China wants to boost its economy and create a regional production chain centred on its manufacturing power which, in my view, is a way of building an "empire" for expanding its economic and political influence (Lo, 2017, chapter 10). From this perspective, the BRI programme is also about exporting Chinese technology and industrial capacity to emerging markets so as to draw the developing economies closer to China's embrace.

Chinese banks and the AIIB have financed infrastructure projects in building highways, railways, ports, airports, power grids, oil and gas pipelines, telecom networks, etc., in the BRI countries. As a result, they have created demand for Chinese capital and industrial goods and services in the recipient countries and generated income for them to trade with China and pay for the Chinese loans and investments. Ideally, when these trade, investment and financing deals are settled in renminbi, the BRI will become a powerful tool for internationalising the renminbi by increasing its acceptance, usage and circulation overseas.

From China's perspective, this could be a win–win outcome. Undoubtedly, China is putting its interests first, but there are also benefits for the BRI countries. China's economic and political leverage will inevitably grow, but that may be a trade-off for countries anxiously seeking economic development but are ignored by the multinational development banks.

Still Going with International Norm

Relating to the political suspicion are concerns that Beijing would use the AIIB as a tool to reshape the global economic architecture by bypassing the global standards established by the existing world order. However, evidence shows that the AIIB has been just another multilateral development bank led by a team of foreign officials and former bankers who come from global institutions. This development is important because it counters the spirit of the AIIB's founding document that clearly states that it would be a financing tool for Beijing's BRI. It also shows that the concerns about the AIIB upsetting the global governance structure have been exaggerated.

Arguably, the shift in the AIIB's focus was a result of its own success. Beijing might originally want to create an institution that would be a quasi-Chinese government fund for financing Chinese industries to export their excess capacity. Within 18 months of China's proposal to set up the Bank in October 2013, 57 countries signed up to become founding members, including many European countries that have high governance standards. The resultant AIIB is simply too big and too diverse to function as a unilateral tool of China's money politics.

The AIIB's first moves were cooperation with the existing order rather than confrontation or competition. In all of its initial lending projects in the BRI countries between 2014 and 2016, it complemented efforts of the World Bank, the Asian Development Bank and the European Bank of Reconstruction and Development by contributing USD1.73 billion to their projects. Most importantly, none of these loans were made in renminbi. Ten years on since its establishment, the AIIB's operations are still predominantly US dollar based.

According to the June 2024 Auditor's Review Report by PricewaterhouseCoopers, the latest available at the time of writing, almost two-thirds of the Bank's funding and borrowing are in US dollars. The euro and pound sterling are the next two major funding currencies. The renminbi's share accounted for less 6%. Such funding currency composition implies clearly that the Bank's lending is not focused on renminbi. This evidence counters the world's concern about Beijing's ambition of using the AIIB to push renminbi internationalisation. It should also serve to allay fears that China is building its own institution to challenge the existing world order of development finance.

Development so far seems to suggest that the AIIB represents an evolution rather than a revolution in development finance. Together with the AIIB, BRI is a bold strategy that must be taken seriously. It may prove to be a long-term stimulus not only for China's growth but also for the growth of the developing world, as the latter badly needs infrastructure investment. The investment opportunities will likely outweigh the risks if China goes by its words on encouraging free trade and abides by international norms and market rules. Of course, if the BRI is a smokescreen for China to advance its self-interest at the expense of the others, it could be a negative disruption for the markets. So far, however, the BRI scheme and the AIIB deserve the benefit of the doubt to be a positive force for the global system.

An Invisible BRI and Disruptions

The strategic objective of the BRI aims at building a massive network of trade and infrastructure by China in the developing world, though it does not exclude the developed world's participation. Obviously, this initiative is crucial for China's traditional exporters of cheap manufactured goods and for the state-owned heavy industries that build infrastructure projects.

However, when it comes to China's economic future, it is pushing hard to develop twenty-first-century technologies, such as blockchain, big data, virtual reality, artificial intelligence and the Internet of Things.[2] Within the BRI framework, building IT networks in the BRI countries is part of the infrastructure investment objective. This linkage between China's high-tech economic future and the BRI's expansion is indeed an invisible Belt and Road Initiative beyond conventional trade and investment. In the grand scheme of things, the BRI is indeed a global framework that could make revolutionary changes to improve the world's trade, investment and technology development in the future.

From a technology perspective, deteriorating Sino-US relations is obstructing these revolutionary changes by breaking the trans-Pacific technological networks that link the two economic giants together. Netware development is heavily concentrated in the Pacific Basin, with the leading netware applications coming overwhelmingly from Chinese and Americans. Companies such as Didi, Baidu, Alibaba, Tencent, Shanda Interactive Entertainment, Mobike Technology, NetEase, Apple, Amazon, Google, Meta (formerly Facebook), Uber, Airbnb and Activision all share a Pacific netware ecosystem. European companies barely register on the radar.

The business model of these online businesses is created by the US and represents the success of Silicon Valley which has evolved from hardware incubation and development to software and netware manufacturing. For example, Apple may design its iPhones in Cupertino, California, but manufacturing and selling the iPhones are not the sources of profit. Apple makes most of its money by putting users into an online services ecosystem based around iTunes and the App Store.

[2] The Internet of Things is the network of physical devices, vehicles, home appliances and other items embedded with electronics, software, sensors, actuators and connectivity which enables these things to connect and exchange data, creating opportunities for more direct integration of the physical world into computer-based systems. The purpose is to increase economic efficiency and benefits with less human intervention.

China's high-tech cities are going the same way. Shenzhen used to make Apple's iPhones, but the production has been relocated to the poorer and cheaper city of Zhengzhou in the Henan province in China many years ago. And despite the Trump administration's effort to reshore iPhone production back to the US, most iPhones are still assembled in China. Huawei and ZTE, which are both Shenzhen-based, have also moved their manufacturing lines to inner and cheaper provinces.

All this underscores a trend of industrial migration, which started in the early 2000s, from the expensive east coast of China to the cheaper inner provinces. This trend can potentially help sustain China's economic growth at an average of 5% for a much longer period than most observers expect, in my view. Meanwhile, Shenzhen, China's Silicon Valley, like California in the US, has evolved into focusing on IT and AI development, social networks, online marketplaces, ecommerce and sharing apps.

Before the trade war, China basically imported all the successful netware business models from the West Coast of the US. Tencent was founded in 1999 as a clone of AOL's ICQ service. Jack Ma founded Alibaba in 2000 with Silicon Valley venture capital and expanded it by merging with Yahoo in China. Robin Li, the CEO of Baidu, worked at Silicon Valley search engine pioneer Infoseek before co-founding Baidu in 2000. These firms have come a long way with close connections with Silicon Valley.

Whether they are Chinese or American firms, the common thread among them is that they are all built on American operating platforms (Android, Windows, iOS or macOS), and programmed in American languages (Java, JavaScript, PHP, Python, Perl and SQL). China is aiming at becoming a leading global technological centre in the twenty-first century. To do so, it will have to connect closely with Silicon Valley and other US technology hubs to be part of the value chain as the US-China technology ecosystem that links champion companies on both sides of the Pacific Ocean is the key to their shared economic future.

That was the development then. Trade war and rising geopolitical tensions between China and the US have destroyed this cooperation model, resulting in disruption in global supply chains, innovation ecosystems and corporate strategies, and increasing global market volatility.

With the US restricting semiconductor exports to China, especially high-end AI chips (such as NVIDIA's A100/H100) and manufacturing equipment (like ASML's EUV machines), China has responded by speeding up domestic chip and increasing tech sector subsidies to achieve self-sufficiency, though it is still lagging in cutting-edge tech production at this stage. This essentially decouples China from the US in global tech development and, thus, effectively breaks up the trans-Pacific technology networks. Meanwhile, the US's friend-shoring push has dragged US firms away from China (e.g. Apple shifting some iPhone production to India/Vietnam), thus disrupting and decoupling the tech supply chains.

To counter the US measures on blocking Chinese investments in quantum computing, AI and biotechnology in America, China has implemented stricter anti-espionage laws and data-usage rules on US firms in, or entering, the China market. These tit-for-tat technology "skirmishes" has fragmented global innovation by reducing academic collaboration (e.g. fewer Chinese STEM students in US, visa restrictions) and creating competing tech standards (e.g. China's BeiDou vs. GPS, 5G protocols).

If the Sino-US tech competition continues to evolve in destructive ways, it could lead to increase in global economic costs and inefficiencies through bifurcation of the global supply chains. In the longer term, the "tech war" between the two largest economies in the world could create parallel technological ecosystems (US-led vs. China-led), with developing markets such as ASEAN and the Middle East as battlegrounds. Politicisation of trade, investment and technology development policies will inflict significant policy and compliance risks on the global system as players will be forced to adapt to shifting geopolitical realities.

Debt-Trap Finance, Myths and Realities

The world is also worried about China shaking up development finance, which is an area of economic prowess dominated by the developed world institutions, including the World Bank, the Asia Development and the European Bank for Reconstruction and Development. Notably, there is a suspicion that China is using "debt-trap" finance through its BRI to mire developing country partners in unsustainable debt-based relationship to advance its economic and geopolitical ambitions.

This view assumes that China could maximise its economic and geopolitical interests by ensnaring its BRI partners in debt distress. But evidence shows that China has not always been able to reap the alleged economic benefits and that it has even been a victim of its lending missteps. Push-back from BRI recipient countries has increased, leading to a slowdown in BRI investments. More importantly, domestic criticism on the BRI has also emerged, scaling back though not stopping President Xi's BRI ambition.

China's increasingly assertive foreign economic policy through its BRI has been criticised as a practice of neo-mercantilism (Blackwell & Tellis, 2015) and as "debt-trap diplomacy" (Chellaney, 2017; Kaleji, 2024). These views argue that China had sought to advance its economic and geopolitical influence by purposely ensnaring some of the developing countries in unsustainable loans-for-infrastructure deals.

The conventional wisdom is that the heavier the debt burden on the recipient country, the greater China's leverage becomes when the country is being forced to sell to China stakes in Chinese-financed projects or hand over management to Chinese state-owned investors. Concerns about China's debt-trap finance have found their way into some countries' foreign policy circle, aggravating the geopolitical tensions (Hurley et al., 2018; The White House, 2018). Critics of China's BRI assume that its economic interests are maximised when its lending partners are in financial distress. However, there is no proof for this claim.

There is no reliable data for tracking the profit and loss of China's BRI projects. But as discussed above, we can use data on the difference between China's new foreign contracts (as a proxy to BRI projects) and completed foreign projects (as a proxy to realised foreign revenues) to gauge the performance of the BRI projects. The data shows that the BRI projects did have difficulties in generating revenues (see Fig. 7.8). The rising gap between the contracted projects and realised revenues raises the suspicion that the newly signed projects just failed to bring in revenues and casts doubt on the alleged profitability of the BRI projects.

Anecdotally, China's lending to Venezuela has been the single most important evidence of its debt-trap finance backfired. Venezuela has been the largest recipient of Chinese official finance, with the China Development Bank doing the bulk of lending. Since China is the world's biggest oil importer and Venezuela has the world's largest oil reserves, the commercial rationale for the loans was strong for financing long-term oil partnership between the two countries.

Yet, with Venezuela in the depths of various economic and political crises since 2013, the China-Venezuela loans-for-oil relationship has gone badly wrong. The collapse of Venezuela's economy means that it has not been able to make loan repayments and even oil shipment to China. In a nutshell, Venezuela has gone from being a geopolitical asset for China in Latin America to being a liability.

Some other BRI projects have also gone wrong. For example, Sri Lanka's Mattala Rajapaksa International Airport, which opened near Hambantota in 2013, is dubbed the emptiest airport in the world. It cost over USD200 billion to build and has capacity for over one million passengers a year. But the most recent data from Travel and Tour World[3]—a digital B2B integrated media platform in the travel and tourism industry—shows that it only handled 7 passengers a week (or 364 on an annual basis). Meanwhile, Hambantota's Magampura Mahinda Rajapaksa Port is also largely idle, as is the multibillion-dollar Gwadar Port in Pakistan. Chinese lending and investment in other BRI countries, including Afghanistan, South Sudan and Angola have also reportedly gone wrong.

All this shows that China debt-trap finance has not achieved its intended purpose of gaining economic and geopolitical benefits through the BRI as many observers have assumed. China might just be following the footsteps of the Western governments, businesses and multilateral development finance institutions in the 1930s and 1970s when they found themselves in unsustainable debt relationships that hurt debtors and creditors alike.

Resistance to BRI investment has also been rising. Notably, Malaysia suspended all foreign direct investment projects, most of which (USD23 billion) were BRI-related, when Dr. Mahathir took over as Prime Minister in May 2018. He then renegotiated in 2019 all the projects signed by former Prime Minister Najib.

The BRI problems have also caught domestic attention in China. Since June 2018, there have been an increase in discontent from policy advisors, academics and even government officials with President Xi's ambitious policy agenda. Some of the criticisms focus on his excessive "foreign aid" to countries in Africa and the Middle East with obvious reference to his BRI projects. The public airing of such a criticism may indicate the emergence of a consensus that Beijing should scale back its BRI ambition.

In the face of international and domestic criticisms about its debt-trap finance approach to push the BRI, senior Chinese leaders seem to want

[3] See *Travel and Tour World*, "Sri Lanka's £162 Million Mattala Rajapaksa International Airport Faces Uncertain Future as It Struggles with Just Seven Passengers Per Week", March 7, 2025. Retrieved from https://www.travelandtourworld.com/news/article/sri-lankas-162-million-mattala-rajapaksa-international-airport-faces-uncertain-future-as-it-struggles-with-just-seven-passengers-per-week/.

to change to a more judicious lending approach since 2019. Indeed, with debt distress in borrower countries on the rise due to overly ambitious investments and poor project planning, they have little choice. Earlier research showed that more than two dozen countries, mostly emerging economies, owed debt equivalent to at least 10% of their GDP to the Chinese government (Horn et al., 2019). Though updates on this data are not available, it is likely that the situation has not improved much as economic volatility and geopolitical risks in the developing nations have increased since 2020. The point is that there is a limit to how much debt countries are willing, or able, to take on before a financial crisis emerge.

When the debtors struggle to repay, the loans have to be renegotiated. While this puts the debtors in a vulnerable political position susceptible to China's pressure/influence, it can also prove costly for the Chinese creditors. China's state banks typically extend loan terms or repayment deadlines and sometimes have little option but to refinance loans at reduced rates or even to forgive debts under Beijing's instruction. Hence, many Chinese officials have signalled a desire to reduce policy loans and foster alternative modes of financing involving private-sector creditors (Wong & Areddy, 2019).

BRI Ambition Scaled Back

Macroeconomic forces have also prompted President Xi to scale back his BRI ambition. When the BRI was launched in September 2013, China enjoyed a current account surplus with huge foreign exchange reserves close to USD4 trillion. Its steel, cement and construction industries were plagued by excess capacity with "hungry" engineering firms looking for new markets. Such a macroeconomic backdrop justified lavish lending to foreign governments in exchange for lucrative construction and engineering contracts. However, China's current account surplus peaked in 2017 at more than 12% of GDP and has fallen to about 1% of GDP in 2024. Greater regulatory scrutiny of BRI projects and more caution on overseas lending have naturally become an economic necessity.

As a result, the BRI has slimmed down indeed, even if it retrains political importance. This can be seen in the declining trend of China's foreign loan data. The growth of China's external loans rose sharply after the BRI was launched in late 2013. It dropped between late 2015 and 2016 when Beijing tightened up on capital controls to stem rampant capital outflows during the market chaos but surged again in 2017 and 2018. During this period, China's policy banks, notably China Development Bank and Export–Import Bank of China, and large state-owned commercial banks were the key players extending large-scale loans for infrastructure and engineering projects in developing countries, which likely included many BRI countries. The surge in foreign loans in 2010 and 2021 (Fig. 7.9) was distorted by the Covid pandemic when China extended foreign loans to help the developing world fight the health crisis. These loans were not likely related to engineering and infrastructure projects.

Discounting this distortion, foreign lending exhibited a downward trend (see Fig. 7.9), reflecting a slowdown in the BRI funding expansion (ambition). Growth in China foreign lending, including to the BRI countries, is likely to stabilise at lower levels going forward as risk assessment and management take precedence over high-risk sovereign loans opportunities.

Note that these numbers have limitations. China does not report any details on foreign lending flows, such as the loans' destinations, purposes and recipients, or any breakdowns between its official lending and private-sector lending. So, it is tricky to draw conclusions from the aggregate data. A lot of loans to foreign engineering and construction projects are hidden in the form of Chinese bank lending to state-owned contractors in the domestic system. While the Chinese government may have tighter

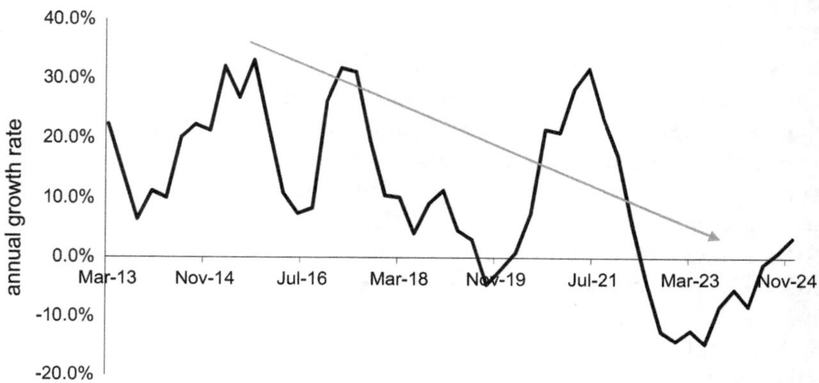

Fig. 7.9 China's overseas lending* (*Note* *Balance of payments data. *Sources* CEIC, author)

scrutiny of these loans and, thus, makes it harder for the recipient countries to abuse the Chinese loans, it also means there are no details on cross-border transactions for monitoring and analysis. The actual foreign lending is almost certainly higher than the official data suggests, though the growth trends should not differ much.

In a nutshell, the BRI faces constraints on both the supply and the demand sides. On one hand, tighter financing and more stringent project controls are forcing Chinese engineering and construction firms to be more vigilant. On the other hand, the recipient countries are becoming more careful about agreeing to Chinese-funded projects, as they seek to avoid becoming financially trapped by Beijing.

The BRI is still moving forward, and China is still signing more countries into the network. The number of BRI countries grew from 54 in 2017 to 150 in 2023. In a way, Beijing's attempts to reset the BRI's direction as a multilateral endeavour that respects international norms are making an impact—even if many European Union members remain wary of China's influence. However, with economic, regulatory and political forces constraining the BRI's expansion and ambition, one should not exaggerate the concerns about its disruption to the global balance of power. There are benefits that the BRI will bring to the global system, and if that is a disruption because it forces the existing powers to rethink their international policies and contribution to the world, it should be seen as a benign disruption.

From BRI to Structural Rebalancing

China's attempt to move from investment-led growth to consumption-led growth is inherently contractionary. If the BRI strategy can help rejuvenate an investment and trade boom in the medium term, it will help lessen this structural drag on China's domestic demand growth and improve investment returns. Hence, the BRI is instrumental in remaking China's growth model.

It is not entirely correct to view the AIIB-facilitated infrastructure investment drive as a way for China to export its excess investment and revive the investment-led growth model, as some China critics have claimed. The rebalancing from investment-led growth to consumption-led growth can only happen very gradually in order to minimise the shock on the economy during the transition period. This is because the marginal propensity to consume[4] (or MPC) is less than 1. This means that one yuan increase in income only elicits less than a yuan increase in consumption. However, one yuan cut in investment will reduce GDP by one yuan (or more, if the knock-on effect of investment in one sector on other sectors is considered).

This will not be a problem in a closed economy because whatever is saved goes back to support investment, which in turn generates GDP growth. But China is not a closed system anymore; or at least it is not as closed as it used to be before economic reforms some 40 years ago. This means that there are leakages from the system where savings could go to buy imports or simply flow out of the country looking for a better home. After all, the national policy under the Xi Jinping government is to reduce the growth reliance on investment so that the savings do not necessarily flow back into domestic investment. Thus, a one-for-one rebalancing from investment to consumption is inherently contractionary for growth.

This is an especially acute problem for China because its MPC is significantly lower than that of many other countries. On average, China's MPC is less than 0.5 (reflecting its high national saving preference), while in many other countries it is higher than 0.6. In other words, if the Chinese government were to push for a fast rebalancing (as some observers argued it should) by cutting investment, say by one yuan, and offset that investment reduction by giving one yuan back to the people, GDP would fall by one yuan (or more depending on the knock-on effect) while private consumption would only rise by less than 50 cents. This would result in a more than 50 cents net contraction in national income.

Hence, the medium-term measures to rebalance the economy should be to cut investment at a very gradual pace, or even to keep the investment-to-GDP ratio stable, and at the same time encourage private consumption growth by boosting the MPC through structural reforms, such as financial liberalisation (to allow inter-temporal consumption choice through borrowing), social safety net improvement (to strengthen consumer confidence) and income growth and redistribution (to reduce income inequality and, thus, raise the spending power of the poor who typically have a higher MPC than the rich).

[4] The marginal propensity to consume is defined as the change in private consumption per unit change in income.

In a nutshell, investment cannot fall too fast; it has to remain large in the short to medium term to generate jobs and income in order to generate consumption. Other structural changes are needed to complement the rebalancing effort. The AIIB and the BRI plans can facilitate this expenditure-switching by boosting infrastructure investment to lessen the negative income shock resulting from China's weak MPC in the rebalancing process. At the same time, they will improve the economic outlook of Asia by boosting regional investment and trade. Finally, as discussed above, evidence so far indicates that the AIIB has been abiding by the international rules of the game instead of upending the order of global development finance.

References

Blackwell, R. D., & Tellis, A. J. (2015, March). *Revisiting US Grand Strategy Toward China* (Council Special Report No. 72). Council on Foreign Relations.

Chellaney, B. (2017, January 23). *China's Debt-Trap Diplomacy*. Project Syndicate.

Horn, S., Reinhart, C., & Trebesch, C. (2019, June). *China's Overseas Lending* (Keil Working Paper, No. 2132). Keil Institute for the World Economy.

HSBC. (2024, October 2). *China's Going Global*. HSBC Global Banking and Markets. https://www.gbm.hsbc.com/en-gb/insights/market-and-regulatory-insights/china-going-global

Hurley, J., Morris, S., & Portelance, G. (2018, March). *Examining the Debt Implications of the Belt and Road Initiative from a Policy Perspective* (CGD Policy Paper 121). Centre for Global Development.

Kaleji, V. (2024, October 23). *China's Debt-Trap Diplomacy in Central Asia*. The Central Asia-Caucasus Analyst. https://www.cacianalyst.org/publications/analytical-articles/item/13823-chinas-debt-trap-diplomacy-in-central-asia.html

Krishnan, A. (2017, January 18). China Defends Pak Corridor After Modi Criticism of Projects. *India Today*. http://indiatoday.intoday.in/story/china-pakistan-economic-corridor-narendra-modi-pakistan-occupied-kashmir/1/860334.html

Lo, C. (2017). *Demystifying China's Mega Trends: The Driving Forces That Will Shake Up China and the World*. Emerald Publishing.

Oliveira, G., Murton, G., Rippa, A., et al. (2020, October). China's Belt and Road Initiative: Views from the Ground. *Political Geography* (Vol. 82).

PTI. (2023, October 19). India Reiterates Opposition to China's Belt and Road Initiative. *The Economic Times*, English Edition. https://economictimes.indiatimes.com/news/india/india-reiterates-opposition-to-chinas-belt-and-road-initiative/articleshow/104562541.cms?from=mdr

Shen. M. (2024, June 13). *More Chinese Firms Keen to Expand Overseas, Survey Finds*. SHINE.CN. https://www.shine.cn/biz/economy/2406139523/

The White House. (2018, June). How China's Economic Aggression Threatens the Technologies and Intellectual Property of the United States and the World. *White House Office of Trade and Manufacturing Policy*.

Wong, C. H., & Areddy, J. T. (2019, April 26). Beijing Appeals for Foreign Funds in Belt-and-Road Adjustment. *The Wall Street Journal*.

CHAPTER 8

Trade War Turning the World Upside Down

China's international trade expansion and rapid technological advancement lie in the heart of the Sino-US tensions as China's ambition to grow assertively clashes with the US's aggressive defence to protect its global power status. Misunderstanding breeds mistrust which has aggravated the tension build-up. However, when the elephants dance, as the saying goes, it is not safe for the chickens. The elephants are the US and China, and the chickens are the rest of the world, notably the smaller emerging economies, who could get crushed. We examine the trade conflict in this chapter and assess the "tech war" in the next chapter.

The Sino-US trade war that started in 2018, and intensified in 2025, is one of the largest disruptions with far-reaching implications on the global system. The trade conflict will not go away because it is not just about economics but also about strategic competition between an emerging power and an incumbent power fighting over technology and national security grounds. In the competition, not just China but also the US is creating significant global disruptive forces, notably through President Donald Trump's mercurial policy approach. While conventional wisdom sees his erratic policies as un-systematic and as acts without thorough strategic considerations, I beg to disagree.

In the trade war environment, both China and the US could be the culprit for triggering a currency war, which could aggravate other economic and financial disruptive forces. There will be collateral damages

C. Lo, *Clash of the Economic Titans: China and the United States*,
https://doi.org/10.1007/978-981-95-2510-2_8

on other innocent by-standers, the "chickens", as well as on the US, despite the US administration's belief that China would be the biggest loser. Despite the increase in trade tension, however, there is no evidence of China shifting to a currency devaluation policy. A stable currency with a strong bias is still Beijing's best foreign exchange policy choice as it strives to make the renminbi a global currency.

Even Partial De-globalisation Would Be Damaging

In the longer term, both China and the US seem to be striving for onshoring the globalised production chains built over the past few decades. China is doing it through import substitution to minimise the foreign share of its industrial base but still wants to pursue multilateralism. The US is doing it via its "America First" policy that essentially reverts to protectionism and isolationism. Even partial success of these initiatives could be damaging for the global system. Why?

Firstly, the breaking up of the global supply chains will likely bring back inflation by reversing the disinflationary forces brought about by globalisation. Secondly, cross-border production chains have been a force for keeping peace and stability as they raise the cost of armed conflicts. Reverting back to national production structures with a domestic focus that disregards global affairs raises the possibility of big countries trying to settle their differences by force.

The increasing assertiveness of China to make its presence felt on the global stage and the aggressiveness of the US to defend its world number one status are raising the geopolitical risk of two dancing elephants crushing the chickens. This risk of the Thucydides Trap unfolding has become more acute since 2010 when China's economic and technological progress becomes noticeable to the world (see Chapter 1) while the US grapples with mounting debt, ageing infrastructure and a political landscape riddled with gridlock. The infrastructure disparity, for example, is particularly striking and threatens to unseat the established superpower (the US).

China has built the largest and most advanced high-speed rail network, which it has exported to many developing countries. However, the US has struggled with outdated roads and unreliable and unsafe public transport. China's rail system spans over 25,000 miles (or over 40,233 kilometres) allowing passengers to travel between major cities like Beijing and Shanghai in just a few hours, which is even faster and cheaper than flying. The fastest train in the US, Amtrak's Acela Express, reaches a mere 240 km/h, is dwarfed by China's CR450, the fastest train in the world with a top speed of 450 km/h. Beyond rail, China's construction of modern airports and smart cities far outpaces the US whose infrastructure is plagued by underfunding and delays.

China has made all these possible by having a high savings rate, which hovers around 44% of GDP, compared to less than 4% of GDP in the US. Crucially, decades of significant public-sector dissaving, i.e. fiscal deficit, in the US have overwhelmed the positive private-sector saving, plaguing America with a chronic (over two decades) current account deficit. By contrast, China has a chronic current account surplus.

It's a Global Imbalance

The difference between their current account balances lays bare the fact that the Sino-US trade war is a global economic imbalance problem where China has too much savings (and too little consumption) while the US has excess consumption (and too little savings). The individual disequilibria have kept the world economic system in an unstable equilibrium for decades with China supplying the US with surplus savings for supporting America's excess consumption. Imposing punitive tariffs on China alone cannot resolve the problem, as US President Donald Trump and his advisors incorrectly believe. The fundamental solution should be for China to reduce savings and increase consumption and for the US to increase savings and reduce consumption. China has been working on its economic restructuring to address this global imbalance. However, by resorting to trade war and protectionism the US is denying its problem and heading in the wrong direction.

The irony is that China's economic rebalancing *per se* is a disruption to the global *status quo* of unstable equilibrium. China was an export-led economy, reflecting its saving surplus, while the American consumer was its largest customer, reflecting the US's saving deficit. However, China has moved away from its export-led growth to domestic-led growth since 2009. This can be seen in the negative contribution of net exports to China's GDP growth most of the time (Fig. 8.1).

Given this fact, it is amazing that so many American politicians and even analysts still think China is export-led economy and have, thus, prescribed punitive tariffs as the solution to "beat" China and turn around the massive US trade deficit with China. Evidence already showed that

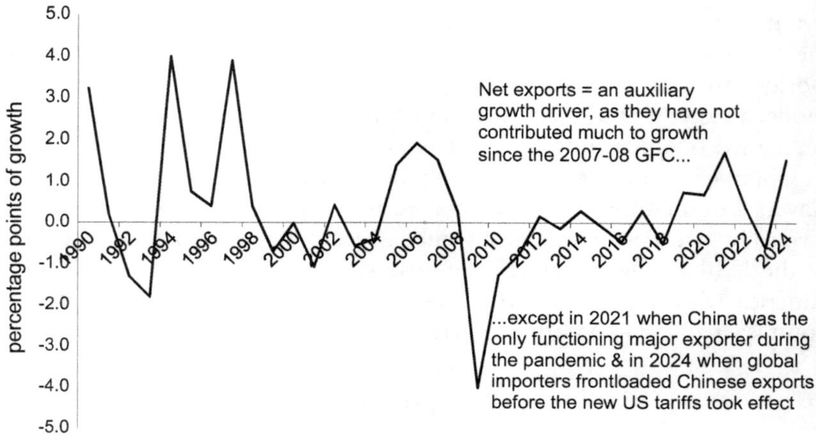

Fig. 8.1 Share of China's net exports contribution to GDP growth (*Sources* CEIC, author)

they did not work, as discussed in Chapter 3, as China's global share of exports has risen since the trade war started in 2018 while that of the US has fallen.

Crucially, in its restructuring process, China has moved up the value-added ladder, shed processing trade and low-value exports and become the centre of the global supply chains by supplying an increasing amount of intermediate goods to the world. This means that China has reduced its role as an input demander and increased its role as an intermediate goods supplier. This structural change in trade dynamics inevitably disrupts the global trade structure. But it should be seen as a benign disruption because it has encouraged international trade growth and division of labour, thus bringing down production costs and enhancing production efficiency.

Meanwhile, the US has remained the world's largest consumer. It still depends heavily on China and Asia to provide low-cost goods for Americans to live beyond their means. From a macroeconomic perspective, this means America still depends heavily on China and other surplus countries, notably Germany and Japan, to fund its twin (current account and fiscal) deficits through heavy buying of US dollar assets, notably Treasury bonds. Mr. Trump has disrupted this global relationship by waging a trade war with China in 2018 (in his first presidency) and with the world in 2025 (in his second presidency).

By using tariffs as the key weapon in the trade wars, Mr. Trump is also inflicting a dangerous disruption to the US and potentially disastrous spillover effects on the global system. Economic theory has long argued that tariffs are better as an industrial policy to nurture infant industries in underdeveloped countries in their early stage of development under an open trade system. But tariffs are ineffective in correcting trade imbalances. This is because tariffs cut imports, but they do not boost exports. US consumption will fall, but without an increase in exports, *ceteris paribus*, US economic growth will fall.

The situation will be worse if other countries retaliate. That could potentially result in a collapse in global consumption and even world depression. This happened before in American history, in 1828 and 1930 when massive US tariff hikes exacerbated existing economic tensions and eventually led to global depression (ET Online, 2025). In 2025, the US under the Trump administration again started a global trade war with massive tariff hikes. What is intriguing is the timing, from 1828 to 1930 to 2025 they are all about 100 years apart. So, the risk of the 2025 tariff war creating a massive disruption to the global system by aggravating the prevailing geopolitical and economic fault lines is real. Time will tell.

Crushing the Chickens

The trade war in 2025, which is still evolving at the time of writing, is especially damaging because it is not just a bilateral trade conflict between China and the US. Mr. Trump announced in April 2025 a reciprocal tariffs framework encompassing all its trading partner countries.[1] It blends a 10% universal tariff with country-specific layers. Tariff rates in the country layers vary widely, with some reaching as high as 49% at the initial stage of the trade war.[2] This framework, if sustained, pushes international

[1] Reciprocal tariffs on imports mean that whatever countries charge the US, the US will charge them the same. For example, when country X charges a 10% tariff rate on imports from the US, while the US only charges a 3% tariff rate on its imports from X, the reciprocal tariff mechanism will raise the US tariff rate on X by 7 percentage points so that the US also charges imports from country X a 10% tariff rate.

[2] In mid-April 2025, Trump raised the reciprocal tariff rate on China to 145%, although this was later lowered back down to 30% in early May as the two countries started trade negotiations.

trade into a new paradigm of import substitution via strategic intervention in market pricing. To put it bluntly, it distorts the international market pricing mechanism and adds to the forces of de-globalisation and protectionism. Open economies, like those in Asia, will suffer the most.

The new tariff framework is a significant expansion of US trade policy that does not simply adjust tariff levels. It also positions the US market strategically for negotiation,[3] disrupts trade flows, distorts international pricing and pushes for onshoring because the framework embraces import substitution. The structure explicitly penalises foreign producers to encourage domestic manufacturing, disregarding the law of comparative advantage in international trade.

Asian economies are the most vulnerable to the reciprocal tariffs because:

1. many Asian countries are small open economies, with export-GDP ratios in excess of 50% and a high percentage of exports to the US (e.g. Vietnam's exports to the US is almost 30% of its GDP in 2024, and Taiwan, Malaysia and Thailand each has exports to the US accounting for more than 10% of their GDP, and
2. most regional countries have higher tariff rates than, and run large trade surpluses with, the US. Mr. Trump made it very clear that he would hit those countries that run large trade surpluses with the US with higher tariffs. Hence, Vietnam, Thailand and China were hit with the highest tariff increases in Trump's initial tariff announcement (Fig. 8.2).

However, the reciprocal tariffs are a wrong policy approach, and it could potentially hurt the US's credibility in the developing world. From a competition perspective, these tariffs could give China the room to increase its global influence, as opposed to what the US intends to do. Many developing economies have higher tariffs out of necessity, not choice. This is because they are not just cash-strapped but also have a lot less administrative capacity than the developed countries to raise revenues.

[3] Trump said in his reciprocal tariffs announcement in April 2025 that these tariff rates could be negotiated down if the targeted countries lower trade barriers to US exports.

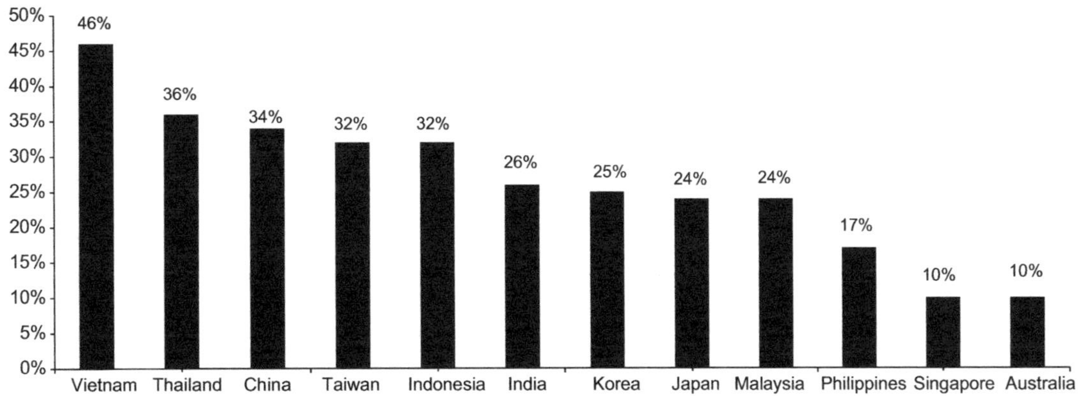

Fig. 8.2 Targeted country-specific tariff rates on Asia, per US announcement on 2 April 2025 (*Sources* The White House, author)

For the developing countries, levying taxes at a limited number of ports of entry is much easier than collecting income, payroll and value-added taxes that make up the bulk of the tax base in advanced economies. Granted, tariffs are a distortion to the developing economies, and their governments know that. However, the fact that they nevertheless keep higher tariffs in place is a sign of their challenging fiscal realities, not of a lack of trade policy acumen.

From a macroeconomic perspective, a sustained sharp rise in tariffs will boost inflation shortly after they are implemented and inflict significant contractionary pressures on economic growth after the inflationary impact is fed through. This increases the risk of stagflation, not just for the Asian open economies but also for the global economy, including the US. The tariffs' indirect negative effects on growth are especially difficult to gauge because they stem from damaging global confidence, asset prices and consequently capital expenditures and trade. But they are a crucial channel for the growth drag to trickle down to the countries. Generally, the more open an economy is, the bigger the growth drag from tariffs will be.

The US reciprocal tariffs have targeted Vietnam in particular because it has served as a jumping board for China to export to the US and eschew US tariffs since the first round of the trade war in 2018. Indeed, Vietnam has been the focus of increasing intra-regional foreign direct investment (FDI) from China (and also Korea and Japan) due to its cheaper manufacturing cost, preferential government policy treatment and improving infrastructure. FDI from these three major Asian economies has far exceeded that from the US (Figs. 8.3 and 8.4). These FDI trends also reflect the impetus of the China + 1 strategy across the multinational business community for hedging against Sino-US political risk (see Chapter 2). Hence, Vietnam's exports to the US, especially in capital goods and computers/computer parts, have grown sharply since 2019.

By imposing lofty tariffs on Vietnam and China's Asian supply-chain partners (Fig. 8.5), the US aims at weakening China's ability to divert trade to other countries for expanding its economic influence and to offset the US tariff impact (see Chapter 2). The prospect for China, to cool trade and political tensions even in the long term is not good because the reciprocal tariff framework is rooted in strategic objectives to compete with China and contain its global expansion.

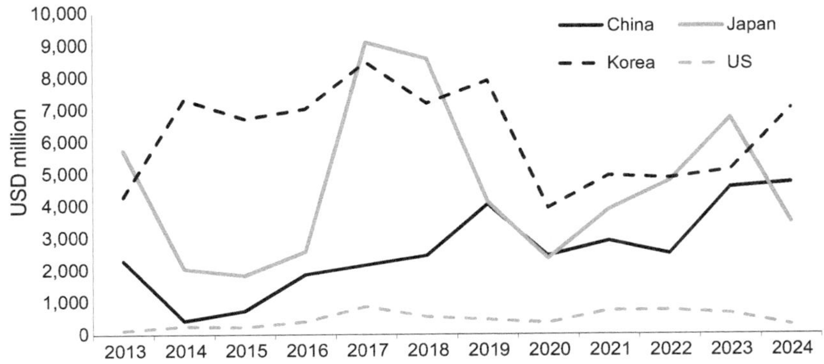

Fig. 8.3 FDI inflows to Vietnam (registered capital) (*Sources* CEIC, author)

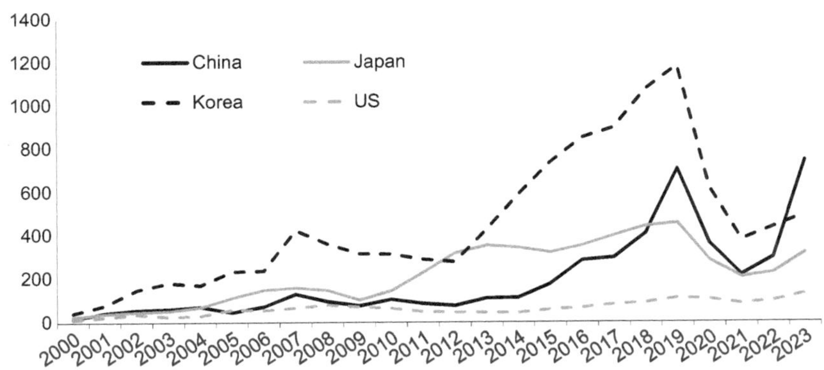

Fig. 8.4 FDI inflows to Vietnam (no. of licensed projects) (*Sources* CEIC, author)

The Chickens Fight Back

The regional countries can negotiate with the US to lower the tariffs. If that fails, they can impose retaliatory measures and devalue their currencies. However, these are the very measures that disrupt supply chains, slow global trade and economic growth and risk triggering another currency

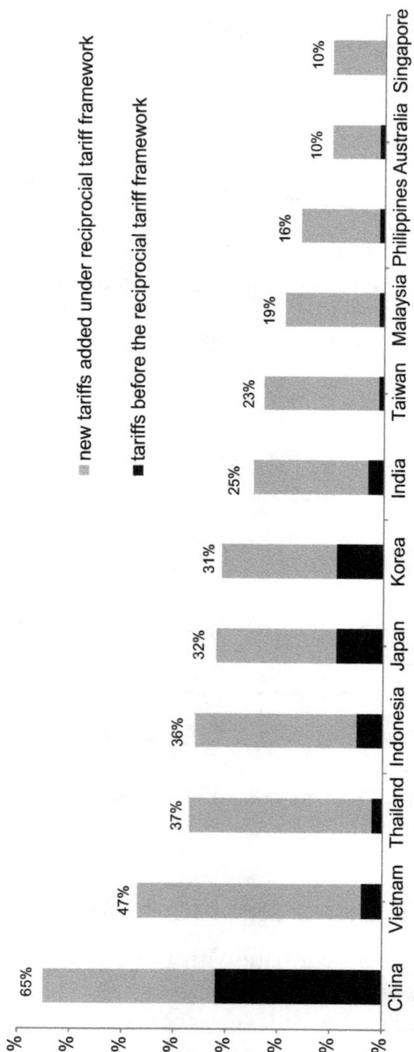

Fig. 8.5 Total tariff rates on Asia under the reciprocal tariff framework (*Sources* The White House, author)

war. The currency situation is especially complicated because other countries cannot depreciate their way out of the growth doldrums if the USD is also weakening at the same time.

Indeed, that was what happened after Mr. Trump announced his intention on imposing reciprocal tariffs shortly after he won the presidential election in January 2025. The expectation of US growth faltering faster under the global tariff war than that of other economies has weighed on the USD exchange rate, nullifying the depreciation effects of other currencies on boosting their exports and thus prompting the other countries to push for more currency depreciation. This means that the competitive devaluation dynamics could worsen if and when the trade war intensifies over time leading to a currency war.

The world also worries about the "elephant's" (China's) exchange rate policy because the correlation between the movement of the regional (especially Asian) currencies and that of China's currency has risen sharply since 2010 (Lo, 2021, pp. 133–134). Throughout the last currency war between 2010 and 2018, China did not devalue. Currency devaluation still is not the optimal strategy for China as Beijing wants to pursue a stable exchange rate policy to foster renminbi internationalisation and build its geopolitical image as a stable and investible country.

However, the People's Bank of China (PBoC) has tolerated more renminbi weakness by pursuing a managed-float exchange rate regime since 2015 as long as the exchange rate movement is gradual and orderly. The purpose of allowing bigger exchange rate adjustments is to lessen the impact of external shocks, like trade war, on the economy and facilitate domestic policy easing to stabilise GDP growth (Lo, 2021, Chapter 8) under the "Impossible Trinity" policy constraint[4] (Lo, 2015, Chapter 1). In the 2018–2019 tariff war episode, the renminbi depreciated by a total 14% against the USD in two years. What this means is that if China allows more renminbi weakness in response to the trade war, it could aggravate the devaluation pressure on other regional currencies.

Boosting domestic sector growth is another way for a country to counter the US tariff drag on growth. Generally, a country that runs a fiscal surplus is well positioned to pursue fiscal expansion. For a fiscal

[4] The Impossible Trinity, also known as the Mundell-Fleming Trilemma, is an economic theory stating that a country cannot control the exchange and the interest rate at the same time under an open capital account. It must choose between an independent monetary policy (i.e. controlling the interest rate) and a fixed exchange rate at any given time.

deficit country, if it runs a current account surplus that overwhelms the fiscal deficit, the resultant twin (fiscal balance + current account balance) surplus will also allow it to pursue fiscal easing and retain investor confidence at the same time. Most regional economies are either running fiscal surpluses or twin surpluses (Fig. 8.6). That gives the region some defensive power to manage the reciprocal tariff shock.

Confused by "Trumponomics"

China's emergence on the global stage has a connection with the US's role in creating disruptive forces via President Trump's "will-they-or-won't-they" and "on-again off-again" policy uncertainty in driving American foreign and trade policies (Davis, 2019). His global policy confusion was manifested most clearly in his dealing with North Korea on the denuclearisation talks in 2017, in the Sino-US trade negotiations between 2018 and 2020, and again in his global tariff war in 2025 when these events created significant volatility to global markets.

In his second presidency that started in 2025, Mr. Trump combined this mercurial policy behaviour with pro-market and protectionist policies (dubbed as "Trumponomics" by financial market players) and created even more confusion and bigger market volatility than his previous policy moves.

For example, global stock markets fell by more than 10% on 3 April 2025 after his announcement of the reciprocal tariff framework. A week later, he softened his stance by announcing to pause the reciprocal tariffs by 90 days. That sent the markets skyrocketing by 10% on the day of announcement, but only to drop by over 5% the next day when he escalated the tariff war with China by increasing tariffs on Chinese imports to 145% (and China retaliated by imposing 125% tariffs on US imports). While many observers think he has no strategic framework for formulating his policies, I think there is much more to the fickle, unpredictable and conflicting pattern in Mr. Trump's negotiation tactics than meets the eye.

The Game Theory in economics provides insights into his behaviour and helps deduce policy and market implications. Let us examine the denuclearisation talks in Mr. Trump's first presidency because it carries important implications for understanding the disruption of the Sino-US trade conflict. Those who are not familiar with the Nash equilibrium concept can refer to the Appendix at the end of this chapter.

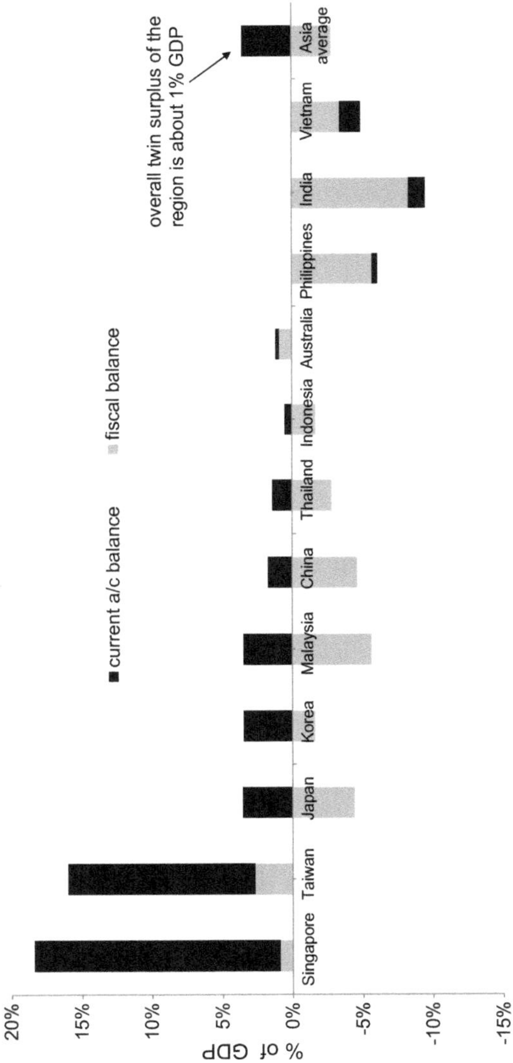

Fig. 8.6 Asian countries' fiscal and current account balances (2023/2024) (*Sources* CEIC, author)

The trouble with understanding Mr. Trump's erratic behaviour is that we tend to think rationally about his negotiations with his counterparts reaching a Nash equilibrium (in the North Korea denuclearisation talks, for example). In Game Theory, a Nash equilibrium is a solution concept of a competitive game involving two or more players in which each player is assumed to know the best strategies of the other players when he/she picks his/her strategy. This also implies an assumption of perfect information in the game. If each player has chosen a strategy and no player can make further gains by changing strategies while the other players keep theirs unchanged, then the prevailing set of strategy choices and the corresponding payoffs constitutes a Nash equilibrium.

Consider two countries, A and B, trying to engage each other in denuclearisation talks. Their moves are in Nash equilibrium if A is making the best decision it can, taking into account B's decision while B's decision remains unchanged; and B is making the best decision it can, considering A's decision while A's decision remains unchanged. In other words, a strategy profile is a Nash equilibrium if no player can do better by unilaterally changing his/her strategy.

We tend to think in a Nash equilibrium framework for working out a solution for the North Korea crisis because there are visible goals for Trump, Kim and all relevant parties:

- All parties want to reduce tensions and avoid a nuclear war.
- Seoul wants to normalise relations with Pyongyang.
- Mr. Trump wants to secure a foreign policy win for his administration.
- Mr. Kim has multiple goals including relief from Washington's economic sanctions, security guarantees of no attack and international recognition of its nuclear power status.
- Beijing wants to avoid the prospect of North/South Korean unification under the US umbrella.
- Russia wants to leverage on this political chaos to increase its influence in North Asia.

So, analysts rationally assume each party, knowing the other party's strategy to get what it wants, would work towards a Nash equilibrium outcome—denuclearisation through political dialogue.

However, what they have missed by thinking in such a way is that these goals may have changed or have been misunderstood, thus introducing imperfect information to the game, so that the initial strategies chosen to achieve them have also changed. There are two cases in point: One is the implicit strategic alliance, which was built in early 2018, between Beijing/Seoul and Pyongyang has emboldened North Korea's Mr. Kim to become more defiant against the US, and two is the difference in the definition of denuclearisation between Washington and Pyongyang.[5]

Trump's Optimal Strategy

In engaging denuclearisation talks with North Korea, Mr. Trump was, in my view, pursuing an optimal (but not commonly understood) strategy in driving for a corner solution for the benefit of the US (please refer to the Appendix for the concept of a corner solution). Theoretically, a corner solution is a special solution to one's maximisation problem in which the quantity of one of the arguments in the maximised function is zero. This occurs when the player is either unwilling or unable to make a trade-off.

For example, when someone says, "I won't buy that at any price" or "I will do this at any cost", these are corner solutions. The word "corner" refers to the fact that if one graphs the maximisation problem, the optimal point will occur at the "corner" created by the budget constraint and one axis.

From Mr. Trump's perspective, given the past Presidents' failure in their approaches to deal with North Korea's nuclear programme, he was unwilling to make the same mistakes. So, he tried to shift North Korea's behaviour away from a predictable Nash equilibrium, which was disadvantageous to the US in political and military terms (due to the past failures). He introduced "noises or imperfect information" to the game by being erratic in order to reach his undisclosed corner solution of gaining full control of the denuclearisation talks and stress-testing Pyongyang's behaviour.

Of course, a non-Nash game is unfamiliar, and uncomfortable, to the world's sedated bureaucrats and political observers. But it is familiar to the

[5] Washington demanded the complete, verifiable and irreversible dismantlement of North Korea's nuclear weapons programme. Pyongyang said it could consider giving up its nuclear arsenal if Washington withdrew its nuclear umbrella of deterrence from South Korea and Japan and withdrew all its troops from South Korea.

seasoned military generals in the US, China, Russia and North Korea. Mr. Kim's best generals should also be familiar with such seemingly irrational antics, unless he has killed them all to reduce any threats to him.

In a non-Nash game, there are many undisclosed objectives from the proponent (or the driver of the game, or the US in our case), i.e. there is imperfect information. Other nations should not lock themselves into commitments with the US and with one another on the basis of the seeming obvious goals (e.g. denuclearisation, peace in Asia, US military withdrawal, trade war, etc.). This also means that at any point in time, anything that seems obvious could be wrong in such a game. And because of this confusion, global markets will be, and have been, wacked with volatility and disruptions.

Relevance to China

Mr. Trump has been playing a similar non-Nash game with China in his trade negotiations. One may wonder what his next unpredictable move would be in shocking the trade negotiation framework to get what he wants? What about an attack on the renminbi, i.e. a currency war alongside a trade war with China?

Before Mr. Trump became the President, US policy for maintaining the dollar's primacy was largely passive, if not conciliatory. Even when it was clear that China was promoting the renminbi as an alternative to the dollar (despite the technical implausibility in the medium-term), the Obama administration did nothing to push back on the Chinese effort. That was because the players were expecting a Nash equilibrium outcome in which China and the US would employ their best strategies to achieve their goals, given their knowledge of the other's strategy.

However, when Mr. Trump came and all bets on a Nash equilibrium were off, as he had gone on the offensive by introducing "imperfect information" to the game through erratic policies and conflicting messages (i.e. making the game non-Nash). The US has a great incentive to play more non-Nash games with China in its attempt to contain China's potential challenge to its global supremacy status. Hence, the Trump policies and their legacy in affecting future policy direction will play a crucial role in creating global disruption.

Damage to the US

The trade war disruption does not only hurt China, but it also hurts the US and other regional economies. China has potential "nuclear options" to hit the US companies operating in China by using regulatory and non-trade barriers. This would be very damaging for the US because it has more investments in China than China has in the US (Fig. 8.7). Estimates by China's State Council White paper in April 2025 showed that total sales of US-invested companies in China amounted to USD491 billion in 2022 while sales of Chinese companies in the US only totalled USD79 billion. Essentially, no US product sold in China, or US company invested in China, would be considered safe from its retaliation.

Since the trade war started in 2018, Beijing has been identifying non-tariff measures that could limit investment or market access by US firms. There are a large number of regulatory tools it could deploy. Evidence from previous economic conflicts shows that the measures on restricting trade and/or tourist flows with Japan, South Korea, Norway, the Philippines, Taiwan and Mongolia, had inflicted economic damages in these economies at little costs to China. The US economy is much bigger and has deeper ties with the Chinese economy, so the potential economic damage from the trade conflict on China could also be larger.

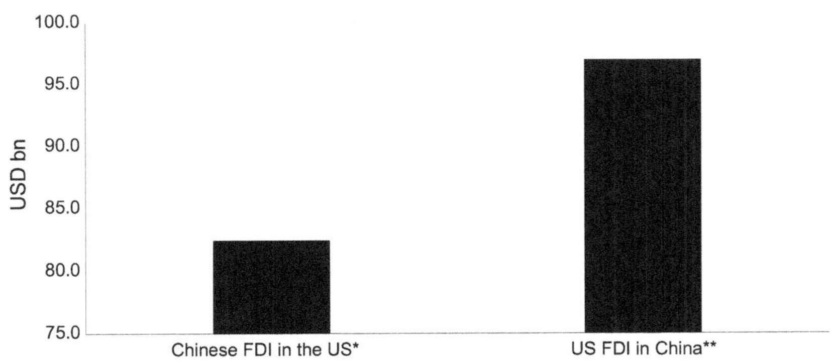

Fig. 8.7 Cumulative foreign direct investment (FDI) (*Notes* *Data started in 2003 through 2023. **Data started in 1985 throgh 2023. *Sources* CEIC, author)

The first targets of Chinese retaliation would likely to be on US products that are less consequential and more replaceable. US aeroplanes by Boeing are a large target. Hollywood is also an easy target, as earnings from the massive Chinese market are increasingly important for American movie makers. Beijing can easily instruct the two state-owned movie distributors to halt or delay distribution of American films or tell video-on-demand companies to reduce the number of US TV shows they stream. It can also tighten censorship requirements, delay films' release dates in China, shorten theatrical release periods or keep movies off screens during lucrative holiday seasons. These latter non-trade barriers have already been put in place for a while and have been a chief complaint by American movie producers.

American pharmaceutical companies are also an easy target. Beijing can easily use targeted regulations to slow approval of foreign drug applications by US companies, hurting their market share in China. Agriculture is another sector where Chinese authorities have enormous regulatory discretion. Excuses such as health and sanitation concerns have already been used to prolong customs checks and quarantine periods to restrict many agricultural imports from America. The regulatory barrier can easily be raised and extend to include US genetically modified crops sold in China, which have been facing delays in the approval process that is already taking years.

American automakers are also a big target in Chinese retaliation. China's car market is the world's largest and one of the most competitive. American brands accounted for only 6% of passenger-car sales in China in 2024, down from 11% in 2018 when the trade war started. Since substitutes from both domestic and foreign cars are readily available and auto brands are usually tied to national identity, cars have been a favourite target in previous disputes.

South Korean and Japanese automakers saw their sales and market share drop sharply in China when their relations with China turned sour in 2017 and 2012, respectively. In both cases, Beijing said consumer outrage, not government action, was the cause for boycotting the foreign cars. But who really knew. Beijing could also easily limit the growth of US automakers by withholding or slowing approvals for new factories or models or distribution licences.

Technology companies are also potential targets for regulatory retaliation. Take Apple Inc., which had USD67 billion in sales in China in 2024 accounting for 20% of Apple's global sales. Beijing could delay issuing network licence for the iPhones and, thus, hurt Apple's launches of new iPhones and sales revenues. Although such action would also hurt the revenue of Chinese suppliers and mobile carriers, Beijing may see that as a price worth paying since it would help Chinese smartphone makers.

If China were to weaponise the tech guidelines to hit American companies, they could easily cause significant difficulties for operating in China and even shutdowns. The Center for Strategic and International Studies argues that the cybersecurity standards purposely used vague language around testing and verification so that Beijing could have broad discretion in assessing and, hence, taking actions against foreign firms (Sacks & Li, 2018). These standards could affect not only tech firms and social media but all businesses that rely on information and communications technology, including retail, fashion, e-commerce, services and manufacturing, etc.

The point is that the destructive power of China's regulatory and non-trade barriers largely operates free of constraints and could virtually hit any sector and any company according to Beijing's discretion. Chinese officials would be happy to comply with Beijing's implicit requests to carry out the retaliation as they see it as their patriotic duty to make life hard for American companies. If China deploys such "nuclear options", no one will benefit, and market risk aversion will soar and the global disruption will be significant.

Meanwhile, a macroeconomic trade weapon China can use is to hit US services imports because the US is the largest source of China's services trade deficit, i.e. China is the largest contributor to the US services trade surplus. China's imports of US services surged more than tenfold from USD5 billion in 2000 to USD55 billion in 2024. Travel dominated this category, comprising 43% of total imports, followed by Intellectual Property (IP) licensing (15%), legal and consulting services (11%), financial services (9%), transport (8%), information and communications technology (5%) and entertainment products (4%). Within travel imports, education-related spending accounted for 71%, followed by leisure travel at 22% and business travel at 7%.

In the 2025 trade war China indeed implemented some of these retaliation tools. They included imposing 125% tariffs on imports of US agricultural products, restricting imports of Hollywood movies, stopping the purchase of Boeing planes, restricting exports to the US of rare earth and other minerals that are crucial for the production of batteries, smartphones, semiconductors, and for the car and aerospace industries. Beijing also issued warnings against travelling to the US and studying in certain states in the US, which amounted to a soft restriction on services exports to the US.

Collateral Damage and Contagion

The Sino-US trade conflict also produces collateral damage on the regional economies. In particular, Asia's export-oriented economies are not immune to tighter US dollar liquidity stemming from risk aversion prompted by the Sino-US trade war. This financial disruption is seen in the decline in Asian currencies against the US dollar when the trade war started in 2018 and again in 2024-early 2025 before Trump's reciprocal tariffs[6] (Fig. 8.8). The collateral damage of the Sino-US trade friction clearly has risk implications on regional growth and asset allocation.

A slowdown in global growth due to the Sino-US trade war will lead to a loss of demand for emerging market (EM) exports. Empirical evidence shows that in Asia, GDP growth of Singapore, Malaysia and Thailand are the most sensitive to shifts in G3 growth (Europe, Japan and the

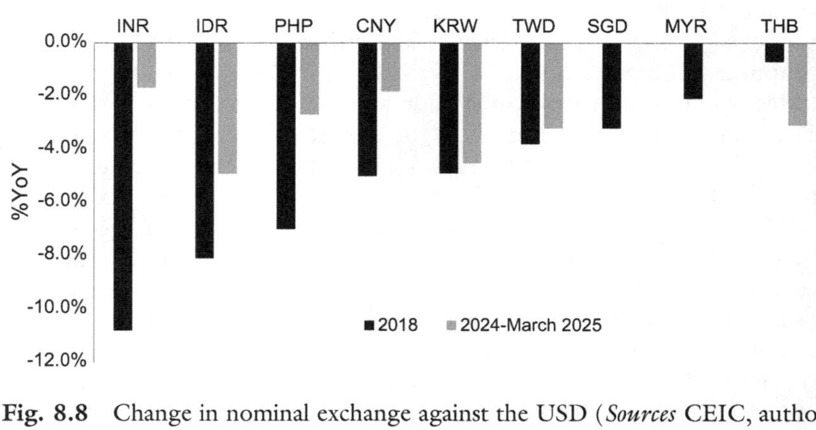

Fig. 8.8 Change in nominal exchange against the USD (*Sources* CEIC, author)

[6] The reciprocal tariffs had a negative impact on the US dollar exchange rate, thus reversing the dollar's strength since the trade tension arose, due to the markets' concerns that the tariffs could push the US into an economic recession eventually and the US Federal Reserve would have to cut interest rates sharply to save economic growth.

US). China is not sensitive due to its large continental economy and the availability of domestic stimulus tools.

The bilateral trade dispute between China and the US could have significant effects on the regional economies through the global supply chain disruption. The potential collateral damage can be estimated by stripping out the foreign value-added content (averaging about 40%) in China's gross exports and reassigning them back to its original source countries to assess these countries' ultimate export exposure to the US.

This means that when China's exports to the US drop due to the trade war, exports from these countries will also fall. My estimation shows that six of the top 10 most-exposed countries are in Asia. The damage on China would be rather limited. From the asset allocation and risk management perspectives, *ceteris paribus*, markets with the highest US-China exposure tend to be hurt the most.

There is also a contagion effect due to the increase in risk aversion, as investors reassess the economic fundamentals of EM and ponder who might be susceptible to financial contagion due to the trade shock. The key economic fault lines under scrutiny include a country's current account balance, fiscal balance, external debt and inflation. When a negative shock hits, a country will likely fall into a crisis or suffer from financial contagion when it has a combination of twin (current account and fiscal) deficits, a large foreign debt and high inflation triggering a loss of confidence.

China has none of these macroeconomic problems, as it has a current account surplus, subdue inflation and a small fiscal deficit and a small foreign debt. Most importantly, the renminbi is not convertible, i.e. not freely tradeable, so that its financial contagion risk is very small. In Asia, there are three Asian economies that have some chronic problems with twin deficits and relatively high inflation. They are India, Indonesia and the Philippines. Hence, they are always more vulnerable than their peer countries to financial contagion, as reflected by the bigger decline in their exchange rates in case of escalation in Sino-US trade tensions (see Fig. 8.8).

Overall, Asia–Pacific economies have more solid fundamentals than many other EM countries, though they are still susceptible to selling pressures from a rise in risk aversion. Crucially, the correlations of the movements between the renminbi and major Asian currencies have increased at the expense of their correlations with the US dollar and the euro in recent years. This suggests that whenever the trade conflict exerts downward pressure on the renminbi, Asia's currencies will also face more depreciation pressure, creating more disruptive forces in the global foreign exchange market.

Cold War Returning?

An increasing worry that is catching global attention is the risk of the geopolitical and trade tensions between China and the US escalating to a new cold war, which could potentially cost dearly not only China and the US but also the world system. If the end of the last Cold War fostered global economic integration, the beginning of the next Cold War between China and the US could potentially produce fragmentation, with long-term impact on even technological innovation and climate change.

Rising Sino-US trade tension is already contributing to a partial economic decoupling that is reverberating across the global system. The breaking up of the global supply chain will be extremely disruptive to the world's production ecosystem by destroying the comparative advantages of different economies and international division of labour.

It is conceivable that the world could be divided into two trading blocs, with each centring on a global power—China and the US. Intra-bloc trade may still thrive, but there might be no links between them. This scenario would be bad enough to unwind many of the globalisation benefits that the world has enjoyed for over two decades.

Continued increase in Sino-US rivalry could unravel the global system. The Trump administration has shown its ability to hurt its targeted countries by using sanctions to deny them access to the US dollar-denominated international payment system. He has even hurt the US's relationship with the ally countries by tariffs in the 2025 trade war. To hedge against this liquidity risk, America's strategic rivals, China and Russia, and even ally, the European Union, are trying to establish alternative payment systems (notably the China Cross-border Interbank Payment System or CIPS which uses S.W.I.F.T. messages and S.W.I.F.T. standards and modelled after the US FedWire).

Such financial fragmentation will disrupt the global technological landscape. This is because restrictions on technology transfers and linkages, justified on the national security basis, will give rise to competing and non-compatible standards, just like the VHS versus Betamax battle in the consumer video market in the late 1970s and 1980s, or more recently like the GSM versus CDMA mobile phone network battle in the 1990s.

It is possible that today's internet will break up into competing domains, giving rise to excessive or cut-throat competition, hurting innovation and leading to higher costs, slower adoption and even inferior products.

A more imminent concern is the disruption to the global supply chains. To avoid being hit by US tariffs, firms producing or assembling from China and exporting to the US are forced to move their production facilities to other unaffected countries. With China standing at the centre of the global supply chains, such a wave of relocation will have long-term disruptive implications for the global system. The broken supply chains will be inefficient as the benefits of the other countries leveraging on China's industrial infrastructure, technology and the size and skill of its labour force will be gone.

Appendix: Nash Equilibrium

In game theory, the Nash equilibrium is a solution concept of a non-cooperative game involving two or more players in which each player is assumed to know the equilibrium strategies of the other players, and no player has anything to gain by changing only their own strategy. If each player has chosen a strategy and no player can benefit by changing strategies while the other players keep theirs unchanged, then the current set of strategy choices and the corresponding payoffs constitutes a Nash equilibrium.

Stated simply, A and B are in Nash equilibrium if A is making the best decision she can, considering B's decision while B's decision remains unchanged, and B is making the best decision he can, taking into account A's decision while A's decision remains unchanged. Likewise, a group of players are in Nash equilibrium if each one is making the best decision possible, considering the decisions of the others in the game as long as the other parties' decisions remain unchanged.

Informally, a strategy profile is a Nash equilibrium if no player can do better by unilaterally changing his or her strategy. To see this, imagine that each player is told the strategies of the others. By knowing the strategies of the other players and treating the strategies of the other players as constant, if any player can benefit by changing his/her strategy, then that set of strategies is not a Nash equilibrium. But if every player does not want to change strategies, or is indifferent between changing and not, then that strategy profile is a Nash equilibrium. In other words, each strategy in a Nash equilibrium is a best response to all other strategies in that equilibrium.

An Example

Consider the following coordination game with two players, two strategies and a payoff matrix shown as below.

- If player 1 chooses strategy A and player 2 also chooses strategy A, they both get 4 credits.
- If player 1 chooses strategy B and player 2 also chooses strategy B, they both get 2 credits.
- If player 1 chooses strategy A and player 2 chooses strategy B, player 1 will only get 1 credit but player 2 will get 3 credits.
- If player 1 chooses strategy B and player 2 chooses strategy A, player 1 will get 3 credits but player 2 will only get 1 credit.

In both of these cases, the two players should cooperate and choose strategy A, and they should have no incentive to change their strategies because if both choose strategy B, each one will be worse off as their payoff will drop from 4 to 2. It is also obvious that if they do not cooperate and each chooses a strategy different from the other, one of them will be much worse off (by getting a payoff of only 1 credit) than if they cooperate and choose the same strategy (both of them will at least get 2 credits).

So, the cooperation between the two players to choose strategy A is a Nash equilibrium as both players have no incentive to change strategies, give the other player does not change. However, if both players choose strategy B though, this is still a Nash equilibrium, even though each player gets less than the (4-credit) optimal payoff, because neither player has an incentive to change strategy due to a reduction in the immediate payoff from 2 to 1 if they do not cooperate.

We have two Nash equilibria in this game, both players cooperate with each other and choose either strategy A (optimal) or strategy B (sub-optimal):

Player 1	*Player 2*	
	Player 2 adopts strategy A	*Player 2 adopts strategy B*
Player 1 adopts strategy A	Player 1 gets 4 credits, Player 2 gets 4 credits	Player 1 gets 1 credit, Player 2 gets 3 credits
Player 1 adopts strategy B	Player 1 gets 3 credits, Player 2 gets 1 credit	Player 1 gets 2 credit, Player 2 gets 2 credits

Source Author

Corner Solution (Winner Takes All)

Technically, a corner solution is a special solution to an agent's maximisation problem in which the quantity of one of the arguments in the maximised function is zero. In non-technical terms, a corner solution is when the player is either unwilling or unable to make a trade-off. In economics when someone says, "I wouldn't buy that at any price" or "I will do this no matter what", those are corner solutions. The word "corner" refers to the fact that if one graphs the maximisation problem, the optimal point will occur at the "corner" created by the budget constraint and one axis.

Practically, a corner solution is an instance where the best solution for a problem, such as maximising profit or utility, or winning a war, or whatever value is sought, is achieved based not on market-efficient actions to maximise the targeted goals/quantities but rather based on brute-force boundary conditions.

For example, if the maximum utility of two goods is achieved when the quantity of goods X and Y are ($X = -2$, $Y = 5$), and the utility function is subject to the constraint that X and Y must be non-negative, i.e. X and Y must be greater than or equal to 0 (one cannot consume a negative quantity of good or sell the good), then the actual solution to the problem would be a corner solution where $X = 0$.

References

Davis, S. J. (2019, September). *Rising Policy Uncertainty* (NBER Working Paper 26243). National Bureau of Economic Research. Cambridge, MA.

ET Online. (2025, April 4). Trump Tariff: Is US Headed Towards Another Great Depression? Expert Cites Two Monumental Mistakes of 1828 and 1930. *The Economic Times*. https://economictimes.indiatimes.com/news/international/global-trends/trump-tariff-is-us-headed-towards-another-great-depression-expert-cites-two-monumental-mistakes-of-1828-and-1930/articleshow/119979255.cms?from=mdr

Lo, C. (2015). *China's Impossible Trinty, the Structural Challenges to the "Chinese Dream."* Palgrave Macmillan.

Lo, C. (2021). *China's Global Disruption: Myths and Reality*. Emerald Publishing.

Sacles, S. and Li, M.K. (2018). *How Chinese Cybersecurity standards Impact Doing Business in China, CSIS Briefs*. Center for Strategic & International Studies, August 2, Washington D.C.

CHAPTER 9

Tech War of the Great Powers

Other than trade and investment, technology is a flash point in the great powers competition and lies in the heart of the China-US hostility. Both countries are locked in neck-and-neck competition to be the leader in future technology. Both are competing for high-tech markets, trying to establish its sphere of influence within the global high-tech landscape. The US is pursuing a decoupling from China to restrict its access to Western advanced technologies. China is pursuing self-sufficiency in technology development through import substitution under its "dual circulation" strategy,[1] emphasising on the need for independent innovation in information technology.

[1] 1 See footnote 1 in Chapter 4.

C. Lo, *Clash of the Economic Titans: China and the United States*, https://doi.org/10.1007/978-981-95-2510-2_9

Since the first trade war with the US in 2018, China has been playing down the tensions with the US by not using any specific terms like "Made in China 2025". However, the technology focus of its industrial policy and global ambition embedded in the "Chinese Dream"[2] have not changed at all. The US is concerned that lavish government aid would enable China to overtake American technological leadership and threaten American national security. Meanwhile, China views Washington's pushback as hostile containment of its global ascent.

Hypes, fears, excessive optimism and pessimism, and misunderstanding about this conflict have aggravated its global disruptive impact and pose risks to both countries and the world. What the tensions are really about is a race for "geo-technological" superiority. Understandably, the US wants to keep its global leadership status, while China is catching up fast and reckons that it must succeed to secure its economic growth and national unity. The rivalry appears to be driving a tech decoupling, which is already manifesting into a global disruption in international trade and supply chains.

The Core of Contention

Information and Communication Technology (ICT) is a central point of contention in the China-US tech competition which extends beyond the simple notion of who is having the most advanced technology. The competition encompasses national security concerns, economic dominance and influence in the digital world. Both countries see ICT as critical for military modernisation and surveillance, hence for being a superpower to enhance national security and global expansion. In the world of technology, who leads in ICT dominates economic power, influences global trade, innovation and market access. Hence, the race to lead in key ICT areas like semiconductors, artificial intelligence (AI) and 5G/

[2] In this nationalistic framework, President Xi Jinping seeks to combine national and personal aspirations in order to "reclaim national pride enhance personal well-being". In economic terms, this amounts to creating incentive compatibility between the state and the people to maximise national and individual interests, subject to political and resources constraints. President Xi is in fact driving home the point of structural rebalancing from export-led growth to consumption-led growth: In his vision, China has been manufacturing and exporting products to meet the consumption appetite of the West for more than three decades. Now China is ready to consume what it produces and to realise the materialistic aspect of the Chinese Dream.

6G technologies is a key driver of the great powers' competition, which could potentially drive the world towards a new Cold War (Jamy, 2023). Winning the race will also be able to affect global standards and influence, which will disrupt global regulatory frameworks and tech governance.

Before the trade dispute erupted, the major American firms in the high-end ICT upstream market worked with downstream Chinese companies, creating a stable supply chain. The US led the market for global server central processing unit, the brains of a computer. American makers of industry-leading microprocessors, such as Intel and AMD, provided licences to Chinese firms, including Hygon and Zhaoxin. The records of patent value and sustainability of US companies far eclipsed their Chinese competitors, with Huawei the sole possible exception. However, the world has been led to believe that China had beaten the US, and other high-tech economies such as Japan and South Korea, in technological advancement, hyping the fears about China taking over the world of technology.

Meanwhile, China has been leveraging on its domestic market to upgrade its ICT sector. Chinese ICT companies are competitive, particularly in wired and wireless communication, server, cloud computing and AI. Many global companies are also attracted by China's huge domestic market, which has contributed significantly to the earnings of many American companies.

However, this Sino-US cooperation did not last for long. Since the trade war in 2018, the US has attacked the Chinese supply chain of core components and business networks. It aims at achieving two goals: forcing the Chinese (1) to retreat from the high-tech industries that the US deems strategic with national security threats, and (2) pay extra political and economic costs by using America's dominant supply position as leverage. Hence, an increasing number of Chinese companies have been put on the Entity List,[3] banning them from accessing American suppliers. In October 2022, the US administration started restricting exports technology goods and semiconductors and computer equipment to China.

In response, China has been deepening its domestic market and opening it up to promote free-trade arrangements, such as the Regional Comprehensive Economic Partnership (RCEP), the ASEAN-led Asia–Pacific trade accord which has yet to be concluded at the time of writing. China has even expressed the intention to join the Comprehensive and Progressive Agreement for Trans-Pacific Partnership (CPTPP), which is a trade arrangement among 11 economies in the Asia–Pacific region. But US President Donald Trump withdrew from it when he took office in 2017. Chinese companies, meanwhile, have engaged actively in global mergers and acquisitions, global talent recruitment and partnerships in third-party markets to fight back the American containment.

China's AI Shock

US restrictions on exports of advanced semiconductor chips to China have forced Chinese AI engineers to innovate faster and use limited computing resources more efficiently to survive, even get ahead of, the competition, shaking up complacency in the industry. While the focus of the markets' attention on Sino-US geopolitical tensions when China launched a new low-cost AI tool, DeepSeek, is relevant, it also misses the point. Economically, it is arguably a welcome development of an ingenious startup emerging to challenge oligopolistic incumbents through dramatic efficiency gains. The more efficient Chinese Large Language Model (LLM) could be a catalyst for boosting global competition and productivity, capital spending and economic growth with benign inflation, just like the 1990 internet boom in the US.

[3] The Entity List is a document provided by the Bureau of Industry and Security (BIS) of the US Department of Commerce that includes the names of foreign persons, government organisations and companies that are subject to specific licence requirements for the export of certain items. These specific licence requirements are in addition to those requirements outlined in the Export Administration Regulations (EAR). The EAR contains a list of names of certain foreign persons—including businesses, research institutions, government and private organisations, individuals and other types of legal persons—that are subject to specific licence requirements for the export, re-export and/or transfer (in-country) of specified items.

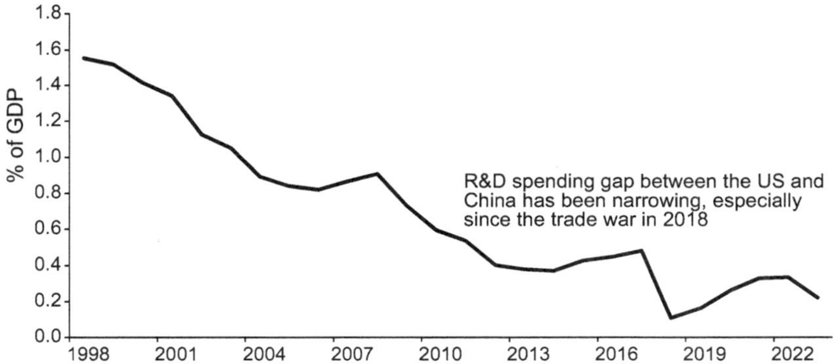

Fig. 9.1 Difference between US and China R&D spending (*Sources* CEIC, author)

A previously unknown Chinese AI startup, DeepSeek, took the tech world by storm in late January 2025 by releasing two open-source LLMs that rivalled the performance of the US-dominant AI tools. The Chinese built the LLMs at a fraction of the cost and computing power most US firms employ. The debut of the Chinese models wiped out nearly a trillion dollars in the stock market capitalisation of listed US technology companies on the day of the DeepSeek announcement, though some of the losses were recovered later.

China's AI progress has shown that the US export restrictions that are meant to impede its tech development had not only failed but might have sped it up. China's research & development spending has caught up quickly with that of the US level, especially since the trade war in 2018 (Fig. 9.1), indicating China's resolve to take on the tech competition with the US. The global implications are far reaching.

Déjà vu and Global Impact

Technology progress with dramatic efficiency gains is not new. The US internet boom between the mid- and late-1990s drove down sharply the price of computing capital relative to the price of output. That boosted investment and productivity growth (Fig. 9.2). If efficiency gains from China's new LLMs reflect a similar phenomenon, it could be a catalyst for driving down the global cost of AI capital and boosting capital spending and productivity growth over time.

Such impact is already emerging in China's domestic market. The race to win consumers has increasingly compelled companies to offer free AI LLM services. In February 2025, tech giant Baidu Inc. made its Ernie AI chatbot free to use in a bid to gain market share. The ubiquity of free AI tools in China is driving companies there to slash prices while also providing little incentive for consumers to pay for any services or subscriptions. The reality is that as AI tools are made increasingly accessible to the public with little or very small product differentiation, consumers are not seeing any difference in the advantages of higher price options.

The AI price wars and the struggles of the service providers to monetise their LLMs that are unfolding in China could have global implications. ChatGPT used to be a standout in the chatbot market, but not anymore. And despite all the money companies like OpenAI are spending, sustainable profitability is looking less guaranteed as competition and market pressures brought about by China's AI shock drive down prices that consumers are willing to pay.

It is only a matter of time before such reality bites in the international market for AI products and services. DeepSeek's blitz of transparency upon launching looks like it was part of a game plan to shake suspicions

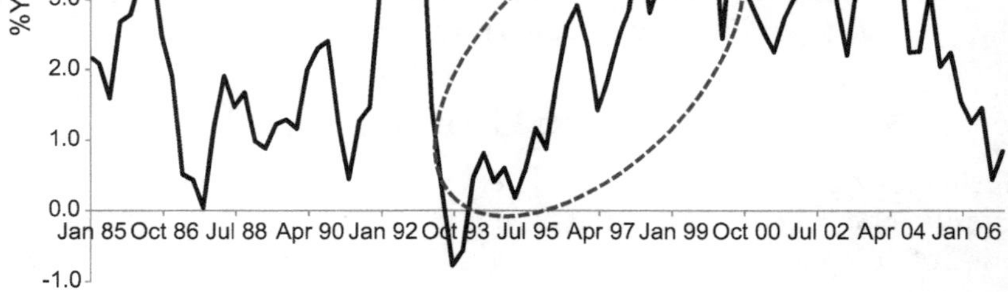

Fig. 9.2 US internet boom (mid- to late- 1990s) boosted labour productivity growth (*Sources* CEIC, author)

about its Chinese origin and penetrate overseas markets where consumers, at least for now, are willing to pay for AI tools. It is unclear whether the DeepSeek shock is a catalyst for a permanent global impact, but it should put Silicon Valley on alert that its pricing power may be doomed.

Such development will exemplify the benign effects of the so-called Jevons paradox on the economy (Rosalsky, 2025). The paradox states that as technological advancement reduces the cost of using a resource, demand for the cheaper and more ubiquitous technology will increase, spurring capital expenditure.[4] In the current context, a cheaper AI resource, triggered by the Chinese competition, should increase its adoption, opening the door to faster LLM-enabled product innovation with wider consumer and business applications. This is already seen happening in China. Over time, this AI transformation could raise productivity and economic growth without pushing up inflation (Betti, 2024).

More than Just Geopolitical Rivalry

Some observers see China's AI progress through the lens of geopolitical rivalry with the US. When the Soviet Union launched the world's first artificial satellite, Sputnik 1, in orbit in 1957, it sparked fears in the US that if America did not speed up technological development, it would fall behind its Cold War adversary. With China now claiming to have built more efficient AI models that can outperform America's leading tech firms, many observers wonder if this is another "Sputnik moment" (Lee, 2019).

This view, while relevant, seems too narrow. The tech sector is dynamic. Competition between nations and firms evolves quickly, with leaders and laggards jostling positions that change frequently. China's challenge to the established American tech leaders shakes up the oligopolistic competition environment in the US-dominated tech industry. This, in turn, raises an acute question about why the US leaders

[4] In economics, the Jevons paradox refers to technological advancements enabling more efficient usage of a resource and driving down its cost and, eventually, increasing the demand for the resource (assuming demand is price elastic). In technology, the Jevons paradox implies that as a technology makes efficient gains, the cost of using the technology declines. The lower cost spurs its consumption and offsets any decreases in the usage of the technology and energy that the efficiency gains might have initially caused. Ultimately, total capital expenditure rises due to the cheaper technology.

have not made similar breakthrough after years of investing billions of dollars.

Groupthink—a phenomenon when a group of players reaches a consensus without critical reasoning or evaluation of the alternatives or consequences—may have prevented US Silicon Valley players from considering alternative approaches and blinded them from seeing potential challengers. However, this may not be the whole story, in my view.

China's AI challenge to US tech dominance has developed quickly, but not unexpectedly. As recent as 2024, various Chinese firms have launched LLMs models boasting exceptional cost-to-performance ratios and sparking a fierce price war among the local AI providers. Beijing's strategic objective on building up China's technology capability has prompted large and small Chinese firms to develop cutting-edge AI models with remarkable cost efficiency, arming the country with tools to become a leading innovator in advanced industries (Atkinson, 2024).

The US has also explored ways to improve efficiency and, thus, lower the costs of AI training (Zewe, 2024). So, it is unlikely that any AI firm failed to realise that lower cost models were feasible. However, despite the inventors' efforts, American AI developers seem to have shown less interest than their Chinese competitors in pushing the innovation frontier. This arguably appears to be a deliberate business choice by US advanced chipmakers and AI developers, made possible by the degree of market control their oligopoly allows them. How so?

It is important to note that AI development goes faster with more computing power, producing more powerful models. So, rapid development of AI has fuelled demand for high-performance semiconductor chips, which are predominately produced by US firms and are put under the US export restriction policy for national security reasons. These sophisticated chipmakers and other tech-related players have strategically aligned themselves across the AI value chain by acquiring, investing in or forming alliances with leading AI developers (Pizio, 2024).

This strategy has ensured that the American AI industry depends on a few giant firms and created an ecosystem with a value chain dynamic that rising demand for computer power increases the profit of every firm in the value chain. Such an approach is typical of an oligopoly and underpins the argument for a deliberate business choice to protect profits by not pushing for lower cost models.

On the other hand, Chinese AI firms operate in a totally different setting. Firstly, there is no oligopoly in China in the AI sector. Secondly, despite the US-led trade restrictions preventing China from buying the advanced semiconductor chips, the export controls have backfired by spurring precisely the innovations that are likely to enable Chinese firms to challenge American AI oligopolies rather than crippling China's AI development.

A Benign Disruption

While China's AI challenge serves as a wake-up call for the US tech giants, it has some benign global macroeconomic impact. Beijing seems to be acting seriously on embracing the benefits of good old-fashioned American competition, while America has been dragging its feet on fixing its tech regulations for fostering competition.

The American big tech companies have argued that their size and dominant market position were competitive advantages that allowed them to push the boundaries of innovation. However, since the Biden administration, the US government has not introduced meaningful legislation to rein in the monopoly power of the American tech giants. Hence, despite building a dominant market position, they have not pushed hard on innovation.

Meanwhile, China has embarked on a sweeping regulatory "cleanup" in the tech sector since President Xi Jinping came to power in 2013, which sparked fears about China "suffocating" private-sector technology development, especially between 2000 and 2022 when Beijing introduced regulations to rein in the runaway growth of the tech sector. Contrary to this common concern among Western analysts, rather than stifling innovation, the regulatory tightening has effectively reduced systemic risk by fixing key loopholes in the Chinese system and increased its efficiency by stabilising China's productivity growth after years of decline.

The reality is that the US mega tech companies have a fiduciary responsibility to their shareholders. So, returns to the company come before the national interest. As innovation is about advancing shareholder value, America's big techs have a bias on embracing monopoly. This contrasts with China, where the returns from the company's innovations are aimed at advancing the national interest ahead of maximising shareholder value.

The AI shock from China shows that the American oligopolistic model is not necessarily good for innovative expansion in the new digital age.

Instead, the companies with the best potential are likely those whose primary fiduciary responsibility is the "animal spirit" of pushing the boundaries of development, not protecting market dominance.

Crucially, US policies designed to impede China's AI innovation have backfired by pushing China to innovate faster, thus introducing market forces back to the US and creating the more open competition that America's AI sector badly needs. This should be a welcome development. Geopolitics might have also pushed China to move faster, but its AI disruption is likely to create spillover effects on boosting global capital investment and economic growth in the longer term after an initial decline in investment effected by the efficiency shock.

The Digital Currency Fight

Related to China's technology progress and innovation is its creation of an official digital currency. China has been working on creating a national digital currency since 2014, but Facebook's intention to launch a cryptocurrency, Libra,[5] in 2019 gave China a push to get ahead of the competition. The People's Bank of China (PBoC), China's central bank, launched in December 2019 a national digital currency called the Digital Currency Electronic Payment (DCEP), involving the Big Four State Banks[6] and Big Three Telecoms companies[7] in Shenzhen and Suzhou as pilots. DCEP is essentially a central bank digital currency (CBDC) which is a digital legal tender in China's monetary system.

In general, cryptocurrencies have raised concerns by global regulators about their potential risks in disrupting monetary policy and financial stability and controlling money laundering, terrorist financing and other illicit usages. However, when the PBoC creates the DCEP, it can see everything and anything because it is the regulator and the clearing house for the digital currency's transactions so that illicit usage can be properly controlled, in principle. By jumping the gun by creating a CBDC, China has inspired many developed world central banks to accelerate

[5] At the time of writing, Libra is still not approved by US regulators. The market assumption is that it will not get approved at all.

[6] The Big Four Banks are the Industrial and Commercial Bank of China, China Construction Bank, Bank of China and Agricultural Bank of China.

[7] The Big Three Telecoms companies are China Telecom, China Mobile and China Unicom.

their research on digital currencies for general usage and to strengthen their regulatory oversight of cryptocurrencies. This competition is not simply on reaping the seigniorage, it is also on the government's ability to regulate and tax the economy globally.

However, the US government, specifically under President Trump and with backing from the Republican-led Congress, has been opposing to create CBDC—like a "digital dollar". This opposition stems from concerns about financial stability, privacy and national sovereignty. Mr. Trump even issued an executive order in January 2025 banning the establishment of a CBDC in America. However, this move looked hypocritical because at the same time he was pushing the idea of establishing a Bitcoin reserve as part of the monetary base. Bitcoin, and cryptocurrencies in general, have their problems in potentially wreaking havoc the financial system and creating systemic risk, as I shall discuss later.

Arguably, the worry about China's DCEP disrupting the global monetary order stems from the strategic competition between China and the US and the lack of trust between the two countries. In the short term, the rise of a Chinese digital currency is not going to undermine the US dollar dominance of global trade and finance, at least the large part that is legal, regulated and taxed. America's deep and liquid capital markets, strong institutions and the rule of law will trump Chinese efforts to achieve any financial dominance in the medium term. Crucially, the fact that despite China's rising economic clout there is still limited, albeit increasing, acceptance of the renminbi by the international community speaks volumes about the renminbi's lack of credibility to replace the US dollar anytime soon.

China will have to sort out its policy for the renminbi's convertibility first before it can push its internationalisation ambition further. It will be a long process for China to sort out its market distortions due to capital controls, lack of transparency, governance problems and restrictions on foreign ownership of Chinese assets before the renminbi could displace the US dollar as the premier global currency. However, DCEP's challenge to the US dollar dominance is real and intensifying as it may serve as a catalyst for prompting changes in China.

When it comes to managing the unofficial and non-mainstream activities, especially those that China and the US do not share any common interests, the threat of a widely used, state-backed, Chinese CBDC could indeed make a big difference to the world order. For example, in the hypothetical case of a US-regulated digital currency which is traceable by

US authorities, if some countries on the American sanction list were to use it to finance illicit activities, the US authorities could potentially block the transactions and catch offenders under US laws.

However, if the cryptocurrency were to come out of China, the US would have little levers to pull. Of course, the US and other Western regulators could ban the use of the Chinese digital currency in their respective jurisdictions, but they would be powerless to stop it from being used/abused in other parts of the world where US regulations do not apply or are not followed closely. This oversight problem could even extend to underground activities in the US and the Western world.

That is why global regulators have a strong incentive to rein in cryptocurrencies by prohibiting their general usage. The regulatory barriers make existing digital currencies highly illiquid and, thus, limit their circulation. Ideally, if the US/West can work with China on regulating digital currencies, the emergence of a Chinese government-backed digit currency, like DCEP, would just be a market development under Chinese regulatory oversight. It should not be a concern for global disruption.

However, this ideal situation would not arise when China and the US (and the West) do not share the same interests. In the hypothetical case of a US-regulated digital currency, the US may be able to prohibit its usage to finance North Korea's nuclear development programme, for example. But it would not be able to do so if the digital currency were run out of China. An incentive incompatibility problem would arise here as China and the US do not share a common policy interest in dealing with North Korea and they do not trust each other when pursuing their respective policies. So, if China were to allow North Korea to use its digital currency, the US cannot do anything about it.

This situation actually constitutes an argument for the US to develop a CBDC, but not uncontrollable cryptocurrencies like Bitcoin, to work with other jurisdictions (including China) on avoiding such incentive incompatibility problem when managing global geopolitical risks. Unfortunately, the competition mentality of great powers, especially when mixed with hostility, is preventing this cooperation from happening.

From the great powers competition perspective, having an official digital currency is also a competition on boosting one's currency as the dominant global reserve currency to advance the country's foreign policy claims. This will be the case as and when China's CBDC, for example, is accepted like the physical renminbi (alongside other currencies) as part of the foreign exchange reserves of other countries, thus boosting the share of the renminbi (both in digital and physical forms) in the global foreign reserves pool. Just as technology has disrupted business and finance, media and politics, a digital renminbi could potentially disrupt America's ability to pursue its broader national interest by leveraging faith and general acceptance in the US dollar. The US certainly wants to defend the *status quo* of a dominant global US dollar when China's DECP is catching up to challenge that dominance.

Chinese President Xi Jinping's Chinese Dream is intended to spread China's global influence through his Belt and Road Initiative (BRI) that covers more than 150 countries (as of 2024) and has extended more than USD1 trillion in foreign loans since inception in 2013. The BRI is supposed to work with the renminbi internationalisation efforts on building an empire for a global renminbi (Lo, 2017, chapter 10). The creation of DCEP is part of this grand expansion plan to facilitate the realisation of the Chinese Dream in the long term. In other words, Beijing hopes that launching DCEP will help boost the BRI and renminbi internationalisation efforts simultaneously. But this has created jittery about an emerging global power, China, shaking up the world system.

Digital Renminbi Challenging King Dollar

China's incentive to climb the global ladder is indeed strong. It overtook the US as the world's largest goods trading country in 2013 and has since been in the top two positions as the world's largest trading nation. There is a clear disconnect between the highest proportion of the world's trade going through China and the trade's denomination in US dollar.

Back in 2009, China launched the renminbi internationalisation programme to promote its foreign trade role. In 2010, just 1.0% of China's foreign trade was denominated in renminbi. That jumped to more than 20% in 2022. The PBoC even set up China's own international payments system, the China International Payment Service (CIPS), in 2015 to facilitate cross-border renminbi settlements and as an attempt to break the dominance of the US dollar-dominated payments system. Participants in CIPS include global banks such as HSBC, Standard Chartered, JPMorgan Chase, Citibank, BNP Paribas, ANZ Banking Group, DBS Bank and Deutsche Bank.

However, the results of internationalisation via foreign trade expansion have been exaggerated because the amount of renminbi trade settlement has concentrated in Hong Kong, the Special Administrative

Region (SAR), where 90% of renminbi trade settlement has taken place. Excluding the SAR, the expansion of renminbi trade settlement has not been as spectacular as the China optimists touted (Fig. 9.3). The bulk of the renminbi trade settlement comes from Hong Kong also means that the usage of the yuan is still limited in other countries.

On the international payments front, compared to SWIFT,[8] the US-dominated messaging system for international payments, CIPS is much smaller. It only had 168 members as of 2024 (though up from 90 in 2018), compared to SWIFT's membership of more than 11,500. SWIFT data also shows that the renmimbi's share of international payments has been stuck in less than 5% over the years (though it was up from less than 2% in 2019), despite 15 years of internationalisation efforts.

The International Monetary Fund (IMF) added the renminbi to its Special Drawing Right (SDR) basket, an international reserve asset, in October 2016. That was indeed an international recognition of China's progress on financial liberalisation. SDR inclusion has also made the renminbi an official reserve currency, though a minor one, as the SDR is held by all IMF member central banks in their foreign exchange reserves. While the renminbi's share in total global reserves has moved up slowly

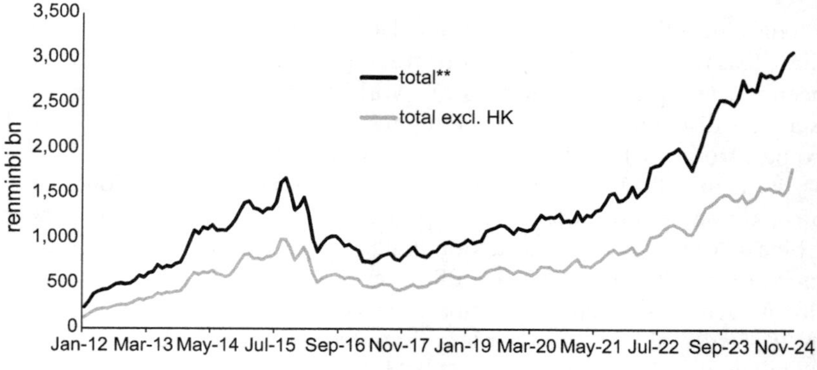

Fig. 9.3 Renmimnbi trade settlement* (*Notes* *Data in 3-month moving average. **Mainland China + HK + Taiwan. *Sources* CEIC, author)

[8] Society for Worldwide Interbank Financial Telecommunication (SWIFT) provides a network that enables financial institutions worldwide to send and receive information about financial transactions in a secure, standardised and reliable environment.

and steadily from zero per cent in 2009, it has remained tiny and stagnant under 2.5% (Fig. 9.4).

To further push the international usage of the renminbi, China undertook numerous financial liberalisation efforts since 2017. They include expanding the Stock Connect scheme, which links the Hong Kong stock market with the Shanghai stock market, to include the Shenzhen stock market for direct trading without foreign exchange controls, reforming the renminbi-US dollar fixing mechanism[9] to make the renminbi-US dollar exchange rate more market-driven, establishing various connect schemes, including the Bond Connect, Wealth Management Connect, Mutal Funds Connect to allow direct bond trading and sales of wealth management products between Hong Kong and Mainland China, just to name a few.

Meanwhile, the BRI aims at bolstering trade and investment between China and more than 150 countries. Under the Initiative, China would provide large loans to fund expansion of the foreign trade network and

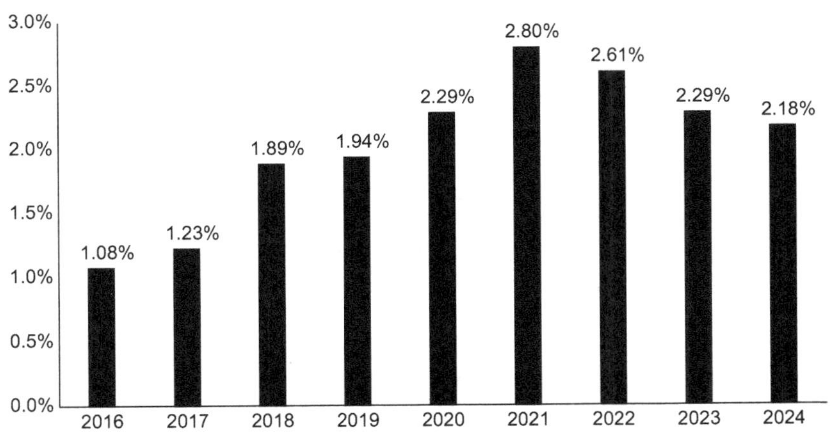

Fig. 9.4 Renminbi's share in global foreign exchange reserves (*Sources* IMF COFER, author)

[9] Every morning, the PBoC sets a so-called daily midpoint fix for the renminbi-US dollar exchange rate, based on the renminbi's previous day closing level and quotations taken from inter-bank dealers. The exchange rate is allowed to trade within a narrow band of 2% above or below the day's mid-point rate (the fixing).

international infrastructure projects, such as power grids, industrial parks, railways, water works and highways. Economically, the spending of huge sums of renminbi loans and investments abroad is a way to internationalise the Chinese currency. Politically, it allows China some leverage over the recipient countries by tying their economic being to Chinese influence.

However, despite China's push for renminbi financing, there was not much acceptance. While there is not a precise, definitive number for the exact amount of BRI loans denominated in renminbi, and despite China's efforts to promote the use of the yuan in BRI financing, the lack of acceptance of renminbi-denominated loans can be seen in the fact that the bulk of the loans extended by and funding of the Asia Infrastructure Investment Bank (AIIB) are denominated in the US dollar (see Chapter 6). This creates another disconnect between China's economic prowess and the international usage of the renminbi as a funding currency. In most cases, the countries involved only used the US dollar as the funding currency even though China was providing the funds for their trade and investment projects.

Despite more than 15 years of internationalisation efforts, and despite China's rising economic and financial clout, the slow BRI development and the renminbi's small international role are certainly dissatisfactory and frustrating for China's superpower ambitions. To speed up and deepen these internationalisation efforts, China needs to create a significant non-trade demand for the renminbi so that it will be used as an investment and a funding currency by the BRI and other countries. To create this secondary demand, China has to create the incentive for holding and trading the renminbi, and for that to happen the renminbi will have to fungible, among other fundamental conditions that it will have to fulfil (Lo, 2017, chapter 9).

Beijing hopes that the launching of DCEP will help boost the BRI and renminbi internationalisation efforts. By coming in as an easily accessible exchange of value with clear international ambitions, China's digital currency could indeed boost its effort to challenge the dominance of the US dollar by fulfiling the fungible condition. The PBoC created DCEP with several purposes, including promoting renminbi internationalisation in the BRI policy environment, improving the convenience of renminbi cross-border payments, enhancing the renminbi as a tool for international trade settlement and invoicing and as a store of value.

Thus, it is clear that DCEP was created as part of the financial infrastructure to achieve the Chinese Dream. Arguably, the erosion of the basic functions of money (as a unit of account, a medium of exchange and a store of value) of the G3 currencies (the US dollar, the euro and the Japanese yen) since the Global Financial Crisis in 2008–2009 has opened up a window of opportunity for the renminbi to rise to challenge the world's monetary order (Lo, 2017, chapter 10). And Facebook's (now Meta) intention to launch Libra just gave China a push to jump the gun and launch its official digital currency, as China was afraid that Libra might threaten its internationalisation efforts. The Chinese CBDC will likely keep the global monetary and payments systems on their toes in the years to come.

Is China Closing the Technology Gap?

Turning to technology, typically countries with strong technology industries earn big incomes from licensing their technology to firms in other countries and earn revenues from patents, trademarks and copyrights. However, China's intellectual property right (IPR) earnings, while catching up with those of Japan's, still trail those of the US by a significant margin (Fig. 9.5). It also runs a chronic IPR payments deficit while the US runs a huge surplus (Fig. 9.6). From these perspectives, China is not really closing the technological gap with the US as quickly as many China optimists think.

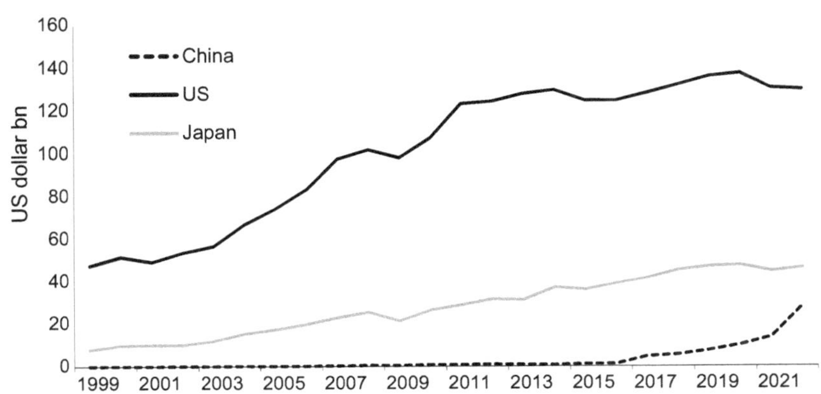

Fig. 9.5 Intellectural property rights earnings (*Sources* CEIC, author)

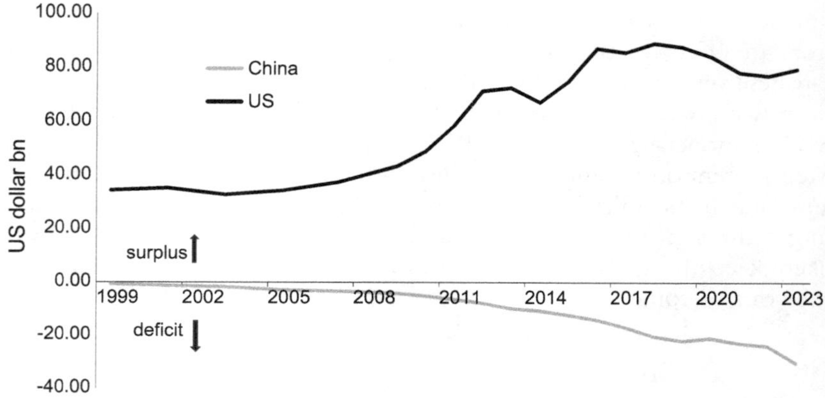

Fig. 9.6 Intellectural property rights payments balance (*Sources* CEIC, author)

A caveat of this argument is that China's industrial policy may just be aiming at being self-sufficient but not exporting its IPR and generating IPR revenues. China's intellectual property (IP) system tends to focus more on the quantity of patents and trademark applications, particularly utility models; they have lower protection periods and retention rates, indicating potentially lower IP quality and value. The US tends to have a higher proportion of invention patents associated with more complex innovations; these have longer protection periods and tend to contribute to higher IP value. All these data and factors do not vindicate that view that the US is at imminent risk of losing a technological race to China, though the Chinese challenge is arising quickly.

Here Comes the Disruption

The technology race aspect of the Sino-US trade war argues that the competition has mutated from the macro level (in terms of market volatility) when it started in 2018 to the micro level (in the technology sector) to date. Crucially, this tech war will not go away. The risk to the world is that US technological protectionism, manifested in an aggressive foreign policy to contain China, would prompt an aggressive Chinese resistance that would hurt the world by disrupting the global technology supply chain, creating a contractionary spiral in global trade and investment dynamics and boosting long-term inflation.

US President Donald Trump's "America First" policy approach has increasingly been seen by China as hostility to its ascent in the global system. On one hand, this could create a benign unintended consequence for China by rallying more domestic support for Chinese President Xi Jinping's structural rebalancing efforts. On the other hand, China's hardliners could hijack this hostility perception and push for defending national security and reversing the opening-up policy.

In America, those hawkish voices in the Trump administration calling for decoupling and isolating China through a new Cold War could risk hurting the US more, in my view, just like the trade protectionist measures backfired on the US and gave China more international expansion opportunities (see Chapter 2). Evidence speaks volume about this potential development. As of 2023, 145 countries had more trade with China than with the US, including more than fifty countries in Africa and Asia.

If the US tries to isolate China, and if these trading partners do not follow, or even cut their US exposures, the US will end up isolating itself. This revives the argument that the US would have a better chance of changing China's behaviour through a multilateral mechanism, such as the Comprehensive and Progressive Agreement for Trans-Pacific Partnership[10] (CPTPP) than an unilateral hawkish foreign policy and an erroneous trade policy. However, Mr. Trump rejected this approach on day one when he came to office in his first presidency in 2017.

Fighting Back

Meanwhile, China is not sitting on its hands. In addition to short-term tit-for-tat tariff retaliation and some export restrictions on key materials to the US to fight the trade war, it has also pursued a long-term policy to counteract the US trade-tech war that conventional wisdom has overlooked until recently: China's export expansion to other markets, notably

[10] The CPTPP) is a free-trade agreement between 12 countries: Australia, Brunei, Canada, Chile, Japan, Malaysia, Mexico, New Zealand, Peru, the UK, Singapore and Vietnam. It aims at promoting trade, investment and economic growth by reducing tariffs and addressing non-tariff barriers.

Asian (see Chapter 2) and the BRI countries, offsetting the fall in exports to the US, and significant increase in research and development (R&D) spending to cut reliance on technology imports. In terms of the trade strategy, China has been exporting more to the BRI countries than to Europe and the US (Fig. 9.7) both because of trade expansion into these countries and, more crucially, a steady increase in the number of BRI countries, from 54 in 2017 to more than 150 in 2024.

China's tech strategy to tackle the US's long-term export restrictions on technology goods and know-how aims at substituting technology goods imports by local production. Thus, it has boosted R&D spending, which is almost matching the level of spending in the US (Fig. 9.8). It has also poured billions into its microchip industry (He, 2024), notably by creating the USD95 billion "Big Fund"—the China Integrated Circuit Industry Investment Fund—to invest in domestic semiconductor companies to reach the national goal of achieving self-sufficiency in the semiconductor industry (Fig. 9.9).

All the available evidence shows that the US tech export restriction had only bolstered China's resolve to become tech self-sufficient, which is one of the key policy objectives in its dual circulation development strategy to counter external exigencies and global demand shift. China's efforts to boost tech development are already showing results, with its dominance in the global electric vehicles market being a notable example (see Chapter 3).

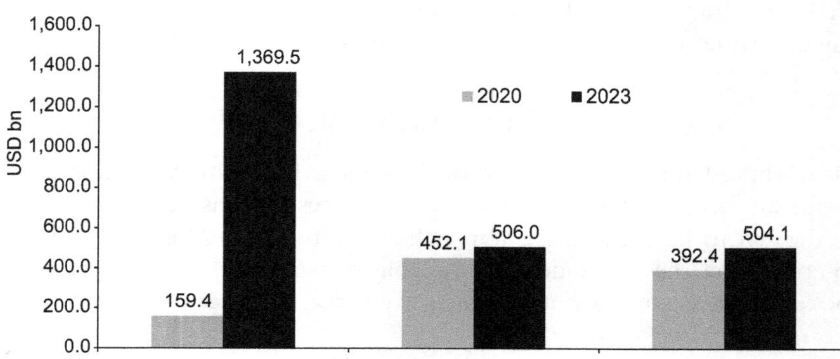

Fig. 9.7 China's exports to the BRI countries have far outpaced those to Europe & the US (*Sources* CEIC, author)

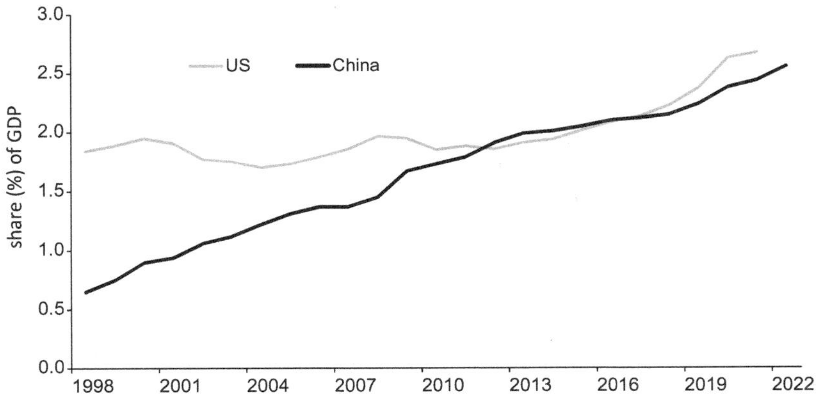

Fig. 9.8 China's R&D spending is catching up with the US level (*Sources* CEIC, author)

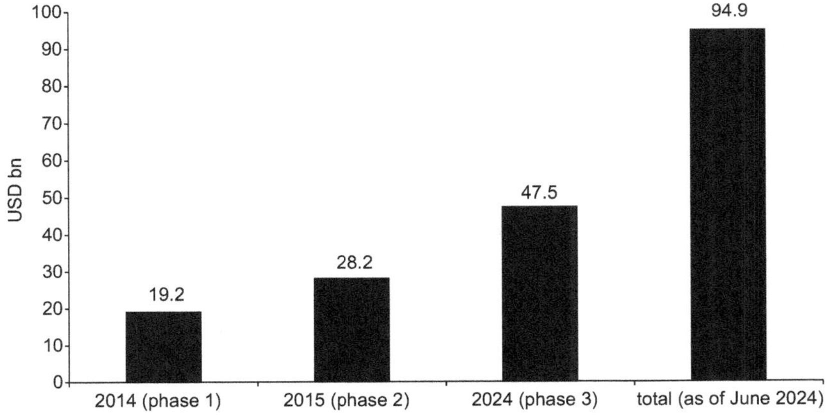

Fig. 9.9 Growth of the "Big Fund" (*Sources* CEIC, author)

Even in the production of advanced semiconductor chips, China's rapid progress has repeatedly shocked the world by refuting the conventional view that its semiconductor industry would continue to stumble at the technology frontier due to the US-led tech export restriction policy. The 7-nanometer chip powering its high-end Huawei smartphone, released in August 2023, showed that China's self-sufficiency in semiconductor design (by HiSilicon, owned by Huawei) and manufacturing capabilities (by SMIC) were catching up at an alarming pace that no one had expected before.

China's ability to mass produce 5 nanometer chips has fuelled talk of likely further leaps in next-generation chips. Furthermore, Huawei and SMIC are already shipping their new microchip—Ascend 910C for artificial intelligence, rivalling the omnipresent US-made H100 microchip by Nvidia, which is banned by the US to export to China for national security reasons (Lin & Huang, 2024; Liu, 2024). Granted, these new chips are still a generation behind the developed world's cutting-edge 3-nanometer chips. However, they show that China can move fast despite the US-imposed obstacles.

The China Offensive and Limitations

Aggravating the global disruption risk that stems from the Sino-US tech war is China's resolve to push its internet ventures abroad by trying to replicate the success of the products and playbooks they used in their domestic market. While China deems such a move commercially driven, America sees it as a direct challenge to its global leadership. Indeed, Chinese firms are the only credible challengers to the global hegemony of US internet companies: essentially, only American and Chinese companies appear on lists of the world's most valuable publicly traded internet companies and private startups.

Nevertheless, the global expansion of Chinese internet firms is often less visible, partly because it has focused on operating in poor or non-English-speaking countries. While the Chinese firms are not likely to challenge Google or Meta (formerly Facebook) seriously by gaining much market share in the developed world countries, especially under Mr. Trump's draconian protectionist policy, they may become a formidable force in the developing world, especially in Asia.

With per-capita GDP of around USD12,000, China's income level is closer to most countries in Asia, Africa, the Middle East and Latin America. Crucially, China and these developing countries share many things in common, making them easy to accept each other as partners. For example, fewer people have credit cards or access to traditional financial institutions in these countries than in America and Europe, making it easier for mobile payments to take off in the developing world; and

China's Alibaba and Tencent are world leaders in mobile payments. Retail networks tend to be less mature, and labour cheaper, so online retail can easily take a higher share of the overall retail sales business; and Chinese firms are e-commerce experts for retail. Furthermore, fewer people own computers, making smartphones and their applications the primary way for their people to access the internet and connect with each other.

Most of the large Chinese internet companies (with the exception of Baidu) have been actively making overseas acquisitions and investments funded by their large profits from their domestic market in China. Their aggressive overseas investment activity, especially in acquiring controlling foreign stakes, has often transform what started off as acquisitions in the tech business into Chinese-controlled diversified business companies.

Online retail is not the only sector in which Chinese firms are directly and increasingly challenging the US internet companies. Their footprints are seen in travel, transportation, media and entertainment. Didi Chuxing, a ridesharing service, ousted Uber in China in March 2018. Before that, it raised USD4 billion in 2017 to fund its expansion under its own brand in Mexico, Australia, Brazil, Japan and Taiwan.

China's aggressive overseas expansion is readily seen in the macroeconomic data also, with Chinese overseas investment particularly active in sectors like automotive, real estate, energy and metal and mineral assets (see also Chapter 6). In particular, in 2023, China's overseas investment hit a record high, with a significant increase in deal value and a notable shift in the types of companies being acquired.

Chinese firms are also developing new products with which US companies do not or cannot compete. One such notable product is the so-called content aggregation apps, which pull together news, photos and videos that are optimised for a particular user's interests. ByteDance, the developer of news aggregation app Jinri Toutiao and other social media apps, notably TikTok, became the flash point of China-US technology contest in 2024 and 2025 and prompted the US government to threaten to ban the app unless TikTok is sold to an American company. At the time of writing, the sale is still under negotiation amid the global tariff war that Mr. Trump initiated in early 2025.

The key reason why the Chinese companies are so successful is their willingness and eagerness to adapt to the local demand conditions by localising their products. While American firms like Amazon and Uber offer the same branded experience and product features across all markets globally, Chinese firms tailor-made what look like homegrown products to cater for local culture and tastes and preferences. They also localise their services so intensively that the local users often do not know that Chinese companies are behind these services.

In many cases, the Chinese firms take control of the local companies that have already developed local products and brands. Such willingness to localise shows that Chinese companies are flexible to blend in with the idiosyncratic market conditions, giving them an edge to compete with, and challenge, American firms which prefer the consistency of operating a standard global platform.

However, it is a different story when it comes to expansion in the developed markets, notably Europe and the US, due to government regulations, branding and the need for local adaptation. For example, after a great deal of fanfare around the expansion of its cloud services, Alibaba had to halt its expansion in the US in 2018 because it was unable to effectively compete with Amazon Web Services, Google Cloud and Microsoft Azure. To expand in other markets, Chinese internet companies often have to come up with workarounds. ByteDance, for instance, offers separate versions of TikTok in China and abroad. The apps function identically but the Chinese version is censored to comply with Chinese regulations.

Countries and regions like the EU and the US are increasing regulatory pressure on Chinese tech companies, particularly regarding data privacy and security. For example, the EU's General Data Protection Regulation requires all firms operating in the EU market to comply with its rules. This makes it difficult for the Chinese firms to adapt locally due to the different regulatory requirements by the Chinese authorities. Developed markets are also saturated with established players. This not only makes competition very keen but also forces China's tech giants to adapt their business models and strategies and reporting requirements to suit the specific needs and preferences of advanced country consumers which are quite different from those underlying the Chinese business and regulatory frameworks.

The Disruption and Opportunity Cost

This evidence explains why the expansion of Chinese tech companies has faced more obstacles in the developed world and is, thus, less successful than their expansion in the developing world. While it may be too simplistic to argue that China is posing an imminent challenge to the US in technology, it may not be an overstatement that China could create a global disruption in its technology competition with America by disrupting the global technological landscape. This is because restrictions on technology transfers and linkages, justified on national security basis, will break up compatibility between different tech systems and give rise to competing and non-compatible standards. The situation will be like the GSM versus CDMA mobile phone network battle in the 1990s. It is possible that the internet, and technological development as a whole, could be broken up into competing domains, giving rise to cut-throat competition, hurting innovation and leading to higher costs, slower adoption and even inferior products.

This risk of global disruption was echoed by Eric Schmidt, the former executive chairman of Alphabet, who argued for a "bifurcation" of the global internet into "a Chinese-led internet and a non-Chinese internet led by America" (Kolodny, 2018). In such a world, American and Chinese internet companies would divide up the technology space between them with the US taking the rich countries and China taking the poor countries.

It is a matter of time for such bifurcation of the technology space to unfold. Before that day of technology "divorce", what will possibly happen are two things. Firstly, Chinese internet companies will become established global players with significant strengths in some services, such as online retail and mobile entertainment. That will shape the internet experiences of many more people in developing countries.

However, they will also have to contend with significant American influence in those markets. Chinese firms will no doubt also try to break into the developed markets and may probably be able to deliver on occasional success, but they will not likely displace any of the major US incumbents especially with the increasing number of regulatory and trade obstacles put up by the US and the Western world against Chinese expansion.

Secondly, the tech competition between China and the US is a global disruption that the world has to live with, and it is hard to predict the winner of the ICT competition. Chinese ICT companies are competitive in fibre optics and wireless communications, while the US is more competitive in satellite technology since it has matured and highly cost-effective supply chains. Despite China's lead in the 5G development, the competitive landscape for the development of 6G, slated for 2025 to 2030, is still highly uncertain. It is unlikely that any one party will gain full advantage in this long-term competition.

The geopolitical complications resulting from this competition of the great powers are matter of national interest allocation rather than a matter of right or wrong. In the digital age, economies will prosper or wither depending on their capacity to adapt to the next ICT revolution against the complicated geopolitical backdrop. Inevitably, in a world of an intensifying China-US geo-technological rivalry, no country can play Mr. Nice Guy by pleasing both countries. Every country, especially small and medium-sized economies, will be forced to take sides, in my view.

In the grand scheme things, under such circumstances, this geo-technological rivalry will make it more difficult for countries to tackle the substantial global challenges such as poverty reduction, terrorism, climate change, money laundering and digital governance. A far better result would be for the two major powers to find ways to cooperate to maximise mutual benefits for all stakeholders and players and to minimise the damage of zero-sum competition. However, given the lack of trust in the two sides, the Sino-US "tech cold war" is likely to get colder as the manifestation of economic and political ideological differences between the two countries unfolds.

References

Atkinson, R. D. (2024, September 16). *China Is Rapidly Becoming a Leading Innovator in Advanced Industries*. Information Technology & Innovation Foundation, Hamilton Center on Industrial Strategy.

Betti, F. (2024, June 28). *How China's Shifting Industries Are Reshaping Its Long-Term Growth Model*. World Economic Forum, Annual Meeting of the New Champions, Dalian, People's Republic of China.

He, L. (2024, May 28). *China Is Pumping Another $47.5 Billion into Its Chip Industry*. CNN Business, MarketPlace Asia, Hong Kong. https://edition.cnn.com/2024/05/27/tech/china-semiconductor-investment-fund-intl-hnk/index.html

Jamy, S. H. (2023, September 13). *US-China Tech War: Semiconductors at Heart of Competition Driving World Towards New Cold War*. Strategic Vision Institute. https://thesvi.org/us-china-tech-war-semiconductors-at-heart-of-competition-driving-world-towards-new-cold-war/

Kolodny, L. (2018, September 20). *Former Google CEO Predicts the Internet Will Split in Two—And One Part Will be Let by China*. CNBC. https://www.cnbc.com/2018/09/20/eric-schmidt-ex-google-ceo-predicts-internet-split-china.html

Lee, K. F. (2019, December 3). China's Sputnik Moment and the Sino American Battle for AI Supremacy. *Asia Society Magazine*.

Lin, L., & Huang, R. (2024, August 14). Huawei Readies New Chip for AI Use. *The Wall Street Journal*. Also on online edition: Huawei Readies New Chip to Challenge Nvidia, Surmounting U.S. Sanctions, *The Wall Street Journal*, August 13. https://www.wsj.com/tech/ai/huawei-readies-new-chip-to-challenge-nvidia-surmounting-u-s-sanctions-e108187a

Liu, Q. (2024, February 6). China on Cusp of Next-Generation Chip Production Despite US Curbs. *Financial Times*, Hong Kong.

Lo, C. (2017). *Demystifying China's Mega Trends: The Driving Forces That Will Shake Up China and the World*. Emerald Publishing.

Pizio, A. D. (2024, October 6). *Nvidia, Microsoft, SoftBank, and Cathie Wood's Ark Invest Are Betting Big on This AI Startup*. The Motley Fool. https://www.fool.com/investing/2024/10/06/nvidia-microsoft-softbank-and-cathie-woods-ark-inv/#:~:text=It%27s%20a%20corporate%20structure%20that,invested%20a%20reported%20%24250%20million

Rosalsky, G. (2025). *Why the AI World Is Suddenly Obsessed with a 160-Year-Old Economics Paradox*. Planet Money, National Public Radio Network. https://www.npr.org/sections/planet-money/2025/02/04/g-s1-46018/ai-deepseek-economics-jevons-paradox

Zewe, A. (2024, November 22). *MIT Researchers Develop an Efficient Way to Train More Reliable AI Agents*. MIT News, Massachusetts Institute of Technology. https://news.mit.edu/2024/mit-researchers-develop-efficiency-training-more-reliable-ai-agents-1122

CHAPTER 10

Digital Currency Competition and Disruption

The competition between China and the US in the realm of digital currencies reflects their intense rivalry in technology, finance and global influence. Both nations are advancing their own digital currency initiatives with different approaches, driven by economic, geopolitical and strategic motivations. China has pushed forward with creating a central bank digital currency (CBDC) that forms part of the country's legal tender. The US has taken an approach that relies on private-sector initiatives to digitise and create cryptocurrencies that are off the regulatory radar.

Bitcoin seems to have special support by US President Donald Trump who wants to create a "Bitcoin reserve" as part of the country's currency reserves. This move has some important implications for the US monetary policy, systemic stability and, hence, the dollar's global supremacy. In my view, Bitcoin could even accelerate the decline of the dollar's influence, but not in the way that many analysts see. By default, this will boost the status of other currencies including that of the renminbi. Let us first see what the potential problems are that Bitcoin could create and hurt the dollar's supremacy.

Mr. Trump's strong support for developing the cryptocurrency market, with a proposal to create a "strategic bitcoin reserve" (SBR), and the launching of cryptocurrency exchange-traded funds in the US since 2024 have boosted the market's interest in Bitcoin as an investment and a

C. Lo, *Clash of the Economic Titans: China and the United States*, https://doi.org/10.1007/978-981-95-2510-2_10

reserve asset. Already, on the sovereign level, El Salvador adopted Bitcoin as legal tender in September 2021 (alongside US dollar that it has been using since 2001). Bhutan also developed state-owned Bitcoin mining operation in 2019. Both countries have Bitcoin in their currency reserves. On the corporate level, the most notable is NASDAQ-listed MicroStrategy's accumulation of Bitcoin since 2020 to build a strategic reserve, with the market estimating that the company had held 461,000 bitcoins as of mid-January 2025, compared to Tesla's holding of 9,720 bitcoins.

Misunderstandings

However, there are some misunderstandings about Bitcoin's merits and impact. If not clarified, they could distort investment and policy decisions. Firstly, if Bitcoin were widely adopted as a global reserve currency, the view goes, it could undermine the dollar's global reserve currency status and create systemic instability. This view is flawed because Bitcoin is priced in US dollar—holding Bitcoin is holding US dollars in a different form. In other words, Bitcoin is no different from anything that is priced off the US dollar in a transaction. For Bitcoin to be a global currency, it would need to be the basis that is not priced off any currencies for global invoicing and pricing, which is clearly not the case and may not be the case in the future, in my view (see below).

Secondly, the view that an SBR could protect a country from debasing its currency due to excessive money printing and the SBR could act as a store of wealth is also flawed. This is because Bitcoin's fixed supply (at 21 million, to be fully mined by 2140 or earlier) is equivalent to a fixed money stock that would deprive central banks of countercyclical policy ability. It is simple economics.

If you fix nominal variables (Bitcoin here), real output has to adjust violently to absorb economic shocks. In case of an economic recession, when Bitcoin cannot be increased, economic output will go into a free fall. It was this problem of rigid money supply that led to the demise of the Gold Standard in 1933 and the Bretton Woods System in 1971, as they deprived governments of the ability to counteract large negative economic shocks, financial crises and price deflation. If the government cannot prevent recession or financial crisis, the system and its asset markets will collapse, triggering a currency crisis and destroying wealth instead of safeguarding it as the SBR advocates think.

Thirdly, it is an exaggeration to argue that Bitcoin would dominate the financial system through the network effect—that is the more people use it, the more valuable it will become—like the US dollar. Bitcoin is still not accepted as a payment means in daily economic life despite more than 16 years of development. This shows that the network effect has not happened, despite all the euphoria. Take Tesla and its CEO Elon Musk. The company accepted Bitcoin payments for its cars in March 2021 but only to stop doing that after two months. Elon Musk, who ironically is a cryptocurrency advocate, owns no bitcoins or any other cryptocurrencies.

The broader point is that although there have been many cryptocurrency payment apps being created in recent years to promote its use, none of them has made it to the world's daily transactions and payments, except for some selective and/or underworld transactions. There was a parallel development in the early 2010s when some large players, including governments, were pushing the use of gold as an alternative to fiat money as a medium of exchange for daily transactions. Many gold ATM machines and settlement mechanisms were installed around the world during those years. But they all failed and disappeared because of low public acceptance and the inconvenience of using gold for transactions. Bitcoin may likely face the same outlook but with additional risks of network failure and power outage that will paralyse transactions.

Fourthly, Bitcoin can be programmed to reform the financial sector and payments system to improve efficiency and lower costs. This assertion is wrong because it is the Distributed Ledger Technology (DLT, which encompasses blockchain) behind Bitcoin, not Bitcoin, that can revolutionise the financial and payments systems. And the DLT is not unique to Bitcoin.

Central Bank Digital Currency (CBDC), which China is developing earnestly, and BRICS Pay—an experimental cross-border payments system in the member countries, also uses DLT. However, unlike Bitcoin, which has no proper supervision and regulatory control to protect the financial system from abuse, fraud, theft or other forms of financial crime, CBDC is a legal tender and BRICS Pay is a regulatory framework for cross-border transactions. So, what is unique and new about Bitcoin?

The crux of the matter lies in the institutional strength of the financial system. When the public enjoys sound legal and economic systems, with an effective government, good consumer protection laws, sound monetary policy and government guarantees like deposit insurance against bank failure, Bitcoin's decentralised and untraceable anonymous design has little to offer. To look at it from a different angle, when the US is pushing for the usage of Bitcoin, one would question the institutional strength of its system underlying the US dollar's supreme currency status.

Considerations for Investment & Reserve Asset

The common factors for investors and official institutions to consider the merits of Bitcoin are liquidity, safety and return. Central banks have an additional consideration—international medium of exchange. The dollar possesses all these factors that make it the global reserve currency.

Liquidity is obviously crucial for private investors to ensure an efficient market for converting an asset into cash without significant price volatility. Similarly, for central banks, viable reserve assets must also have high liquidity so that they can reliably be liquidated without aggravating market volatility in times of systemic financial stress. Bitcoin's trading volumes, though large, are still significantly less than that of traditional assets because of the lack of market depth. This also makes it susceptible to price manipulation, swings in market sentiment, rumours, etc.

Safety refers to the stability and predictability of an asset's value. This, in turn, is related to its price volatility which is a measure of risk. Reserve assets must have low risk to retain their value when unexpected shocks hit the system, causing market failure to price assets. Safety is also a crucial characteristic for most private investors. Bitcoin clearly fails in the safety aspect for being a reserve asset and an investment, as its price volatility is far higher than the traditional assets (Fig. 10.1). It is even questionable if Bitcoin is an asset, though it is investible.

There is an income stream associated with a financial asset. Granted, there are assets with zero yield, such as commodities, but they have practical use for production or consumption. Bitcoin has neither income stream nor practical use. So arguably, it commands a price and is traded mainly due to speculation, hence its violent and random price movement. This brings up the other problem, store of value, which needs low risk and predictability.

Some argue that Bitcoin risk could be hedged by global players with risk management experience, including asset managers, banks and investment funds, providing liquidity and hedging tools. The question is whether they would still provide liquidity and market pricing and at what price for hedging in times of economic stress, such as the Great Financial Crisis in 2008?

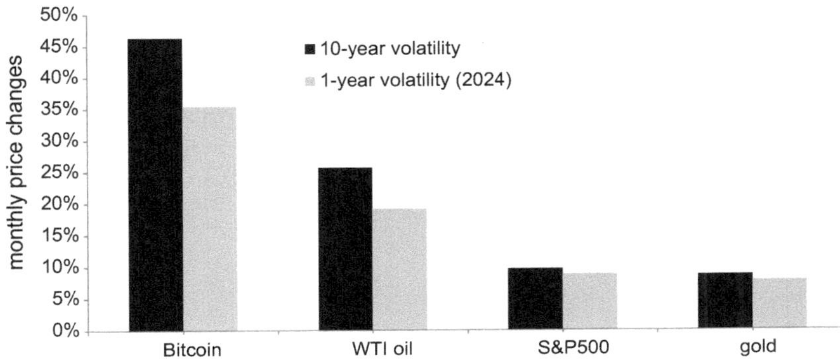

Fig. 10.1 Bitcoin's long (10-year) and short (1-year) price volatilty far exceeds traditional assets (*Sources* Forbes, author)

Bitcoin also has an outsized concentration risk compared to tradition assets due to "whale wallets"—pseudo-players holding massive number of bitcoins—which can move the bitcoin market easily through collusion and manipulation. According to market data, the top 6 whale wallets held 10% of all bitcoins outstanding as of 24 January 2025. And 6,952 bitcoin wallets controlled 58.2% of all available bitcoins, which means that 0.01% of total bitcoin holders have almost 60% of Bitcoin supply (World, 2024).

So, Bitcoin's high returns come with high volatility and high risk which central banks and most rational investors typically avoid in their reserve management and investment strategies. For central banks, since return is of secondary importance behind safety and liquidity, they require robust regulatory oversight to manage reserve assets. The regulatory environment for cryptocurrencies is still evolving, with many countries having no clear cryptocurrency regulatory frameworks and existing regulations remaining inconsistent across countries.

Such uncertainty and inconsistency pose regulatory arbitrage and operational risks, making it difficult and unlikely for the world's major central banks to use Bitcoin as a reserve asset. In a broader sense, while DLT underlying Bitcoin is designed to be secure and transparent, the cryptocurrency ecosystem is fraught with moral hazard risks, including fraud, hacking, money laundering and operational failures. The lack of intrinsic value and the reliance on speculative interest ultimately undermine Bitcoin's merits as a reliable reserve asset and investment.

Finally, to become a reserve asset, Bitcoin needs to function as an international medium of exchange. Typically, the composition of trade and financial flows determines the asset and currency composition of foreign reserves. For the foreseeable future, cross-border payments will likely remain denominated and transacted in major and emerging fiat currencies, like the five SDR currencies (US dollar, euro, yen, pound sterling and renminbi).

Bitcoin's Future

Despite high returns and growing liquidity, Bitcoin must overcome many obstacles to become an eligible reserve asset and investment. To start, it must acquire a legal status and play a substantial role in the global monetary system with wide acceptance as a medium of exchange and store of value. Mr. Trump's proposal for setting up an SBR offers a vision for modernising the US financial system, with potential benefits of enhanced efficiency and lower cost. However, Bitcoin is not the key to deliver that financial reform. It is the digitalisation process with the DLT that will ultimately revolutionise the US and global financial and payments systems.

Bitcoin does have its merits and potential, but they have been hyped at this stage. Continued regulatory and infrastructure development in the crypto market will gradually address the concerns about bitcoin. The day for Bitcoin (and other digital assets) to replace traditional assets in the global system will come, and Mr. Trump's cryptocurrency advocacy may help, but it will not likely come anytime soon.

The Chinese Digital Competition

In the great powers' competition on the digital currency arena, China's CBDC approach seems to be more concrete and better thought out than the US private-sector Bitcoin approach. China's CBDC can also drive renminbi internationalisation in the longer term to compete with the dollar for global influence. It also addresses many questions that other monetary authorities are asking, such as operating and managing a retail network by the central bank (which is not equipped to do so), transparency and anonymity of users, etc.

China is the world's first country to create an official digital currency called Digital Currency Electronic Payment (DCEP). The People's Bank of China (PBoC), the central bank, has spearheaded its development with an aim to create a new form of renminbi that meets the public's demand for digital cash in the era of a high-tech economy. Supported by a retail payment infrastructure that has been built since the beginning of the millennium and proven reliable, efficient, adaptive and open, the DCEP system crystallises China's ambition to build a high-tech digital economy that will enhance financial inclusion and make the monetary and payment systems more efficient.

DCEP is issued by the central bank and is, thus, the same legal tender as the physical form of renminbi. It adopts a centralised management model and a two-tier operational system (Fig. 10.2), coexists with the physical form of RMB and acts as a substitute for cash in circulation or base money (M0).[1] The PBoC has a target of replacing 10% of M0 by DCEP, but it has no timetable for achieving that. As a retail-type CBDC, DCEP mainly serves to meet domestic retail payment demand. The international role of DCEP is not a policy priority at this stage.

As Fig. 10.2 depicts, the PBoC sits at the top of the DCEP operational system. It issues DCEP to authorised operators, which include designated commercial banks and e-payment platforms such as Alipay and WeChat Pay, and manages DCEP throughout its life cycle. These designated agents have to deposit an equivalent amount of paper renminbi at the PBoC for each unit of DCEP they receive. Meanwhile, authorised operators and other financial institutions in the system are engaged in the exchange and circulation of DCEP to the public.

The 14th Five-Year Plan for Financial Standardisation, released in February 2022, made DCEP the focus of development on building smart cities and a digital national economy. In support of this policy ambition, many provincial governments have sped up their efforts to carry out the central government plans since early 2022.

[1] Base money or the monetary base (M0) is the total amount of money created by the central bank. This includes the total amount of notes and coins circulating in public, plus the currency that is physically held in the vaults of commercial banks, and the commercial banks' reserves held at the central bank.

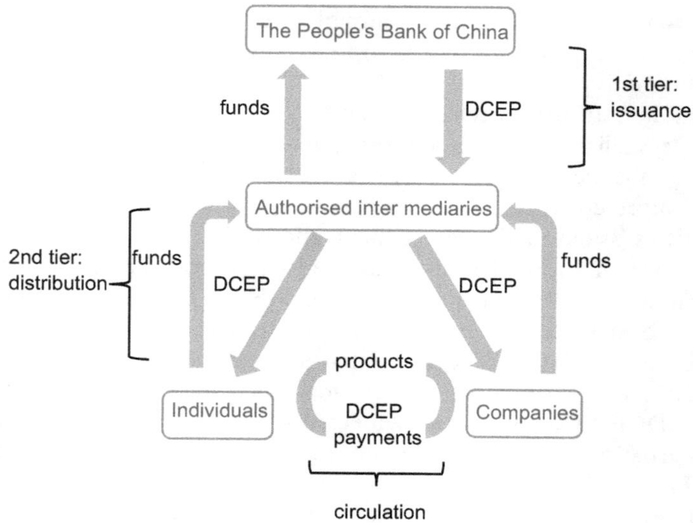

Fig. 10.2 The two-tier system of DCEP (*Source* Author)

Controlled Anonymity

A unique feature of China's digital renminbi at this stage of development is its "controlled anonymity", as opposed to the "untraceable anonymity"[2] of the private-sector cryptocurrencies including Bitcoin. Arguably, this feature resolves many developed markets' central banks' headache of striking a balance between regulatory control, systemic stability and users' privacy/anonymity, though many private-sector (retail) users may still be wary of the public sector's ability to monitor and trace their transactions and even movement.

The controlled anonymity works through the two-tier system discussed above. Chinese users of DECEP do not have any digital renminbi account with the PBoC. This saves the hassle of having the Chinese central bank to

[2] Technically, the anonymity of private cryptos, like Bitcoin, is still traceable, as illustrated by the Colonial Pipeline ransom case in June 2021, where US officials successfully traced and accessed one of the hackers' Bitcoin wallets and recovered most of the Colonial ransom. Retrieved from https://www.cnbc.com/2021/06/08/bitcoin-btc-price-slides-as-us-seizes-most-of-colonial-ransom.html.

run retail-banking operations, which are not a central bank basic function. However, the subject of having the central bank running retail-banking operations is often an issue in CBDC discussions and considerations by many other central banks.

In China's DCEP design, the authorised institutions see only the part of the digital transactions that they handle—for example, when their clients deposit, withdraw or transfer funds or make payments using digital renminbi. This is the "anonymity" part. However, the PBoC sees the transactions of all the authoritised institutions if it needs/wants to, and it does not share this information with the public. This is the "controlled" part.

The two-tier system and controlled anonymity are likely to be the central features of the digital renminbi when it is rolled out nationally later.[3] The current stage of digital renminbi development is domestic-oriented with no policy intention to expand its usage beyond China's borders, though the groundwork for furthering renminbi internationalisation in digital forms has been laid as a by-product of China's digital revolution through the digital Belt and Road Initiative (see Chapter 2). Indeed, China's push for the digital Belt and Road Initiative underscores the worry by the West about China spreading its digital technology to the developing world threatening, or even displacing, the influence of the Western democracies and the systems they have built there.

Disrupting the Global Payments System

A key political aspect for China's digital disruption to the world and challenge the US global leadership relates to the role that digital currencies play in military conflicts, notably their ability to erode the effectiveness of US economic sanctions. The 2022 Russo-Ukrainian crisis, which is still ongoing at the time of writing, showed clearly that military conflict could escalate global economic warfare.

Throughout the crisis, the US has imposed economic sanctions against Russia. One of those actions is banning it from using the Society for Worldwide Interbank Financial Telecommunications (or SWIFT) for international payments clearance. This essentially shuts Russia out from most of its international transactions and all of its transactions using the

[3] At the time of writing, Beijing still does not have a timeline for rolling out the digital renminbi nationally.

US dollar. Here is where China comes in, linking geopolitics with China's digital disruption to the world system and challenge the US.

The US-led Western sanctions have pushed Russia to work more closely with China's cross-border payments system and use the renminbi for almost all of its foreign transactions to offset the blow of the financial sanctions. In the longer term, the Sino-Russian cooperation on cross-border payments could increase the impact of the Chinese digital disruption to the US dollar-centric global payments system by breaking it up when the number of countries that use the Chinese payments system increases. Indeed, such an incentive has increased due to countries' attempt to reduce the US dollar risk of being sanctioned at the US's discretion.

Furthermore, as the Russo-Ukrainian crisis mounts, China has taken the opportunity to revive its petro-yuan initiative, which dated back to 2018, by actively persuading Saudi Arabia to accept renminbi for China's oil import from the kingdom. If the two countries eventually agree to this arrangement, they will certainly use China's Cross-border Interbank Payment System (CIPS) instead of the US dollar-based SWIFT. Some other countries, especially in the developing world, may follow suit in their trade with China. This will give the renminbi and the Chinese digital platforms a boost in their global influence at the expense of the US dollar and dollar-centric payments system. It will also force the world to reorient its international transaction mechanisms and the underlying technical, regulatory and institutional frameworks to accommodate the digital renminbi mechanism.

The unprecedented amount of sanctions against Russia by the US and its partner countries have raised questions about whether the Russians might use digital/crypto currencies to bypass those sanctions (McBride et al., 2022; Nolsoe & Pop, 2022). Any success by the Russians to do so would be a disruption to the global monetary order and geopolitics. That is because as the Russo-Ukrainian crisis has pushed Russia closer into China's economic and financial embrace, it has also linked the Chinese digital platforms to the impact of the war and shows others that there is an alternative to the US dollar-based SWIFT system for cross-border payments. Such a linkage could disrupt significantly the global dollar-based financial system by undermining the US dollar's supremacy in the long term.

China may not have planned to challenge the US dollar system this way and so soon, but the opportunity arising from the Russo-Ukrainian crisis has presented itself for China's exploitation to pursue its long-term policy of digitalisation and globalisation of the renminbi. China indeed has strong economic and geostrategic reasons to work with Russia to challenge the US dollar-based global payments system. The Sino-Russian-US triangular relationship during the Cold War[4] gives important hints for this potential political-economic development.

During the Cold War, the US embraced China in an "economic marriage of convenience" to counter the Soviet military threat. However, the trade war and technology competition that have shattered Sino-US relationship since the first Trump presidency has become a factor breaking up the China-US geopolitical and economic marriage. Meanwhile, a comparable strategy that the US used in the Cold War to counter the Soviet Union has brought China and Russia to a similar "marriage of convenience" with the Russo-Ukrainian crisis as a catalyst.

Economically, Russia has the natural gas that an energy-hungry, coal-dependent China needs. China, with its surplus savings, ample foreign capital, growing military might and an expanding Belt and Road Initiative (BRI) network, offers Russia added clout to buttress its territorial ambitions. Strategically, both countries, rightly or wrongly, are convinced that the US seeks to contain their supposedly peaceful rise on the global stage. The Russo-China joint statement signed on 4 February 2022 before the start of the Winter Olympics in Beijing shows clearly that both sides share the same view that America poses an existential threat to their developments.[5]

The battle of the China-Russia-US competition will mostly be fought in the economic arena. Today, a weaker US economy (with an average GDP growth rate and labour productivity gains of 2.0% and 2.7% a year, respectively, between 2020 and 2022) is facing a rising China (whose GDP and productivity growth averaged 4.5% and 2.2% a year, respectively, in the period). This is in sharp contrast to the Cold War clash between a strong America and a faltering Soviet Union. As for Russia, it is no threat to China, as China's GDP is 9.5 times that of Russia (in 2024) and the gap is expected to remain in the foreseeable future.

[4] The Cold War was the geopolitical, ideological and economic struggle between two global powers, the US and the USSR. It started in 1947 at the end of the Second World War and lasted until the dissolution of the Soviet Union in December 1991.

[5] See *USC US-China Institute* report on February 4, 2022. Retrieved from https://china.usc.edu/russia-china-joint-statement-international-relations-february-4-2022.

With this economic backdrop, Russia can still give what China wants to counter the US—by being a partner who can destabilise the Western alliance and deflect America's strategic resources away from its China-containment policy. From China's perspective, a Sino-Russian marriage could facilitate China's ascendency to global power status, helping President Xi Jinping to achieve his "Chinese Dream" ambition.

Challenging the US

Dollar dominance is not just about what currency to use, but also about the clearing and payments systems. In recent years, from China to Europe and the Middle East there is a growing incentive to diversify US dollar risk exposure by shifting away from the US dollar-based payments system, the SWIFT.

In particular, Russia introduced its System for Transfer of Financial Messages (SPFS) in 2014; China set up its Cross-Border Inter-Bank Payments System (CIPS) in 2015; the EU developed the European Payments Initiative (EPI) in 2020. In early 2021, an affiliate of the People's Bank of China (PBoC), the Digital Currency Institute, launched the Multiple Central Bank Digital Currency Bridge Project (or m-CBDC Bridge project) in tandem with the Hong Kong Monetary Authority, the Bank of Thailand and the Central Bank of the United Arab Emirates. This involves a CBDC project for cross-border payments endorsed by the Bank for International Settlements Innovation Hub Centre in Hong Kong.

All these systems are built to compete with, or bypass, the US dollar-based system. China is at the forefront of this competition, having leapfrogged the developed world in the fintech race since the early 2000s (Chorzempa, 2018). China is the world's largest cashless economy with the most advanced digital payments network processing more than USD700 trillion a year of cashless payments since 2015, compared with about USD110 trillion in Europe and USD 140 in the US (Fig. 10.3). The creation of China's official digital currency, DCEP, in 2019 has consolidated its digital revolution.

There is strong economic interest in China and Russia working together even before the Russo-Ukrainian crisis, and the war with Ukraine only cemented their relationship tighter. Russia's Eurasia Economic Union (EEU) overlaps China's BRI route in Central Asia and Eastern Europe. Reflecting the growing economic relationship is the rise in Sino-Russian trade (Fig. 10.4) and the fact that Russia has reduced the dollar

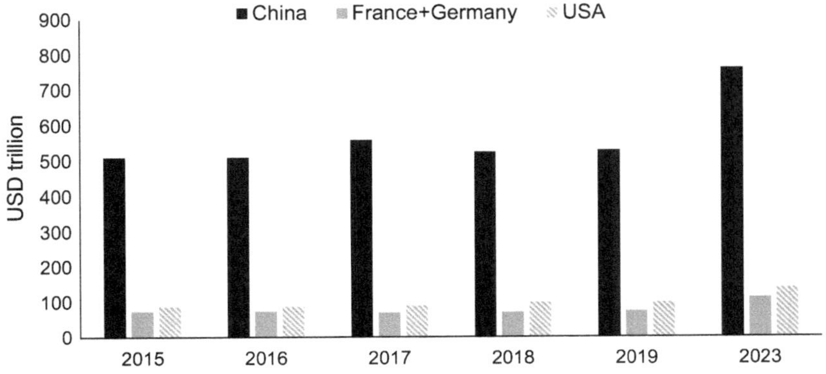

Fig. 10.3 Value of cashless payments (*Sources* BIS, author)

share of its foreign exchange reserves to almost zero per cent and over 99% of the foreign exchange trading in the Russian forex market are in renminbi since the US-led sanctions were imposed. Some of Russia's other foreign currency assets and gold are also held in China (Abay, 2022).

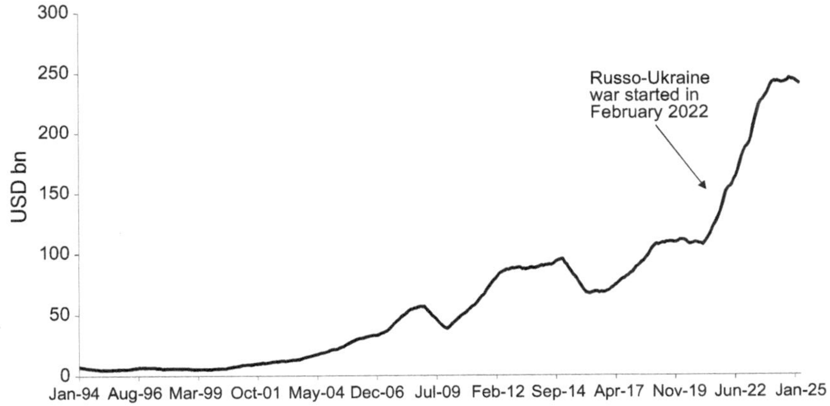

Fig. 10.4 Rising China-Russia trade* (*Note* *Exports + imports, 12-month rolling sum. *Sources* CEIC, author)

Deepening cooperation between China and Russia could strengthen China's international payments system, CIPS. Arguably, this is a key area where China may decouple from the US by breaking up the current US-centric international payments system. However, complete decoupling is still not likely to happen, in my view, because as long as China still engages with the external sector and foreign capital, as stipulated by its dual circulation policy, it will remain part of the dollar-based payments system. In the future, a multipolar world of cross-border payments systems may emerge.

The US dollar's dominance in the global financial and trade system has enabled the US to police cross-border transactions and payments and, thus, to advance its global political and economic interests. However, if China's digitalisation enables other countries to engage in international transactions using DCEP, that would be totally outside the US surveillance and, thus, erode its global control. China's digital sovereign currency would also make international loans and aid faster, more transparent and traceable. When the recipient countries use DCEP to pay for Chinese trade or infrastructure investments, they will replace the dollar and dollar-related technology. This is potentially a long-term development, but it is happening.

The point is that when there is enough acceptance and usage of the digital renminbi in a separate jurisdiction or region, it is conceivable that a trade and finance system parallel to the US dollar system could gain critical mass, chipping away the dollar's dominance and forcing changes in the global tech regulatory and financial regimes. It is clear that when China sets up CIPS, pushes digital revolution, creates DCEP, implements the digital BRI and launches the m-CBDC Bridge project, they are all aimed at building a renminbi bloc of finance, trade, investment and technology mainly with, but not limited to, the developing world.

Thus, digitalisation has potentially created a whole new ballgame for China to advance its interests in the global stage, making the digital renminbi a possible contender to challenge the dollar's hegemony in the longer term. China's incentive to reduce the dollar risk is, arguably, stronger than any other countries because deterioration in Sino-US relations has made Beijing very worried about Chinese banks' exposure to the US dollar-centric financial system. The possibility of cutting off Chinese banks' access to US dollar clearing, like what the US has done to Russia since the 2022 Russo-Ukrainian crisis, is seen as the "nuclear weapon" for the US to dismantle China's expansion strategy. Although going down this route would be apocalyptic for the world and the US, China is unwilling to take that chance.

Generally, cooperation between China and other countries to establish alternative international payments systems to the US dollar-dominated SWIFT system could increase the world's incentive to reduce the global dominance of SWIFT, leading to an eventual breakup of the global US dollar-centric system. However, China's CBDC alone is not a silver bullet to its economic problems as many of them are structural (notably a distorted financial system with an underdeveloped financial market) and, hence, cannot boost China and its currency to become a global leader like the US. Ultimately, China needs to establish the renminbi's global credibility to gain acceptance in digital or physical form.

Disrupting the Banking System

China's CBDC can also potentially disrupt (or break up) the global correspondent banking model that underpins most cross-border payments. This banking model exists because each country's payments system operates in a highly monopolised domestic environment. It uses only domestic currency, has high barriers of entry that limit the number of participants and does not clear cross-border transactions directly. Instead, domestic banks use correspondent banks for settling international payments.

Consider a cross-border transaction between banks A and B in two different countries, and they are not a participant in each other's settlement system. They use a correspondent bank that has settlement accounts in both A and B's settlement systems. In reality, this process often involves not just one, but many intermediaries in different jurisdictions, thus making the payments process lengthy and costly.

Thus, this model is expensive and inefficient because it has to go through intermediaries operating in different countries (Fig. 10.5). Cross-border differences in regulatory controls (on anti-money laundering, counter terrorist financing, due diligence, etc.) and operational and technical standards (as simple as different operation hours and time zones) impose high compliance and operational costs on international settlements. This payments model also relies on using the US dollar as a conduit currency for cross-rate transactions in the foreign exchange market.

Official digital currencies, such as China's DCEP, could reduce these costs and inefficiencies by using DLT, such as Blockchain, to standardise

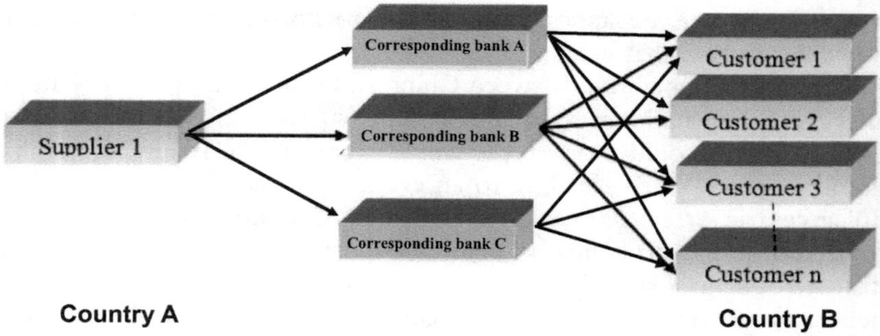

Fig. 10.5 The correspondent bank model (*Source* Author)

operational and settlement systems across different institutions, countries and time zones by creating one single global network that could allow cross-border payments settlement almost instantly. The resultant cost-efficient peer-to-peer payments transfers using official digital currencies could replace the inefficient correspondent banking model. China's DCEP is a pioneer in this revolutionary process.

Digital Renminbi Internationalisation

A fungible digital renminbi with DLT could be an efficient medium of exchange for international transactions. This is the fundamental basis for the renminbi to challenge the dominance of the US dollar. Theoretically, DCEP could facilitate renminbi internationalisation by improving the convenience of renminbi cross-border payments and enhancing its attractiveness as a tool for trade invoicing, settlement and store of value. However, before it can reach that stage, China will have to sort out the renminbi convertibility and related reform issues first. This means that China's largely inconvertible capital account will limit the digital renminbi's benefits for cross-border transactions, virtual banking and investment. It will have to liberalise the capital account further to realise DCEP's advantages.

Thus, using DCEP to boost the internationalisation of renminbi is a long-term development as well as a tall order since the process also involves many structural changes for China. Contrary to the views of many observers, Beijing does not have any policy to push DCEP into the global system in the short term. Nevertheless, to prepare for development in the future, it does have plans for large-scale cross-border testing in addition to its experiment in the domestic market. The launching of the mBridge project by the PBoC in Hong Kong in 2021 with the Bank for International Settlements, the Monetary Authority of Hong Kong, the Central Bank of Thailand and the Central Bank of the United Arab Emirates is the first major step.

The mBridge is a project to explore the potential of using digital currencies and DLT for delivering real-time, cheaper and safer cross-border payments and settlements (BIS, 2021). Arguably, this is a serious effort of China to challenge the US dollar-centric global payments system and the dollar's global reserve currency status. Since 2020, China has also been working on an interoperability project of integrating DCEP with Hong Kong's Faster Payment System[6] with an ultimate goal for launching DCEP in Hong Kong. The PBoC has stated that it would follow the "do no harm" principle[7] in cross-border testing and would ensure compliance of all procedures with local regulations.

China's DCEP is the largest and the most public testing ground for the efficacy of a CBDC. The DCEP system interacts with commercial banks, payments providers, artificial intelligence and big data vendors, other central banks, and multinational banks and companies. The DCEP experiment is way ahead of many other advanced countries' research and development on CBDC. China's interest in the cross-border functionality of DCEP and its relatively advanced stage of development give it a first-mover advantage in creating official digital currency. Such advantage could potentially make China a leader for setting standards in CBDC development globally.

To be fair, there is still a large gap between the potential and actual use of renminbi outside of China, despite steady albeit slow, increases in renminbi bank deposits, renminbi-denominated bonds issued, the share

[6] All banks and e-wallet operators in Hong Kong can participate in the Faster Payment System (FPS). The FPS enables their customers to make cross-bank/e-wallet payments easily, by entering the mobile phone number or the email address of the recipient, with funds transferred from the sender's account to the recipient's account instantly.

[7] The "do no harm" principle is a fundamental ethical concept in healthcare, emphasising the duty to avoid causing harm to patients or others. The principle is also applied to other fields, including humanitarian aid and leadership. It encourages careful consideration of potential negative impacts before taking action, aiming to minimise harm and prioritise well-being.

of China's trade settled in renminbi and the foreign exchange turnover share of the renminbi. Before making the renminbi more convertible and all the necessary structural changes to go with it (Lo, 2021, chapter 10), digitising the renminbi will not help change much the Lilliputian role of the yuan in the global system. Beijing likely understands these daunting challenges, and hence it does not have a timetable for a full-scale launch of DCEP and its internationalisation. So, the dollar's global supreme status is safe, for now that is. Nevertheless, the digital renminbi's disruption to the global system, whether good or bad, has started and will get bigger.

References

Abay, E. G. (2022, March 1). *Around 35% of Russia's Accessible Assets are in Country, China*. Anadolu Agency. https://www.aa.com.tr/en/asia-pacific/around-35-of-russias-accessible-reserves-in-country-china/2519923

BIS. (2021, September). *Inthan-LionRock to mBridge: Building a Multi CBDC Platform for International Payments*. Bank for International Settlements, BIS Innovation Hub, Hong Konf SAR Centre, Hong Kong.

Chorzempa, M. (2018, April 26). *How China Leapfrogged Ahead of the United States in the Fintech Race*. Peterson Institute for International Economics, China Economic Watch.

Lo, C. (2021). *China's Global Disruption: Myths and Reality*. Emerald Publishing.

McBride, C., Talley, I., & Norman, L. (2022, March 30). What to Know as U.S., Allies Put Sanctions on Russia. *The Wall Street Journal*. https://www.wsj.com/articles/russia-ukraine-sanctions-11645819467

Nolsoe, E., & Pop, V. (2022). Russia Sanction List: What the West Imposed Over the Ukraine Invasion. *Financial Times*, London and Brussels. https://www.ft.com/content/6f3ce193-ab7d-4449-ac1b-751d49b1aaf8

World (2024, November 5). *The Biggest BTC Whales: Who Owns the Most Bitcoin?* https://world.org/articles/popular-cryptos/who-owns-the-most-bitcoin

CHAPTER 11

Creeping Renminbi Internationalisation Challenges King Dollar

Since started in 2009, China's renminbi internationalisation programme has been seen as a move to challenge the US dollar's global supremacy and shake up the global monetary system, although China officially disagrees with this view. Some cynics even argued that by internationalising the renminbi, Beijing was preparing for future currency wars by making the renminbi more convertible and more readily available in the foreign exchange market.

The logic is sound, but it misses the key point, in my view, about the great powers' competition for being the host country of the world's reserve currency. The main point is that the creeping progress of renminbi internationalisation is already eroding the US dollar's global influence without any discernable signs. This is another example, I would argue, of China rising to the global stage while the West is sleeping on the wheel.

China is showing its ambition of using the renminbi to foster a new monetary order by internationalising the renminbi even before its capital account is fully opened. The erosion of the basic money functions of the three major global currencies (yen, euro and US dollar) since the 2008–2009 Global Financial Crisis (GFC) has opened a window of opportunity for the renminbi to increase its global influence. Granted, the pace of progress has been slow, and the delivery of internationalisation results are not in China's control. Indeed, Beijing has reduced its internationalisation

C. Lo, *Clash of the Economic Titans: China and the United States*, https://doi.org/10.1007/978-981-95-2510-2_11

efforts since 2016 due to changes in the global economic environment (Lo, 2021, pp.168–174).

Contrary to the common belief, renminbi internationalisation is never a top policy priority on Beijing's agenda (Windsor & Halperin, 2018), although it is an important policy goal. While China has strong motives for internationalising the renminbi, how fast and how effective it can deliver tangible results are totally different matters. Structurally, it will take a mindset, or even a regime, change for China to boost the renminbi to become a global currency and unseat the dollar's supremacy. This is not practical in the foreseeable future—despite years of progress on capital account liberalisation and structural reforms, the renminbi is not ready to become the world's reserve currency (Lo, 2017, Chapter 10).

This also means the disruption of the renminbi to the world's monetary order will not be as serious as most observers have feared. From a geopolitical perspective, the US's own policy actions could ironically help China to erode the dollar's global status. This will especially be so if the Trump administration's propensity for threats and coercion, willingness to betray friends and allies, and disregard for rules and norms is to continue into the future.

It Starts with Oil

One of China's efforts to push renminbi internationalisation is the talk with Saudi Arabia about pricing crude oil in renminbi. The dialogue has increased the market's debate about Beijing's motives to shake up the US dollar-based international payments system by promoting the usage of the renminbi and the Chinese cross-border payments system—the China International Payment System, or CIPS. If major oil-producing countries were to price some oil trades in renminbi, other countries may follow. This could sharply increase the volume and scope of using the renminbi in international payments, thus threatening the US dollar's global currency status in the long term.

No one expects China to displace the dollar-centric global financial system anytime soon simply because the renminbi is not ready to do so. However, the point is that gradual renminbi internationalisation will force changes in the global financial system and allow renminbi assets to become a class of their own, thus increasing the yuan's global influence slowly but surely.

Since 2018, China has been in talks with Saudi Arabia on settling some oil trades in renminbi. It has even set up a local oil futures exchange with contracts denominated in renminbi. Many market players see this as China's first step towards nudging the global oil trade to the renminbi from the US dollar, thus creating a "petro-yuan" system to challenge the "petro-dollar". Meanwhile, the Russo-Ukrainian crisis since 2022 (which is still ongoing at the time of writing) has pushed Russia to trade oil with China using the renminbi and CIPS instead of the dollar and the SWIFT (Society for Worldwide Interbank Financial Telecommunications).

If Saudi Arabia and Russia were to work with China, the amount of renminbi-denominated oil trades could rise sharply and transactions could go through China's payments system, CIPS, at the expense of US dollar and the SWIFT system. This would be a serious challenge to the dollar-based global financial system as, arguably, the dollar's global reserve currency status is largely based on its importance in the energy and commodity markets.

Linchpin of Dollar Supremacy

One of the staples of the past four decades, and an anchor sustaining the dollar's global reserve currency status, was a global financial system based on the petro-dollar. This was a world in which oil producers would sell their products to the US and the rest of the world for dollars. They would recycle the proceeds into dollar-denominated assets by investing in dollar-bloc markets, thus propping up the dollar as the world's reserve currency. This has made the oil market, and by extension the global commodity market, a linchpin for sustaining the US as the world's undisputed financial superpower (Fig. 11.1). If that linchpin were to break, the dollar's status would start to crumble.

With China slowly challenging the dollar, Saudi acceptance of renminbi in oil trades could help chip away at the supremacy of the dollar by gradually weakening that linchpin. The question is whether Saudi Arabia would want to do that when it is also a major US ally. Arguably, Saudi Arabia has an incentive to get closer to China, although it also has to balance this with its US interests. It has become increasingly unhappy with US security commitments to defend the kingdom. Meanwhile, China has strengthened its relationship with Saudi Arabia in recent years by increasing investment in, and military cooperation with, the kingdom (Kalin, 2022).

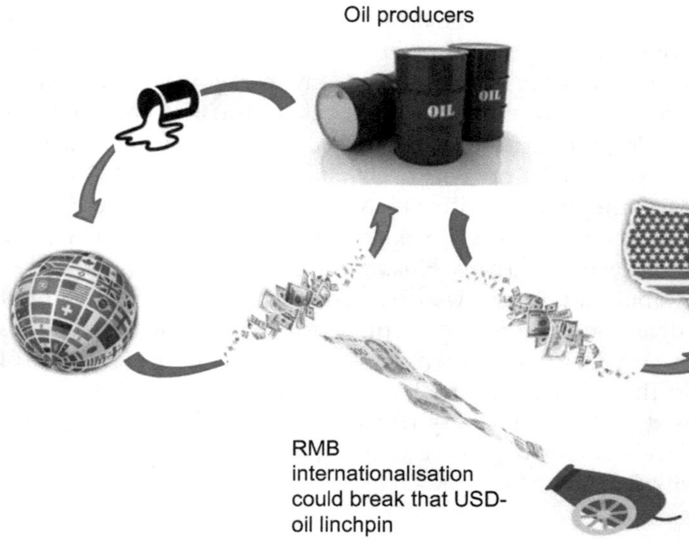

Fig. 11.1 Linchpin of the dollar's supremacy (*Source* Author)

One way for Saudi Arabia to balance its interests between China and the US would be to trade oil with China (and probably also with Asia) in renminbi using CIPS, while continuing trading oil with the rest of the world in US dollars via SWIFT. Saudi has had spasmodic talks with China on renminbi-priced oil contracts since 2018. These discussions have accelerated since March 2022 amid rising geopolitical tensions.

The Petro-Yuan's Threat

How big a threat will the petro-yuan be to the dollar-based payments system? It is impossible to give an accurate answer at the time of writing as it will take time for the petro-yuan oil talks to conclude. However, we may get some clues from public information on the relationships and oil trades between China and other major oil producers. Some market players initially estimated that switching the oil trade from the dollar to the renminbi could move up to USD1 trillion worth of transactions out of the dollar a month (Salameh, 2018).

Now consider the SWIFT data on global payments currencies. In March 2025 (the latest data available at the time of writing) the renminbi was ranked the fourth most widely used currency for global payments, accounting for 4.13% of the total, ahead of the Japanese yen's 3.9% and behind the pound sterling's 6.6% (Fig. 11.2).

Since about USD150 trillion worth of payment messages move through SWIFT worldwide every year, or USD12.5 trillion a month, the renminbi's 4.13% would amount to about USD516 billion a month. If we add the estimated monthly USD1 trillion of oil trade that would be settled in renminbi, the yuan's share of global payments would rise to more than 12% in the SWIFT system, beating the pound sterling's 6.64% by a wide margin to become the third most widely used payments currency, *ceteris paribus*.

The impact on CIPS would be more dramatic. According to the CIPS website, the Chinese system processed about USD61 billion worth of payment messages a day, or USD 1.22 trillion a month (or USD14.6 trillion a year), assuming 20 business days a month. Adding USD1 trillion

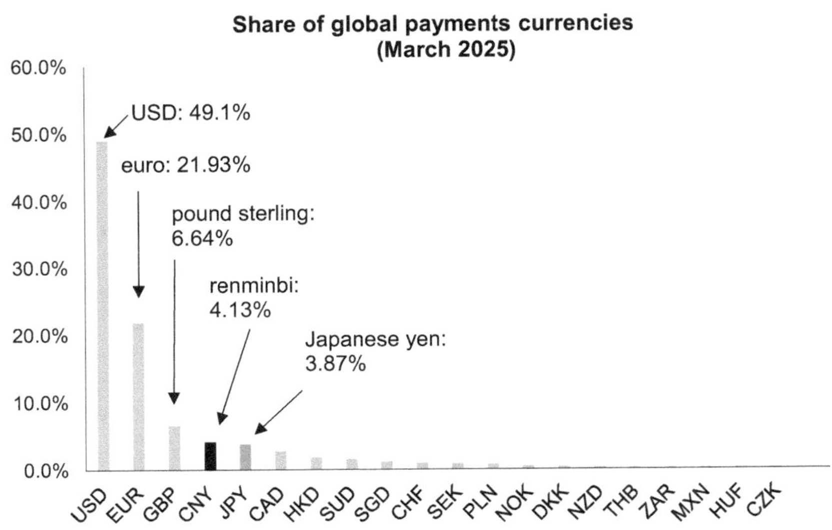

Fig. 11.2 Share of global payments currencies (March 2025) (*Source* SWIFT, author)

would almost double its payment processing capacity to USD2.22 trillion a month.

However, it could go further. If Saudi Arabia and Russia start using renminbi for oil trade, other countries would likely follow. At this point, Russia, Iran, Venezuela and Indonesia are already settling some (and all, in Russia's case) of their oil trades with China in renminbi. The volume, and the scope of using renminbi for international payments, could grow as more countries diversify out of US dollar risk.

The Dollar's Boiling Frog Fable

Of course, no one expects the petro-yuan to displace the petro-dollar and the dollar-based payments system anytime soon. The process is like the boiling frog fable, which is already reflected in the slow erosion of the US dollar's share in the global foreign reserve pool from almost over 85% in the 1970s to less than 58% now. There are indeed strong theoretical and practical reasons to expect these trends will continue and the renminbi's challenge to the US dollar hegemony to be a drawn-out process.

To make the renminbi attractive for payments, China will need to liberalise its financial markets and its capital account much more than what it has done so far. In practice, this means allowing foreigners to trade Chinese assets without capital or bureaucratic controls. While China has been liberalising its capital account for years, the pace has been grudgingly slow. Nevertheless, the difficulty for opening up quickly is that given China's large debt overhang (with the debt-to-GDP ratio estimated at over 280% in 2023), liberalising its capital account would risk a debt-currency crisis pulling the rug from under the Chinese system.

A major obstacle for renminbi oil trading is that the major oil and gas producers in the Middle East have currencies pegged to the US dollar, including Saudi Arabia, the United Arab Emirates, Oman and Qatar. Kuwait's currency is pegged to a basket of currencies dominated by the dollar. These pegs acted as a stability anchor for these countries when the US was the world's largest oil importer.

Nevertheless, with China replacing the US as the world's largest oil importer and with the US turning into a net oil exporter since 2021, this change in the oil demand and supply dynamics is challenging the stability anchor and, hence, the sustainability of these currency pegs. Nevertheless, inertia could keep these pegs intact for a long time, especially when paying for oil in renminbi—or any currency other than the dollar—raises a foreign exchange risk that these oil-producing countries have not faced in decades. Moreover, despite years of financial reforms, China still does not have a large derivatives market to provide sufficient tools for hedging renminbi exchange risk.

A Gold-Backed Yuan

If Saudi Arabia decides to trade oil with China in renminbi, it will add momentum to the petro-yuan trading that is already happening between China and Russia and some other oil-producing countries including Indonesia, Iran and Venezuela (see Chapter 9). When more players choose to trade oil and other products with China in renminbi, that could help build a critical mass for yuan trading over time. China is trying to encourage this development by using gold for building up the petro-yuan system. The trick is to back the renminbi oil trade with gold. This is indeed a condition that Beijing promised Riyadh in their talks since 2018 about trading Saudi oil with China in renminbi.

A gold-backed petro-yuan does not require full renminbi convertibility to function because only the amount of renminbi that is used in the oil trade is convertible into gold. Therefore, it allows China to simultaneously retain control of the capital account and boost the internationalisation of the renminbi. This measure is instrumental in building up the petro-yuan system because making the yuan convertible into gold effectively turns it into a globally investable asset for foreign renminbi owners, thus boosting international confidence in and demand for the Chinese currency. Over time, if a gold-backed renminbi is rolled out on a large scale, it could make renminbi assets an independent asset class and deepen its internationalisation process and China's onshore capital markets.

If such a strategy succeeds in getting Saudi Arabia to buy into the petro-yuan initiative, many other countries may follow. This would change the dynamics of the oil trade and could tilt the geopolitical balance towards China. Countries might be able to evade economic sanctions under the US dollar system by using the renminbi and CIPS, thus greatly weakening the US global surveillance ability and influence. Generally, a shift towards renminbi-dominated payments will also disrupt the USD-dominated SWIFT payments system.

Ultimately, China needs to establish the renminbi's global credibility for it to gain acceptance. That will take a long time. However, it appears that China's disruption to the future global payments system is already becoming a reality even before the renminbi becomes a global currency (see Chapter 9), as China is building the infrastructure for incorporating the yuan in the global system. A petro-yuan could allow China to accelerate the internationalisation process while retaining full control of its capital account. Sustaining and growing the petro-yuan network also means that China would accumulate more gold for a gold-backed renminbi as an insurance for foreign investors and businesses to accept the currency.

Furthermore, China will need to create more yuan-denominated investible assets besides gold to increase the foreign incentive to use the currency. Only when non-trade demand for renminbi rises can China deepen its internationalisation efforts (Lo, 2017, pp. 209–212). That will require China to further develop its onshore capital markets, including renminbi hedging instruments, to accommodate large foreign fund flows.

A Significant Step Forward

Developments in late March 2023 showed that renminbi internationalisation moved a significant step forward, with Brazil, Saudi Arabia, France and ASEAN countries joining the game. While this could boost China's effort to build a financial infrastructure for the renminbi to become a global currency, Beijing is not in a hurry. Instead, it has employed a "salami-slicing tactics" for internationalising the yuan. Such a strategy will slowly erode, not replace, the US dollar's global dominance in the medium term.

This implies that countries may increasingly trade with China using renminbi, but they still use the dollar in trade with most of the rest of the world. It is important to note that when there is enough penetration of the renminbi in a separate jurisdiction, a payments system parallel to the US dollar system could gain critical mass, re-orientating the world's payments systems and the underlying technical, regulatory and institutional frameworks to accommodate the renminbi over time.

Here is what happened in March 2023 that marked an important step forward for renminbi internationalisation:

- 27 March—Saudi Arabia announced that Aramco would build oil refineries with China for RMB 83.7 billion.

- 28 March—China and France completed their first LNG trade using renminbi, involving 65,000 tonnes of LNG from the UAE.
- 29 March—Saudi Arabia joined the China-led regional security and trade club, the Shanghai Cooperation Organisation, improving diplomatic relationship and advancing talks on trading oil in renminbi.
- 29 March—China and Brazil struck a deal to ditch the US dollar and use the renminbi in cross-border transactions.
- 30 March—ASEAN leaders considered reducing the usage of the US dollar, euro, pound sterling and Japanese yen in financial transactions and move to settlements in local currencies.
- 31 March—At the Boao Forum in Hainan in China, Malaysia revived a former proposal to create an "Asian Monetary Fund" to reduce dependence on the US dollar.

Incentive to Diversify Out of the Dollar

The relevance of these developments to the progress of renminbi internationalisation is that they underscore the efforts of other countries over the years to diversify out of the US dollar exposure by shifting away from the dollar-based payments system, SWIFT. Notably,

- in 2014, Russia introduced its System for Transfer of Financial Messages (SPFS)
- in 2015, China set up its Cross-Border Inter-Bank Payments System (CIPS)
- in 2020, the EU developed the European Payments Initiative (EPI)
- and in early 2021, China's Digital Currency Institute, an affiliate of the People's Bank of China, launched the Multiple Central Bank Digital Currency Bridge Project (or m-CBDC Bridge) together with the Hong Kong Monetary Authority, the Bank of Thailand and the Central Bank of the United Arab Emirates, to explore cross-border payments using the digital renminbi. The Bank for International Settlements Innovation Hub Centre in Hong Kong endorses the project.

The incentive for diversifying out of the US dollar system has grown over time due to fears about US sanctions. The US has imposed more

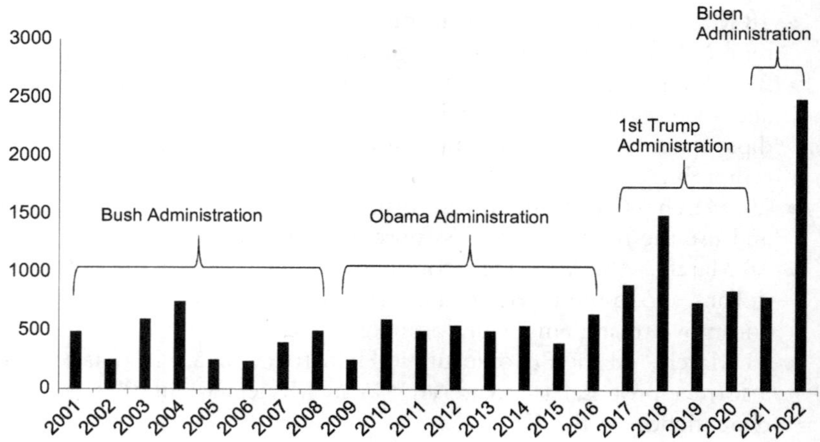

Fig. 11.3 Number of new US sanctions by year (*Source* Compiled from US Treasury by author)

than 10,000 unilateral sanctions on foreign entities over the past 20 years. The sanction efforts have intensified under the Biden administration (Fig. 11.3). Arguably, the effect is a "de-dollarisation" of trade, with China picking up the slack through internationalisation.

The Salami-Slicing Tactics

Individually, these developments do not dent the dollar's global supremacy. Take the China-Brazil agreement, which received much international attention, to replace the US dollar in most of their bilateral trade settlement by the renminbi. Sino-Brazil total trade totals about USD182 billion a year. Furthermore, China's cumulative investment in Brazil since the 1990s is about USD150 billion.

Now consider SWIFT. Using the data from the above discussion, SWIFT processes about USD150 trillion worth of payment messages worldwide a year. If we assume all the China-Brazil trade and investment payments were made in renminbi, that will cut USD332 billion worth of payments from SWIFT, or only about 0.22% of its annual total.

However, China is using a "salami-slicing" tactics by taking small steps to encourage countries in the developing world, not just Brazil, to use renminbi for cross-border payments. It is already trading with Russia in renminbi (due to the Western sanctions on Russia) and doing some oil trades with countries like Indonesia, Iran and Venezuela in renminbi. Among the BRICS countries, the three largest ones—China, Russia and Brazil—are now working together on using renminbi for cross-border payments. They are the world's largest commodity exporters and importers, and their cooperation could draw many other countries to the renminbi payments mechanism over time.

The point is that while each small individual agreement or alliance does not have much impact on the US dollar-dominated global payments system, cumulatively they could produce some material impact on favouring the renminbi global influence by eroding the US dollar influence. To see this, consider the following.

Using the oil market's estimate from the discussion above, let us assume USD1 trillion worth of oil transactions would switch out of the dollar each month (or USD12 trillion a year) into the renminbi. Meanwhile, official data shows that Sino-Russian trade totals about USD245 billion a year and rising.

Adding these amounts to the Sino-Brazilian annual trade and investment data would suggest that about USD12.6 trillion worth of cross-border payments (USD332 billion + 12 trillion + 245 billion) could move from US dollar (SWIFT) to renminbi (CIPS). That would cut the SWIFT's annual payments processing by 8.4% (USD12.6 trillion out of SWIFT annual processing of USD150 trillion) but boost that of CIPS by over 86% (= USD12.6 trillion out of CIPS' annual total of USD14.6 trillion).

These tactics for internationalising the renminbi could further erode the declining share of the US dollar in global official reserves and boost the share of the renminbi (Fig. 11.4), as the volume and the scope of using renminbi for international payments could grow when more countries diversify out of US dollar risk. If China gets its economic and reform policies right, that could even boost global confidence in the renminbi and speed up the momentum of the yuan's internationalisation.

China's internationalisation tactics highlight the development that Brazil, China, Russia—the world's largest commodity and energy exporters and importers—are already working together on renminbi cross-border payments. As discussed, due to international sanctions, Russia is conducting its Chinese trade in renminbi. In March 2023, China

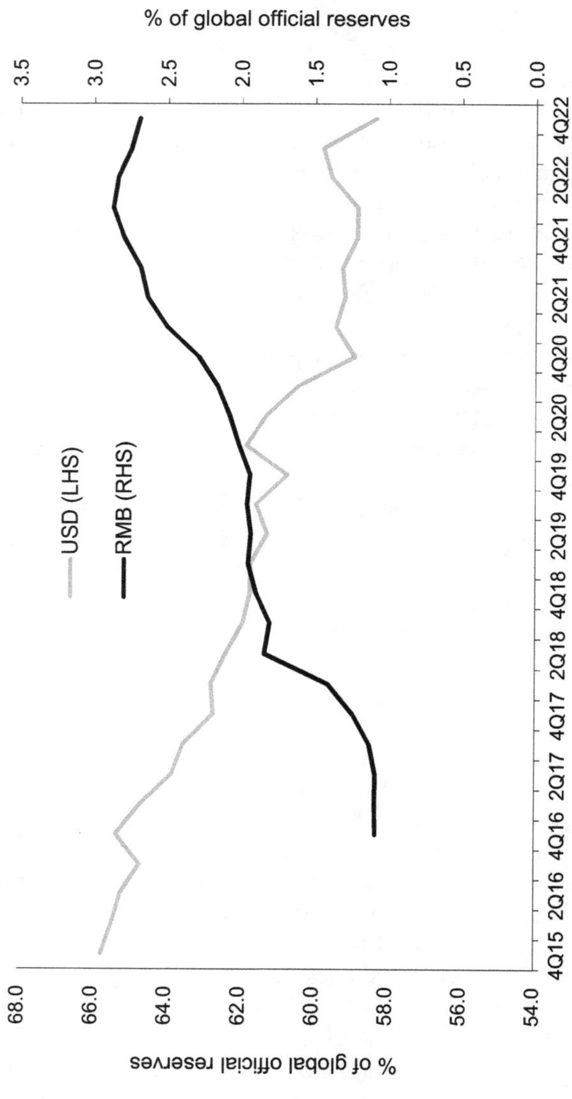

Fig. 11.4 Shares of USD and renminbi in global reserves (*Source* IMF, author)

and Brazil struck a deal to drop the US dollar and use the renminbi directly in cross-border transactions (Tang, 2023).

Furthermore, expansion of the BRICS bloc and China's increasing trade and investment flows with Africa are acting to deepen the renminbi's creeping internationalisation and reinforce China's salami-slicing tactics. These developments also lend credence to the argument that over time when there is enough penetration of the renminbi in a separate jurisdiction, a payments system parallel to the US dollar system could gain critical mass, re-orientating the global payments systems and the underlying technical, regulatory and institutional frameworks to accommodate the renminbi.

Add in the BRICS...

In 2024, Saudi Arabia, Iran, Ethiopia, the United Arab Emirates, Argentina and Egypt joined the BRICS bloc, originally made up of Brazil, Russia, India, China and South Africa (hence the BRICS acronym). Some 20 other countries, including major emerging economies such as Nigeria, Venezuela and Indonesia, have also been keen to join.

Before the BRICS expansion, China renewed discussion with Saudi Arabia on trading oil in renminbi in early 2023. Then in March, as discussed above, a series of events involving France, Brazil, Argentina (Wong, 2023), ASEAN countries and Saudi Arabia, boosted the incentive for other countries to use the renminbi for cross-border transactions. The BRICS expansion builds upon this momentum by broadening the renminbi network for cross-border payments using CIPS and boosting the chance of trading oil and other commodities in renminbi.

The shift towards CIPS may happen faster than expected because half of the six new BRICS members, and some of the 20 countries that want to join BRICS (notably Nigeria, Indonesia, and Venezuela), are major commodity/oil producers. As discussed above, a limited shift of oil trade and cross-border trade to using the renminbi could boost the renminbi's status in global payments significantly, threatening to overtake other major currencies like the Japanese yen and the pound sterling to become one of the top three most widely used global payments currency in the SWIFT system.

... AND AFRICA

China's burgeoning trade relationship with Africa is another emerging force for boosting renminbi internationalisation. China runs a large trade surplus with Africa (Fig. 11.5). This means that African demand for renminbi to pay for the Chinese imports far exceeds the supply of renminbi it receives by exporting to China. China has built the financial infrastructure for enabling renminbi cross-border payments with Africa by signing bilateral currency swap agreements[1] with key countries, including South Africa (RMB30 billion since 2015), Egypt (RMB18 billion since 2016) and Nigeria (RMB15 billion since 2018). These agreements allow the countries to borrow from the PBoC the specified amount of renminbi to pay for their Chinese imports directly without using the US dollar as the conduit currency (Perez-Saiz & Zhang, 2023).

China also set up offshore renminbi clearing banks in South Africa and Zambia in 2015, and Mauritius in 2022. In May 2023, it established

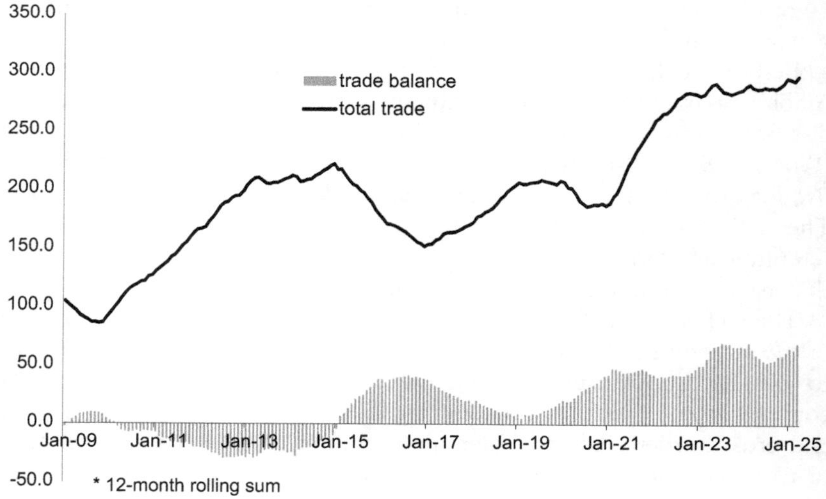

Fig. 11.5 China-Africa trade* (USD billion) (*Note* *12-month rolling sum. *Source* CEIC, author)

[1] These currency swap agreements are renewable every three years.

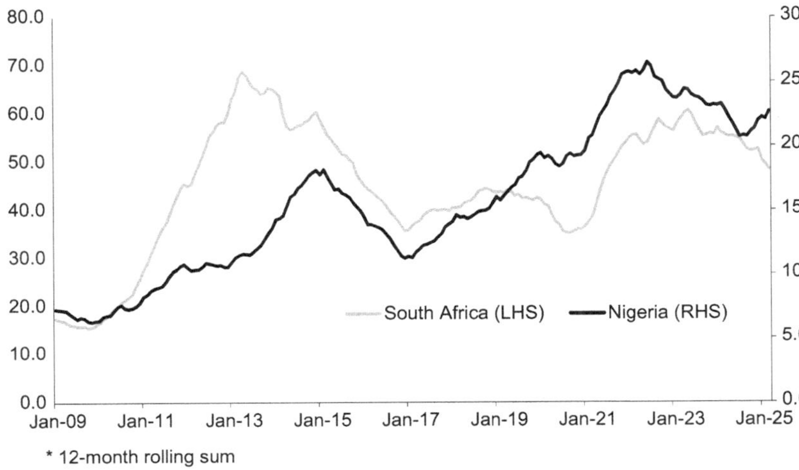

Fig. 11.6 China trade with South Africa & Nigeria* (USD billion) (*Note* *12-month rolling sum. *Source* CEIC, author)

a China-Africa cross-border settlement centre in Yiwu in its Zhejiang province to facilitate direct renminbi cross-border payments. Kenya, Tanzania and Ghana could soon sign currency swaps with China due to their rising Chinese imports.

SWIFT data shows that countries with close China trade ties have taken up renminbi trade settlement quickly. In this regard, South Africa and Nigeria have big potential for increasing the share of renminbi-denominated trade due to their rising trades with China (Fig. 11.6); they are already the largest and second largest importers, respectively, of Chinese goods in Africa.

Gold and Renminbi Bonds

Ethiopia could also see a significant increase in renminbi-denominated cross-border payments due to the potential of increasing its gold export to China and large imports from China (almost 30% of its total imports). As I argued above, gold is instrumental in building up the petro-yuan in the renminbi internationalisation process to eventually challenge the dominance of the petro-dollar system. As a strategy to boost confidence in the renminbi, China could extend its pledge to back oil trade with Saudi Arabia to other countries and other types of international trade in the future.

Such a strategy will boost China's demand for gold and allow major gold exporters, such as Ethiopia, to increase trade with China using the renminbi. Official data shows that China's gold reserve has risen sharply in recent years (Fig. 11.7). This may signal that Beijing is preparing for gold-backed renminbi internationalisation. Some other major emerging market central banks, notably those in Singapore, India and Turkey, have also increased their gold reserves sharply since early 2023, indicating an increase in the incentive to diversify out of US dollar risk exposure.

Meanwhile, creating more renminbi assets, such as renminbi-denominated bonds, is a crucial step towards internationalising the yuan and challenging the dollar. This is because the availability of those assets will create an incentive for countries to use, hold and invest the renminbi that they have accumulated. Renminbi-denominated bonds issued by African (and other developing nation) governments and companies may likely be a new development in this step.

Notably, Egypt, a new member of BRICS that has limited access to international capital markets, was the first African economy to issue a

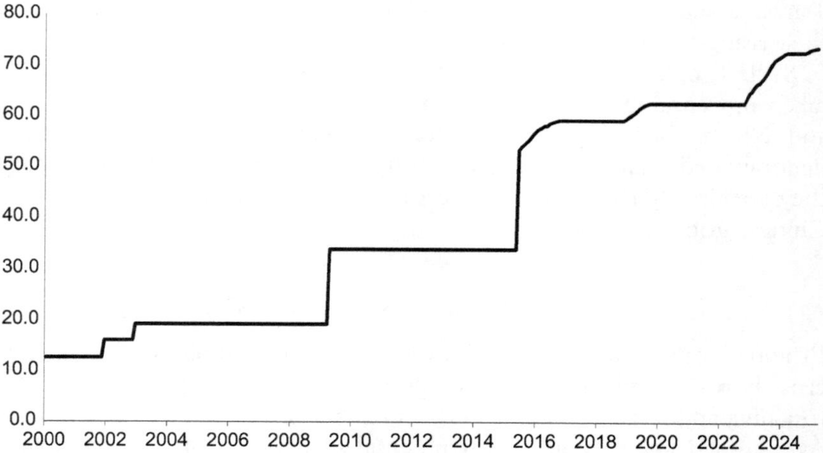

Fig. 11.7 China's gold reserves (million onces) have been rising as renminbi internationalisation moves ahead (*Source* CEIC, author)

Panda bond[2] to finance green and social projects in May 2023. Already, more than 5% of Cameroon, Kenya and Tanzania's external debt is denominated in renminbi. With the US increasingly weaponising the US dollar through the usage of financial sanctions, there is a good incentive for African (and other) countries to reduce their US dollar risk and shift to the renminbi in cross-border transactions and issuing renminbi-denominated bonds.

An Offensive Move by Stealth

China's issuance of US dollar-denominated sovereign bonds in Saudi Arabia in November 2024 could be seen as another creeping step of renminbi internationalisation. Arguably, this is an offensive move to challenge the US dollar hegemony through "a dollar for a dollar" strategy (see below) that expands China's geopolitical influence and hits the US's financial foundation without any visible signs. The crux of this strategy is that China issued those dollar bonds at comparable interest rates to US Treasury bonds and was able to attract significant demand from international, including sovereign, investors.

The implication is that as China issues more dollar sovereign bonds at rates comparable to US Treasuries, it will redirect demand for US dollar bonds away from the US to Chinese bonds, making it harder for the US to fund its twin (current account and fiscal) deficits and strengthening China's influence in the global dollar system. Furthermore, the Belt and Road Initiative (BRI) could become a crucial tool for further expanding such strategy if and when China lends to developing economies the dollar proceeds it raises from issuing bonds in dollars and have them repaid in renminbi.

What happened was China issued USD2 billion sovereign bonds in Riyadh, Saudi Arabia, on 20 November 2024. While the issuance did not attract much market attention (because most players, in my view, were sleeping on the wheel or the story did not fit the China-bashing agenda of the media), there could be far-reaching implications on the US dollar bond market and, by implication, funding for the US twin deficits.

2 A Panda bond is a renminbi-denominated bond issued by a non-Chinese entity sold in China.

This is thus another signal of progress for the renminbi's internationalisation and expansion of China's global influence that has been ignored by mainstream debates.

Intriguing Thoughts

The dollar sovereign bond issuance raises some intriguing thoughts which most observers have failed to notice. Firstly, the Chinese bonds, with maturities of three and five years, were almost 20 times oversubscribed, compared to the usual over-subscription rate of two to three times for US Treasury bond auctions. Such strong demand for USD Chinese sovereign debt likely underscores a global displeasure with the US international leadership and diversification out of US dollar.

Secondly, the interest rate spread of the Chinese bonds was just one to three basis points[3] over that of comparable US Treasuries. This implies that China (with an S&P credit rating of A+/A-1) was able to borrow in US dollar at almost the same interest rate as the US government (which has a higher S&P credit rating of AA+/A-1).

Thirdly, the Chinese bonds were issued in Riyadh—an unusual move as sovereign bonds are typically issued in major financial centres like London, New York and Tokyo. This could mean closer ties between Saudi Arabia and China which have been in talks about renminbi-based bilateral oil trading.

Eroding Funding for the US's Twin Deficits

Crucially, by issuing dollar bonds though in a small financial centre, China is directly competing with US Treasuries for funding by paying almost the same interest rate. This has two implications. Firstly, the strong demand for the Chinese bonds seems to signal that China could eventually become an alternative manager of dollar liquidity in the global system.

Secondly, if China starts issuing more dollar sovereign bonds and can price them at rates similar to those on US Treasuries, it will provide an option for investors and countries to invest their dollars in Chinese government bonds. Given the stock of dollars, one dollar that goes

[3] A basis point is a unit of measure in finance to describe the percentage change in the value or rate of a financial instrument. One basis point is equivalent to 0.01% (i.e. one–one hundredth of a per cent) or 0.0001 in decimal form.

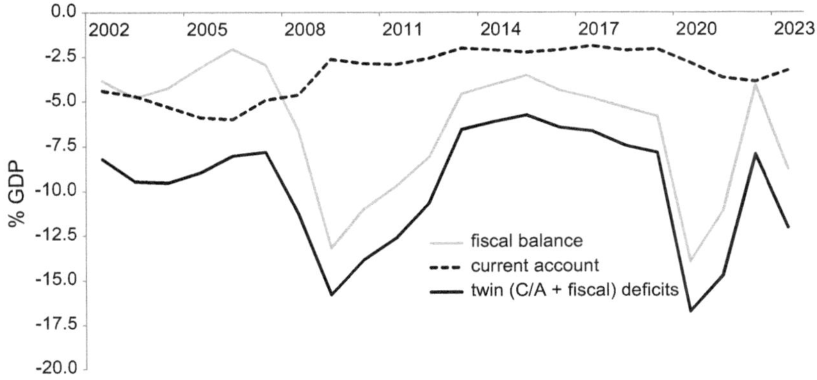

Fig. 11.8 US twin deficits require persistent funding from the world's saving (*Source* CEIC, author)

to buying Chinese bonds instead of US Treasuries is a dollar less for financing the US's massive (12.1% of GDP) twin deficits (Fig. 11.8).

Since the US government needs to constantly sell Treasury bonds to fund these deficits, the emergence of China as a dollar sovereign bond issuer who can direct dollar liquidity away from the US could potentially pose financial problems for the US government and, eventually, erode the US's "exorbitant privilege".[4]

Nudging Internationalisation Forward

China's choice of issuing the US dollar-denominated sovereign bonds in Riyadh and the fact that the Saudis agreed to it can be seen as another step nudging renminbi internationalisation forward. The importance lies in Saudi Arabia's role in the global petro-dollar system, as discussed above. The success of this Chinese dollar bond issuance in a financial centre outside the major ones demonstrates that China had already amassed

[4] This "exorbitant privilege" refers to the benefits the US has due to its own currency (the US dollar) being the international reserve currency. One key benefit is that the US would not face a balance of payments crisis because its imports are purchased in its own currency (US dollar).

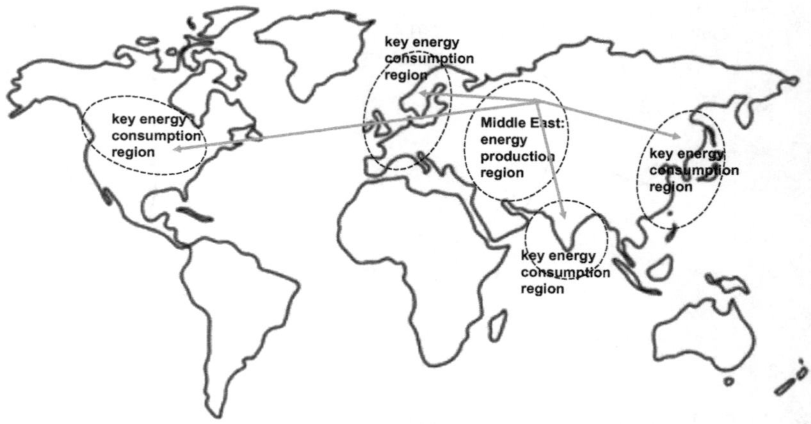

Fig. 11.9 Strategic importance of the Middle East in China's expansion strategy (*Source* Author)

sufficient influence to redirect US dollar liquidity in the heart of the petro-dollar system. Should the Americans not worried?

The Middle East is of particular strategic importance to China's game plan due to its connectivity with the major oil-consuming regions. Establishing a major influence in the Middle East will give China an edge in trading with the major energy consumers on the BRI route and beyond (Fig. 11.9).

"A Dollar for a Dollar" Strategy

The option for Saudi Arabia and other oil-producing countries to invest their billions of dollars of reserves in the Chinese government instead of the US government suggests that China could effectively use the US dollar to hit back at the US in the context of Sino-US geopolitical tensions. Such an approach would be akin to "an eye for an eye" manifested as "a dollar for a dollar" strategy. Should oil-producing countries invest in China's dollar bonds instead of recycling their revenues into US Treasuries, China would effectively be bidding dollars away from the US in the global market, thus hitting the US by inflicting funding pressure on its twin deficits.

While the US Federal Reserve (Fed) could still print more dollars, China would increasingly influence where those dollars would flow. The dollar-for-dollar strategy could potentially weaken the dollar's network effect—when everyone uses it, then everyone else uses it—and increase the renminbi's global impact at the expense of the dollar's hegemony in the long term.

Enter the Belt & Road Initiative

One may wonder what is the point of China issuing dollar bonds and adding to the huge pile of dollars that it has amassed through its current account surplus? Subtly, such dollar bond issuance lays bare China's motive for accumulating US dollar to advance its renminbi internationalisation programme through the BRI network.

Out of the 195 countries in the world, 150 are part of the BRI. Crucially, many of these owe dollar-denominated debts to the US government or other developed world lenders. China could use its US dollar to help the BRI countries pay off their dollar debts to the developed world and arrange for them to repay China in renminbi, or through other bilateral arrangements such as strategic resources.

This would be a "one-stone-kills-three-birds" move that would allow China to

(1) use its excess dollars.
(2) to help its partner countries reduce their USD risk exposure, and
(3) deepen its integration with BRI countries, and, by corollary, alienate them from the US.

China's help would make strategic sense for the BRI countries also as it could help them escape the dollar debt trap, reduce their dollar risk exposure (including that of US sanctions) and improve relations with the main country helping their development: China.

Geopolitical Implications

China's sovereign dollar bond issuance programme in effect makes it an intermediary at the heart of the dollar system. While the dollars still make their way back to the US through the US government borrowing to fund its twin deficits, there is now an alternative route to flow back to the US through China's borrowing. This alternative builds Chinese rather than American influence in the global system and undermine the US's ability to finance itself as well as to monitor the global system.

How Might the US Respond?

One response would be to threaten sanctions against countries or institutions that buy China's sovereign dollar bonds. Indeed, there are signs of the US doing so. On 30 November 2024, then US President-elect Donald Trump wrote on his social media platform, Truth Social, demanding that BRICS member countries commit to not creating a new currency or supporting another currency that would replace the dollar or face 100% tariffs (Honderich, 2024).

However, such scare tactics only showed that dollar assets would not be safe from US political interference and, thus, could encourage countries to diversify out of the dollar, further eroding its network effect. This can already be seen as an after-effect of US sanctions against Russia, which created some impetus for countries to move out of the dollar together.

Another option would be for the US Fed to raise interest rates to attract demand for US Treasuries. However, China could easily match that and nullify the impact. Crucially, raising rates by the Fed for this reason would be self-defeating. This is because it would increase the US government's borrowing costs when it is already struggling with financing the massive twin deficits, potentially creating economic and financial crises.

On the contrary, were China to pay higher interest rates to attract demand for its sovereign dollar bonds, it could dry up demand for US Treasuries. This could force the US to respond by also raising rates, which would disrupt its financial and economic systems. From this, one can see how destructive and clever this a-dollar-for-a-dollar strategy could become.

The US could go for the "nuclear option" of shutting China out of all US dollar transactions. However, this would hurt the US at least as much as China due to the complicated crisscrossing relations between China, the US and the world. It would effectively fragmentate the global financial and trade system and undermine the dollar's role as the global reserve currency—an outcome the US is trying to avoid.

From a global investment perspective, the creeping influence of the renminbi can be seen to be building the foundation for making Chinese assets a standalone asset class in the long term, rather than part of the emerging market asset class. The rise of China as a manager of dollar liquidity could influence the future demand for US Treasuries and US interest rate levels. There is little the US can do to avoid its global influence being eroded in some shape or form.

Geopolitical tensions and strategic competition between the two big powers will continue for the foreseeable future. On a positive note, thinking about all this in the Game Theory framework, if China's strategy is to force the US to contemplate every possible uncomfortable outcome, the drive for both players to reach a "Nash equilibrium" (where a player will stick with their chosen strategy and have no incentive to deviate from it, after considering the opponent's best strategy) could lead to constructive competition in the future. That might mean that the unpleasant implications financial markets have feared may not materialise.

The US will just have to come to terms with the reality of living alongside China.

Is King Dollar in Danger?

This is the ultimate question for assessing the "clash of the Titans" in their competition for global power in the modern days. Good news for the dollar is that its global supremacy will remain safe for some years due to what financial market players called "TINA"—There Is No Alternatives. This means practically there are no viable challengers to the US dollar as the world's dominant reserve currency, despite the increase in global incentive to diversify out of the dollar. From a general equilibrium economic perspective, the dollar will likely become a weak currency in the long term when the global economy starts correcting the prevailing saving-investment imbalance.

Concerns about the US dollar's dominance as a global reserve currency are not new. They were first raised in the 1960s by Valéry Giscard d'Estaing, the French finance minister who accused the US of abusing the dollar's "exorbitant privilege". More recently, doubts over the dollar's supremacy increased again with the US-led sanctions against Russia since 2022, as the sanctions have raised the fear about who's next and, thus, boosted the global incentive to reduce US dollar exposure.

Particularly disconcerting was the simultaneous sell-off in the dollar and US Treasury bonds when US President Donald Trump started the global trade war in 2025. This phenomenon runs counter to their (US dollar and Treasuries) traditional safe-haven roles during times of high market volatility and rising risk aversion. Even when the US was at the epicenter of the 2007–10 subprime crisis,[5] investors still flocked to the safety of the dollar and US government bonds.

Although the share of the dollar in global reserves had fallen from a peak of about 85% in the early 1970s to about 58% in 2024, according to the International Monetary Fund's (IMF) data, it was not the currencies of the major economies like Europe, Japan and China that gained at the dollar's expense. Rather, it was the other smaller currencies, such as Canadian and Australian dollars, that gained global reserves shares at the expense of the US dollar (Fig. 11.10).

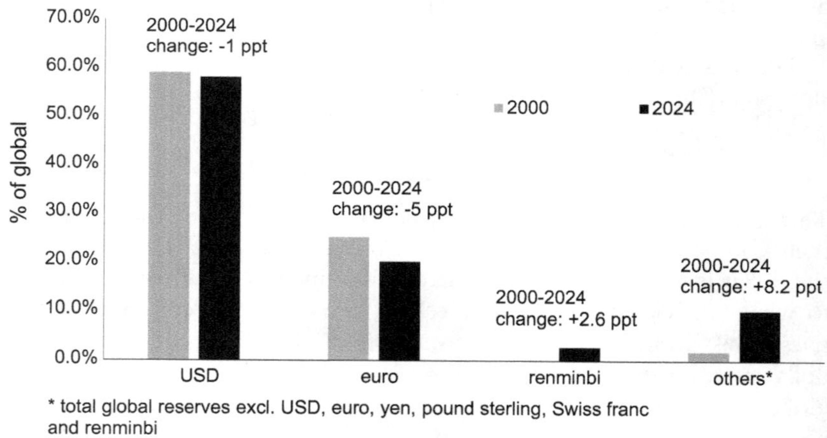

Fig. 11.10 The share of other smaller currencies* in global reserves has surged since 2000 (*Note* *Total global reserves excl. USD, euro, yen, pound sterling, Swiss franc and renminbi. *Source* IMF, author)

[5] The US subprime mortgage crisis occurred between 2007 and 2010. It was caused by the widespread default of high-risk mortgages, leading to a severe economic recession that spilled over to the world economy and resulted in the Great Financial Crisis (GFC). The subprime crisis was triggered by the bursting of the housing bubble, which was fuelled by low interest rates and lax lending practices in the years before the eruption of the crisis when many homeowners defaulted on their mortgages. The US-originated crisis eventually led to a cascade of events that brought down financial institutions and triggered the GFC.

Since the turn of the millennium, global reserve managers have been diversifying out of the dollar into smaller currencies and gold. IMF data shows that the global allocation of foreign exchange reserves to the minor non-US dollar currencies rose from less than 2% in 2000 to 10% in 2024. This increase occurred in two waves. The first wave started with the eurozone's debt crisis in 2011, which exposed the fundamental flaws in the monetary union and, hence, hurt public confidence in the euro as a global reserve currency. The euro's share of global reserves peaked at about 28% in 2010 and has stabilised at around 20% since 2015.

The second wave coincided with the growing geopolitical tensions between China and the US since around 2017. This has hurt global sentiment in the renminbi as a global reserve currency. Despite more than doubling its share in the global reserves pool since 2016, the renminbi's share remains stuck at below 3% of the global total (see Fig. 11.4). The Russo-Ukrainian war has aggravated the worries of central bank reserves managers about the Sino-US geopolitical rivalry. The draconian US-led sanctions against Russia have raised concerns about whether China is still an "investible" market (a subject that we shall examine in the next chapter).

Aside from these other fiat currencies, central banks have also been diversifying into gold. This process has also accelerated since the Russo-Ukrainian war in 2022. With all of Russia's hard currency reserves being frozen by the US-led sanctions and all Russian international transactions being shut out of the SWIFT system, central banks around the world have become much more aware of the benefits of holding physical gold as a hedge against such US sanction risk.

The Practicality of "TINA"

Although these other smaller currencies account for the majority of the gains in global reserves shares at the expense of the dollar's share since 2000 (see Fig. 11.10), their markets are small and relatively illiquid. It will, thus, not be possible for global reserve managers to increase much further their allocation to these currencies. Meanwhile, the tradeable size of the gold bullion market is also small (estimated at about USD3.5 trillion) relative to the total global foreign exchange reserves pool of USD14 trillion and storing and transporting bullion are practical problems. All this makes it difficult for the gold bullion to become a major reserve asset to rival the dollar.

The renminbi's Lilliputian role in global finance means that to challenge the US dollar, China needs to develop deep and liquid domestic financial markets and make the renminbi fully convertible with an open capital account. Once confidence in the financial system builds, foreign businesses will be more willing to accept the renminbi as a form of payment and investors and reserve managers will become more comfortable with holding assets denominated in renminbi. However, it could take years, and possibly decades, before any of this happens (if at all).

Since the creation of the Special Drawing Rights (SDR)[6] in 1969 as an alternative reserve asset, the euro has come the closest to rivalling the dollar. However, the euro's ascent was disrupted by the 2011 debt crisis. Also, Russia's experience warns the other countries that holding euros is no better than holding dollars when it comes to collective Western sanctions because Russia's euro assets are frozen and transactions in euros are shut out of the SWIFT along with the US dollar assets and transactions.

Weakening the King Dollar

While TINA can keep King dollar's throne until some viable alternatives are found to replace the US dollar's supreme status, there is another way for the rest of the world to wean itself off US assets and erode the dollar's global influence. That will happen when the world starts to correct the saving-investment imbalance by stopping to generate so much excess savings. The global economy has been kept in an unstable equilibrium with excess savings in the current account surplus countries flowing to fund excess investments in the deficit countries.

Official data shows that China, the eurozone, Japan and Gulf Cooperation Council (GCC) members[7] are running large current account surpluses amounting to an aggregate current account surplus of more than USD1 trillion on an annualised basis. By definition, these excess

[6] The SDR is an international reserve asset created by the IMF to supplement the official reserves of its member countries. The SDR is not a currency. It is a potential claim on the freely usable currencies of IMF members. So, SDRs can provide a country with liquidity. The SDR basket includes five currencies, namely, US dollar, pound sterling, euro, yen and renminbi.

[7] The Gulf Cooperation Council (GCC) is a regional organisation comprising six Arab states: Bahrain, Kuwait, Oman, Qatar, Saudi Arabia and the United Arab Emirates. Its primary goals are to enhance coordination and integration among its members, promoting economic, political and social cooperation.

savings must find their way to economies that are deficient in savings and running current account deficits. The US has run a chronic and large current account deficit for decades, making it the largest, deepest and most liquid market that can absorb such a large pool of surplus savings (Fig. 11.11). Other deficit economies are simply too small to take in the vast amount of excess savings being generated (Fig. 11.12).

The day of reckoning will come as and when the world's saving countries start spending more on their domestic economies and, thus, reducing the pool of excess savings to fund the US current account deficit. In the short term, the US trade war in 2025 has put pressure on large surplus countries like China and Europe to significantly increase domestic spending to counteract the negative impact on their economic growth. In the long term, there is an increasing intention for the world to start correcting the unsustainable global saving-investment imbalance as the willingness to fund the US current account deficit wanes. The point is that if a greater portion of global surplus savings are directed inward to fund domestic spending, that will leave less to flow abroad (to fund the US deficit).

A reduction in excess savings in the rest of the world will mean one of two things for the savings deficient US economy: higher bond yields or a weaker dollar. With an open capital account, the US is subject to the "impossible trinity" policy constraint, i.e. with free flow of capital,

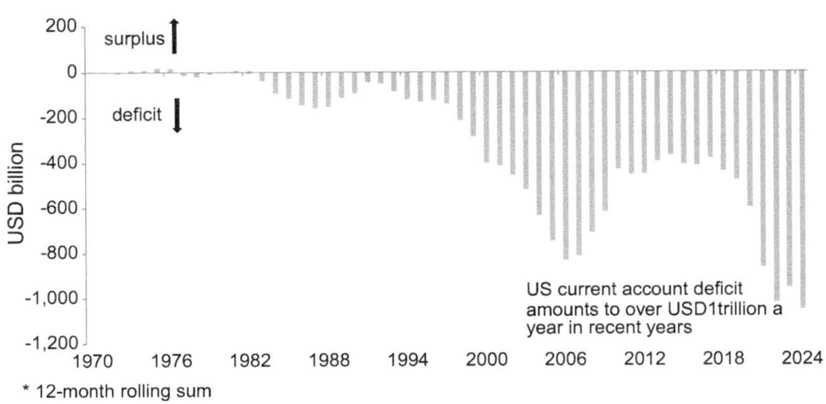

Fig. 11.11 US chronic current account deficit* reflects its savings deficit (*Source* CEIC, author)

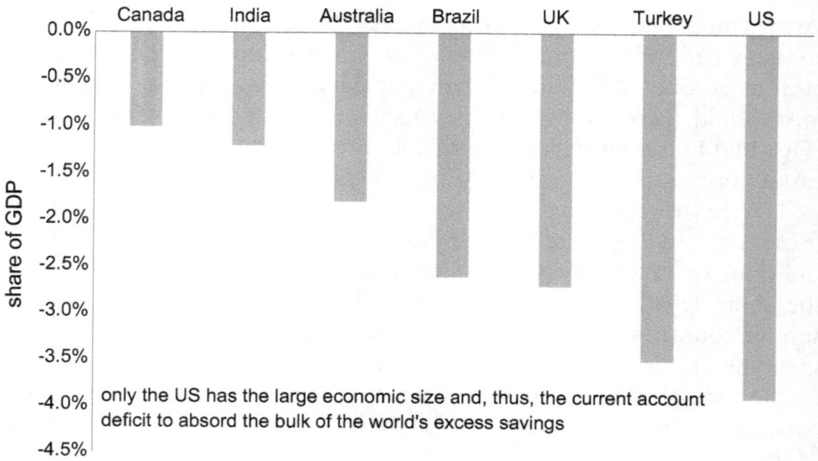

Fig. 11.12 Top current account deficit countries (2024) (*Note* *12-month rolling sum. *Source* Trading economics, author)

the authorities can either control interest rate or exchange rate, not both. As the Fed policy choice has been to target interest rates and not the dollar, US bond yields will be largely determined by the stance of Fed policy (Fig. 11.13). That will leave the dollar to bear the brunt of less excess savings from overseas flowing into the US. In other words, as the Fed needs to keep US interest rates low in the long term, the US dollar exchange rate will come under continued downward pressure as demand for US dollar falls on less attractive returns, *ceteris paribus*.

So, both cyclical (short-term) and structural (long-term) forces are negative for the dollar. This also means that even without the challenges from the renminbi's creeping internationalisation and Beijing's "a dollar-for-a-dollar" strategy, the US dollar is likely to be a weak currency in the long term. That will be a sign of the King dollar's declining influence on the global stage, although the renminbi is not ready to overtake the dollar's global supremacy.

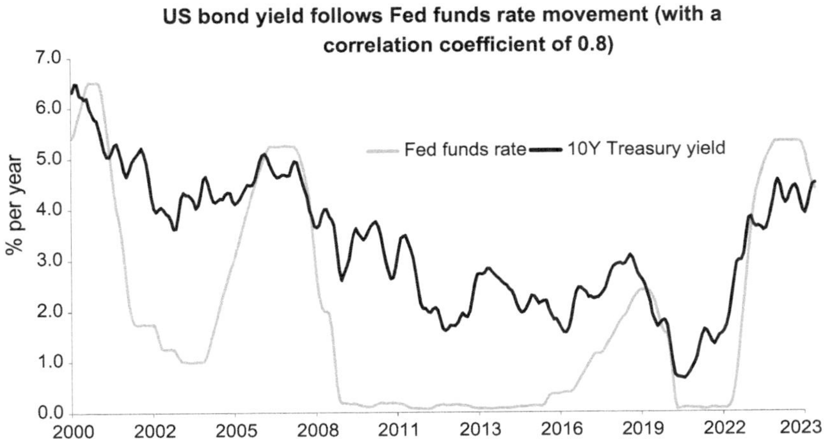

Fig. 11.13 US bond yield follows Fed funds rate movement (with a correlation coefficient of 0.8) (*Source* CEIC, author)

References

Honderich, H. (2024). Trump threatens 100% tariff on Brics nations if they try to replace dollar. *BBC News*, 2 December. Retrieved from https://www.bbc.com/news/articles/cgrwj0p2dd9o

Kalin, S. (2022). As Saudi Arabia Cools on the U.S., It warms to China. *The Journal, Wall Street Journal Podcast*, March 17. Full transcript retrieved from https://www.wsj.com/podcasts/the-journal/as-saudi-arabia-cools-on-the-us-it-warms-to-china/46e7073c-88b3-4708-8440-e4f72c863e3f

Lo, C. (2017). *Demystifying China's mega trends: The driving forces that will shake up China and the world*. Emerald Publishing.

Lo, C. (2021). *China's global disruption: Myths and reality*. Emerald Publishing.

Perez-Saiz, H., & Zhang, L. (2023). Renminbi usage in cross-border payments: Regional patterns and the role of swaps lines and offshore clearing banks. *International Monetary Fund*. IMF Working Papers Vol. 2023, Issue 077. 31 March.

Salameh, M. G. (2018). The Petro-yuan: A momentous game changer for the global energy markets, the global economy and sanctions. In *International Association for Energy Economics*, IAEE Energy Forum, Third Quarter (pp. 29–33).

Tang, F. (2023). China's yuan makes Brazilian inroads, as 'de-dollarisation reflects cracks' in US currency settlements. *South China Morning Post*, 3

April. Retrieved from https://www.scmp.com/economy/china-economy/article/3215857/chinas-yuan-makes-brazilian-inroads-de-dollarisation-reflects-cracks-us-currency-settlements

Windsor, C., & Halperin, D. (2018). RMB internationalisation: Where to next? *Reserve Bank of Australia Bulletin*. September.

Wong, K. (2023). Argentina to settle Chinese imports in yuan as China marches into South America to dethrone US dollar. *South China Morning Post*, 27 April. Retrieved from https://www.scmp.com/economy/global-economy/article/3218577/argentina-settle-chinese-imports-yuan-china-marches-south-america-dethrone-us-dollar?module=inline&pgtype=article

CHAPTER 12

Is China Un-investible (Collapsing)?

In the great powers' competition for global supremacy, many global players have doubts about the sustainability of the Chinese system and argued that China had become an un-investible country due to problems in the banking system, the property market, an ageing population, the high debt burden, a weak private business environment, an opaque business framework with poor governance, the lack of rule of law, a corrupted government... the list goes on. The concerns stemming from these doubts then become not just a savage China challenging a rules-based US but also an eventual implosion of the Chinese system upending the world system.

Many observers have also compared China's problems with Japan's in the early 1990s and argued that China had fallen into a trap of "Japanification" with decades of debt-deflation and zero growth unfolding. Believing this is the case, these observers have suggested China to implement quantitative easing (QE) as a policy prescription to save its economy from collapsing and, by implication, the global economy from the apocalyptic China effect. Following on from this view, some others have argued that China was already in decline and would be replaced by India as an emerging economic power.

Many of these opinions seem to have developed into conventional wisdom since the pandemic. They sound legitimate and logical. Nevertheless, careful and balanced analyses of China's role in the evolving global

C. Lo, *Clash of the Economic Titans: China and the United States*, https://doi.org/10.1007/978-981-95-2510-2_12

environment reveal that many of these arguments were just conventional views with no wisdom. Many of them have shown partial understanding of China's economic and policy evolution. Others are, as often, just biased by focusing on the stock of China's problem but ignoring the improvements that China has made in recent years. In the following, we assess these debates and views from some other angles that many observers have overlooked (either intentionally or unintentionally).

While bearish sentiment on China is not new, it has risen to new high since the Covid-19 pandemic with many global investors arguing (even at the time of writing—three years after the pandemic) that China had become un-investible. The bearishness is understandable, given China's weak economic growth momentum and financial and property market woes, and the disappointment with the government's policy response to these problems since it re-opened the economy in April 2023.

However, these concerns are also examples of the lack of understanding by many observers about China's economic and policy development. Even many so-called financial experts (those highly paid fund managers and analysts working in the financial markets) got China's cyclical problems confused with structural issues, with the media aggravating the confusion (He, 2023), while China's structural transformation was in fact still on track according to evidence.

Conventional but No Wisdom

The conventional wisdom in 2023 was that Beijing's policy in handling the Covid-19 health crisis was flawed. Such a policy mistake, the view goes, had intensified the country's economic weakness that portends a serious long-term problem that will unfold in the post-pandemic years (Goodman, 2023; Kynge, 2023). America's narrative about China at the time had even changed to a "wounded dragon" from a "peer competitor", with former President Joe Biden reportedly calling China a "time bomb" in economic problems (Eaglen, 2023; Galbraith, 2023; Gao, 2023).

The "time bomb" talk about China is not new. Many market observers have long-predicted banking and debt crises in China. However, China has defied these dire predictions by keeping the "ticking debt bomb" from going off. Furthermore, the view that China's huge debt burden had restricted Beijing's options to deal with the country's problems is myopic, as I have repeatedly argued elsewhere with evidence that China's debt is a manageable problem and is not a constraint on Beijing's macroeconomic policy management (Lo, 2021, Chapter 6).

The problem with the conventional analysis on China's debt problem is that it has mainly focused on the liability side of the economic balance sheet. The debt debate has overlooked the asset side, which shows that some local governments are investing in productive investments and improving their financial stability (Lo, 2021, Chapter 7). The crucial combination of a closed capital account, the self-funded nature of China's debt and a strong political will to reduce debt has kept a long-predicted debt-currency crisis in China at bay, and it should continue to minimise such risk. China will likely allow market forces to play a bigger role in its future debt-reduction efforts.

The slow growth that China has experienced since Covid-19 and the government's post-Covid insufficient policy easing stance is a policy choice. As Beijing quits the old debt-fuelled supply-expansion growth model, it has refused to return to the old playbook of massive reflation and is willing to tolerate slower growth rates. Perhaps more dangerous than misreading China's debt problem is a lack of insight in the world opinion into the nature of China's development. This shallow understanding can lead to a misunderstanding of China and its debt dynamics and other economic challenges, and lead to poor investment decisions and policy reactions.

There's More than Meets the Eye

Let us see how distorted public information and reports have aggravated the world's bearishness on China's economic future after the pandemic. Arguably, partial information and analysis like what we discuss here are prevalent in the US political circle and lead to misinformed policy decisions by the administration to continue to use trade wars to hit China, thinking that China is still an export-led economy when, in fact, it is not (see Chapter 1).

The economic problems in China that the world dwelled on after Covid-19 were mainly cyclical problems, which could be resolved by policy stimulus. The economic malaise was, thus, a matter of Beijing's overly cautious policy but not of its inability to boost growth as most of the world's opinions saw. Crucially, China's economy was not in a dire state as the media painted. The economic data spoke volume about exaggerated pessimism fanned by erroneous and biased information.

Take the international trade numbers, which even China critics agree that they do not (cannot) lie.[1] The sharp drop in 2023–2024 in the value of China's imports, a widely reported indicator of domestic demand growth, was misleading because in volume terms imports continued to grow (Fig. 12.1). This meant that physical demand was still growing but falling prices had depressed the value of imports.

Urban per-capita expenditure growth also outpaced per-capita income growth in 2023, suggesting a recovery in urban consumer demand funded by household saving (Fig. 12.2). The recovery might not be as strong as the market expected, but this data implied that the loss of consumer confidence might not be permanent, as many observers and the media loosely assumed it was. So, more assertive policy easing could revive confidence and boost consumer spending.

Furthermore, per-capita disposable income grew faster than nominal GDP since 2023 (Fig. 12.3), suggesting that the share of output accruing to households was rising, not falling as it is wrongly perceived. The combination of rising personal income and consumption funded by saving

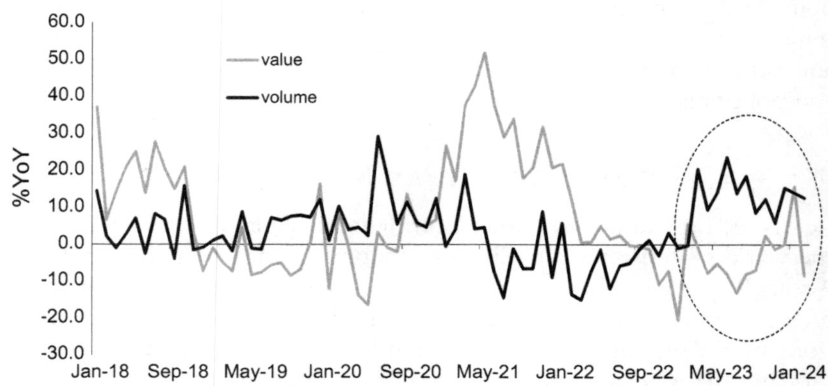

Fig. 12.1 China's import value fell in 2023–2024 but volume continued to rise (*Source* CEIC, author)

[1] This is because one can always cross-check China's trade data with those of China's trading partners. For example, data of China's imports from the US can be cross-checked with data of US exports to China.

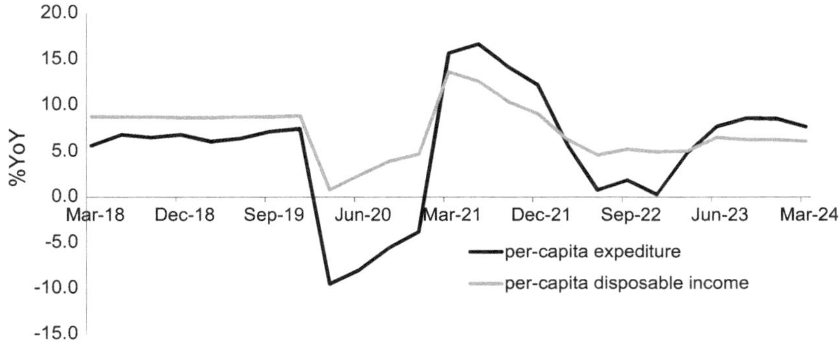

Fig. 12.2 Household expenditure > income growth => no economic collapse (*Source* CEIC, author)

means that policy stimulus could effectively boost household consumption by improving the economic outlook and reviving public confidence. This underscores the argument that it was Beijing's policy choice not to massively reflate the economy but not that it ran out of policy options.

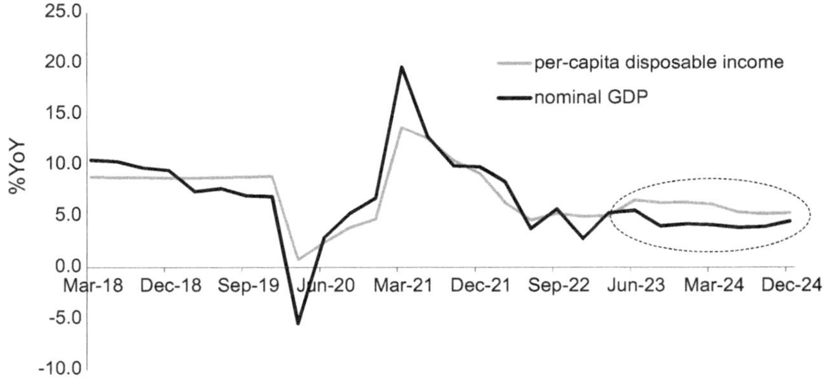

Fig. 12.3 China's household disposable income growth > nominal GDP growth (*Source* CEIC, author)

Structural Transformation

Meanwhile evidence shows that China's structural transformation is ongoing, albeit slowly, but not derailed as many China critics told us. There is nothing new about the world's view that China has too much savings and that it will need structural rebalancing to put more income in the hands of the consumer so that consumption can take over investment as the long-term growth driver. So, the slogan of "invest less, consume more" has become conventional wisdom.

However, there is something wrong with this slogan. This is because China still needs investments in many underdeveloped parts of the country to create income and consumption growth. Consumption alone is not a panacea for saving the Chinese economy, as many observers have blindly assumed and argued. Does China need more televisions and furniture but fewer flats/houses to put them in, should China have more cars for consumers but worse roads, fewer petrol stations, trains and other transport means?

The reason why the Chinese saving rate is so high is because they have incomes. Where do these incomes come from? A large part is from jobs created by investments. So, contrary to conventional wisdom, the average Chinese household is not income constrained; otherwise, it would not be able to save so much. Simple economics tells us that saving should equal investment in the long run. This also implies that high saving should lead to high investment. Hence, blindly following the "invest less, consume more" mantra makes no sense for a high-saving country that still have areas for development.

Furthermore, high savings should naturally lead to high debt because financial intermediation, mainly by banks in China's debt-financed growth model, channels savings into investments by transforming savings into debt. This happens as soon as the savings are lent out for funding investment (Lo, 2017, pp. 111–114). Thus, high debt, by creating a future income stream through investment, is not necessarily an evil for China unless it is not backed by any assets or is backed by bad assets.

What's New?

Recognising this investment-consumption cycle and past reform errors, Beijing made a tactical shift in its structural reform direction under its broad "dual circulation" strategy in the second half of 2020. The new tactics favour "hard tech" over "soft tech"[2] development and engage the private sector as a driver for innovation. This approach should revive industrial migration to the interior provinces, a trend started in 2005 but was interrupted in 2013, with high value-added industries leading the way. Data shows that this resumption is already happening (Fig. 12.4). When properly implemented, the continuation of industrial migration should not only revive GDP growth momentum but also raise productivity in the long term with the new industries tapping cheaper and idle resources in the poorer provinces inland.

China's post-Covid economic recovery has been fragile, but the problems are mainly cyclical and can effectively be resolved by aggressive fiscal expansion facilitated by monetary easing. It is a matter of the government's calculated easing move. The structural transformation is still ongoing with renewed investment growth focusing on high-value manufacturing and high-tech industries. In the new economy, Beijing's key tasks lie in improving education, health care and the labour market structure by matching jobs to skills, in providing for the elderly, in curbing pollution and controlling climate change and, at the same time, in cutting the debt-to-GDP ratio.

An Economic Paradox

These efforts are tall orders and there is no guarantee that they will succeed. However, they are on China's policy agenda and will be implemented over time. Excess pessimism based on misinformed narratives does not help understand this matter. Nevertheless, there is an economic paradox that has puzzled the world, including many people in China.

Evidence shows that China has decisively shifted from a growth-maximising model to a growth-quality model. This shift involves a "creative destruction" process that is inherently contractionary. However, it conflicts with Beijing's "common prosperity" policy which needs continued economic expansion at an average GDP growth rate of around 5% a year between 2020 and 2035 to achieve the policy's goal of doubling per-capita income. These policy conflicts have created a

[2] Hard tech refers to the production of hardware and components that caters for the country's strategic and high-tech development. Soft tech refers to the e-commerce development that caters for non-strategic consumption demand.

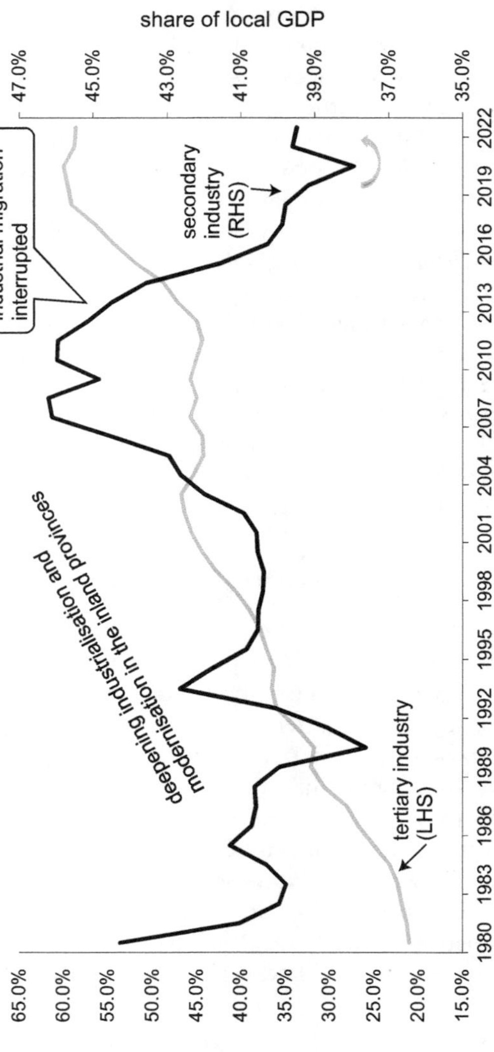

Fig. 12.4 Industries migrating inland* (*Source* CEIC, author)

paradox—Beijing's deflationary structural reform policy clashes with its reflationary growth needs to double per-capita GDP by 2035.

Domestically, the paradox is also about Beijing's focus on re-industralising the economy by creating a high-tech system at the expense of consumption. This could risk damaging growth before reaping the benefits of economic restructuring. Externally, such a policy could worsen trade and geopolitical tensions, especially with the US. Crucially, China's economic reform model is based on strategic usage of market forces to change the economy under state guidance. However, many foreign players, including politicians and the media, have assumed that the market is the driver of such changes.

Arguably, China's economic paradox is attributable to the change by President Xi Jinping in the government's policy objective function to improving growth quality rather than maximising growth rates, subject to the policy constraints imposed by structural reforms and debt reduction. The Xi administration wants to focus on "high-quality development" and "new quality productive forces" by retreating from the old economy of polluting industries, infrastructure investment and property investment. While the latter helped lift China from poverty to middle-income status, the new policy direction aims at escaping the middle-income trap and pushing China to a rich-income status by structural rebalancing towards a high value-added manufacturing and high-tech economy.

Hence, Chinese officials have little incentive to revive the old economy. This is notably the case in relation to the real-estate slump since 2022, as success would do little to improve their political standing while failure could end their careers. Had the authorities eased policy decisively after the pandemic, consumer confidence and private-sector "animal spirits"[3] could have been restored, instead of leaving them stuck in the doldrums (Figs. 12.5, 12.6). The crux of the policy problem since Covid-19 has been the obstruction by the leadership's structural policy directives of forceful cyclical policy easing. Hence, economic growth has suffered.

[3] In economics, "animal spirits" refers to the emotional and psychological factors that affect economic decisions, particularly investment and spending behaviour. These factors include optimism, pessimism, confidence and fear. They can be as powerful as rational factors in shaping economic outcomes but are not always predictable and quantifiable, hence the term animal spirits.

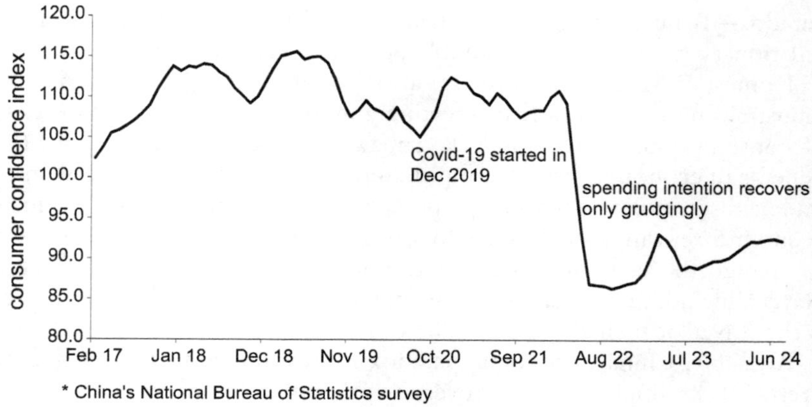

Fig. 12.5 China's consumer willingness to spend* has not recovered to pre-Covid level (*Note* *China's National Bureau of Statistics survey. *Source* CEIC, author)

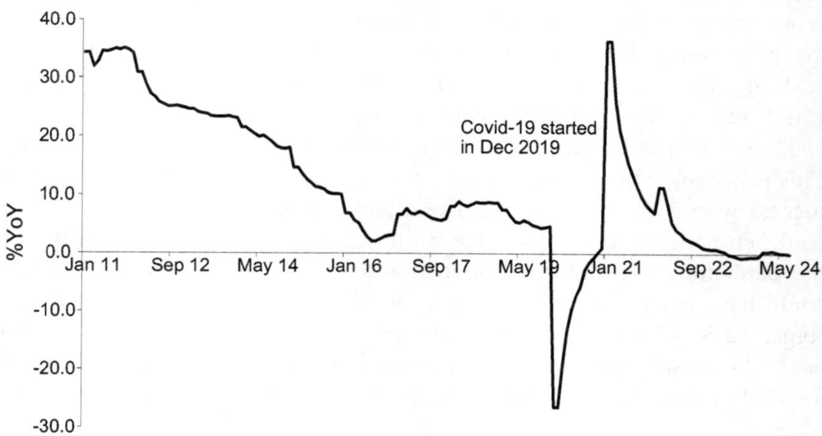

Fig. 12.6 China's private-sector investment growth (*Source* CEIC, author)

A Revolutionary Change…

Now let us examine China's changing reform tactics that have been misunderstood by many observers and politicians. What is revolutionary about President Xi's approach is the forceful change in the political and economic incentives that had governed China for over four decades. In March 2018 the Communist Party revised the constitution to remove the presidential term limit at the National People's Congress. Many players in the West saw this as a significant setback on governance that threatens to nudge China towards dictatorship. However, it was probably China's only option to manage daunting reforms in the face of significant incentive problems that threatened to derail the country's long-term growth. The decision to centralise power was taken because decentralisation had been tried before in China, but it failed to move the country forward as intended.

In the two decades before Mr. Xi took office, Beijing delegated more autonomous power to the regional governments to encourage them to try out economic reforms. They were allowed to own businesses and run major regional affairs, including land allocation, business development, infrastructure construction, local fiscal policy and law making and enforcement. The central government also encouraged regional governments to compete to get rich. GDP growth became the predominant political objective with appointment and promotion of government officials being tied to local growth performance.

This decentralised framework created an incentive scheme of "chasing growth at all costs". It also gave rise to powerful provincial officials, who acted like regional "warlords", defying central government decrees and indulging in rent-seeking and corruption. Indeed, Chinese bureaucrats have a long history of skillfully resisting orders from above and abusing power. It should perhaps not be surprising that the decentralised power structure that evolved after Deng Xiaoping failed (Lo, 2015, pp. 70–80).

Having inherited a corrupt system with strong regional defiance, Mr. Xi faced a high risk that his reforms intended to pull China out of the middle-income trap would fail. That, in turn, risked the political demise of the Communist Party under the system's incentive distortions and corruption. According to the Transparency International Corruption Index—which ranges between 0 (highly corrupt) and 100 (entirely clean)—in the 20 years before Xi Jinping took office, China was very corrupt. The index averaged only 33 under both the Jiang Zemin and

Hu Jintao administrations between 1995 and 2012. But it has risen to above 40 since Mr. Xi came to power (Fig. 12.7), reflecting some initial success of his new policy focus, including the draconian anti-corruption campaign.

…That is Not Obvious

From Mr. Xi's perspective, there is a link between leadership power and reform implementation. His vision for the future is not to reduce state intervention but to refine the role of the state in the economy. The new economic model is a strategic mix of the state driving changes and market forces being used as a tool to make the changes.

Thus, the need for greater leadership power, as reflected in the elimination of the presidential term limit, has become a key element of Mr. Xi's implementation efforts. He has moved forcefully to change incentives away from single-mindedly maximising growth to targeting multiple policy goals, such as maintaining GDP growth, alleviating poverty, reducing financial risk and protecting the environment.

By replacing the old, simple, incentive with a complex set of priorities (which is impossible to optimise simultaneously), Mr. Xi has created a high-pressure political environment to break local defiance and ensure strict compliance with central decrees. Under this multi-priority system, local officials do not know the best way to satisfy Beijing's multiple goals. So, they simply comply with the orders rather than trying to be creative and defiant. Eliminating the presidential term limit also made it clear to the local officials that there are no alternative power centres for them to appeal to, and that waiting for Xi to pass from the scene is not an option, except when he dies. To survive and thrive required pledging loyalty to Xi.

The New Reform Tactics

In 2020, Beijing made a tactical shift of its dual circulation policy to tackle intensifying domestic and geopolitical challenges, in particular Sino-US competition. To achieve common prosperity under the new reform tactics, China has reiterated its policy of increasing (not stifling, as many observers said) the role of the private sector in the economy. High value-added manufacturing and innovation driven by the small- and medium-sized enterprises are to serve as the engines for raising China's

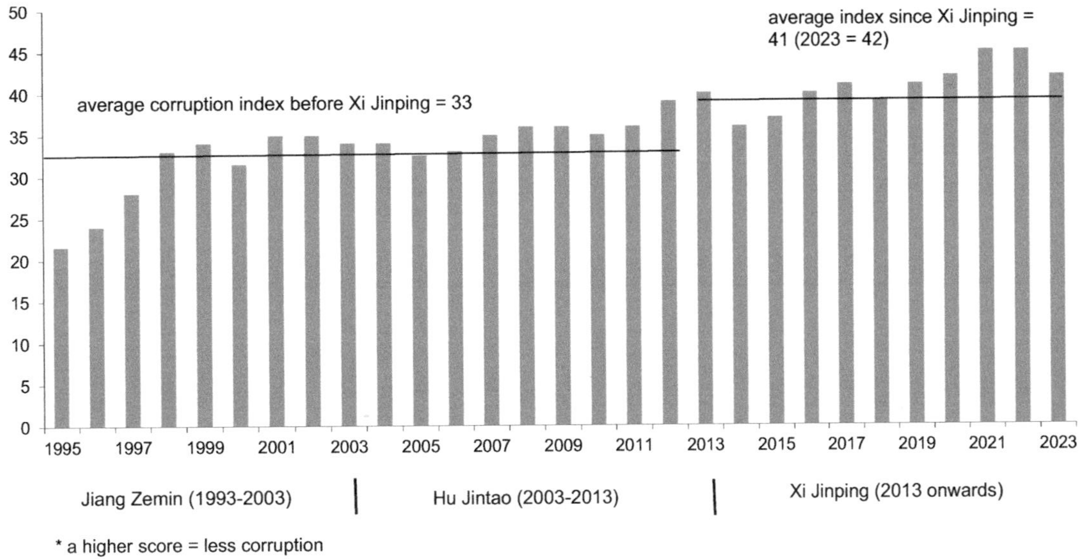

Fig. 12.7 China's corruption index* (*Note* *A higher score = less corruption. *Source* Transparency International, author)

productivity. This is different from the Western interpretation of Beijing's policy to re-centralise power by marginalising the market mechanism.

Since the National People's Congress in March 2024, Mr. Xi has advocated for unleashing "new quality productive forces" to stimulate "future industries"[4] under the guidance of a "new national system" of coordination and capital allocation. This new policy incorporates both market forces and state guidance and is the latest iteration in China's long-term development policy.

Technology is a "new quality productive force" (in addition to the classical ones of labour and capital) to generate disruptive breakthroughs. The goal is not simply to produce incremental improvement in existing technologies. Previous industrial policy efforts mainly focused on achieving competence, self-sufficiency or global market share in established technologies. The new generation of development policies focuses on future industries that are nascent or do not yet exist.

These ambitions will be realised through a centralised "new national system" for coordinating public- and private-sector resources, led by the new Central Science and Technology Commission (CSTC), for funding scientific research and innovation. Chinese leaders are prepared to tolerate some inefficiency and waste as a cost for producing champions in the process. Local governments are doing everything they can to foster emerging industries, from combining venture capital with public investment to attracting scientific talent that are threatened by America's scrutiny of Asian scientists (Wagner, 2021).

OECD data shows that China had gained more than 2,400 scientists in 2021 when the US suffered a net loss of scientists under the US's new China-containment policy (Bier, 2023). If this is a strategy that America hopes to use to out-compete, or contain, China in the technology race, it is not working. It has actually backfired on the US (Hu et al. 2024). The data speaks volume about that.

The US National Science Foundation (NSF) data shows that the global share of China's papers published in scientific and technological journals already surpassed those by the US as early as in 2018, with the Chinese

[4] The list of "future industries" published by the Ministry of Industry and Information Technology in January 2024 includes manufacturing, information, materials, energy, space and health, and on the technology side includes humanoid robots, nano-manufacturing, quantum computing, nuclear fusion, hydrogen energy, exploration of the moon and Mars, deep-sea mining and genetic engineering.

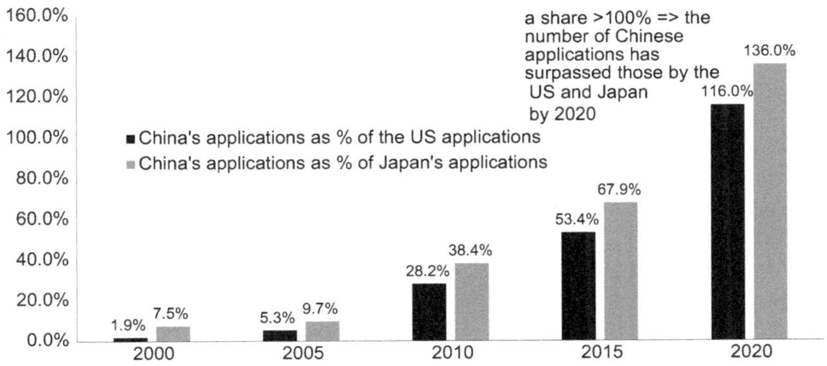

Fig. 12.8 Number of patent cooperation treaty (PCT) applications by China as a share of US and Japan applications (*Source* World Intellectual Property Organization, author)

papers increasing from 5.0% of the world total in 2000 to 20.7% in 2018 surpassing the 16.6% by the US. The leap in the number of patent cooperation treaty (PCT) applications by China as a percentage of the US's and Japan's applications was even more specular, with Chinese applications surpassing those by the US and Japan in 2020 (Fig. 12.8).

The China Risk

However, the problem with this rebalancing strategy is that the old and new economies are deeply intertwined. If the old economy falters too quickly, it will also hinder the rise of the new. This can already be seen in the battered property market since 2022, which has wiped out jobs and destroyed household wealth and public confidence, significantly damaging private-sector spending.

Shifting to a high-tech economy needs steady and reasonably strong GDP growth and healthy public finances so that the government can invest in new industries, retrain workers and establish social safety nets to minimise the shock on the labour market. Without a robust economy, the transition risks "killing the goose that lays the golden egg". However, China is accelerating its shift to cutting-edge technologies as its economy loses growth momentum and the local governments run into debt problems. This backdrop makes its structural transformation risky.

Beijing's single-minded focus on producing advanced-technology products has driven local authorities to over-invest in sectors that Mr. Xi favours, notably electric vehicles and solar panels. This has created an incentive problem of what some researchers called "low productivity innovation drive", when local officials inflate the number of patents and innovations by encouraging junk patents (Ang et al., 2023). This leads to wastage and excess capacity, forcing producers to export goods and exacerbating trade and geopolitical tensions, especially with the US.

The failure to recognise China's economic paradox creates risks for the world too. Those who focus only on China's economic problems worry the country may make aggressive military moves (like attacking Taiwan) as its power wanes, a perspective that could lead to a vicious cycle of mutual antagonism and geopolitical risk (Hass, 2024). China indeed faces strong growth headwinds amid its structural rebalancing process, but predictions about China imploding and becoming un-investible are mostly based on partial understanding of China.

This brings up another concern about China, which has developed since the end of the pandemic, that it is following the Japanese footsteps by falling into a balance sheet recession soon. This has even led some "experts" to advocate quantitative easing (QE) as a policy prescription for China to save its economy from the falling into the Japanese economic quagmire of debt-deflation and decades of lost growth. The global disruption stemming from a Chinese balance sheet recession and a QE policy could be significant due to China's vital role in the global supply chains and increasing importance in the world's financial system and investment flows. So, how serious is the risk of a balance sheet recession in China, and is QE the solution for it?

What is a Balance Sheet Recession?

A balance sheet recession results when high levels of private-sector debt force individuals and companies to focus on debt reduction by cutting spending and investment. This is unlike a recession caused by business cycle fluctuations or macroeconomic policy tightening. Bursting of an asset bubble in a high-debt economy may trigger a balance sheet recession which would destroy wealth and confidence, forcing economic agents to cut spending to deleverage and create a debt-deflation spiral and prolonged economic stagnation. Japan's experience since 1990 has been a prime example.

Financial engineering adds to the problem by:

(1) transforming debt into financial instruments and selling to investors as assets and
(2) funding asset churning that pushed most of the developed world into a balance-sheet-recession adjustment after the 2007–2008 subprime crisis.

China's economy does exhibit some balance sheet recession symptoms. However, data and evidence show that only a limited amount of wealth in China is destroyed, China's debt is simple, there is limited financial engineering, and China's economic balance sheet does not look impaired.

Talks about China falling into a balance sheet recession has emerged since its post-Covid economic recovery has lost momentum and "animal spirit" have failed to recover. Notably, the resulting drop in confidence has caused private-sector investment to decline steadily (see Fig. 12.6). This not only deprives the economy of growth momentum but also reflects a balance-sheet-recession symptom of loss of confidence forcing economic agents to cut spending and minimise debt rather than maximise profit or utility.[5]

The Curse of Debt-Deflation

In a balance sheet recession, trouble starts with high debt accumulation. When an asset bubble bursts, it destroys wealth and impairs the economy's balance sheet. Public confidence collapses, forcing the private sector to cut spending to reduce debt and the impaired financial institutions to cut lending. Credit implosion ensues.

Unless external demand comes to rescue via a surge in the trade surplus or there is massive fiscal stimulus, private income falls, pushing up the debt-to-income ratio (or debt burden) and aggravating the debt-reduction effort. This soon creates a vicious debt-deflation cycle with spending cuts leading to income contraction, raising the debt burden and forcing the private sector to cut spending further to reduce debt (Fig. 12.9).

[5] The term utility here is used in an economics context, meaning the total satisfaction or benefit a consumer derives from consuming a good or service. Economic theories assume that a typical consumer is rational and strive to maximise her/his utility.

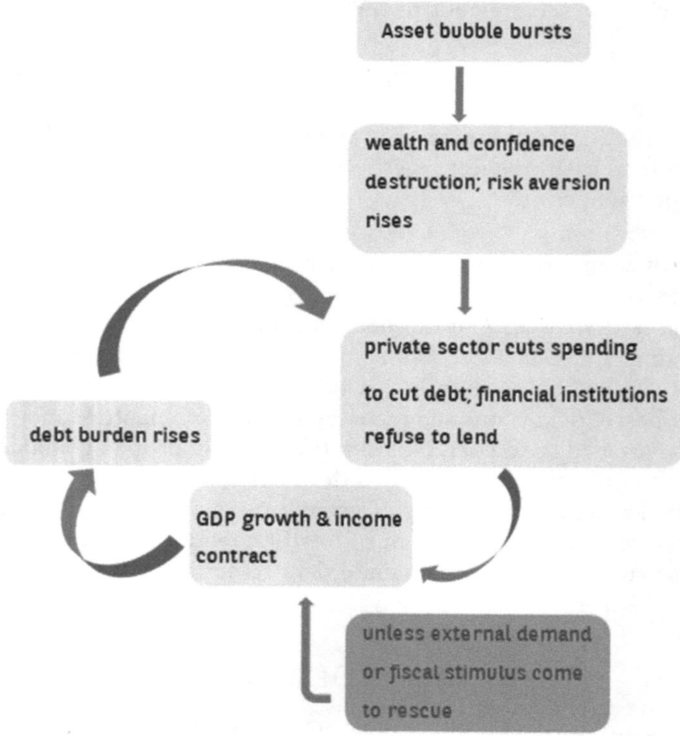

Fig. 12.9 A debt-deflation spiral of balance sheet recession (*Source* Author)

The crux of the problem is wealth destruction and risk aversion forcing the private sector to deleverage and the impaired financial institutions to cut lending. Financial engineering adds to the root of the problem that laid behind the 2007–2008 subprime crisis, which eventually led to the Global Financial Crisis (GFC) and pushed the developed world, notably the US, into a balance sheet recession (Lo, 2010, Chapter 1).

In a highly indebted system, financial engineering transforms debt into investment products which become assets when sold to the public. Many players also borrow to engage in asset churning. These transactions inflate the value of the asset side of the balance sheet, prompting players to borrow more to fund the churning and inflating the asset values further.

As the party goes on, such financial engineering activities and debt-funded investments do not create any real assets but only create asset bubbles like building a pyramid upside down on sand.

When the asset bubble bursts, the debt-fuelled assets deflate. Initially, the value of the liability side of the economy's balance sheet remains unchanged but the value of the asset side collapses, making companies insolvent and impairing the system's balance sheet. Later, when companies go bust, the value of the liability side also goes to zero, causing the economy's balance sheet to implode and pulling the rug from under the financial system. In the absence of new sources for growth, prolonged economic stagnation ensues.

While much of the financial engineering is absent in China, it exhibits some classic balance sheet recession symptoms, including high debt, a loss of confidence, a bad property market, high-risk aversion cutting consumption and bank lending, and system-wide deleveraging. These similarities have prompted some observers to compare China with Japan's experience after its asset bubble burst in 1990 and argue that China is falling into balance sheet recession (Daniel, 2023).

Really? Let us assess the hallmarks of balance sheet recession—debt, wealth destruction, financial engineering, loss of confidence and deleveraging—in China's perspectives to get a better understanding.

Debt Risk

China has a high debt ratio (Fig. 12.10), but as I have argued elsewhere it is not dire (Lo, 2017, Chapter 5). China has persistently defied predictions of a debt-currency crisis because its debt is self-funded,[6] its capital account is relatively closed and Beijing is pursuing a selective "implicit guarantee" policy to uphold systemic confidence. This combination makes China's debt a manageable risk. The China debt debate has been distorted by many observers' ignorance about the asset side of China's economic balance sheet and financial innovation that have positive impact on growth. Meanwhile, conventional wisdom has exaggerated China's debt problem (Lo, 2021, Chapters 6 and 7). The point is that China's debt is not going to cause an economic balance sheet implosion as many China critics have assumed it would.

[6] China has a small foreign debt of 13.6% of GDP (in 2022), compared to a national saving rate of over 40% and foreign exchange reserves of 19% of GDP.

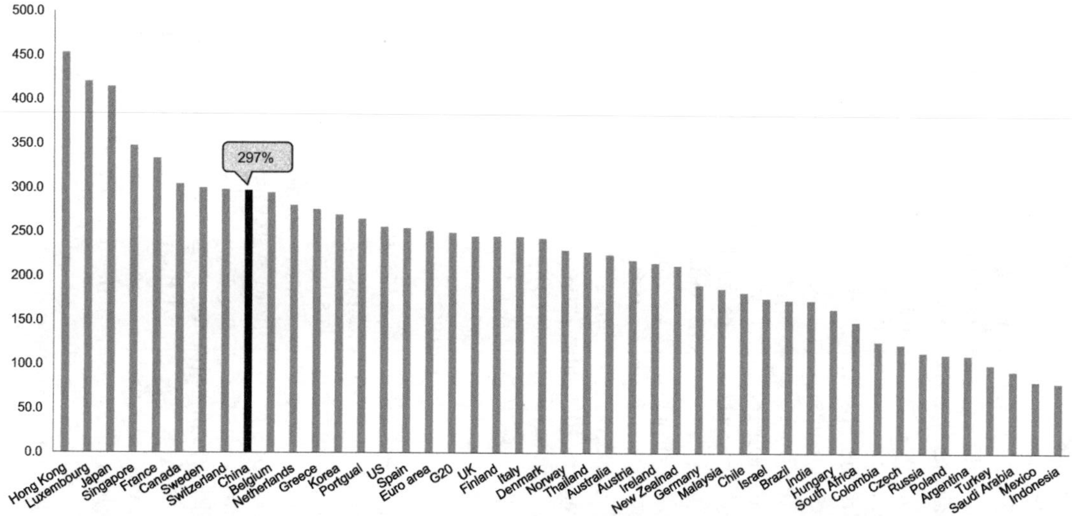

Fig. 12.10 Debt-to-GDP ratio (%) for non-financial sector (2022) (*Source* BIS, author)

Wealth Destruction

The wealth effect from the stock market on China's private-sector spending is limited because the bulk of Chinese assets is not held in financial assets but in property. And despite the property market woes, there is limited wealth destruction and little risk of large-scale negative equity on mortgages.

Estimates of the share of Chinese household's financial assets (including stocks and bonds and products in insurance, trusts and wealth management) range between a mere 20% and 30% of total wealth. China's stock market (CSI300) dropped by only 6.8% during the pandemic (2020–2022). Hence, the negative wealth effect of the stock market on Chinese household is limited.

About three-quarters of China's household wealth is held in property. The decline in housing prices throughout Covid was also limited, thanks to Beijing's restrictive property market measures, including lending restrictions and at least 30% down payment for the first home and 60% for the second before the relaxation after 2022. Thus, property market correction in China typically comes from contraction in transaction volumes but not in price crash. Here too, wealth destruction has been contained.

Financial Engineering

Overall, China's housing market indebtedness is not high. Despite a rising trend, mortgage loans account for only about 20% of total bank loans. Crucially, there are no financial derivatives, such as collateralised debt obligations (CDOs) and asset-backed securities (ABS), and no organisations such as the Fannie Mae and Freddie Mac in the US, for leveraging up the housing market. Hence, few residential mortgage loans are in negative equity.

China's immature credit system and limited financial innovation have also barred many high-risk buyers from entering the property market. Thus, it is unlikely for China to experience a 2007–2008 subprime crisis US-style housing crash and a "Minsky Moment", which is an abrupt and significant drop in asset values because of rampant speculation funded by borrowed funds on the back of prolonged economic prosperity,[7] that would lead to massive wealth destruction.

Loss of Confidence and Deleveraging

Hence, it is not high debt and massive wealth destruction, but the combination of a bad property market and three years of Zero-Covid policy[8] (that caused prolonged, severe and disruptive quarantine and lockdowns), that has killed public confidence in China. Crucially, deleveraging in China is a policy decision. It is not forced by any bursting of asset bubbles triggering a collapse in confidence and private-sector spending.

Beijing launched a debt-reduction campaign as early as in 2013 to end the unprecedented post-GFC credit expansion. In 2017, it curtailed shadow banking activities and forced state-owned enterprises (SOEs) to cut their leverage ratios. In 2018, regulators imposed sweeping rules to rein in commercial banks' wealth management products, which was closely related to underground financing activities, to reduce systemic risk. All these efforts resulted in a fall in China's debt ratio between 2017 and 2019 (Fig. 12.11). The campaign was only shelved in 2020 when Covid-19 hit.

Crucially, China has persevered with its debt-reduction resolve through tough times (Fig. 12.12) by upholding the financial de-risking policy between 2018 and 2021, despite the trade war with the US (which started in 2018) and the Covid-19 health crisis (which erupted in late 2019). This deleveraging resolve sets China apart from other financial crisis countries whose governments left it too late to deal with the debt problem.

[7] There are three kinds of borrowers in the Minsky world. (1) The hedge borrower (who can repay principal and interest from cash flow), (2) the speculative borrower (who can only repay interest and needs to roll over the principal by further borrowing) and (3) the Ponzi borrower (who can repay neither interest nor principal and must borrow, or sell assets, to meet the interest bill). Professor Minsky argued that prolonged and robust growth would breed economic complacency and increase the number of speculative and Ponzi borrowers. They are the culprits who cause asset bubbles that eventually burst with devastating economic effects.

[8] China's Zero-Covid Policy is an attempt to prevent any community spread of the coronavirus. To achieve this goal the country has enacted some draconian measures, implementing a strategy of using strict, targeted lockdowns and mass testing. Entire neighbourhoods have been sealed off across the country.

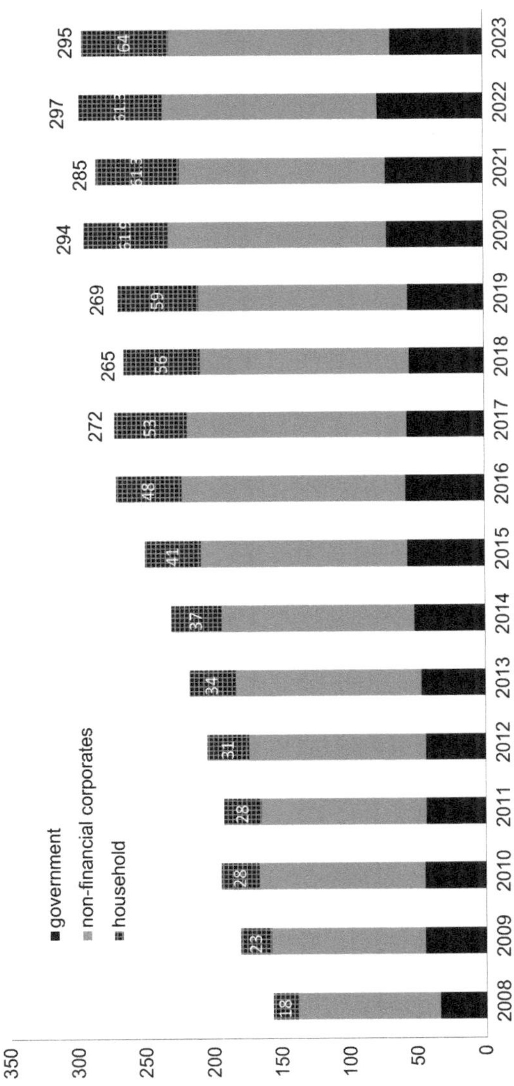

Fig. 12.11 China's debt-to-GDP ratio (%) (*Source* BIS, author)

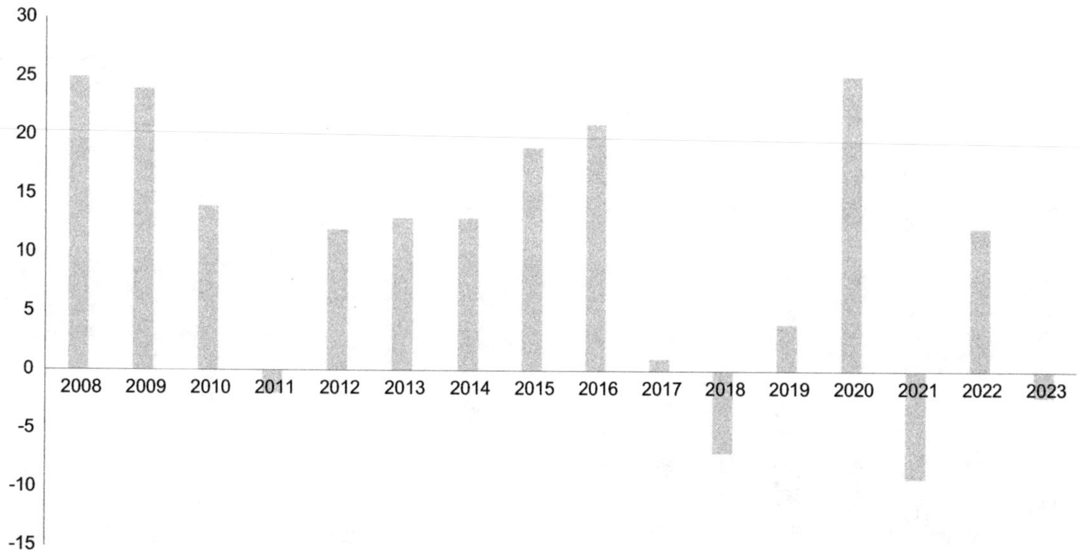

Fig. 12.12 Year-over-year change in China's domestic debt-to-GDP ration (%) (*Source* BIS, author)

Growth Sources

How about growth sources, the lack of which is a key tenet of balance sheet recession? As I argued earlier, China's "dual circulation" development strategy, implemented since 2020, is re-discovering and deploying new resources for sustaining long-term growth to counter external exigencies and global demand shift. It focuses on supply chain security, high-value manufacturing, high-tech development and new infrastructure, including inter-city railway, research and development on energy and environmental technology, 5G/6G networks, artificial intelligence and Internet of Things.

This strategy is reviving the industrial migration trend, which was started in 2005 but was interrupted in 2013,[9] to the interior provinces where untapped and cheaper resources are available, with high value-added industries leading the way (See Fig. 12.4). If China gets this new development strategy right, it could make the economy more productive and create sustainable growth momentum, leaving the balance sheet recession an even more remote possibility. The world should reassess China's growth outlook based on its new structural reform direction but not dwell on the stock of its past problems.

Nevertheless, owing to the balance sheet recession concern, there were voices in 2023–2024 advocating that China should implement (or had already implemented) QE to dig the economy out of the Japanese-style debt-deflation doldrums. Evidence and economic theories show that this policy suggestion lacked understanding about China's policy and system environment and, thus, missed the point.

China's nominal interest rate was far above zero and its real interest rate still had room to fall to address the economy's liquidity trap problem. Beijing must ease monetary policy further and for longer to resuscitate economic growth because the Chinese system's credit flows were clogged and misallocated. Structural policy, not QE, should be used to repair China's impaired monetary transmission mechanism and capital misallocation. Given that nature of China's post-Covid economic problems, monetary easing is necessary but not sufficient for boosting the economy. Fiscal policy must do heavy lifting to revive growth momentum.

[9] The process was interrupted in 2013 when the reform policy focused on shifting the economic growth drivers from investment and manufacturing to services and consumption.

Why QE?

Strictly speaking, QE is an unconventional form of monetary easing implemented when the nominal policy interest rate hits zero, thwarting the central bank's ability to stimulate growth via interest rate cuts. In such circumstances, the central bank can buy assets from the private sector (or even the government) and pay for these assets by creating "central bank reserves". This is referred to as "printing money", though technically the central bank does not have to print any banknotes.

Typically, the central bank either sets a target for the quantity of assets it will buy at any price, or it sets a target for the price of an asset and buys however much is needed to hit that price. The purposes are:

- To flood the system with liquidity to reduce the term premium and risk-free yield (or, simply put, interest rates) for as long as needed to encourage risk-seeking behaviour to revive economic activity, and
- As a forward guidance, to signal that interest rates will stay lower for longer to boost aggregate demand.

Conditions in China

In 2023–2024 when those QE voices were the loudest, China's interest rates were still far above zero. So, there was still room for the People's Bank of China (PBoC) to cut interest rates before considering QE. Generally, when the PBoC buys government bonds in the open market, it is easing monetary conditions in a positive, not zero, interest rate environment. Such a move is liquidity management, like open market operations (OMO), and not QE. It is amazing, and a puzzle to me, that so many of those financial experts calling for China to implement QE have no such basic economic knowledge.

Some observers have also argued that the expansion of the PBoC's balance sheet since 2023 (Fig. 12.13) indicated the start of QE. This view shows ignorance about how China conducts its monetary policy. The PBoC's balance sheet expansion is mostly driven by its mid-term lending facility[10] (MLF) injections and relending.[11] These operations are not system-wide easing, but QE is. They are targeted injections limited to PBoC-designated sectors and banks as directed by Beijing.

From a policy management perspective, trading government bonds directly on the secondary market enables the PBoC to engage in a so-called "operation twist"—as the US Federal Reserve and the European Central Bank occasionally do—to sell (or buy) short-term securities and buy (or sell) long-term securities simultaneously to bring down (or raise) long-term interest rates. Such trades do not expand the central bank's balance, so it is not QE as some analysts have mistaken.

With no evidence that China has suffered from a balance sheet recession, as discussed above, and traditional monetary policy tools are still available, why would China need to implement QE?

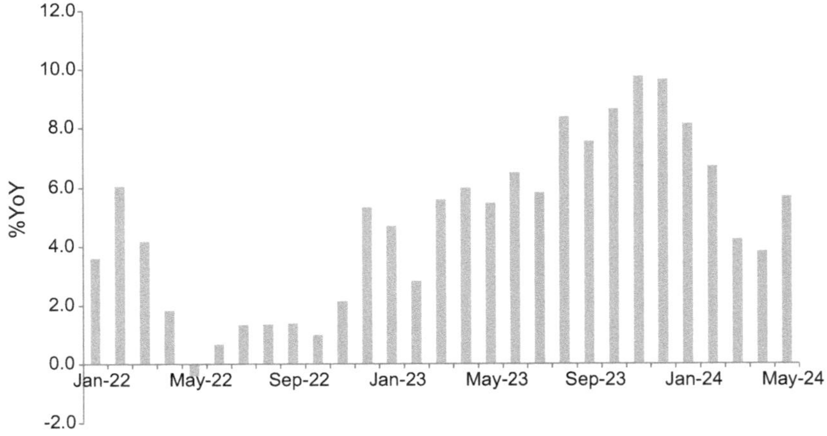

Fig. 12.13 PBoC's balance sheet growth (*Source* CEIC, author)

[10] A mid-term lending facility (MLF) is a monetary policy tool used by the PBoC (and generally by central banks) to provide medium-term liquidity to financial institutions through borrowing money from the PBoC for a specific period, typically between 1 and 5 years.

[11] Relending refers to the process of a bank or financial institution re-lending funds that it has received from the PBoC (or generally from another lender) to its own customers. This involves taking on the credit risk of the borrower, who then uses the funds for their own purposes.

Cost Versus Benefits

Proponents of QE for China have also overlooked its uncertain economic benefits and hefty costs. QE relies on asset price inflation to create a wealth effect on consumption and investment. However, this may not work as intended when a loss of confidence leads to high-risk aversion and destroys consumption and investment appetite, leaving the liquidity idling in the system. This is indeed the case in China since the pandemic. With interest rates remaining positive, traditional monetary policy tools, not QE, still have a role to play in resolving the problems.

QE, the argument goes, also has the benefit of weakening the renminbi exchange rate. This would help boost China's exports, increase its capacity utilisation and end deflation. This argument is flawed, and the perceived benefits are marginal, as evidence shows.

Firstly, the RMB exchange rate is not a major factor affecting China's competitiveness. This is seen in the continued increase in China's global export market share despite economic and geopolitical shocks (Fig. 12.14) and disregarding exchange rate fluctuations. The resistance among West economies to surging exports of China's electric vehicles (EV) is an indication of China's competitive strength[12] in this emerging industry of the world. To protect their automotive industries, the US,[13] Europe[14] and Canada have imposed significant import tariffs on Chinese EVs.

Secondly, contrary to the conventional wisdom, China no longer relies on exports to drive growth, as I have argued throughout this book. Since the 2007–2008 GFC, net exports have been only an auxiliary growth force in China's economy; in many years, they actually dragged on GDP growth (see Chapters 1 and 7).

[12] Whether the competitiveness is achieved through comparative advantage or government subsidies is irrelevant here. The point is that China's EVs are super-competitive, with prices 40% and 125% below those of Western brands in various markets.

[13] In May 2024, the US announced tariffs of 102.5% on Chinese EV imports.

[14] In June 2024, the EU also announced provisional tariffs on Chinese EV imports up to 40% on top of the existing 10%. The EU's new tariffs are still provisional at the time of writing because they may be reduced if Chinese producers can prove that they get lower subsidies than the EU has estimated. Also, if China can reach an agreement with the EU to reduce the volume of Chinese EV exports to Europe, the new tariffs may not be implemented at all.

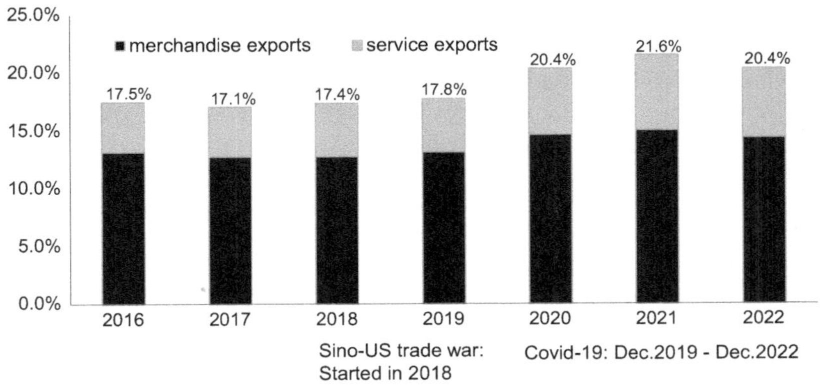

Fig. 12.14 China's share of merchandise & service exports in global markets (*Source* Statista, author)

The point is that if the renminbi exchange rate were to be used as a tool to generate some material growth momentum for the economy, it would have to fall significantly (e.g. by 20–40% according to my calculations) to boost China's exports to help GDP growth. However, such a devaluation would exacerbate trade tensions and cause financial chaos in the global markets, something that Beijing will not want to do.

QE Not a Solution

Crucially, but not widely known, China's monetary transmission mechanism has broken down since the Covid-19 health crisis, reflecting incomplete reforms of the country's monetary policy framework. From a cyclical perspective, this means Beijing must ease monetary policy more and longer than in the previous cycles for it to have the same impact on growth. In the longer term, it will have to implement more financial reforms, reducing its "implicit guarantee" policy further to address the moral hazard problem and truly liberalising interest rates to allow the monetary pricing tools to work properly.

Beijing also needs to correct the rent-seeking incentive and regulatory arbitrage problems in the financial sector so that credit can flow to where it is needed most but not to inefficient sectors. These incentive problems have led to an excess capacity conundrum, which has arisen as misallocation of capital creates excess capacity in one part of the economy while starving the other, efficient, part of credit (Lo, 2015, pp. 96–108).

A regulatory (or interest rate) arbitrage that distorted credit flows was "round tripping" of bank loans, which was quite a prevalent practice in 2023–2024.[15] Here, banks lend to large companies to fulfil the banks' regulatory requirements for loan growth. So, narrow money supply M1 increases. Then the banks turn around and offer the borrowers a time deposit rate above the loan rate, enticing them to deposit the loan back in a time deposit. As a result, there is no net increase in M1 for funding economic activities. However, M2 increases due to the increase in corporate time deposits, but those funds remain idle in the system.

QE cannot fix such incentive problem. Microeconomic and structural policy solutions are needed. Indeed, Beijing has been implementing regulatory reforms since 2017 to deleverage and de-risk the financial system, and by attacking the various forms of the incentive problem. In 2024, it cracked down on round tripping of loans by banning banks from offering fixed deposit rates higher than the lending rates.

Since 2023, the situation in China has been one of a liquidity trap when there is liquidity in the system, but it is not taken up due to a loss of confidence. The impaired monetary transmission mechanism only rubs salt into the wound. All this has led some market players to compare China's economic woes after the pandemic with Japan's post-bubble situation in the 1990s that plunged the Japanese economy into three decades of debt-deflation and lost economic growth.

The comparison is wrong, in my view, because China has not fallen into a balance sheet recession as Japan did. However, the sharp change in the world's opinion in Japan since early 2024—that it is finally moving out of a long-running debt-deflation spiral into a wage-price "virtuous" inflation cycle—contains some lessons for China to avoid the risk of falling into a debt-deflation spiral (more discussion on this in the next chapter).

[15] For a stylised example of incentive problems creating systemic financial distortion, see Lo (2015, pp.115–120) in Bibliography.

A Lesson from Japan

The biggest lesson is to keep the real interest rate (r) low for long enough to drive a persistent negative gap between the real interest rate and the real GDP growth rate (g) to sustain economic growth in a debt-deflation environment. Experience suggests that a prolonged (r-g) gap of around – 200 basis points is needed[16] (Heylen et al. 2024).

The economic logic is simple: A large and sustained (r-g) gap is crucial to rekindle "animal spirits" and revive private-sector spending, thus reflating the economy. In this regard, the Bank of Japan's persistent monetary easing created a large (r-g) gap averaging more than – 400 basis points (or 4 percentage points) in 2022 and 2023. And that finally delivered an average nominal growth rate of over 3.0% in the period (compared to an annual average of – 0.4% in the 2000s) and turned around market expectations on Japan's economic outlook.

However, China has continued to avoid aggressive easing after the pandemic amid concerns about the negative impact on structural reform and debt-reduction efforts. This policy stance was like Japan's in the early 1990s, which kept it from acting in a timely and forceful manner after the country's asset bubble burst. The resulting financial damage was followed by more than three decades of lost growth. Such policy misstep lays bare the consequences of a policy failure to deal proactively with the loss of wealth and confidence.

To revive the economy, China needs to pursue aggressive monetary easing to create a wide (r-g) gap to revive animal spirits, private investment and consumer spending. China's (r-g) gap, averaging only – 120 basis points in 2023 (Fig. 12.15), was too small for keeping growth momentum steady.

Arguably, China's economic problems were primarily self-inflicted by insufficient cyclical policy support to counteract the deflationary forces from the country's structural creative destruction process as it strived to develop new industries to drive economic growth. Generally, since interest rates have not hit the zero bound in China, traditional monetary policy tools remain appropriate. Indiscriminate flooding of liquidity through QE cannot fix the incentive problems and structural distortions. It will even aggravate the excess capacity problem in the inefficient sectors without

[16] Empirical research suggests that the – 200 basis points (r-g) gap could be kept for as long as a decade to sustain GDP growth.

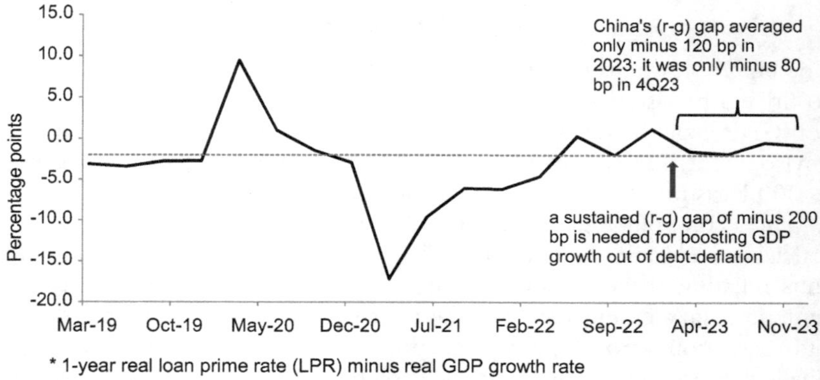

Fig. 12.15 China's (r-g) gap* is too small for boosting GDP growth under debt-deflation (*Note* *1-year real loan prime rate (LPR) minus real GDP growth rate. *Source* CEIC, author)

correcting the capital misallocation problem that starves the efficient sectors of credit.

To avoid falling into a prolonged debt-deflation quagmire, China needs monetary easing to facilitate fiscal expansion to boost growth, not QE under the prevailing economic backdrop. This is simply a Keynesian policy prescription for getting out of a liquidity trap: when the private sector is not spending, the public sector must step in to pick up the slack.

In the next chapter, we shall examine in more details the optimism on Japan (that has emerged since 2024) and assess the views that India's economy will overtake China's soon.

References

Ang, Y. Y., Jia, N., Bo, Y. et al. (2023). China's low-productivity innovation drive: Evidence from patents. *Comparative Political Studies*, Social Science Research Network (SSRN), 24 September.

Bier, D. (2023). *Abandoning the US, more scientists go to China*. The Cato Institute, April 11.

Daniel, W. (2023). *China is 'entering a balance sheet recession' as borrowers shy away from new debt in a potential replay of Japan's 'lost decades'*. Fortune. June 30.

Eaglen, M. (2023). *It's time to retire the term "Near-Peer" competitor when it comes to China*. American Enterprise Institute, June 6.

Galbraith, J. (2023). America's 'new' China narrative: A wounded dragon. *Project Syndicate*, August 17. Retrieved from https://www.project-syndicate.org/commentary/new-us-narrative-about-chinese-decline-by-james-k-galbraith-2023-08

Gao, L. (2023). Biden calls China a 'ticking time bomb' over economic problems. *NBC News*, London, August 11. Retrieved from https://www.nbcnews.com/news/world/biden-calls-china-ticking-time-bomb-economic-problems-rcna99397

Goodman, P. (2023). China's stalling economy puts the world on notice. *The New York Times (Digital Edition)*, August 11.

Hass, R. (2024). Organizing American Policy Around "Peak China" is a Bad Bet. *China Leadership Monitor*, Fall 2024 Issue 81, September 1.

He, L. (2023). China's economy is in trouble. Here's what's gone wrong. *CNN Business*, Hong Kong, August 23. Retrieved from https://edition.cnn.com/2023/08/21/economy/china-economy-troubles-intl-hnk/index.html

Heylen, F., Mareels, M., & Van Langenhove, C. (2024). Long-run perspectives on r−g in OECD countries: An empirical analysis. *Journal of International Money and Finance, 145*, 103093.

Hu, A., Zhou, S., & Xie, Y. (2024). *Study on the national conditions of modernization with Chinese characteristics*. Springer and Tsinghua University Press, October 2024 (pp. 243–272).

Kynge, J. (2023). China has fallen into a psycho-political funk. *Financial Times (Digital Edition)*, Opinion Chinese politics & policy, August 12.

Lo, C. (2010). *China after the subprime crisis: Opportunities in the new economic landscape*. Palgrave Macmillan.

Lo, C. (2015). *China's impossible trinty, the structural challenges to the "Chinese Dream."* Palgrave Macmillan.

Lo, C. (2017). *Demystifying China's mega trends: The driving forces that will shake up China and the world*. Emerald Publishing.

Lo, C. (2021). *China's global disruption: Myths and reality*. Emerald Publishing.

Wagner, C. (2021). Intense scrutiny of Chinese-born researchers in the US threatens innovation. *The Conversation*, United Kingdom Edition, January 26. Retrieved from https://theconversation.com/intense-scrutiny-of-chinese-born-researchers-in-the-us-threatens-innovation-153688

CHAPTER 13

A Reluctant Economic Superpower

Even before China can prove itself with its economic restructuring and policy initiatives, its economic superpower aspirations have already been challenged. Some players in the financial and political domains are predicting China's downfall or collapse, and argue that Japan would revive (Lazard Asset Management, 2025; Reidy, 2024) or even India would rise (Chakravorti & Dalmia, 2023; Rogers, 2025; Srivastava, 2022) to challenge and eventually replace China as the next economic superpower.

Data and evidence seem to indicate that there might be more hype than truth behind these views. Most importantly, there is an assumption behind all the great powers competition views that China wants to be an, if not the, economic superpower. Has anyone questioned if this assumption is correct? Does China really want to be a superpower and why does it want to move up the global league? These are not obvious questions as the conventional wisdom in the West has assumed. They are the ultimate questions that the world should seek answers for when dealing with China's emerging power. In this final discussion on better understanding China's role in shaping and disrupting the global economy, let us address these crucial questions and the views on Japan's and India's challenges to China.

C. Lo, *Clash of the Economic Titans: China and the United States*,
https://doi.org/10.1007/978-981-95-2510-2_13

The Optimists' Views

Is Japan's economic vigour rising again? Will India's economy overtake China's soon? These are two big questions that have raised significant global attention after the pandemic, and many financial market players have bet a large amount of money on the Japanese and Indian stock markets based on their convictions on these markets.

Global investor optimism that Japan was finally moving from a long-running debt-deflation spiral into a wage-price "virtuous" inflation cycle pushed the Japanese stock market to record highs in early 2024, although the uptrend seems to have lost momentum by the end of the year (Fig. 13.1). In contrast, there was significant pessimism about the outlook for China, prompting many observers to compare Japan's economic and policy experience between the late 1980s and the 1990s with China's post-Covid situation and to wonder if China was sleepwalking into a Japan-style economic quagmire.

There was similar optimism about India. For years, China has been the world's favourite growth story. That changed in late 2023 when investors shifted their focus to India. A record amount of portfolio investment flowed into US-based Indian exchange-traded funds (ETFs) in late 2023, boosting India's total stock market capitalisation to overtake Hong Kong as the world's fourth largest at that time.

However, the optimism on these two countries seems to have faded later as both the Japanese and Indian stock markets have fallen since 2025

Fig. 13.1 Nikkei 225 index rose to record high in November 2024 (*Source* CEIC, author)

(see also Fig. 13.8). Has the world changed its mind on these countries, and why?

Japan's Turnaround

Despite some parallels, notably insufficient policy easing, ageing population and a persistent high debt-to-GDP ratio (at more than 290% in 2023), China's economic backdrop today is quite different from Japan's 30 years ago, making it unlikely that it will fall into a Japan-style balance sheet recession, as discussed in the last chapter. However, why has the world turned optimistic on Japan but remained bearish on China? The answers also contain lessons for China to minimise the risk of falling into a debt-deflation spiral.

An expected macroeconomic regime shift from deflation to inflation, improvement in corporate earnings and corporate governance reforms (such as increasing the number of external or independent board members and shareholder advocacy) have fuelled optimism in Japan's outlook since late 2023 (Komatsu, 2023). The yen's sharp depreciation, due to the monetary policy divergence between Japan and the US that has opened a large negative interest rate differential between the two countries, and pessimism on China's outlook have encouraged global investors to refocus on Japan. The sharp fall in the yen exchange rate has also added to imported inflation in Japan since 2022, contributing to the change in the expectation from deflation to inflation.

Japan had been mired in deflation for three decades. This saw nominal GDP growth fall from an annual average rate of 5.4% in the 1980s to 1.9% in the 1990s and then to − 0.4% in the 2000s. However, nominal growth started to rise after 2012 (except in 2020 when Covid hit), averaging 1.4% a year between 2012 and 2019 and rising to 3.1% between 2021 and 2023.

This turnaround in nominal GDP growth reflected the Bank of Japan's (BoJ) persistent accommodative monetary stance that kept its negative interest rate policy (NIRP) throughout the US tightening cycle in 2022 and 2023. The policy divergence created a large gap between Japan's real interest rate (r) and real GDP growth (g), averaging over − 400 basis points (or 4 percentage points) in 2022 and 2023 (Fig. 13.2). That (r-g) gap was significantly wider than the − 200 basis points gap that experience suggests as necessary for sustaining economic growth in a debt-deflation environment (Heylen et al., 2024).

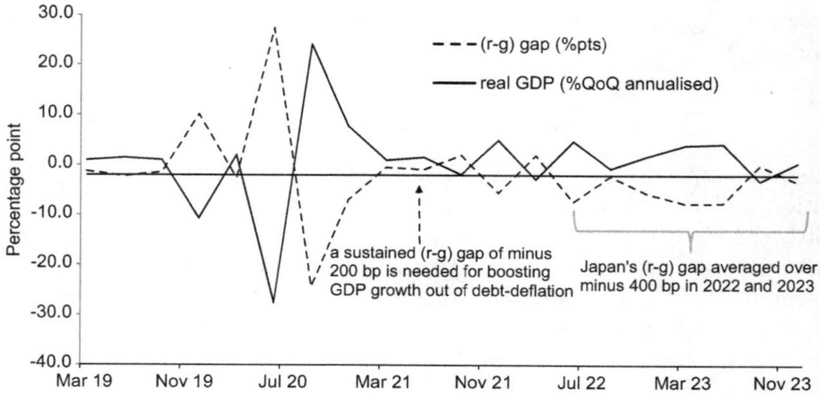

Fig. 13.2 Japan's (r-g) gap is conducive to boosting growth (*Source* CEIC, author)

Theoretically, a large and sustained (r-g) gap is crucial to rekindle animal spirits and revive private-sector spending to help reflate the economy. BoJ research indeed shows that Japanese companies and households are starting to respond to the stimulative effects of its persistent ultra-easy monetary policy by changing their pricing habits. Companies are abandoning their reluctance to change prices and lift wages while unions and workers are starting to ask for, and actually getting, pay increases (Kazuo, 2023; Shuichiro et al., 2023). Notably, Japan's biggest labour union group Rengo successfully negotiated a pay increase of 5.3% in March 2024 (up from 3.8% in March 2023). The increase was significantly above market expectation of 4.0% and had not been seen for over 30 years.

These developments prompted the market to expect a structural change in the Japanese wage negotiation behaviour. Optimists expect that the "Shunto" annual wage negotiation[1] process between workers and employers would set into motion a cycle of rising wages, which should stimulate consumer spending, lift prices sustainably and help pull Japan out of a decades-long economic morass.

[1] In Japan, "Shunto" refers to the annual spring wage negotiations between major companies and labour unions that take place in March. These negotiations determine wage increases and working conditions for the new fiscal year that begins in April.

Structural Factors Boosting Japan's Wages

Research also shows that there might have been a structural change in Japan's labour market with labour shortage pushing up wage growth (Nishioka, 2023). While Japan's prime working age population has continued to rise, mainly due to the increase in participation by female and older workers, the limits are in sight. More than half of the female labour force is already working and, crucially, the old age participation rate, which rose from 20% in 2010 to 26% in 2021, is stagnating (Fig. 13.3).

There is also evidence that occupational mobility in Japan is rising. As approximated by the combined rate of workers joining and leaving their companies, labour mobility rose to a post-Covid high of 4.21% in January 2024. That was significantly above the 5-year average of 3.8% (Fig. 13.4). This should facilitate wage negotiations for higher pay.

Japan's demographic problem of shrinking labour supply limiting GDP growth has been well-known. However, in recent years financial markets have taken this long-term negative structural factor as a short-term positive bet on the revival of a wage-price spiral. Market players expect Japanese firms to pass on the increase in labour cost to selling prices, thus improving companies' earnings outlook. Against this change in the expectations on Japan, what puzzles me is the pessimism on China when Chinese wages are still growing, core inflation rate is still around 2%

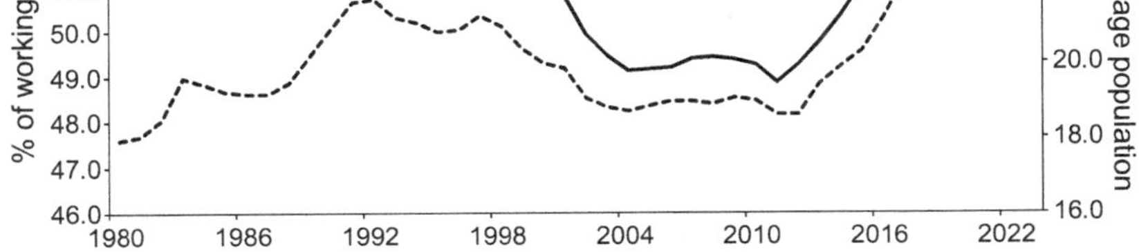

Fig. 13.3 Japan's old-age & female labour participantion rate (*Source* CEIC, author)

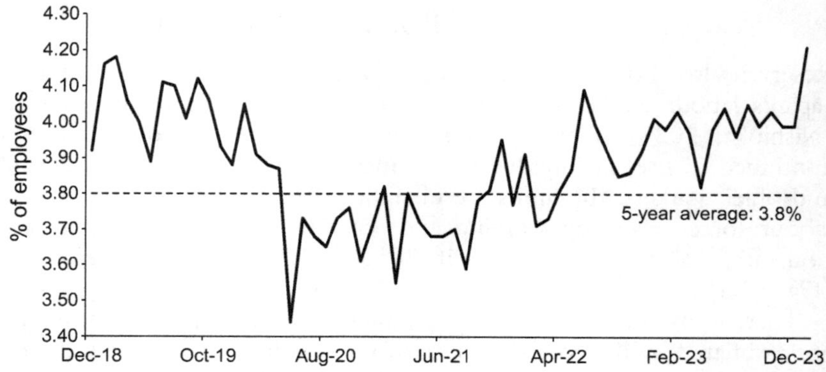

Fig. 13.4 Japan's total accession & separation rates rising to post-Covid high (*Source* CEIC, author)

and there are still underdeveloped areas in the country that can generate growth impetus through industrial migration (see Chapter 11).

Mind the (r-g) Gap

For Japan to get out of debt-deflation, the rise in wages would need to be translated into more consumption rather than higher household saving or debt-reduction. Firms would need to pass on the higher labour costs to selling prices. This would prompt workers to negotiate for more pay increases, setting off a wage-price spiral to generate sustainable economic reflation.

There is more for economic management policy to do to facilitate a sustained economic turnaround. BoJ policy would need to remain accommodative to keep the (r-g) gap large at − 200 basis points or more to prevent economic growth momentum from faltering. This means that despite the BoJ's exit from its ultra-easy monetary policy in March 2024, it would still need to keep real interest rates negative to revive corporate sector dynamism and boost capital expenditure, or capex, to lift productivity and sustain nominal GDP growth.

The prospect of these developments helps explain the markets' optimism on Japan. Time will tell if they unfold as expected.

A Policy Lesson for China

Insufficient policy easing after the Covid-19 health crisis has been a key factor behind China's sluggish economy as policymakers have continued to avoid aggressive easing amid concerns over the negative impact of massive reflation on structural reform and debt-reduction efforts. This policy stance is like Japan's in the early 1990s when similar concerns prevented the Japanese government from acting in a timely and forceful manner after the country's epic bubble burst. The resulting financial damage was followed by three decades of lost growth.

Japan's policy misstep should serve as a wake-up call for China, as it lays bare the consequences of a policy failure to deal proactively with the destruction of wealth and confidence. Notably, the BoJ did not cut interest rates until more than a year after stock prices collapsed (Fig. 13.5). Even when the economy was struggling with price deflation after the asset bubble burst, Japanese policymakers still focused predominately on debt reduction and fiscal austerity, with Japan's net fiscal stance in the 1990s barely expansionary. Such ultra-conservative policy stance aggravated the economic stagnation amid insufficient monetary stimulus (Posen, 1998).

Thus, Beijing's self-imposed policy constraints risk similar consequences. Without any forceful countercyclical policy help, the economy must go through a prolonged cleaning process at an enormous economic

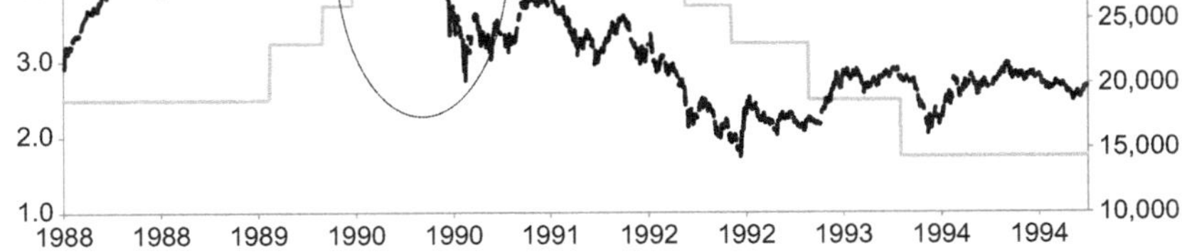

Fig. 13.5 The BoJ only cut interest rate more than a year after the stock market crash (*Source* CEIC, author)

and social cost. However, there is a key difference between Japan then and China today that could keep China's picture from becoming as dire as many observers fear.

China has not suffered from the devastating collapse of asset bubbles as Japan did. This can be seen from the fact that China's stock market did not collapse as much as Japan's did from the market peak (Fig. 13.6). Hence, Chinese households, companies and banks are unlikely to suffer a massive balance sheet recession. As discussed in Chapter 12, China's economic problems are primarily self-inflicted by insufficient cyclical policy expansion to counteract the deflationary forces from the country's structural creative destruction process. This policy misstep was aggravated by the draconian Zero-Covid Policy which was scrapped by Beijing at the end of 2022.

The lesson for China's monetary policy is clear—it needs to pursue aggressive monetary easing to create a wide (r-g) gap to revive animal spirits for boosting private investment and consumer spending, all of which are still lacking at the time of writing despite two years of "incremental easing" policy[2] between 2022 and 2023. Unlike Japan, China's (r-g) gap was too narrow, averaging only − 120 basis points in 2023 (see Chapter 11, Fig. 15). This reflected Beijing's conservative easing stance in the post-Covid recovery period on the back of its deleveraging and structural reforms directives that have deprived the economy of growth impetus.

Supply-Side Expansion Alone Won't Work

At the National People's Congress in 2024, Beijing doubled down on its emphasis on self-sufficiency and manufacturing upgrades, pledging to increase fiscal support for technological development and upgrading equipment. Support for the consumer sector remained very limited. The reason for using such a policy mix that focuses on boosting the supply side of the economy is Beijing's expectation that a rise in manufacturing capex

[2] China's "incremental easing" policy refers to a series of small steps and piecemeal measures taken by the Chinese central bank and the government to stimulate economic growth after the Covid-19 health crisis. The measures involved a combination of monetary and fiscal policies.

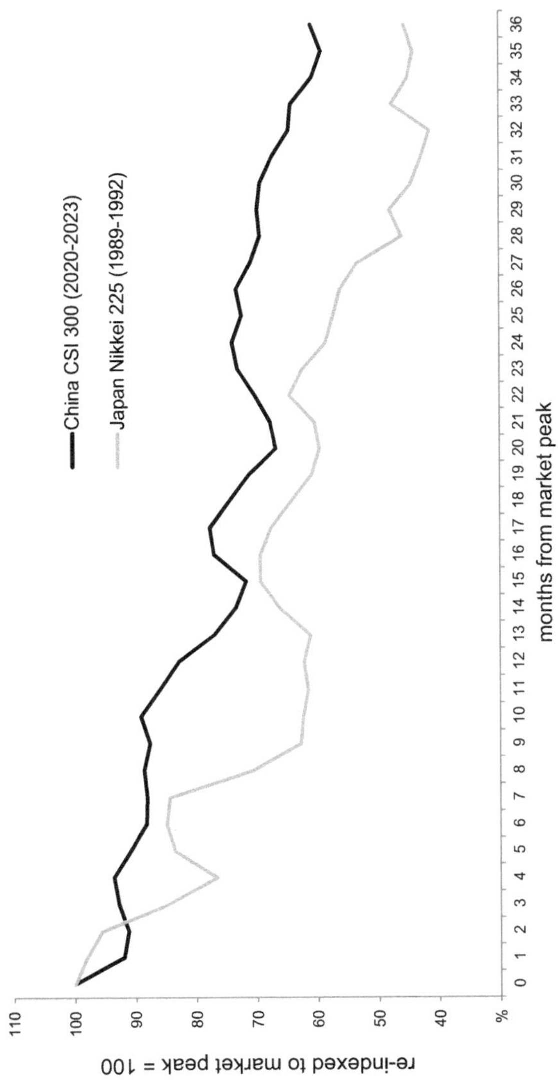

Fig. 13.6 China did not suffer from the devastating asset bubble collapse as Japan did (*Source* CEIC, author)

will create more jobs and boost income growth and, thus, consumption. This supply-side expansion policy has been China's policy habit since economic reforms started over four decades ago.

However, Japan's experience between 1996 and 2005 showed that while increasing capital expenditure helped lift productivity in tradeable sectors and boost manufacturing, the uplift for consumption was limited. Insufficient demand led to a decline in wage and disposable income growth (Fig. 13.7). Such an outcome was mostly due to the loss of confidence, a problem that also applies to China after the pandemic.

This is thus evidence for arguing that supply-expansion policy alone—the focus of the Chinese policy makers—is not enough to reflate the economy without expansionary demand management policy support when there is a loss of confidence. In other words, China needs to sustain aggressive policy easing to boost both demand and supply, but not just focusing on the supply side, to turn around public sentiment and consumption confidence. Such policy is especially important given that China's monetary transmission mechanism looks impaired after Covid-19 (see Chapter 11).

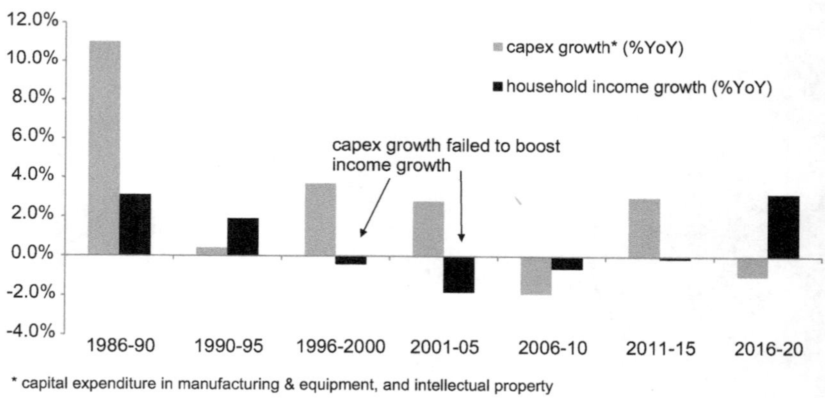

Fig. 13.7 Japan: Increase in manufacturing capex failed to reflate income growth (*Note* *Capital expenditure in manufacturing & equipment, and intellectual property. *Source* Morgan Stanley, author)

Optimism on India

Over to India. Few descriptions better capture the changing views of financial markets and the media regarding the Indian and Chinese economies than the S&P 2023 report entitled "China slows, India grows" (Tan, 2023). Since the re-opening of the two economies after the pandemic lockdowns in 2022, China has grappled with weakening economic momentum and a falling stock market. By contrast, India has seen strong economic growth and rising stock prices, though the stock market strength has faded since late 2024 (Fig. 13.8).

With an annual growth of 7–8%, India is expected to become the world's third-largest economy by the end of 2030. Some observers are even talking about India overtaking China and the US to become the world's largest economy in the not-too-distant future and the Indian rupee to become the world's alternative reserve currency (Garcia-Herrero, 2024; Panagariya, 2023; Modi, 2024). Really? Euphoria is in the air.

Why is the world so optimistic about India? Comparing India with China, many investors have argued that what makes India grow keeps China weak, propelling India ahead of China and arguing for a shift of

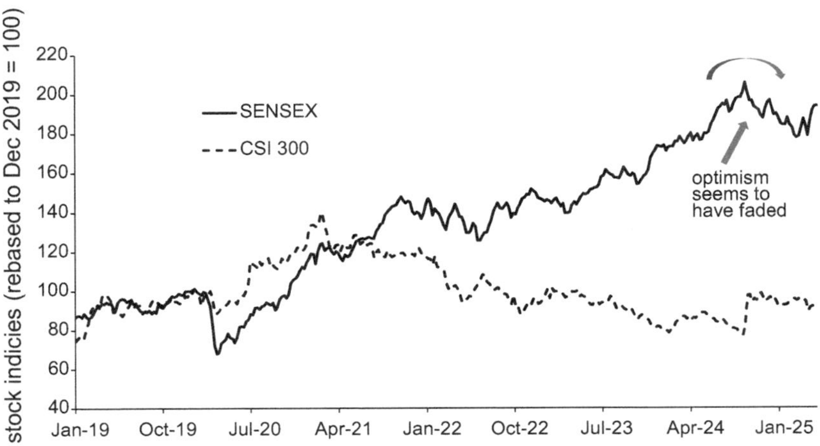

Fig. 13.8 Indian stocks (SENSEX) have outperformed Chinese stock (CSI 300) since 2022 (*Source* CEIC, author)

investment to India from China. Let us assess this line of thinking with data and evidence.

India's Advantages...

Indeed, India has some significant advantages over some major countries, including China. The most notable one is demographics. United Nations data shows that India overtook China as the world's most populous country in April 2023, with over 43% of its population under the age of 25 compared to only 28.5% in China. Its workforce is also significantly younger than China's.

Geopolitically, the US and Europe bicker with China over trade and subsidies, resulting in higher tariffs and export restrictions on tech goods to China. Together with rising labour costs and regulatory risk in China, these factors have incentivised many multinational companies to hedge the "China risk" by moving to other countries, notably Asia and that includes India. Reflecting this trend is the sharp slowdown in foreign direct investment (FDI) in China since 2022 (Fig. 13.9), though there is no conviction for net FDI outflows from China anytime soon (see Chapter 3).

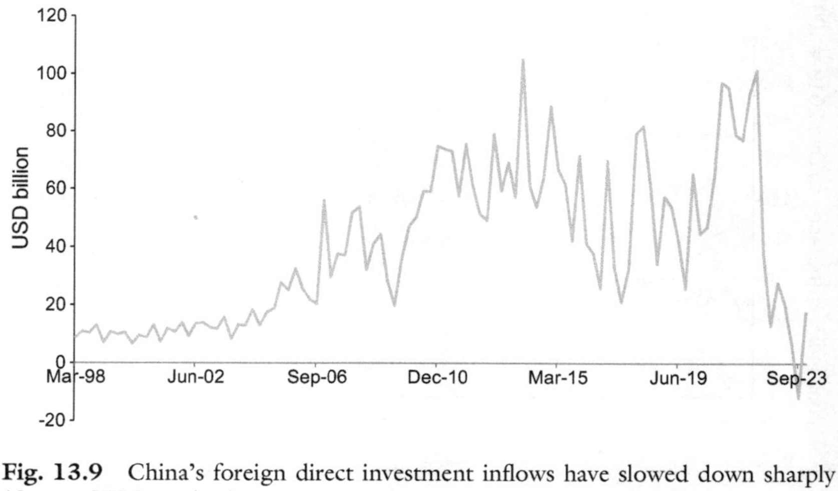

Fig. 13.9 China's foreign direct investment inflows have slowed down sharply (*Source* CEIC, author)

The Indian government's ambitious economic reform agenda is also boosting its economy.[3] Prime Minister Narendra Modi's administration has introduced various reforms in recent years to improve the country's investment climate. As a result, India's business sector has enthusiastically embraced initiatives like "Make in India", "Self-Reliant India" and "Digital India".

Augmenting its supply-side strengths is India's cheap labour. According to the OECD, the average wage (measured in purchasing power parity terms) is about one-third and 10% of those in China and the US, respectively. This implies that there is significant scope for catch-up growth in India.

These favourable factors have prompted a sea-change in the world's opinion, favouring India as a leading alternative to China as the top manufacturing and investment destination. However, the comparison begs the question of how big, and realistic, are these advantages for India to grow and overtake the economies of China and the US?

... Versus Reality

While India's growth potential is clear, there are reasons to believe that the market is too optimistic, with partial understanding of what is happening between India and China. Take demographics. India's advantage over China does not seem to be as significant as many observers think. The United Nations' population statistics show that India's fertility rate, at two births per woman, has fallen below the replacement rate[4] of 2.1, though it is still higher than China's fertility rate of 1.2.

Separately and crucially, World Bank data shows that India's total labour force participation rate was just 55.3% in 2023, compared to China's 66.4%; and its 32.7% female labour force participation rate was far lower than China's rate of 60.5%. The overall quality of India's labour force is also lower than that of China's. World Bank research shows that 97% of Chinese aged 15 and older were literate as of 2020 (the latest data available), but India's literacy rate was only 76% in 2022. So, the gap in

[3] The Center for Strategic & International Studies (CSIS) has produced an Indian Reforms Scorecard for tracking India's reforms. It is available from it website, https://indiareforms.csis.org/.

[4] The replacement rate is the rate of birth per female that is needed to keep the population of a country stable over time.

quality-adjusted labour costs between India and China is much smaller than simple nominal-terms comparison implies. Furthermore, China has more developed roads, ports, airports and infrastructure links than India has. This makes manufacturing and exporting goods from China more cost-effective than from India, as many multinational companies can attest.

Crucially, India's corruption level is more serious than in China, according to Transparent International's Corruption Perception Index (CPI), which ranges between 0 for very corrupt and 100 for very clean. Between 1995 (when the index was first calculated) and the 2019 pandemic, India's CPI averaged 33 while that of China averaged 35. This indicates that China was persistently less corrupt than India. Notably since 2019, China's index has improved while that of India's has worsened (Fig. 13.10). Higher corruption is a deterrent for investment inflows and business operations, *ceteris paribus*.

While India benefits from China's geopolitical tensions and trade frictions with the developed world, its protectionist policies could be offsetting this geopolitical advantage. World Trade Organization research shows that India's barriers to trade are much higher than China's, while

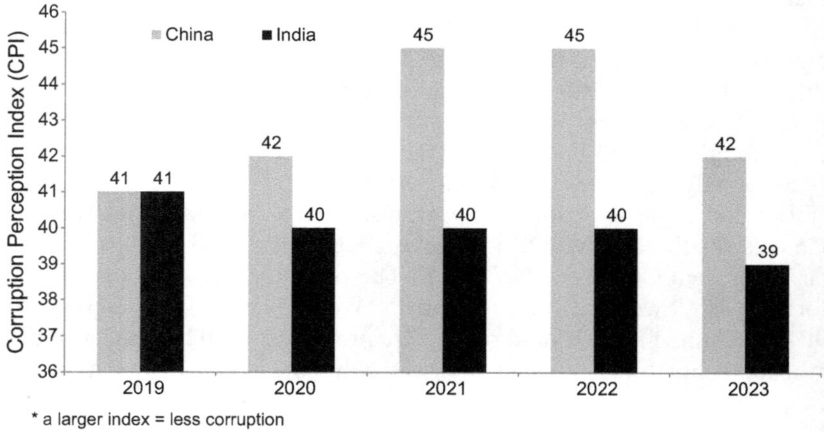

Fig. 13.10 China's corruption* has improved while that of India's has worsened since Covid-19 (*Note* *A larger index = less corruption. *Source* Transparency International, author)

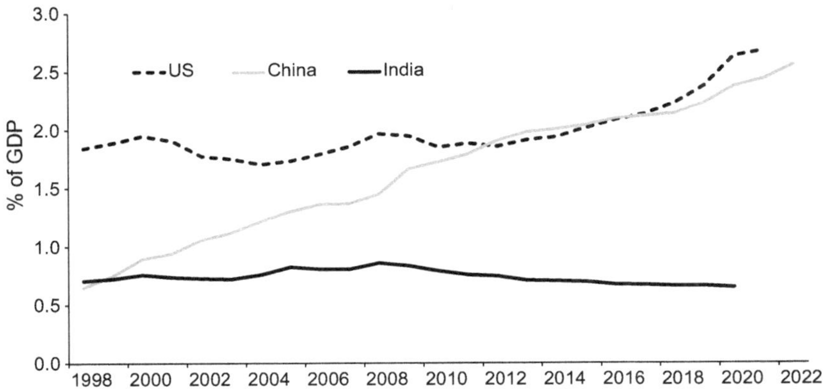

Fig. 13.11 India has the lowest R&D spending compared with China and the US (*Source* CEIC, author)

OECD data indicates that India commands no advantages over China in attracting FDI. This is because India's regulatory restrictions on FDI flows is comparable to that of China's—both countries scored an OECD FDI restrictiveness index[5] (between 0 for open and 1 for closed) of 0.21 in 2020 (the latest data available).

When it comes to technological advancement and competition, which affects not only future growth potentials, but also military power, research and development (R&D) spending is of paramount importance. However, India is spending much less on R&D (as a per cent of GDP) than China, whose R&D spending is catching up quickly to the US levels (Fig. 13.11).

The Future

India has many challenges to overcome. It needs a multifaceted approach to implement sweeping structural reforms, flight corruption, invest in better infrastructure, raise educational standards and increase R&D

[5] The OECD's FDI restrictive index gauges the restrictiveness of a country's foreign direct investment rules by looking at four main types of restrictions: foreign equity restrictions, discriminatory screening or approval mechanisms, key foreign personnel restrictions and operational restrictions.

spending. These are tall orders, but they are essential for India to live up to the expectation of becoming the world's next economic superpower. The relevant point to China is that blind optimism on India, or excessive pessimism on China, based on partial analysis of the countries' development does not help understand China's position in the world's geopolitical economic environment and that could lead to wrong, or even dangerous, policy reactions and business decisions.

From an investment angle, the optimism may not necessarily reflect expectations of India's structural and economic superiority, as many observers have casually assumed. It may simply reflect a tactical rotation away from China over worries about the Chinese debt situation and property crisis when the Chinese economy is stuck in post-Covid cyclical doldrums. At the time of writing, many foreign investors seem to think that India's economy does not to have to be larger than China's for its financial market to deliver higher returns, especially when the Chinese market is out of favour.

However, when China recovers, the euphoria over India will likely fade, leaving the two countries to compete for investment flows based on their relative fundamental strengths. To be fair, an investment decision does not have to be on either India or China. If investors want to capture the potential of these two large economies, they should invest in both based on their different structural and economic backdrops. Of course, there are also far-reaching geopolitical policy implications, but I shall leave it for other experts to explore.

A Wrong Perception of China

US President Donald Trump seems to play a role in fostering the common assumption that China wants to be an economic superpower by competing with the US and other powers, like Japan and India that we discuss in this chapter. Indeed, with the US administration pursuing an unpredictable strategy, China seems to position itself as a force for global stability. This has created a perception that it wants to fill the vacuum left by an increasingly erratic, self-centred and isolationist US under Trump's rule.

That could be a wrong perception. From China's perspectives, trying to replace the US as the "international police" would be a costly and dangerous move because the economic cost of doing so will be colossal. China can ill afford to spare the resources when it is pursuing massive domestic economic restructuring. Having watched the US play the role of international police, China knows well that being a global superpower would drain its resources from domestic needs and inevitably draw it into many international conflicts that it would prefer to avoid. Look at the US. Its basic infrastructure, most notably roads, bridges, airports, water system, electric grid, etc., badly needs repairment and improvement (ASCE, 2025). But nothing has been done for decades, arguably because most resources have been diverted to advance the US's foreign claims and interests by being the global leader.

That is why despite its proposals for fostering global initiatives on security, development and civilisation, and a vision of multipolarity in which all countries cooperate equally, China has spent very limited efforts on taking the lead to realise these goals. It has also been trying to avoid being involved in any crises beyond its immediate neighbourhood. This hesitancy to lead seems to suggest that China may not want to be a global economic superpower. Furthermore, the Chinese political DNA seems to be built on protecting territorial integrity and the country's "properties" whatever they may include, rather than global expansion.

This understanding runs in sharp contrast to the common Western thinking that China's core national interest is to replace the US as the global leader. Most observers do not seem to understand that China does not have a core national interest. It has several core interests that are all domestic-orientated. They include sustaining the regime legitimacy and security, continuing the improvement on Chinese living standard, distributing wealth more evenly to minimise the risk of systemic instability, and even re-unifying Taiwan with the Mainland.

These goals, from Beijing's perspective, are best served by keeping a cold peace with the US rather than confronting it to become the world's powerhouse. Confrontation will only deplete resources that China needs to tackle its domestic challenges, including rebalancing the economy from supply-expansion to demand-driven growth and high-tech development. China also needs to get ready for possibly losing one of its largest trading partners, the US as it reverts to isolation. Trump's punitive tariff war against China since his first presidency in 2018, which was intensified in his second presidency in 2025, is a wake-up call for the Chinese leaders to speed up economic rebalancing.

The Chinese Motives to Move Up

The intensifying Sino-American rivalry has prompted the Chinese leaders to think that domestic innovation is a strategic necessity to counter external exigencies. Beijing's "dual circulation" strategy (see Chapter 1 for discussion), which aims at sustaining China's growth through expanding demand and reducing reliance on (but not relinquishing) exports, is a result of a change in its strategic thinking from cooperating with the US to preparing for "struggle", as many senior leaders put it, under intense geopolitical tensions.

Hence, while the dual circulation was designed as a defensive strategy in the beginning, it has also acquired an offensive tactic in recent years through trade, investment and diplomatic expansion to fend off US "attacks", thus clashing with the US's global interest. China is particularly keen on building resilient supply chains for critical technologies to circumvent US chokepoints. It has been redirecting a significant share of national resources towards promoting domestic technology development and innovation. A prime example is the policy to shrink the property sector to free up capital and resources for other national strategic objectives.

Essentially, China's foreign policy strategy aims at creating an external environment that is conducive to domestic economic development. This is a non-combative approach that dates back to early leaders like Mao Zedong's "strategic stalemate"—an enduring equilibrium where American pressure becomes manageable and China buys time to catch up to the US—and Deng Xiaoping's "hide your strength, bide your time"—a strategy of opening up to the world while maintaining a low profile and learning from advanced nations to secure China's independent position between the US and the Soviet Union. President Xi Jinping has revived these mantras for navigating the combative policies of the US.

So, China's strategic development objective is not really aimed at filling a void left by the US in global leadership, in my view. Aware of the US's economic and military superiority, President Xi is seeking to avoid direct confrontation while holding China's ground in a protracted, all-encompassing competition. To do so, he knows China must be freed from being held hostage by advanced economies for critical inputs such as advanced semiconductors and aircraft engines. He is also aware of the weakness of China's original innovation capabilities (Dohmen, 2024).

Hence, instead of just focusing on boosting domestic technology development and innovation, China is also eager to seize opportunities to set the global governance agenda for emerging technologies while remaining rather conservative in leading any broader global initiatives.

Under the "internal circulation" efforts of the dual circulation strategy, China has successfully developed low-cost artificial intelligence models, most notably DeepSeek, that rival those from top US developers. This achievement has created a strong incentive for it to move up the global technology ladder and advocate that a handful of rich countries should not be allowed to monopolise the technologies that will determine the world's economic future. China's advocation has received strong support from the developing world, which has voted on its feet by accepting Chinese technologies as the predominant source for building their own systems especially since the Covid health crisis.

Regional Partnership Challenging the US

In building up its regional influence, China views Russia as practically the most important strategic partner and the Sino-Russian alignment as a geographical and strategic necessity. It has also been de-escalating tensions with India, another large, nuclear-armed neighbour, despite all the structural and historical stains on their relationship.

Beyond these immediate neighbours, China has sought to mobilise the Global South[6] behind reforms to multilateral institutions. When China talks about ushering in an "orderly multipolarity", it is seeing a new international order in which the non-Western world has much more clout. Hence, it has been a strong advocate of the BRICS expansion, and of proposals to redistribute voting shares within Western-dominated development finance institutions.

From this perspective, China does have a subtle foreign policy interest in challenging US influence in the developing world by building major infrastructure and addressing long-ignored development needs in the developing world without making any demands for democracy, human rights and accountability. China also does not offer any security guarantees, like the Western democracies often do. Instead, it offers roads,

[6] Global South is a term that refers to a group of countries in the Southern Hemisphere that are characterised by lower levels of economic development and often face economic and political challenges of poverty and systemic instability, and the legacy of colonisation.

bridges and other infrastructure aids (including technologies) in return for accessing critical raw materials and opening new markets for its state-owned enterprises and private companies at a time when Europe and the US are closing their doors.

For China, Mao Zedong's "strategic stalemate" and Deng Xiaoping's "hide your strength bide your time" are the most realistic strategies in the foreseeable future. Hence, it has only assumed a limited leadership role without directly confronting the US and its allies. While China is keen on pursuing wide-ranging economic statecraft in developing countries, it remains reluctant to engage directly with complex security matters elsewhere in the world. It knows the US is still the central player, and usually by default, in many global affairs. It has no intention to uproot the US-led liberal international order and replace the US as the global superpower, as many in the West have assumed. Rather, it just wants to pursue its national interests pragmatically.

A Reluctant Powerhouse

Nevertheless, even by just pursuing partial or limited global leadership, China will inevitably create significant disruption to the global economy because it will have to deal with big challenges, both domestically and externally, under an increasingly hawkish and unpredictable US.

From a geopolitical perspective, China cannot keep playing a limited leadership role forever as it expands into the non-Western world to counter the US containment policy. Sooner or later, China will have to develop a global foreign policy and get involved deeper in international affairs. Crucially, as the US keeps an erratic policy in global affairs, China will find it increasingly difficult to sustain its commercial engagement with many countries without deeper involvement in global geopolitics.

How China will handle this challenge will depend on how others perceive its actions and respond to them. Crucially, the US will not sit idly by and watch China increase its influence at the expense of US interests. This can readily be seen in the moves by the Trump administration to impose drastic costs on those countries and entities who do business with China.

From an economic perspective, China is striving to implement a domestic economic rebalancing. This is a process that will have significant global consequences. Shifting from a supply-expansion growth model to a demand-driven one will take years. Meanwhile, China's ambition to remain a global manufacturing powerhouse is already causing tensions with Europe and some developing countries whose domestic manufacturers are struggling to compete with Chinese national champions, like the electric-vehicle maker BYD and the solar panel manufacturer Tongwei Solar. Countries may abhor the US's coercive and erratic policy style, but they are also wary of Chinese competition. Chinese leaders will need to "cross the river by feeling the stones"—navigate uncertainty cautiously by taking one step at a time—as Deng Xiaoping famously said.

China will continue to grow, but it will likely remain largely a self-centred and reluctant superpower. Its domestic political economy argues for a restrained foreign policy focusing primarily on its immediate neighbours and commercial opportunities in the non-Western countries, notably Global South. All this takes us back to what I discussed in Chapter 2 about China's new worldview under its dual circulation policy framework where its internal circulation sits in the centre of Asia, engaging regional and global capital, financial and technological markets for enhancing domestic growth and driving regional growth.

In a new paradigm of erosion of US power shifting the geopolitical pendulum towards multipolarity, China will increasingly and inevitably become the centre of gravity in the global economy. How the geopolitical and economic forces will playout world is uncertain. What is certain is that China's disruptive forces will continue, making it imperative for us to better understand the economic evolution and global aspirations of China to manage the potential volatility of its emergence.

References

ASCE. (2025). *A comprehensive assessment of America's infrastructure*. American Society of Civil Engineers, 2025 Report Card for America's Infrastructure. March. Retrieved from https://infrastructurereportcard.org/wp-content/uploads/2025/03/Full-Report-2025-Natl-IRC-WEB.pdf

Chakravorti, B., & Dalmia, G. (2023). Is India the world's next great economic power? International Business, *Harvard Business Review*, September 6.

Dohmen, H. (2024). Assessing China's AI development and forecasting its future tech priorities. *Atlantic Council*, Strategic Insights Memo, September 18.

Garcia-Herrero, A. (2024). India's economy can overtake China's if it can stay on track. *Nikkei Asia*, Hong Kong, April 12. Retrieved from https://asia.nikkei.com/Opinion/India-s-economy-can-overtake-China-s-if-it-can-stay-on-track

Heylen, F., Mareels, M., & Van Langenhove, C. (2024). Long-run perspectives on r − g in OECD countries: An empirical analysis. *Journal of International Money and Finance, 145*, 103093.

Kazuo, U. (2023). Wages and prices: Past, present, and future. *Bank of Japan*, Speech at the Meeting of Councillors of Keidanren (Japan Business Federation) in Tokyo, December 25.

Komatsu, M. (2023). *Corporate governance reform points to opportunities ahead in Japan equities*. Nikko Asset Management, 27 December. Retrieved from https://en.nikkoam.com/articles/2023/corporate-governance-reform-points

Lazard Asset Management. (2025). *A Tale of two economies: Japan's revival and China's uncertain future*. May 7. Retrieved from https://www.lazardassetmanagement.com/sg/en_us/research-insights/investment-insights/investment-research/japan-revival-china-uncertain-future

Modi, J. (2024). Indian rupee is now aiming to be world's alternate reserve currency. *The Economic Times*, April 20. Retrieved from https://economictimes.indiatimes.com/markets/forex/indian-rupee-is-now-aiming-to-be-worlds-alternate-reserve-currency/articleshow/109453703.cms?from=mdr

Nishioka, S. (2023). Severe labor shortage puts upward pressure on wages in Japan. *Japan Research Institute, 6*(3), 1–8.

Panagariya, A. (2023). How India's economy will overtake the U.S.'s. *Time Ideas, Time*. July 28. Retrieved from https://time.com/6297539/how-india-economy-will-surpass-us/

Posen, A. (1998). Restoring Japan's economic growth. *Peterson Institute for International Economics*. September. ISBN: 978-0-88132-262-0 (p. 214).

Reidy, G. (2024). How a fading Japan regained its superpowers. *Bloomberg UK*, Tokyo. April 25. Retrieved from https://www.bloomberg.com/opinion/features/2024-04-24/how-japan-regained-its-superpowers-and-recovered-from-recession

Rogers, J. (2025). Indian economy has potential to surpass China in near future. *DD News*, 12 May. Retrieved from https://ddnews.gov.in/en/indian-economy-has-potential-to-surpass-china-in-near-future-jim-rogers/#:~:text=Economy%20%7C%20Jim%20Rogers-,Indian%20economy%20has%20potential%20to%20surpass%20China%20in%20near%20future,to%20ace%20investor%20Jim%20Rogers

Shuichiro, I., Takuji, K., Yoshiyuki, K., Taichi, M., & Tomoyuki, Y. (2023). Firms' recent price-setting stance: Evidence from the tankan. *Bank of Japan Review*, 2023-E-2, February.

Srivastava, D. K. (2022). Indian economy by 2050: In pursuit to achieve the $30 trillion mark. Economic Watch, Macro-fiscal Unit, *EY India*, August.

Summary Retrieved from https://www.ey.com/en_in/insights/tax/economy-watch/indian-economy-by-twenty-fifty-in-pursuit-to-achieve-the-thirty-trillion-dollar-mark#:~:text=As%20per%20OECD%27s%20baseline%20projections,terms%20by%20the%20late%202040s

Tan, E. (2023). China slows, India grows. *S&P Global Ratings*, Credit conditions Asia-Pacific Q1 2024, November 28. Retrieved from https://www.spglobal.com/_assets/documents/ratings/research/101590079.pdf

Index

A

"a dollar for a dollar" strategy, 9, 245, 248, 256
America First, 126, 131, 158, 201
American shield, 138
animal spirit, 86, 88, 192, 267, 275, 289, 296, 300
Artificial intelligence (AI), 8, 13, 23, 28, 34, 35, 44, 49, 73, 74, 146–148, 184–192, 204, 227, 283, 311
Asia Infrastructure Investment Bank (AIIB), 122, 143–145, 153, 155, 198
Asian Infrastructure Investment Bank, 41, 122
Association of Southeast Asian Nations (ASEAN), 37, 44, 47, 58, 61–64, 66, 69, 113, 131, 138, 148, 186, 236, 237, 241

B

balance of payments, 67, 103, 106, 247
balance sheet recession, 9, 274–277, 283, 285, 288, 295, 300
basic surplus, 101, 102
beggar-thy-neighbour, 39
Belt and Road Initiative (BRI), 4, 7, 8, 16, 29, 37, 41, 43, 44, 46–53, 76, 80, 100, 103, 113, 122, 124, 129–131, 133, 135–146, 148–153, 155, 195, 197, 198, 202, 221, 222, 245, 248, 249
Bitcoin, 40, 193, 194, 211–216, 218
Bitcoin reserve, 8, 193, 211
boiling frog fable, 9, 234
Brazil, Russia, India, China and South Africa (BRICS), 71, 213, 239, 241, 244, 250, 311
Brexit, 42
BRI vision, 49, 137

C

capital account, 7, 40–42, 79–86, 88–90, 92–97, 101, 107, 122, 123, 135, 167, 226, 229, 230, 234–236, 254, 255, 261, 277

C. Lo, *Clash of the Economic Titans: China and the United States*, https://doi.org/10.1007/978-981-95-2510-2

Central Bank Digital Currency (CBDC), 8, 192–194, 199, 211, 213, 216, 217, 219, 222, 225, 227
chatbot, 188
ChatGPT, 188
China Inc, 20, 23
China Initiative programme, 34
China International Payment Service, 195
China + 1, 64, 72
Chinese Dream, 29, 44, 137, 184, 195, 198, 222
Chinn-Ito index, 93
collabetition, 59, 73, 74
common prosperity, 265, 270
comparative advantage, 3, 4, 36, 73, 162, 178, 286
Comprehensive and Progressive Agreement for Trans-Pacific Partnership (CPTPP), 186, 201
controlled anonymity, 218, 219
controlled liberalisation, 7
control problem, 25
correspondent banking model, 225, 226
creative destruction, 120, 265, 289, 300
creeping internationalisation, 9, 241, 256
Cross-border Interbank Payment System (CIPS), 178, 195, 196, 220, 222, 224, 230–233, 235, 237, 239, 241
cryptocurrency, 8, 40, 192–194, 211, 213, 215, 216, 218
current account, 2, 3, 36, 51, 85, 101–103, 106, 109, 116, 142, 151, 159, 160, 168, 177, 245, 249, 254, 255

D

debt-deflation, 9, 259, 274, 275, 283, 288–290, 294, 295, 298
debt trap, 6, 8, 50, 130, 249
decoupling, 3, 6, 7, 58–64, 66, 67, 70, 72–74, 125, 126, 135, 148, 178, 183, 184, 201, 224
DeepSeek, 8, 186–189, 311
de-globalisation, 7, 14, 15, 43, 59, 61, 67, 70, 116, 130, 135, 162
development finance, 7, 49, 50, 100, 101, 122, 124, 145, 148, 150, 155, 311
digital BRI, 43, 44, 46, 47, 224
digital currency, 8, 192–194, 198, 199, 211, 216, 219, 222, 225–227, 237
Digital Currency Electronic Payment (DCEP), 192–195, 198, 216, 217, 219, 222, 224–228
digital currency war, 9
digital renminbi, 8, 9, 195, 218–220, 224, 226, 228, 237
Digital Silk Road, 44–46
diminishing marginal returns, 108, 118
Distributed ledger technology (DLT), 213, 215, 216, 225–227
dollar supremacy, 231
dual circulation, 14, 43, 44, 48, 60, 61, 63, 66, 73, 130, 131, 135, 136, 183, 202, 224, 264, 270, 283, 310, 311, 313

E

Electric vehicles (EV), 21, 28, 74–77, 134, 202, 274, 286
Entity List, 186
European Dream, 42
excess capacity, 24, 51, 103, 108, 116, 136, 137, 145, 151, 274, 288, 289

external circulation, 14, 15, 61, 63, 130, 135

F
FDI Restrictiveness Index, 124, 307
financial engineering, 25, 275–277
Foreign direct investment (FDI), 7, 61, 64, 66–72, 99, 101, 102, 104, 106, 114–117, 124, 125, 164, 304, 307
free trade zones, 80, 84
friend-shoring, 63, 67, 73, 74

G
G3, 40, 43, 62, 63, 176, 199
Galapagos Island Syndrome, 23
giant sucking sound, 36, 57
global disruption, 26, 30, 81, 130, 172, 175, 184, 194, 204, 207, 274
Global Financial Crisis (GFC), 18, 25, 40, 41, 199, 229, 252, 276, 280, 286
global imbalance, 159
globalisation, 4, 15, 80, 87, 158, 178, 221
Global South, 16, 311, 313
gold-back renminbi, 235
great power competition, 2
groupthink, 190
Gulf Cooperation Council (GCC), 71, 254

H
Health Silk Road, 44–48, 66
hybrid economy, 17

I
implicit capital controls, 7
implicit guarantee, 123, 277, 287
import substitution, 57, 60, 158, 162, 183
Impossible Trinity, 79, 82, 95, 97, 167, 255
incentive, 4, 7, 8, 21, 25, 42, 59, 64, 72, 75, 80, 86–90, 95, 100, 109–111, 118, 130, 142, 172, 180, 184, 188, 194, 195, 198, 220, 222, 224, 225, 231, 236, 237, 241, 244, 245, 251, 267, 269, 270, 274, 287–289, 311
industrial migration, 147, 265, 283, 298
Information and Communication Technology (ICT), 184, 185, 207, 208
internal circulation, 14, 15, 48, 63, 130, 311, 313
internationalisation, 23, 44, 81, 82, 92, 116, 193, 195, 196, 198, 199, 226, 228, 229, 235, 236, 238, 239, 246
internet bifurcation, 46
invisible hand, 21, 24–26

J
Japanification, 259
Jevons paradox, 189

K
key man risk, 25

L
lesson for China, 300
Libra, 192, 199
liquidity trap, 283, 288, 290
local protectionism, 25

M

marginal propensity to consume, 154
m-CBDC Bridge, 222, 224, 237
medium of exchange, 40, 42, 199, 213, 214, 216, 226
middle income trap, 5, 26
migrant workers, 13
Minsky Moment, 279
Multiple Central Bank Digital Currency Bridge Project, 222, 237
mutual fund recognition scheme, 85

N

network effect, 213, 249, 250

O

onshoring, 3, 67, 73, 74, 162
operation twist, 285
over-invoicing, 89, 90
Overseas direct investment (ODI), 69, 72, 99, 100, 102, 103, 107–120, 123, 124, 126, 127

P

petro-dollar, 231, 234, 243, 247
petro-yuan, 220, 231, 232, 234–236, 243
protectionism, 15, 57, 58, 73, 114, 116, 125, 130, 135, 158, 159, 162, 200

Q

Qualified Domestic Institutional Investor (QDII), 84, 85
Qualified Foreign Institutional Investor (QFII), 83–85
quantitative easing, 9, 40, 259, 274

R

rebalancing, 8, 39, 43, 60, 80, 153–155, 159, 184, 201, 264, 267, 273, 274, 309, 312
reciprocal tariffs, 161, 162, 164, 167, 168, 176
Regional Comprehensive Economic Partnership (RCEP), 186
regionalism, 7, 14, 43, 59, 61, 67, 73, 135
renminbi internationalisation, 9, 59, 71, 80, 84, 86, 93, 95, 109, 116, 129, 135–137, 145, 167, 195, 198, 216, 219, 226, 229, 230, 236, 237, 242–245, 247, 249
Renminbi Qualified Foreign Institutional Investor (RQFII), 83, 85
reshoring, 67, 73, 74, 131
reverse supply chains, 7, 59
(r-g) gap, 289, 298, 300
round tripping, 288

S

salami-slicing tactics, 236, 241
savings-investment imbalance, 2, 3, 9
sleeping on the wheel, 27, 33, 45, 135, 229, 245
Society for Worldwide Interbank Financial Telecommunications (SWIFT), 23, 41, 59, 135, 196, 219, 220, 222, 225, 231–233, 235, 237–239, 241, 243, 253, 254
Special Drawing Rights, 41, 196, 254
special economic zones, 86
stock connect scheme, 84, 85, 91–95, 197
store of value, 40, 41, 198, 199, 214, 216, 226
Strategic bitcoin reserve (SBR), 211, 212, 216

strategic stalemate, 310, 312
structural transformation, 260, 264, 265, 273
subprime crisis, 25, 26, 39–41, 123, 252, 275, 276, 279
superpower, 1, 2, 6, 9, 10, 26, 27, 30, 35, 36, 39, 61, 158, 184, 198, 231, 293, 308, 309, 312, 313
supply chains, 3, 4, 15, 21, 23, 28, 46, 47, 58–62, 64, 66, 67, 69, 70, 72, 114, 116, 130, 135, 147, 148, 158, 160, 165, 177–179, 184, 185, 201, 207, 274, 283, 310
supply-expansion growth, 261, 312
supply-side expansion, 302
System for Transfer of Financial Messages, 222, 237

T

tech war, 8, 148, 157, 200, 201, 204
There Is No Alternative (TINA), 9, 251, 254
Thucydides Trap, 27–29, 158
trade diversion, 63
trade war, 1–4, 8, 23, 45, 58, 62–64, 70, 74, 113, 125, 131, 135, 147, 157, 159–161, 164, 167, 172–178, 184, 185, 187, 200, 201, 221, 251, 255, 261, 280
Trumponomics, 168
twin deficits, 2, 3, 177, 245, 247, 248, 250
two-tier system, 218, 219

U

untraceable anonymity, 218

V

visible hand, 21, 24

W

weak dollar policy, 3
wealth destruction, 26, 276, 277, 279, 280
wealth management connect scheme, 85
whale wallets, 215

Kolibri 360 GmbH
Ferdinand-Jühlke-Straße 7
99095 Erfurt, Deutschland
produktsicherheit@kolibri360.de